W9-BVM-472

1 BASIC FACTS, SUMS THROUGH 10

Match the set to the number.
Match the number to the number name.

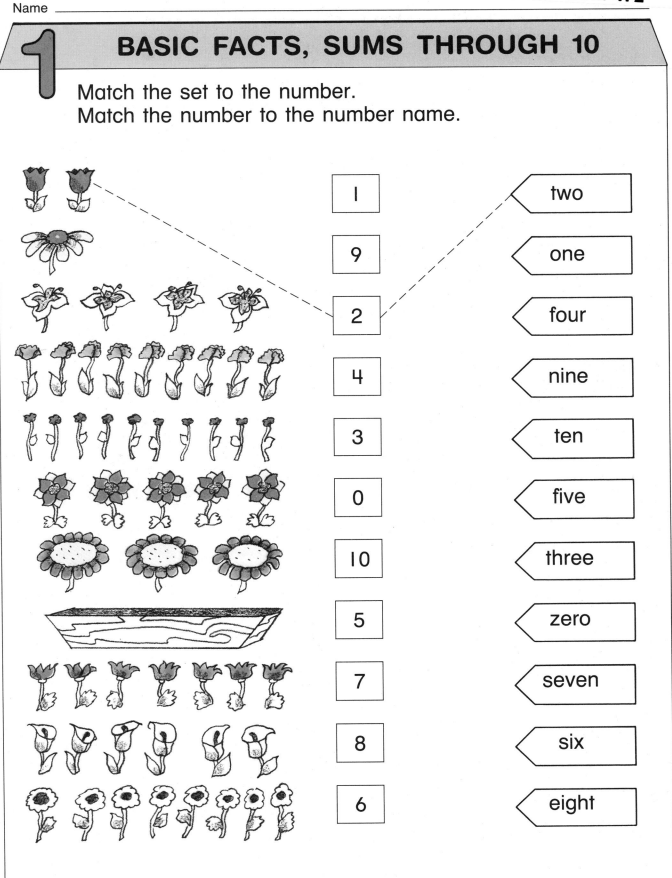

1	two
9	one
2	four
4	nine
3	ten
0	five
10	three
5	zero
7	seven
8	six
6	eight

Write the numbers.

1. 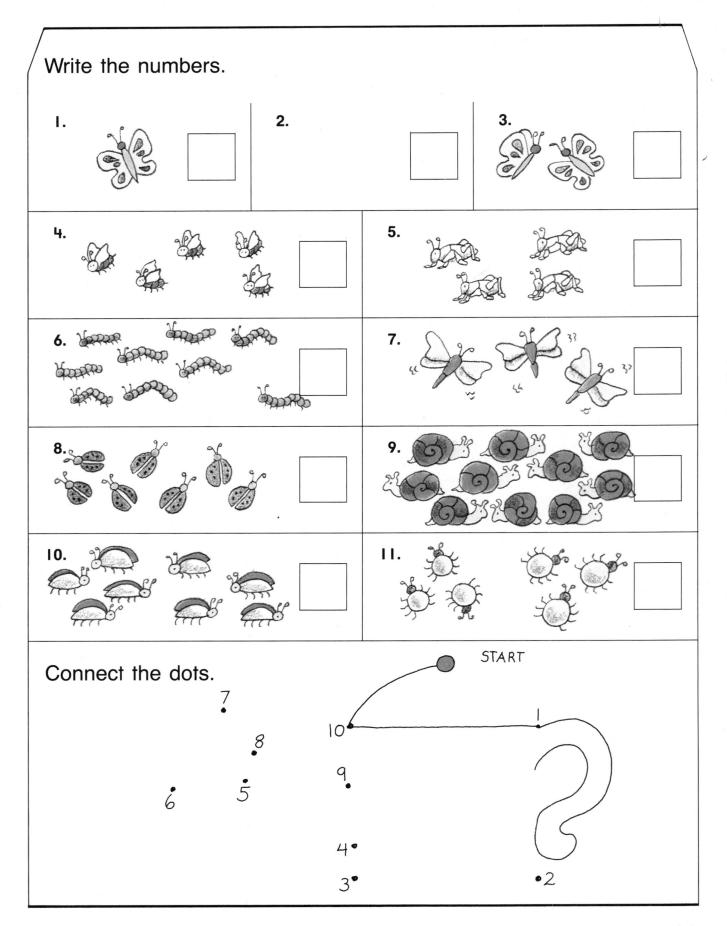 ☐

2. ☐

3. ☐

4. ☐

5. ☐

6. ☐

7. ☐

8. ☐

9. ☐

10. ☐

11. ☐

Connect the dots.

START

Reading and writing numbers, 0 through 10

We started with ___3___ fish.

We bought ___2___ more.

How many fish

do we have in all? ___5___

$3 + 2 =$ ___5___

$$\begin{array}{r} 3 \\ +2 \\ \hline 5 \end{array}$$

Add.

1.
$$\begin{array}{r} 1 \\ +2 \\ \hline \end{array}$$

2.
$$\begin{array}{r} 1 \\ +1 \\ \hline \end{array}$$

3.
$$\begin{array}{r} 2 \\ +1 \\ \hline \end{array}$$

4.
$$\begin{array}{r} 3 \\ +0 \\ \hline \end{array}$$

5.
$$\begin{array}{r} 2 \\ +2 \\ \hline \end{array}$$

6.
$$\begin{array}{r} 0 \\ +2 \\ \hline \end{array}$$

7.
$$\begin{array}{r} 3 \\ +1 \\ \hline \end{array}$$

8.
$$\begin{array}{r} 1 \\ +4 \\ \hline \end{array}$$

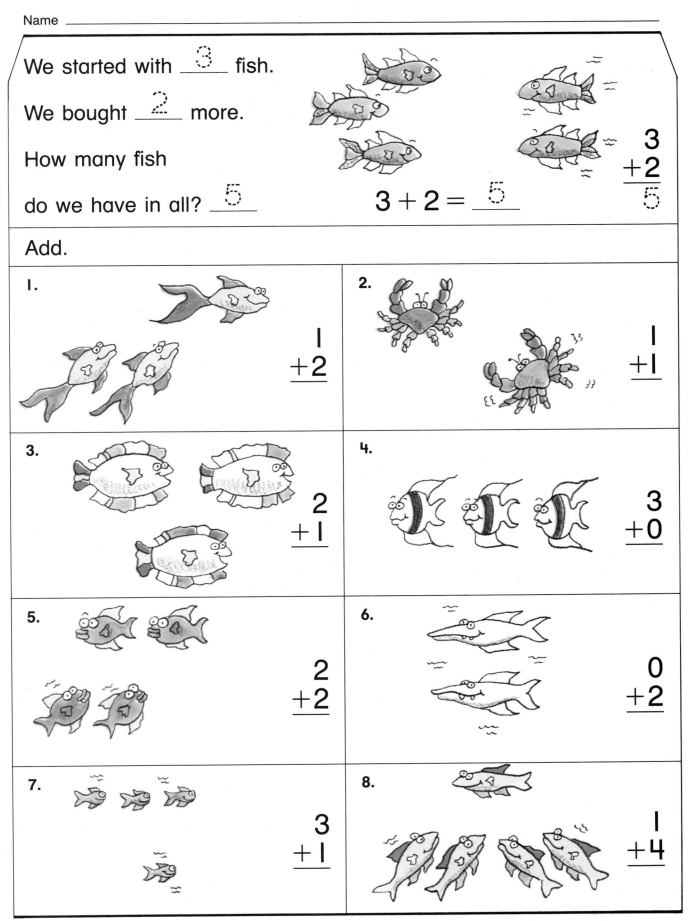

Add.

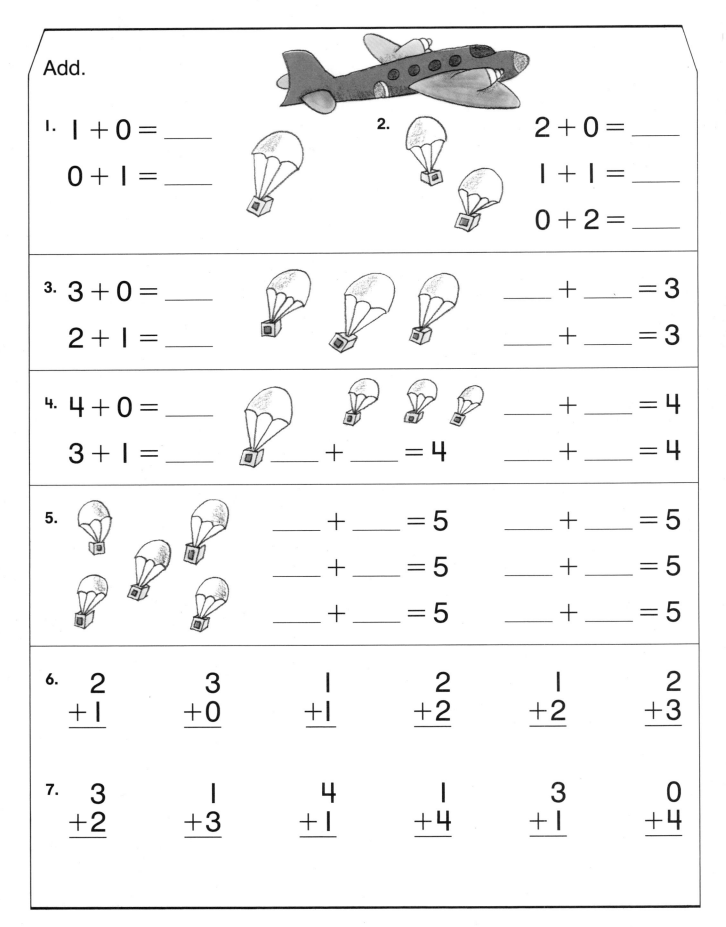

1. $1 + 0 = \underline{}$

   $0 + 1 = \underline{}$

2. $2 + 0 = \underline{}$

   $1 + 1 = \underline{}$

   $0 + 2 = \underline{}$

3. $3 + 0 = \underline{}$

   $2 + 1 = \underline{}$

   $\underline{} + \underline{} = 3$

   $\underline{} + \underline{} = 3$

4. $4 + 0 = \underline{}$

   $3 + 1 = \underline{}$

   $\underline{} + \underline{} = 4$

   $\underline{} + \underline{} = 4$

   $\underline{} + \underline{} = 4$

5. $\underline{} + \underline{} = 5$

   $\underline{} + \underline{} = 5$

   $\underline{} + \underline{} = 5$

   $\underline{} + \underline{} = 5$

   $\underline{} + \underline{} = 5$

   $\underline{} + \underline{} = 5$

6.
$$\begin{array}{r} 2 \\ +1 \\ \hline \end{array} \qquad \begin{array}{r} 3 \\ +0 \\ \hline \end{array} \qquad \begin{array}{r} 1 \\ +1 \\ \hline \end{array} \qquad \begin{array}{r} 2 \\ +2 \\ \hline \end{array} \qquad \begin{array}{r} 1 \\ +2 \\ \hline \end{array} \qquad \begin{array}{r} 2 \\ +3 \\ \hline \end{array}$$

7.
$$\begin{array}{r} 3 \\ +2 \\ \hline \end{array} \qquad \begin{array}{r} 1 \\ +3 \\ \hline \end{array} \qquad \begin{array}{r} 4 \\ +1 \\ \hline \end{array} \qquad \begin{array}{r} 1 \\ +4 \\ \hline \end{array} \qquad \begin{array}{r} 3 \\ +1 \\ \hline \end{array} \qquad \begin{array}{r} 0 \\ +4 \\ \hline \end{array}$$

Addition facts, sums through 5

Add.

$0 + 6 = 6$

$1 + 5 = 6$

___ $+$ ___ $= 6$

___ $+$ ___ $= 6$

___ $+$ ___ $= 6$

___ $+$ ___ $= 6$

___ $+$ ___ $= 6$

___ $+$ ___ $= 6$

1. $1 + 1 =$ ___ $4 + 4 =$ ___ $4 + 2 =$ ___

2. $2 + 2 =$ ___ $5 + 5 =$ ___ $5 + 2 =$ ___

3. $3 + 3 =$ ___ $3 + 4 =$ ___ $6 + 2 =$ ___

4.
$\begin{array}{r} 8 \\ +1 \\ \hline \end{array}$
$\begin{array}{r} 0 \\ +2 \\ \hline \end{array}$
$\begin{array}{r} 4 \\ +0 \\ \hline \end{array}$
$\begin{array}{r} 7 \\ +1 \\ \hline \end{array}$
$\begin{array}{r} 1 \\ +6 \\ \hline \end{array}$
$\begin{array}{r} 9 \\ +1 \\ \hline \end{array}$
$\begin{array}{r} 3 \\ +5 \\ \hline \end{array}$

5.
$\begin{array}{r} 2 \\ +7 \\ \hline \end{array}$
$\begin{array}{r} 4 \\ +3 \\ \hline \end{array}$
$\begin{array}{r} 5 \\ +4 \\ \hline \end{array}$
$\begin{array}{r} 3 \\ +6 \\ \hline \end{array}$
$\begin{array}{r} 2 \\ +8 \\ \hline \end{array}$
$\begin{array}{r} 5 \\ +3 \\ \hline \end{array}$
$\begin{array}{r} 6 \\ +4 \\ \hline \end{array}$

Solve.

6. Jim saw 4 🐕 .

   Jan saw 5 🐕 .

   They saw ___ 🐕 .

   $\begin{array}{r} 4 \\ \oplus\ 5 \\ \hline \ \end{array}$

7. Maria picked 5 🌼 .

   Lynn picked 3 🌼 .

   They picked ___ 🌼 .

Add.

1.
$\begin{array}{r}1\\+9\\\hline\end{array}$
$\begin{array}{r}3\\+6\\\hline\end{array}$
$\begin{array}{r}4\\+2\\\hline\end{array}$
$\begin{array}{r}1\\+2\\\hline\end{array}$
$\begin{array}{r}6\\+1\\\hline\end{array}$
$\begin{array}{r}3\\+7\\\hline\end{array}$
$\begin{array}{r}2\\+2\\\hline\end{array}$

2.
$\begin{array}{r}3\\+2\\\hline\end{array}$
$\begin{array}{r}6\\+2\\\hline\end{array}$
$\begin{array}{r}4\\+1\\\hline\end{array}$
$\begin{array}{r}5\\+2\\\hline\end{array}$
$\begin{array}{r}2\\+6\\\hline\end{array}$
$\begin{array}{r}5\\+1\\\hline\end{array}$
$\begin{array}{r}1\\+8\\\hline\end{array}$

3.
$\begin{array}{r}2\\+1\\\hline\end{array}$
$\begin{array}{r}7\\+2\\\hline\end{array}$
$\begin{array}{r}2\\+8\\\hline\end{array}$
$\begin{array}{r}4\\+6\\\hline\end{array}$
$\begin{array}{r}1\\+7\\\hline\end{array}$
$\begin{array}{r}8\\+2\\\hline\end{array}$
$\begin{array}{r}3\\+1\\\hline\end{array}$

Complete the tables.

4.

Add 3	
2	5
4	
1	
3	
6	
5	
7	

5.

Add 4	
1	5
3	
0	
2	
6	
5	
4	

6.

Add 5	
3	
0	
2	
5	
1	
4	

Addition facts, sums through 10

There are __5__ birds in all.

We saw __2__ birds fly away.

How many birds

are left? __3__

$5 - 2 = \underline{3}$

$\begin{array}{r} 5 \\ -2 \\ \hline 3 \end{array}$

Subtract.

1. $\begin{array}{r} 3 \\ -0 \\ \hline \end{array}$

2. $\begin{array}{r} 3 \\ -3 \\ \hline \end{array}$

3. $\begin{array}{r} 5 \\ -4 \\ \hline \end{array}$

4. $\begin{array}{r} 4 \\ -2 \\ \hline \end{array}$

5. $\begin{array}{r} 3 \\ -1 \\ \hline \end{array}$

6. $\begin{array}{r} 5 \\ -3 \\ \hline \end{array}$

7. $\begin{array}{r} 4 \\ -4 \\ \hline \end{array}$

8. $\begin{array}{r} 3 \\ -2 \\ \hline \end{array}$

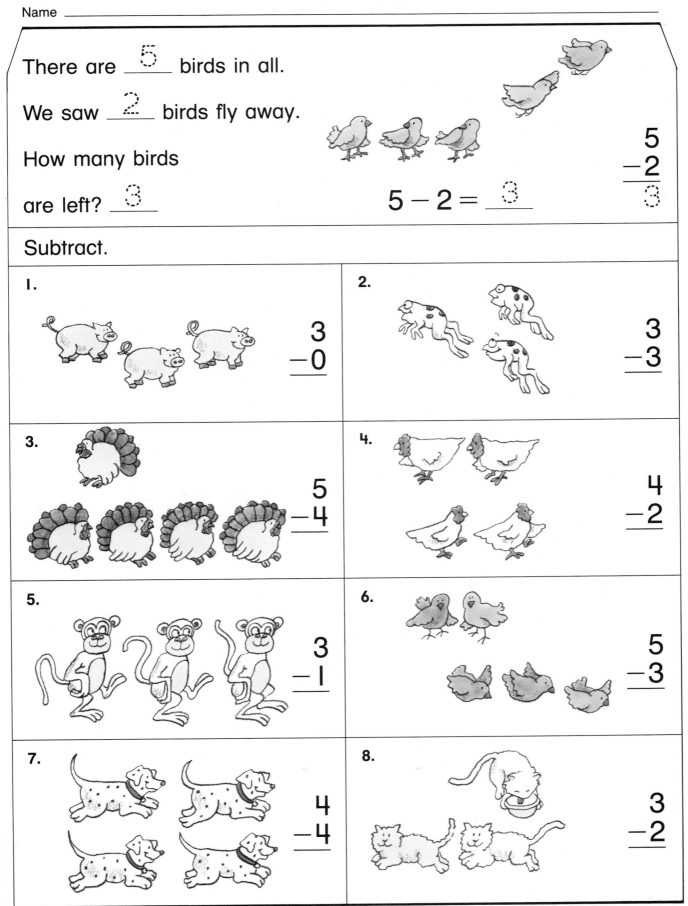

Subtraction facts, minuends through 5

Subtract.

1.  $\begin{array}{r} 5 \\ -1 \\ \hline 4 \end{array}$

2. $\begin{array}{r} 3 \\ -2 \\ \hline \end{array}$

3. $\begin{array}{r} 2 \\ -0 \\ \hline \end{array}$

4. $\begin{array}{r} 4 \\ -0 \\ \hline \end{array}$

5. $\begin{array}{r} 2 \\ -1 \\ \hline \end{array}$

6. $\begin{array}{r} 5 \\ -4 \\ \hline \end{array}$

7. $\begin{array}{r} 2 \\ -2 \\ \hline \end{array}$

8. $\begin{array}{r} 5 \\ -3 \\ \hline \end{array}$

9. $\begin{array}{r} 1 \\ -0 \\ \hline \end{array}$

10. $\begin{array}{r} 4 \\ -1 \\ \hline \end{array}$

11. $\begin{array}{r} 4 \\ -3 \\ \hline \end{array}$

12. $\begin{array}{r} 5 \\ -2 \\ \hline \end{array}$

FIELD TRIP

Write two addition and two subtraction sentences.

$2 + 3 = \underline{}$ $5 - 3 = \underline{}$

$3 + \underline{} = \underline{}$ $5 - \underline{} = \underline{}$

Subtraction facts, minuends through 5

Name _____

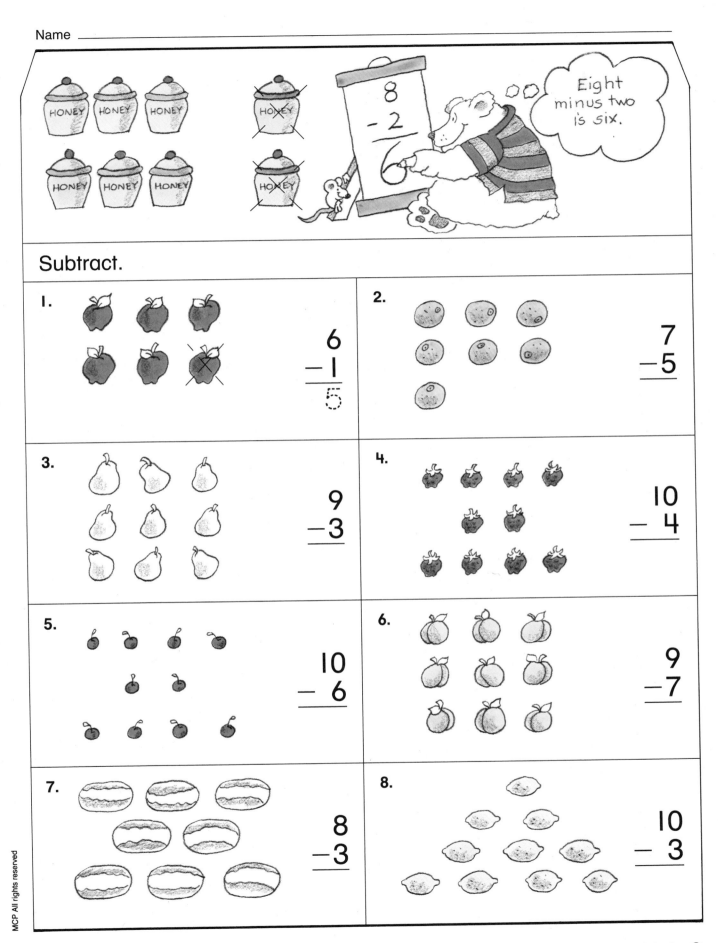

Eight minus two is six.

$$\begin{array}{r} 8 \\ -2 \\ \hline 6 \end{array}$$

Subtract.

1. $$\begin{array}{r} 6 \\ -1 \\ \hline 5 \end{array}$$

2. $$\begin{array}{r} 7 \\ -5 \\ \hline \end{array}$$

3. $$\begin{array}{r} 9 \\ -3 \\ \hline \end{array}$$

4. $$\begin{array}{r} 10 \\ -4 \\ \hline \end{array}$$

5. $$\begin{array}{r} 10 \\ -6 \\ \hline \end{array}$$

6. $$\begin{array}{r} 9 \\ -7 \\ \hline \end{array}$$

7. $$\begin{array}{r} 8 \\ -3 \\ \hline \end{array}$$

8. $$\begin{array}{r} 10 \\ -3 \\ \hline \end{array}$$

Subtraction facts, minuends through 10

(nine) **9**

Subtract.

1. $10 - 3 =$ _____ $8 - 2 =$ _____ $8 - 6 =$ _____

2. $7 - 4 =$ _____ $6 - 3 =$ _____ $10 - 9 =$ _____

3. $10 - 5 =$ _____ $9 - 4 =$ _____ $8 - 7 =$ _____

4. $8 - 5 =$ _____ $10 - 6 =$ _____ $7 - 2 =$ _____

5. $8 - 4 =$ _____ $10 - 1 =$ _____ $6 - 5 =$ _____

6. $9 - 5 =$ _____ $9 - 3 =$ _____ $10 - 2 =$ _____

7.

6	9	7	6	10	9	7
-6	-8	-5	-2	-8	-6	-0

8.

8	6	9	7	10	9	8
-3	-4	-2	-3	-4	-7	-0

Complete the tables.

9.

Subtract 2	
5	3
7	
8	

10.

Subtract 3	
7	4
9	
6	

11.

Subtract 5	
8	
6	
10	

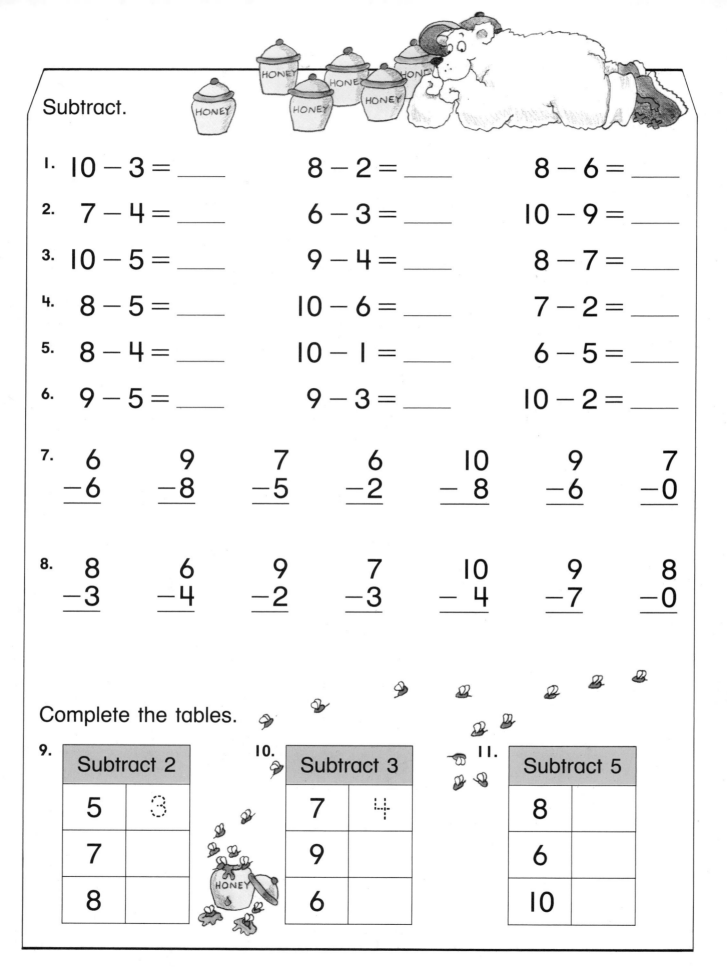

Subtraction facts, minuends through 10

Name _____

Add.

1.

2	1	5	3	6	1	7
$+2$	$+1$	$+2$	$+2$	$+1$	$+4$	$+2$

2.

4	6	2	5	3	4	1
$+1$	$+3$	$+6$	$+1$	$+7$	$+2$	$+9$

3.

0	3	8	1	5	2	4
$+4$	$+3$	$+1$	$+6$	$+0$	$+1$	$+5$

4.

1	8	4	2	7	6	2
$+2$	$+0$	$+3$	$+8$	$+1$	$+4$	$+5$

5.

3	5	1	5	6	8	3
$+4$	$+3$	$+8$	$+5$	$+2$	$+2$	$+1$

6.

7	4	2	3	0	1	9
$+3$	$+4$	$+3$	$+5$	$+7$	$+3$	$+1$

7.

2	3	1	4	1	5	2
$+4$	$+6$	$+5$	$+6$	$+7$	$+4$	$+7$

Addition facts, sums through 10

Subtract.

1.
$$4 - 2$$
$$2 - 1$$
$$7 - 2$$
$$5 - 3$$
$$7 - 1$$
$$5 - 4$$
$$9 - 2$$

2.
$$5 - 1$$
$$9 - 3$$
$$8 - 6$$
$$6 - 5$$
$$10 - 3$$
$$6 - 2$$
$$10 - 1$$

3.
$$8 - 2$$
$$6 - 3$$
$$9 - 8$$
$$7 - 6$$
$$5 - 5$$
$$3 - 1$$
$$9 - 4$$

4.
$$3 - 2$$
$$8 - 0$$
$$7 - 4$$
$$10 - 8$$
$$8 - 1$$
$$10 - 4$$
$$7 - 5$$

5.
$$7 - 3$$
$$8 - 5$$
$$9 - 1$$
$$10 - 5$$
$$5 - 2$$
$$10 - 2$$
$$4 - 3$$

6.
$$10 - 7$$
$$8 - 4$$
$$4 - 0$$
$$8 - 3$$
$$7 - 7$$
$$4 - 1$$
$$10 - 9$$

7.
$$6 - 4$$
$$9 - 6$$
$$6 - 1$$
$$10 - 6$$
$$8 - 7$$
$$9 - 5$$
$$9 - 7$$

Subtraction facts, minuends through 10

Name _____

Add or subtract.

1. $1 + 4 =$ _____

2. $3 + 3 =$ _____

3. $9 - 6 =$ _____

4. $8 + 2 =$ _____

5. $4 + 1 =$ _____

6. $5 + 3 =$ _____

7. $8 - 4 =$ _____

8.
$$\begin{array}{cccc} 4 & 2 & 6 & 9 \\ -2 & +2 & +3 & -7 \end{array}$$

9.
$$\begin{array}{cccc} 4 & 5 & 7 & 8 \\ +4 & -3 & -5 & -2 \end{array}$$

10.
$$\begin{array}{cccc} 10 & 3 & 2 & 7 \\ -\ 8 & +7 & +5 & +2 \end{array}$$

Solve.

11. Dan saw 5 ✈ .
Then he saw 2 more.
How many planes did he see in all?

[5] ⊕ [2]

_____ planes

12. Mary had 6 🍒 .
She ate 3 🍒 .
How many cherries did she have left?

_____ cherries

13. Elena had 8 🍑 .
She gave 3 of them away.
How many peaches were left?

_____ peaches

14. Jim caught 7 🐟 .
Sarah caught 3 🐟 .
How many fish were caught?

_____ fish

Add or subtract.

1.
$$4 - 2$$ $$6 - 3$$ $$8 - 4$$ $$10 - 3$$ $$9 - 3$$ $$8 - 5$$ $$7 - 4$$

2.
$$5 + 2$$ $$3 + 3$$ $$4 + 4$$ $$7 + 2$$ $$5 + 5$$ $$7 - 3$$ $$9 - 4$$

3.
$$10 - 4$$ $$2 + 7$$ $$8 + 2$$ $$6 + 4$$ $$5 - 2$$ $$7 - 6$$ $$6 + 2$$

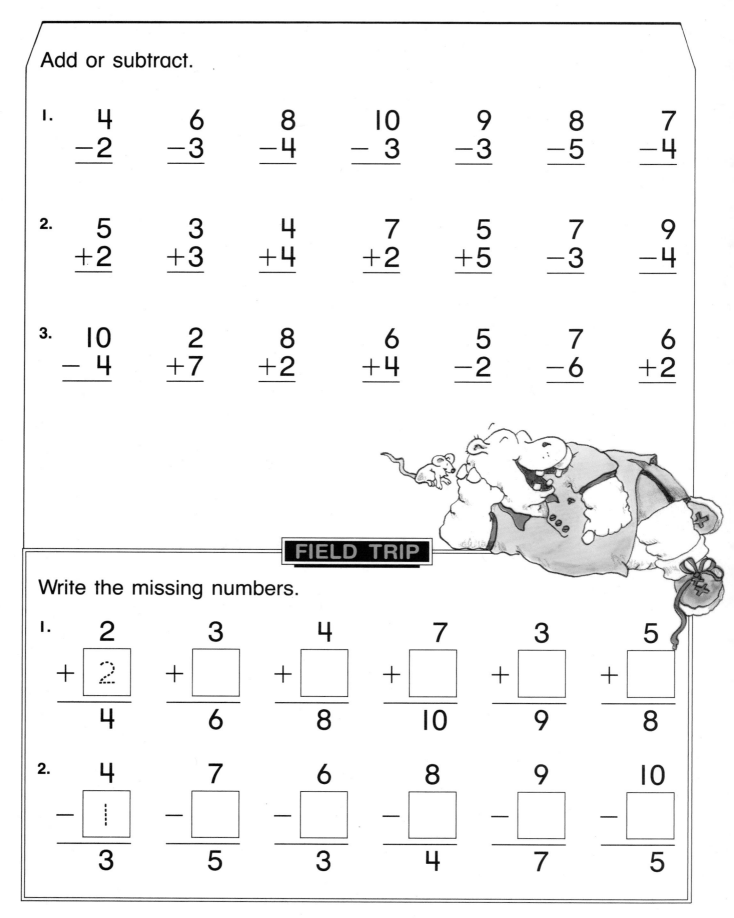

FIELD TRIP

Write the missing numbers.

1.
$$2 + \boxed{2} = 4$$ $$3 + \boxed{\ } = 6$$ $$4 + \boxed{\ } = 8$$ $$7 + \boxed{\ } = 10$$ $$3 + \boxed{\ } = 9$$ $$5 + \boxed{\ } = 8$$

2.
$$4 - \boxed{1} = 3$$ $$7 - \boxed{\ } = 5$$ $$6 - \boxed{\ } = 3$$ $$8 - \boxed{\ } = 4$$ $$9 - \boxed{\ } = 7$$ $$10 - \boxed{\ } = 5$$

Practice, adding and subtracting

Name _____

How much do both cost? __9__ ¢

$$\begin{array}{r} 5¢ \\ +4¢ \end{array}$$

Solve.

1. How much do both cost? ____ ¢

$$\begin{array}{r} 4¢ \\ +3¢ \\ \hline ¢ \end{array}$$

2. How much do both cost? ____ ¢

$$\begin{array}{r} 5¢ \\ +2¢ \\ \hline ¢ \end{array}$$

3. How much do both cost? ____ ¢

$$\begin{array}{r} 8¢ \\ +1¢ \\ \hline ¢ \end{array}$$

4. How much do both cost? ____ ¢

$$\begin{array}{r} 3¢ \\ +7¢ \\ \hline ¢ \end{array}$$

5. How much do both cost? ____ ¢

$$\begin{array}{r} 7¢ \\ +2¢ \\ \hline ¢ \end{array}$$

6. How much do both cost? ____ ¢

$$\begin{array}{r} \square ¢ \\ +\square ¢ \\ \hline ¢ \end{array}$$

7. How much do both cost? ____ ¢

$$\begin{array}{r} \square ¢ \\ +\square ¢ \\ \hline ¢ \end{array}$$

8. How much do both cost? ____ ¢

$$\begin{array}{r} \square ¢ \\ +\square ¢ \\ \hline ¢ \end{array}$$

Problem solving, adding money

(fifteen) **15**

Solve.

1. Aaron had 7¢. He bought a . How much was left? ____ ¢

$$\begin{array}{r} 7\ ¢ \\ -\ 4\ ¢ \\ \hline 3\ ¢ \end{array}$$

2. Dawn had 9¢. She bought a . How much was left? ____ ¢

$$\begin{array}{r} 9\ ¢ \\ -\ 3\ ¢ \\ \hline ¢ \end{array}$$

3. Tina had 8¢. She bought a . How much was left? ____ ¢

$$\begin{array}{r} 8\ ¢ \\ -\ 5\ ¢ \\ \hline ¢ \end{array}$$

4. Rex had 9¢. He bought a . How much was left? ____ ¢

$$\begin{array}{r} 9\ ¢ \\ -\ 4\ ¢ \\ \hline ¢ \end{array}$$

5. Ruth had 6¢. She bought a . How much was left? ____ ¢

$$\begin{array}{r} 6\ ¢ \\ -\ 2\ ¢ \\ \hline ¢ \end{array}$$

6. Jill had 6¢. She bought a . How much was left? ____ ¢

$$\begin{array}{r} 6\ ¢ \\ -\ 3\ ¢ \\ \hline ¢ \end{array}$$

7. Randy had 8¢. He bought a . How much was left? ____ ¢

$$\begin{array}{r} 8\ ¢ \\ -\ 7\ ¢ \\ \hline ¢ \end{array}$$

8. Juan had 9¢. He bought a . How much was left? ____ ¢

$$\begin{array}{r} ¢ \\ -\ ¢ \\ \hline ¢ \end{array}$$

9. Tom had 10¢. He bought a . How much was left? ____ ¢

$$\begin{array}{r} ¢ \\ -\ ¢ \\ \hline ¢ \end{array}$$

10. Tracy had 10¢. She bought a . How much was left? ____ ¢

$$\begin{array}{r} ¢ \\ -\ ¢ \\ \hline ¢ \end{array}$$

Problem solving, subtracting money

Name _____

Solve.

1. Maria picked 3 🍎 .
Sonja picked 4.
How many apples
were picked?

3
$\oplus$ 4

_____ apples

2. Jack had 6 🍐 .
He ate 2.
How many pears
are left?

6
$\ominus$ 2

_____ pears

3. Leah found 10 🐚 .
She gave 3 to Sarah.
How many shells
are left?

_____ shells

4. Eve had 9 🐟 .
She gave 3 to Alan.
How many goldfish
are left?

_____ goldfish

5. Larry found 6 🌰 .
Dino found 3.
How many acorns
were found?

_____ acorns

6. There are 10 🍌 .
The monkey ate 6.
How many bananas
are left?

_____ bananas

7. Mike has 7 pets.
3 of them are cats.
How many pets
are not cats?

_____ pets

8. Jan walked 5 blocks.
She ran 4 blocks.
How far
did Jan go?

_____ blocks

Problem solving, choosing the operation

Solve.

1. Ray had 10¢. He bought a [image]. How much money was left?

_____ ¢

$\bigcirc$ [ ] ¢ [ ] ¢ ¢

2. Lynn saw 4 [frog]. Ben saw 4. How many frogs did they see?

_____ frogs

$\bigcirc$ [ ] [ ]

3. Ted has 3 [duck]. Chan has 5. How many ducks are there in all?

_____ ducks

$\bigcirc$ [ ] [ ]

4. Jill had 9 stamps. She used 7 stamps. How many stamps are left?

_____ stamps

$\bigcirc$ [ ] [ ]

FIELD TRIP

Write in the correct sign.

1. $3 \bigcirc 4 = 7$
   $7 \bigcirc 4 = 3$

2. $6 \bigcirc 2 = 4$
   $2 \bigcirc 4 = 6$

3. $4 \bigcirc 4 = 8$
   $8 \bigcirc 4 = 4$

4. $3 \bigcirc 5 = 8$
   $8 \bigcirc 5 = 3$

5. $8 \bigcirc 2 = 6$
   $6 \bigcirc 2 = 8$

6. $10 \bigcirc 4 = 6$
   $6 \bigcirc 4 = 10$

7. $10 \bigcirc 5 = 5$
   $5 \bigcirc 5 = 10$

8. $8 \bigcirc 2 = 10$
   $10 \bigcirc 2 = 8$

9. $6 \bigcirc 3 = 3$
   $3 \bigcirc 3 = 6$

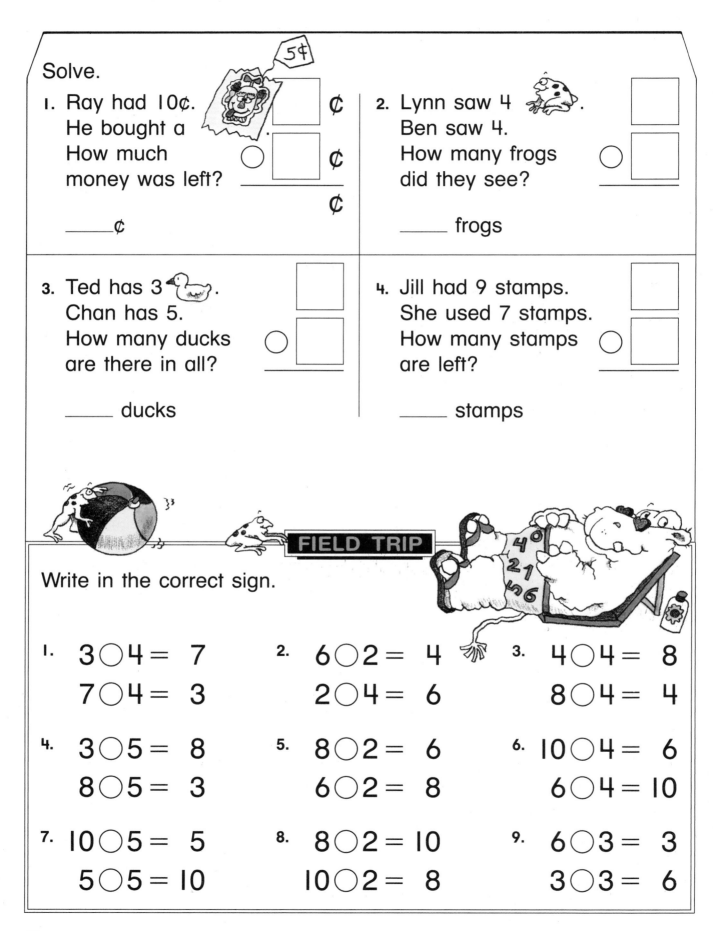

Problem solving, choosing the operation

Name _____

CHAPTER CHECKUP

Match.

1.

2		three
3		five
5		two

Add.

2.
$\begin{array}{r} 1 \\ +1 \\ \hline \end{array}$
$\begin{array}{r} 3 \\ +1 \\ \hline \end{array}$
$\begin{array}{r} 4 \\ +5 \\ \hline \end{array}$
$\begin{array}{r} 3 \\ +0 \\ \hline \end{array}$
$\begin{array}{r} 2 \\ +7 \\ \hline \end{array}$
$\begin{array}{r} 4 \\ +3 \\ \hline \end{array}$
$\begin{array}{r} 1 \\ +4 \\ \hline \end{array}$

3.
$\begin{array}{r} 2 \\ +8 \\ \hline \end{array}$
$\begin{array}{r} 5 \\ +1 \\ \hline \end{array}$
$\begin{array}{r} 2 \\ +5 \\ \hline \end{array}$
$\begin{array}{r} 3 \\ +3 \\ \hline \end{array}$
$\begin{array}{r} 3 \\ +7 \\ \hline \end{array}$
$\begin{array}{r} 2 \\ +4 \\ \hline \end{array}$
$\begin{array}{r} 3 \\ +6 \\ \hline \end{array}$

4.
$\begin{array}{r} 2 \\ +2 \\ \hline \end{array}$
$\begin{array}{r} 5 \\ +5 \\ \hline \end{array}$
$\begin{array}{r} 0 \\ +4 \\ \hline \end{array}$
$\begin{array}{r} 5 \\ +2 \\ \hline \end{array}$
$\begin{array}{r} 3 \\ +5 \\ \hline \end{array}$
$\begin{array}{r} 7 \\ +2 \\ \hline \end{array}$
$\begin{array}{r} 6 \\ +3 \\ \hline \end{array}$

5. $7 + 0 =$ ___ $7 + 3 =$ ___ $5 + 3 =$ ___

6. $3 + 4 =$ ___ $5 + 4 =$ ___ $0 + 8 =$ ___

7. $2 + 3 =$ ___ $4 + 4 =$ ___ $8 + 1 =$ ___

8. $1 + 7 =$ ___ $1 + 9 =$ ___ $4 + 6 =$ ___

9. $3 + 2 =$ ___ $6 + 4 =$ ___ $4 + 2 =$ ___

CHAPTER CHECKUP

Subtract.

1. $\begin{array}{r} 3 \\ -1 \\ \hline \end{array}$ $\begin{array}{r} 2 \\ -0 \\ \hline \end{array}$ $\begin{array}{r} 4 \\ -2 \\ \hline \end{array}$ $\begin{array}{r} 7 \\ -4 \\ \hline \end{array}$ $\begin{array}{r} 6 \\ -3 \\ \hline \end{array}$ $\begin{array}{r} 8 \\ -6 \\ \hline \end{array}$ $\begin{array}{r} 5 \\ -3 \\ \hline \end{array}$

2. $\begin{array}{r} 6 \\ -4 \\ \hline \end{array}$ $\begin{array}{r} 9 \\ -2 \\ \hline \end{array}$ $\begin{array}{r} 10 \\ -\ 1 \\ \hline \end{array}$ $\begin{array}{r} 6 \\ -2 \\ \hline \end{array}$ $\begin{array}{r} 9 \\ -5 \\ \hline \end{array}$ $\begin{array}{r} 8 \\ -3 \\ \hline \end{array}$ $\begin{array}{r} 10 \\ -\ 5 \\ \hline \end{array}$

3. $10 - 2 = \underline{\quad}$ $10 - 3 = \underline{\quad}$ $6 - 6 = \underline{\quad}$

4. $8 - 4 = \underline{\quad}$ $7 - 0 = \underline{\quad}$ $10 - 6 = \underline{\quad}$

Solve.

5. Alex had 9 🍃.
   He gave Liz 3.
   How many leaves
   are left?

   _____ leaves

6. Jeff saw 4 🦋.
   Bill saw 4.
   How many butterflies
   were seen?

   _____ butterflies

7. Hal bought a 🍐 5¢
   and a 🍌 5¢.
   How much did
   both cost?

   _____¢

8. Rose had 8¢.
   She bought a 🐱 2¢.
   How much
   is left?

   _____¢

2 BASIC FACTS, SUMS THROUGH 12

Add.

$$8 + 3 = 11$$

11 is 1 ten and 1 one

1.
$$7 + 5 = 12$$

2.
$$5 + 6$$

3.
$$6 + 6$$

4.
$$9 + 3$$

5.

8	5	4	9	7	9	3
$+4$	$+7$	$+4$	$+2$	$+4$	$+3$	$+8$

6.

4	4	5	3	2	6	7
$+7$	$+8$	$+6$	$+9$	$+9$	$+5$	$+5$

Complete the wheels.

1.

Wheel 1 (center 3): +8, +3, +5, +6, +7, +9, +4, +2

Wheel 2 (center 5): +2, +4, +7, +0, +5, +3, +1, +6

Add.

2.
$\begin{array}{r} 7 \\ +2 \\ \hline \end{array}$
$\begin{array}{r} 9 \\ +1 \\ \hline \end{array}$
$\begin{array}{r} 8 \\ +4 \\ \hline \end{array}$
$\begin{array}{r} 5 \\ +5 \\ \hline \end{array}$
$\begin{array}{r} 4 \\ +7 \\ \hline \end{array}$
$\begin{array}{r} 6 \\ +6 \\ \hline \end{array}$
$\begin{array}{r} 9 \\ +3 \\ \hline \end{array}$

3.
$\begin{array}{r} 4 \\ +5 \\ \hline \end{array}$
$\begin{array}{r} 6 \\ +3 \\ \hline \end{array}$
$\begin{array}{r} 2 \\ +7 \\ \hline \end{array}$
$\begin{array}{r} 8 \\ +2 \\ \hline \end{array}$
$\begin{array}{r} 3 \\ +9 \\ \hline \end{array}$
$\begin{array}{r} 7 \\ +5 \\ \hline \end{array}$
$\begin{array}{r} 3 \\ +6 \\ \hline \end{array}$

4.
$\begin{array}{r} 8 \\ +3 \\ \hline \end{array}$
$\begin{array}{r} 5 \\ +6 \\ \hline \end{array}$
$\begin{array}{r} 4 \\ +6 \\ \hline \end{array}$
$\begin{array}{r} 7 \\ +4 \\ \hline \end{array}$
$\begin{array}{r} 3 \\ +8 \\ \hline \end{array}$
$\begin{array}{r} 6 \\ +4 \\ \hline \end{array}$
$\begin{array}{r} 9 \\ +2 \\ \hline \end{array}$

5.
$\begin{array}{r} 4 \\ +8 \\ \hline \end{array}$
$\begin{array}{r} 6 \\ +5 \\ \hline \end{array}$
$\begin{array}{r} 3 \\ +7 \\ \hline \end{array}$
$\begin{array}{r} 5 \\ +4 \\ \hline \end{array}$
$\begin{array}{r} 7 \\ +3 \\ \hline \end{array}$
$\begin{array}{r} 2 \\ +8 \\ \hline \end{array}$
$\begin{array}{r} 5 \\ +7 \\ \hline \end{array}$

Name _____

Add.

1.
$$\begin{array}{r} 9 \\ +1 \\ \hline \end{array}$$
$$\begin{array}{r} 7 \\ +3 \\ \hline \end{array}$$
$$\begin{array}{r} 5 \\ +4 \\ \hline \end{array}$$
$$\begin{array}{r} 8 \\ +2 \\ \hline \end{array}$$
$$\begin{array}{r} 6 \\ +5 \\ \hline \end{array}$$
$$\begin{array}{r} 3 \\ +7 \\ \hline \end{array}$$
$$\begin{array}{r} 4 \\ +8 \\ \hline \end{array}$$

2.
$$\begin{array}{r} 5 \\ +7 \\ \hline \end{array}$$
$$\begin{array}{r} 8 \\ +4 \\ \hline \end{array}$$
$$\begin{array}{r} 2 \\ +8 \\ \hline \end{array}$$
$$\begin{array}{r} 3 \\ +6 \\ \hline \end{array}$$
$$\begin{array}{r} 7 \\ +4 \\ \hline \end{array}$$
$$\begin{array}{r} 2 \\ +9 \\ \hline \end{array}$$
$$\begin{array}{r} 6 \\ +4 \\ \hline \end{array}$$

Complete the tables.

3.

Add 6	
2	8
4	
6	
3	
5	

Add 4	
4	8
5	
7	
8	
6	

Add 3	
5	
7	
4	
9	
6	

Add 5	
5	
7	
4	
6	
3	

Solve.

4. Ken has 9 🐚.
   He found 3 more.
   How many shells
   does Ken have?

   _____ shells

5. Megan picks 5 🌸.
   Rich picks 6 🌸.
   How many flowers
   do they have?

   _____ flowers

Add.

1. $7 + 2$ $1 + 9$ $4 + 6$ $3 + 8$ $6 + 4$ $5 + 4$ $1 + 8$

2. $6 + 6$ $8 + 2$ $7 + 3$ $3 + 7$ $5 + 6$ $9 + 1$ $4 + 7$

3. $1 + 1 = \underline{\quad}$ $8 + 4 = \underline{\quad}$ $2 + 8 = \underline{\quad}$

4. $2 + 2 = \underline{\quad}$ $7 + 5 = \underline{\quad}$ $9 + 3 = \underline{\quad}$

5. $3 + 3 = \underline{\quad}$ $6 + 5 = \underline{\quad}$ $8 + 3 = \underline{\quad}$

6. $4 + 4 = \underline{\quad}$ $5 + 7 = \underline{\quad}$ $9 + 2 = \underline{\quad}$

7. $5 + 5 = \underline{\quad}$ $2 + 9 = \underline{\quad}$ $4 + 8 = \underline{\quad}$

FIELD TRIP

Circle pairs of numbers.

Sums of 11

2	5	3	8
9	7	4	4
2	6	2	7
6	5	8	3

(There are 8 pairs.)

Sums of 12

4	8	2	5
9	3	8	7
8	9	6	6
4	7	7	5

(There are 7 pairs.)

Name _____

How many cherries
are there? __12__

How many are
crossed out? __4__

How many are left? __8__

$$\begin{array}{r} 12 \\ -4 \\ \hline 8 \end{array}$$

Subtract.

1.
$$\begin{array}{r} 11 \\ -5 \\ \hline \end{array}$$

2.
$$\begin{array}{r} 12 \\ -6 \\ \hline \end{array}$$

3.
$$\begin{array}{r} 12 \\ -3 \\ \hline \end{array}$$

4.
$$\begin{array}{r} 11 \\ -2 \\ \hline \end{array}$$

Subtract.

5.
$$\begin{array}{r} 11 \\ -3 \\ \hline \end{array} \quad \begin{array}{r} 11 \\ -8 \\ \hline \end{array} \quad \begin{array}{r} 11 \\ -7 \\ \hline \end{array} \quad \begin{array}{r} 11 \\ -4 \\ \hline \end{array} \quad \begin{array}{r} 12 \\ -3 \\ \hline \end{array} \quad \begin{array}{r} 12 \\ -9 \\ \hline \end{array} \quad \begin{array}{r} 12 \\ -6 \\ \hline \end{array}$$

6.
$$\begin{array}{r} 11 \\ -5 \\ \hline \end{array} \quad \begin{array}{r} 11 \\ -6 \\ \hline \end{array} \quad \begin{array}{r} 12 \\ -5 \\ \hline \end{array} \quad \begin{array}{r} 12 \\ -7 \\ \hline \end{array} \quad \begin{array}{r} 11 \\ -9 \\ \hline \end{array} \quad \begin{array}{r} 12 \\ -4 \\ \hline \end{array} \quad \begin{array}{r} 12 \\ -8 \\ \hline \end{array}$$

Subtract.

1. $8 - 1 =$ ___ $11 - 6 =$ ___ $10 - 1 =$ ___

2. $10 - 2 =$ ___ $9 - 1 =$ ___ $12 - 8 =$ ___

3. $11 - 4 =$ ___ $12 - 7 =$ ___ $8 - 2 =$ ___

4. $9 - 0 =$ ___ $10 - 9 =$ ___ $10 - 4 =$ ___

5. $11 - 5 =$ ___ $8 - 7 =$ ___ $12 - 5 =$ ___

6. $10 - 3 =$ ___ $12 - 6 =$ ___ $8 - 3 =$ ___

7. $12 - 9 =$ ___ $9 - 5 =$ ___ $11 - 2 =$ ___

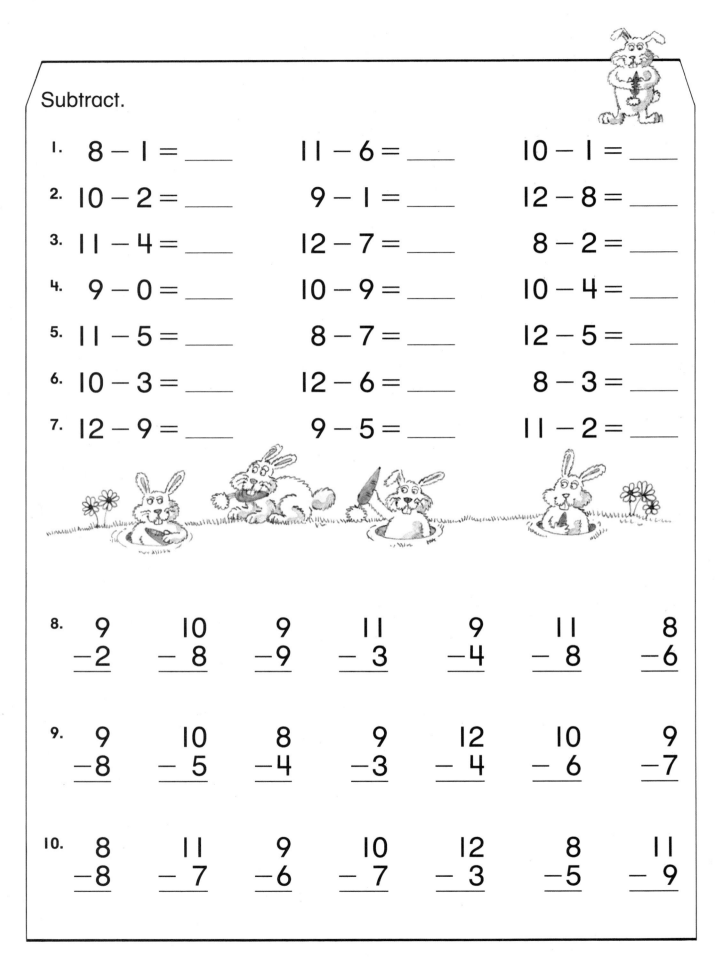

8.
$$\begin{array}{c}9\\-2\\\hline\end{array}\quad\begin{array}{c}10\\-8\\\hline\end{array}\quad\begin{array}{c}9\\-9\\\hline\end{array}\quad\begin{array}{c}11\\-3\\\hline\end{array}\quad\begin{array}{c}9\\-4\\\hline\end{array}\quad\begin{array}{c}11\\-8\\\hline\end{array}\quad\begin{array}{c}8\\-6\\\hline\end{array}$$

9.
$$\begin{array}{c}9\\-8\\\hline\end{array}\quad\begin{array}{c}10\\-5\\\hline\end{array}\quad\begin{array}{c}8\\-4\\\hline\end{array}\quad\begin{array}{c}9\\-3\\\hline\end{array}\quad\begin{array}{c}12\\-4\\\hline\end{array}\quad\begin{array}{c}10\\-6\\\hline\end{array}\quad\begin{array}{c}9\\-7\\\hline\end{array}$$

10.
$$\begin{array}{c}8\\-8\\\hline\end{array}\quad\begin{array}{c}11\\-7\\\hline\end{array}\quad\begin{array}{c}9\\-6\\\hline\end{array}\quad\begin{array}{c}10\\-7\\\hline\end{array}\quad\begin{array}{c}12\\-3\\\hline\end{array}\quad\begin{array}{c}8\\-5\\\hline\end{array}\quad\begin{array}{c}11\\-9\\\hline\end{array}$$

Subtraction facts, minuends through 12

Subtract.

1.

11	11	11	11	11	11	11
$-\ 3$	$-\ 5$	$-\ 9$	$-\ 4$	$-\ 7$	$-\ 6$	$-\ 8$

2.

12	12	12	12	12	12	12
$-\ 3$	$-\ 5$	$-\ 6$	$-\ 8$	$-\ 4$	$-\ 7$	$-\ 9$

Complete the wheels.

3.

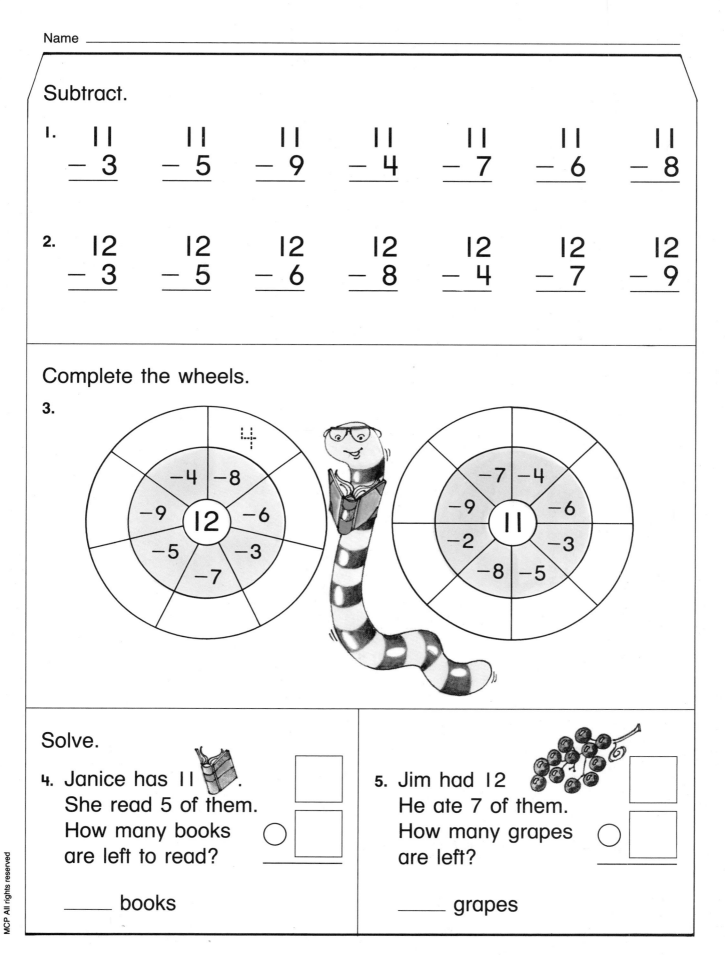

Left wheel center: 12; spokes: -4, -8, -6, -3, -7, -5, -9 (one filled answer: 4 for -8)

Right wheel center: 11; spokes: -7, -4, -6, -3, -5, -8, -2, -9

Solve.

4. Janice has 11 📖.
She read 5 of them.
How many books
are left to read?

○ ☐
☐

_____ books

5. Jim had 12 🍇
He ate 7 of them.
How many grapes
are left?

○ ☐
☐

_____ grapes

Subtract.

1. $10 - 3 =$ _____ $8 - 2 =$ _____ $10 - 8 =$ _____
2. $9 - 1 =$ _____ $11 - 3 =$ _____ $11 - 5 =$ _____
3. $11 - 4 =$ _____ $10 - 4 =$ _____ $9 - 3 =$ _____
4. $10 - 7 =$ _____ $12 - 3 =$ _____ $12 - 5 =$ _____
5. $8 - 7 =$ _____ $10 - 5 =$ _____ $12 - 6 =$ _____
6. $11 - 2 =$ _____ $12 - 8 =$ _____ $10 - 2 =$ _____
7. $12 - 4 =$ _____ $10 - 9 =$ _____ $11 - 6 =$ _____
8. $10 - 1 =$ _____ $11 - 7 =$ _____ $12 - 9 =$ _____
9. $11 - 8 =$ _____ $12 - 7 =$ _____ $10 - 6 =$ _____
10. $9 - 7 =$ _____ $9 - 5 =$ _____ $11 - 9 =$ _____

FIELD TRIP

Use these numbers to write four number sentences.

| 5   11   6 | 4   12   8 |

$5 + 6 = 11$ $4 +$ ___ $= 12$

___ $+$ ___ $=$ ___   ___ $+$ ___ $=$ ___

$11 - 6 = 5$ ___ $-$ ___ $=$ ___

___ $-$ ___ $=$ ___   ___ $-$ ___ $=$ ___

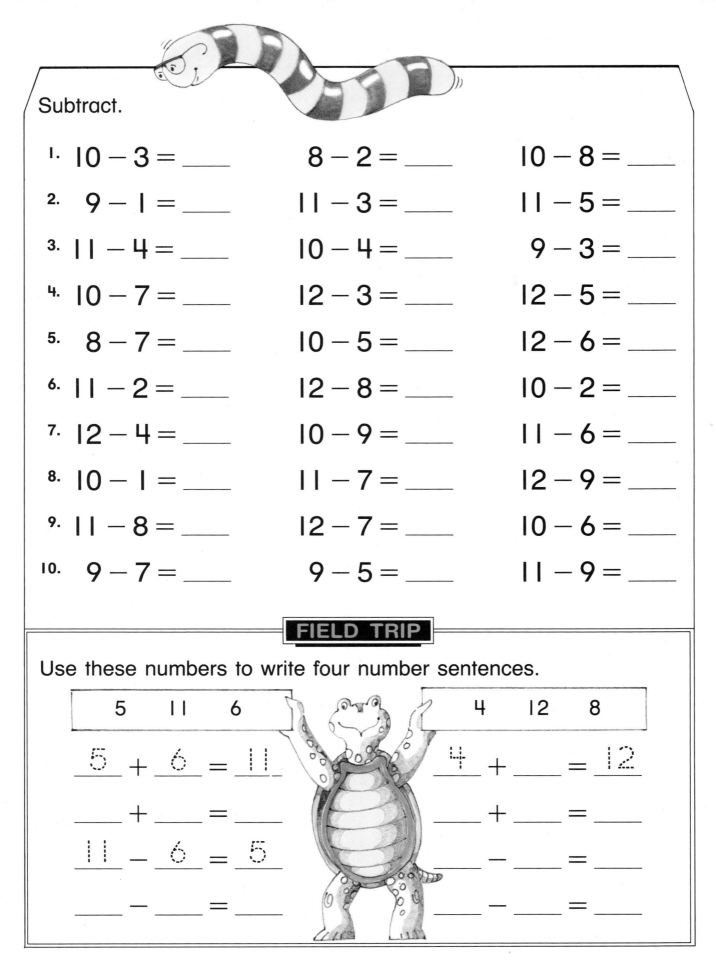

Match.

1. | $7+2$ | $5+6$ | $3+5$ |

8   9   11

2. | $4+8$ | $5+5$ | $4+3$ |

10   7   12

3. | $12-3$ | $10-5$ | $11-3$ |

8   9   5

4. | $12-8$ | $11-4$ | $12-6$ |

7   6   4

Add or subtract.

5.
$\begin{array}{r} 1 \\ +5 \\ \hline \end{array}$
$\begin{array}{r} 6 \\ +5 \\ \hline \end{array}$
$\begin{array}{r} 0 \\ +7 \\ \hline \end{array}$
$\begin{array}{r} 10 \\ -2 \\ \hline \end{array}$
$\begin{array}{r} 11 \\ -2 \\ \hline \end{array}$
$\begin{array}{r} 3 \\ +9 \\ \hline \end{array}$
$\begin{array}{r} 2 \\ +7 \\ \hline \end{array}$

6.
$\begin{array}{r} 11 \\ -4 \\ \hline \end{array}$
$\begin{array}{r} 10 \\ -5 \\ \hline \end{array}$
$\begin{array}{r} 4 \\ +8 \\ \hline \end{array}$
$\begin{array}{r} 12 \\ -7 \\ \hline \end{array}$
$\begin{array}{r} 12 \\ -3 \\ \hline \end{array}$
$\begin{array}{r} 5 \\ +6 \\ \hline \end{array}$
$\begin{array}{r} 11 \\ -3 \\ \hline \end{array}$

7.
$\begin{array}{r} 12 \\ -9 \\ \hline \end{array}$
$\begin{array}{r} 11 \\ -5 \\ \hline \end{array}$
$\begin{array}{r} 9 \\ +3 \\ \hline \end{array}$
$\begin{array}{r} 3 \\ +7 \\ \hline \end{array}$
$\begin{array}{r} 1 \\ +9 \\ \hline \end{array}$
$\begin{array}{r} 10 \\ -7 \\ \hline \end{array}$
$\begin{array}{r} 12 \\ -3 \\ \hline \end{array}$

8.
$\begin{array}{r} 12 \\ -5 \\ \hline \end{array}$
$\begin{array}{r} 11 \\ -8 \\ \hline \end{array}$
$\begin{array}{r} 2 \\ +9 \\ \hline \end{array}$
$\begin{array}{r} 11 \\ -6 \\ \hline \end{array}$
$\begin{array}{r} 7 \\ +4 \\ \hline \end{array}$
$\begin{array}{r} 5 \\ +7 \\ \hline \end{array}$
$\begin{array}{r} 8 \\ +4 \\ \hline \end{array}$

Add or subtract.

1. $2 + 9 = \underline{\quad}$
2. $5 + 7 = \underline{\quad}$
3. $8 + 3 = \underline{\quad}$
4. $10 - 1 = \underline{\quad}$
5. $11 - 4 = \underline{\quad}$
6. $12 - 6 = \underline{\quad}$
7. $7 + 5 = \underline{\quad}$
8. $8 + 2 = \underline{\quad}$
9. $4 + 7 = \underline{\quad}$
10. $10 - 5 = \underline{\quad}$
11. $12 - 9 = \underline{\quad}$
12. $6 + 5 = \underline{\quad}$

13.
$$\begin{array}{cccc} 9 & 4 & 11 & 3 \\ +1 & +8 & -9 & +8 \end{array}$$

14.
$$\begin{array}{cccc} 6 & 12 & 11 & 12 \\ +4 & -7 & -5 & -8 \end{array}$$

15.
$$\begin{array}{cccc} 12 & 3 & 9 & 5 \\ -3 & +7 & +3 & +5 \end{array}$$

16.
$$\begin{array}{cccc} 8 & 10 & 12 & 11 \\ +4 & -6 & -5 & -3 \end{array}$$

17.
$$\begin{array}{cccc} 10 & 3 & 11 & 6 \\ -8 & +9 & -7 & +6 \end{array}$$

FIELD TRIP

Write the correct sign.

$$\begin{array}{cccccc} 8 & 12 & 4 & 6 & 7 & 5 \\ \bigcirc 3 & \bigcirc 7 & \bigcirc 5 & \bigcirc 6 & \bigcirc 4 & \bigcirc 5 \\ \hline 5 & 5 & 9 & 0 & 11 & 10 \end{array}$$

Practice, adding and subtracting

I nickel	I penny
(nickel image)	(penny image)
5 cents	I cent
5¢	I¢

(coins) ___9___ ¢

Five, six, seven, eight, nine. I have 9 cents.

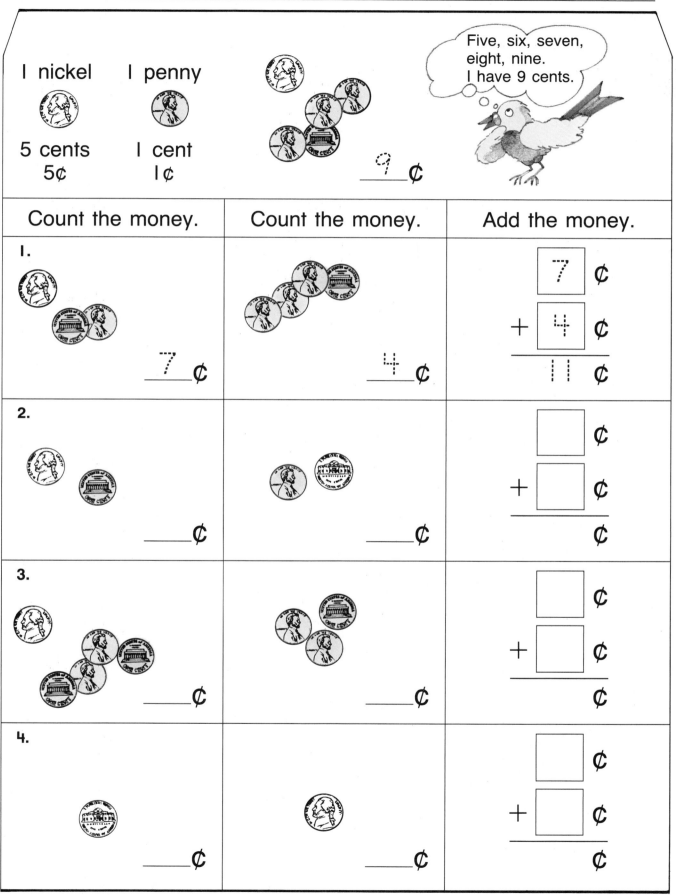

Count the money.	Count the money.	Add the money.
1. (coins) ___7___ ¢	(coins) ___4___ ¢	$\begin{array}{r} 7 \\ +\ 4 \\ \hline 11 \end{array}$ ¢
2. (coins) ____¢	(coins) ____¢	$\begin{array}{r} \square \\ +\ \square \\ \hline \end{array}$ ¢
3. (coins) ____¢	(coins) ____¢	$\begin{array}{r} \square \\ +\ \square \\ \hline \end{array}$ ¢
4. (coin) ____¢	(coin) ____¢	$\begin{array}{r} \square \\ +\ \square \\ \hline \end{array}$ ¢

Problem solving, adding money

Count the money. How much is spent? How much is left?

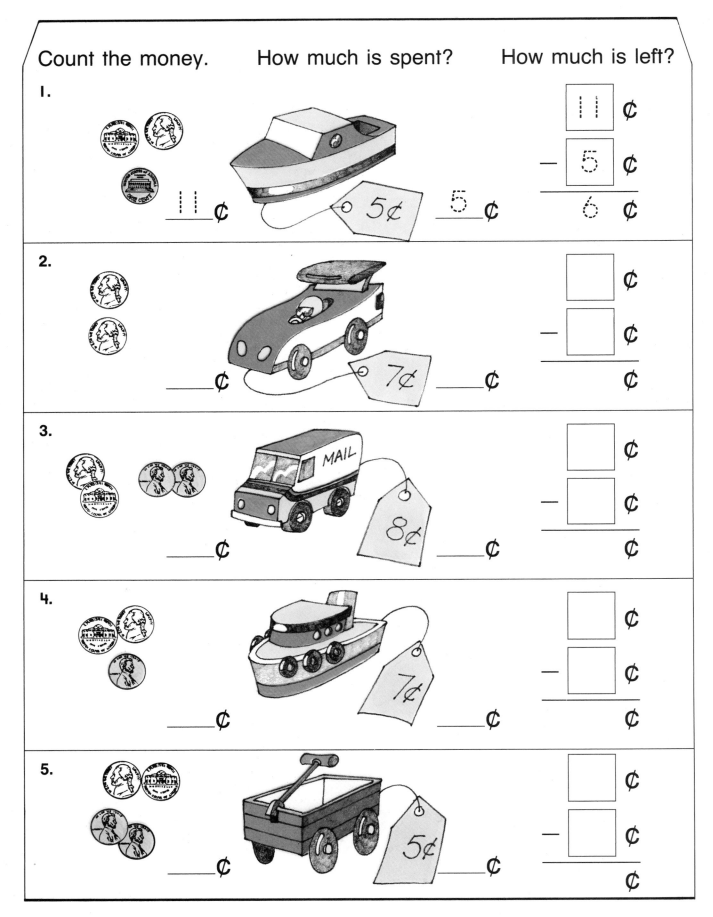

1. 11 ¢ 5¢ 5 ¢

$$\begin{array}{r} 11\ ¢ \\ -\ 5\ ¢ \\ \hline 6\ ¢ \end{array}$$

2. ___ ¢ 7¢   ___ ¢

$$\begin{array}{r} \square\ ¢ \\ -\ \square\ ¢ \\ \hline \square\ ¢ \end{array}$$

3. ___ ¢   MAIL 8¢   ___ ¢

$$\begin{array}{r} \square\ ¢ \\ -\ \square\ ¢ \\ \hline \square\ ¢ \end{array}$$

4. ___ ¢ 7¢   ___ ¢

$$\begin{array}{r} \square\ ¢ \\ -\ \square\ ¢ \\ \hline \square\ ¢ \end{array}$$

5. ___ ¢ 5¢   ___ ¢

$$\begin{array}{r} \square\ ¢ \\ -\ \square\ ¢ \\ \hline \square\ ¢ \end{array}$$

Problem solving, subtracting money

Solve.

1. Dick had 11 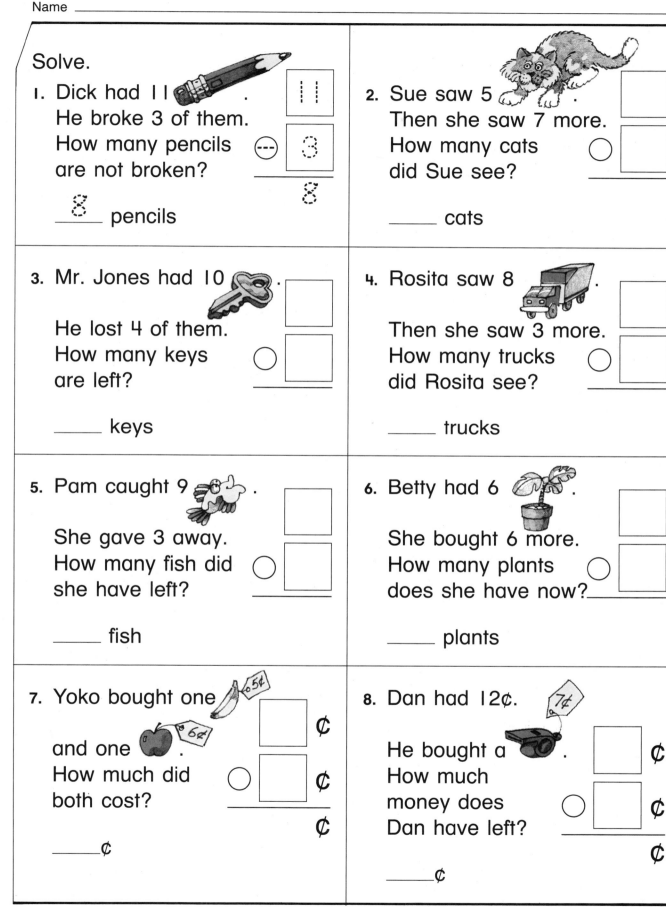. He broke 3 of them. How many pencils are not broken?

_____ pencils

2. Sue saw 5 . Then she saw 7 more. How many cats did Sue see?

_____ cats

3. Mr. Jones had 10 . He lost 4 of them. How many keys are left?

_____ keys

4. Rosita saw 8 . Then she saw 3 more. How many trucks did Rosita see?

_____ trucks

5. Pam caught 9 . She gave 3 away. How many fish did she have left?

_____ fish

6. Betty had 6 . She bought 6 more. How many plants does she have now?

_____ plants

7. Yoko bought one 5¢ and one 6¢. How much did both cost?

_____ ¢

8. Dan had 12¢. He bought a 7¢. How much money does Dan have left?

_____ ¢

Solve.

1. Ed saw 5 🦆 .
Carla saw 4.
How many ducks
did they see?

$\begin{array}{r} 5 \\ \oplus\ 4 \\ \hline 9 \end{array}$

__9__ ducks

2. Doug had 12 .
He planted 7.
How many seeds
does he have left?

_____ seeds

3. Steve had 11 🍊 .
He ate 2 of them.
How many oranges
are left?

_____ oranges

4. Mr. Smith had 7 🐄 .
He bought 4 more.
How many cows
does he have now?

_____ cows

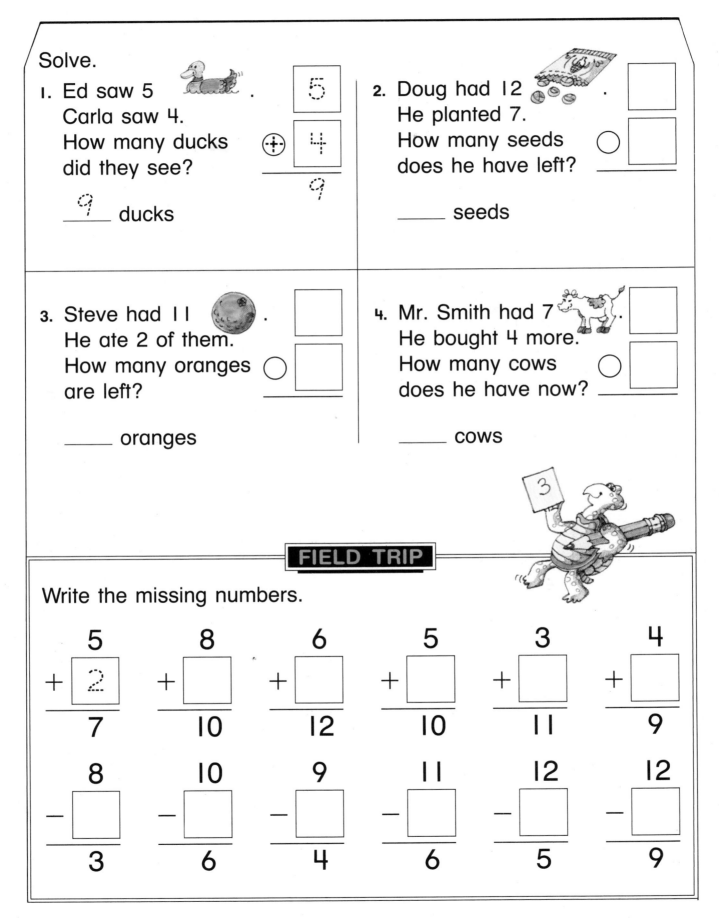

FIELD TRIP

Write the missing numbers.

$\begin{array}{r} 5 \\ +\ 2 \\ \hline 7 \end{array}$
$\begin{array}{r} 8 \\ +\ \square \\ \hline 10 \end{array}$
$\begin{array}{r} 6 \\ +\ \square \\ \hline 12 \end{array}$
$\begin{array}{r} 5 \\ +\ \square \\ \hline 10 \end{array}$
$\begin{array}{r} 3 \\ +\ \square \\ \hline 11 \end{array}$
$\begin{array}{r} 4 \\ +\ \square \\ \hline 9 \end{array}$

$\begin{array}{r} 8 \\ -\ \square \\ \hline 3 \end{array}$
$\begin{array}{r} 10 \\ -\ \square \\ \hline 6 \end{array}$
$\begin{array}{r} 9 \\ -\ \square \\ \hline 4 \end{array}$
$\begin{array}{r} 11 \\ -\ \square \\ \hline 6 \end{array}$
$\begin{array}{r} 12 \\ -\ \square \\ \hline 5 \end{array}$
$\begin{array}{r} 12 \\ -\ \square \\ \hline 9 \end{array}$

Problem solving, adding and subtracting

CHAPTER CHECKUP

Add.

1.
$$\begin{array}{r} 1 \\ +9 \\ \hline \end{array}$$
$$\begin{array}{r} 8 \\ +4 \\ \hline \end{array}$$
$$\begin{array}{r} 8 \\ +3 \\ \hline \end{array}$$
$$\begin{array}{r} 5 \\ +6 \\ \hline \end{array}$$
$$\begin{array}{r} 3 \\ +9 \\ \hline \end{array}$$
$$\begin{array}{r} 3 \\ +7 \\ \hline \end{array}$$
$$\begin{array}{r} 5 \\ +7 \\ \hline \end{array}$$

2.
$$\begin{array}{r} 6 \\ +5 \\ \hline \end{array}$$
$$\begin{array}{r} 9 \\ +3 \\ \hline \end{array}$$
$$\begin{array}{r} 4 \\ +8 \\ \hline \end{array}$$
$$\begin{array}{r} 2 \\ +9 \\ \hline \end{array}$$
$$\begin{array}{r} 6 \\ +6 \\ \hline \end{array}$$
$$\begin{array}{r} 7 \\ +4 \\ \hline \end{array}$$
$$\begin{array}{r} 3 \\ +8 \\ \hline \end{array}$$

Subtract.

3.
$$\begin{array}{r} 11 \\ -2 \\ \hline \end{array}$$
$$\begin{array}{r} 11 \\ -9 \\ \hline \end{array}$$
$$\begin{array}{r} 10 \\ -7 \\ \hline \end{array}$$
$$\begin{array}{r} 10 \\ -3 \\ \hline \end{array}$$
$$\begin{array}{r} 11 \\ -5 \\ \hline \end{array}$$
$$\begin{array}{r} 11 \\ -6 \\ \hline \end{array}$$
$$\begin{array}{r} 12 \\ -6 \\ \hline \end{array}$$

4.
$$\begin{array}{r} 12 \\ -4 \\ \hline \end{array}$$
$$\begin{array}{r} 12 \\ -8 \\ \hline \end{array}$$
$$\begin{array}{r} 11 \\ -7 \\ \hline \end{array}$$
$$\begin{array}{r} 11 \\ -4 \\ \hline \end{array}$$
$$\begin{array}{r} 12 \\ -5 \\ \hline \end{array}$$
$$\begin{array}{r} 11 \\ -3 \\ \hline \end{array}$$
$$\begin{array}{r} 12 \\ -7 \\ \hline \end{array}$$

Solve.

5. Kay had 11¢.
She spent 6¢.
How much money
does she have
left?

☐ ¢
○ ☐ ¢
___ ¢

___ ¢

6. Dan bought a ruler
for 7¢ and an
eraser for 5¢.
How much money
did he spend?

☐ ¢
○ ☐ ¢
___ ¢

___ ¢

ROUNDUP REVIEW

Add or subtract.

1. $1 + 2 =$ ___ $9 - 3 =$ ___ $1 + 5 =$ ___

2. $7 - 4 =$ ___ $8 - 2 =$ ___ $3 + 3 =$ ___

3. $2 + 4 =$ ___ $6 - 1 =$ ___ $9 + 3 =$ ___

4. $5 + 3 =$ ___ $7 + 5 =$ ___ $6 + 4 =$ ___

5.
$$\begin{array}{ccccccc} 9 & 4 & 2 & 5 & 8 & 9 & 10 \\ -4 & +4 & +7 & +5 & -5 & -6 & -\ 5 \end{array}$$

6.
$$\begin{array}{ccccccc} 11 & 12 & 10 & 9 & 6 & 11 & 12 \\ -\ 3 & -\ 5 & -\ 2 & +1 & +3 & -\ 6 & -\ 8 \end{array}$$

7.
$$\begin{array}{ccccccc} 5 & 8 & 6 & 4 & 3 & 10 & 12 \\ -5 & +3 & +5 & +8 & +7 & -\ 7 & -\ 9 \end{array}$$

Solve.

8. Adam saw 4 🦁 and 5 🐯 .
How many animals did Adam see?

___ animals

9. Molly had 11 🥜 .
She ate 4.
How many peanuts did Molly have left?

___ peanuts

36 (thirty-six)   Cumulative review

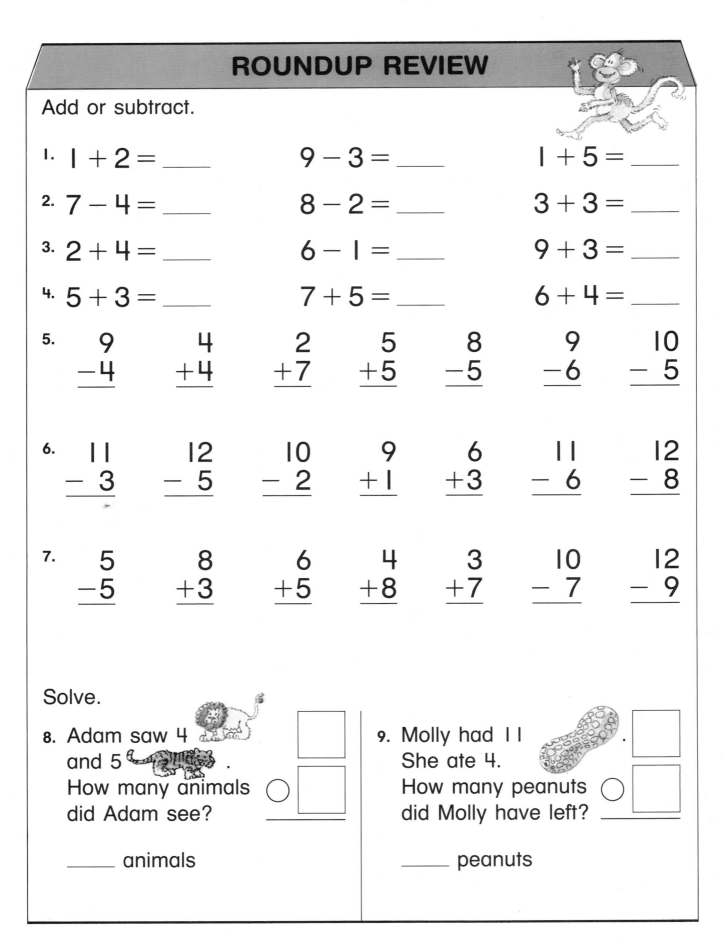

ADDITION, SUMS THROUGH 18

3 Write the numbers.

$10 + 1 =$ _____
eleven

$10 + 2 =$ _____
twelve

$10 + 3 =$ _____
thirteen

$10 + 4 =$ _____
fourteen

$10 + 5 =$ _____
fifteen

$10 + 6 =$ _____
sixteen

$10 + 7 =$ _____
seventeen

$10 + 8 =$ _____
eighteen

Match.

19	fifteen	10 + 5
15	nineteen	10 + 2
12	twelve	10 + 9
11	fourteen	10 + 3
13	eleven	10 + 1
14	thirteen	10 + 4
17	sixteen	10 + 8
16	eighteen	10 + 7
18	seventeen	10 + 6

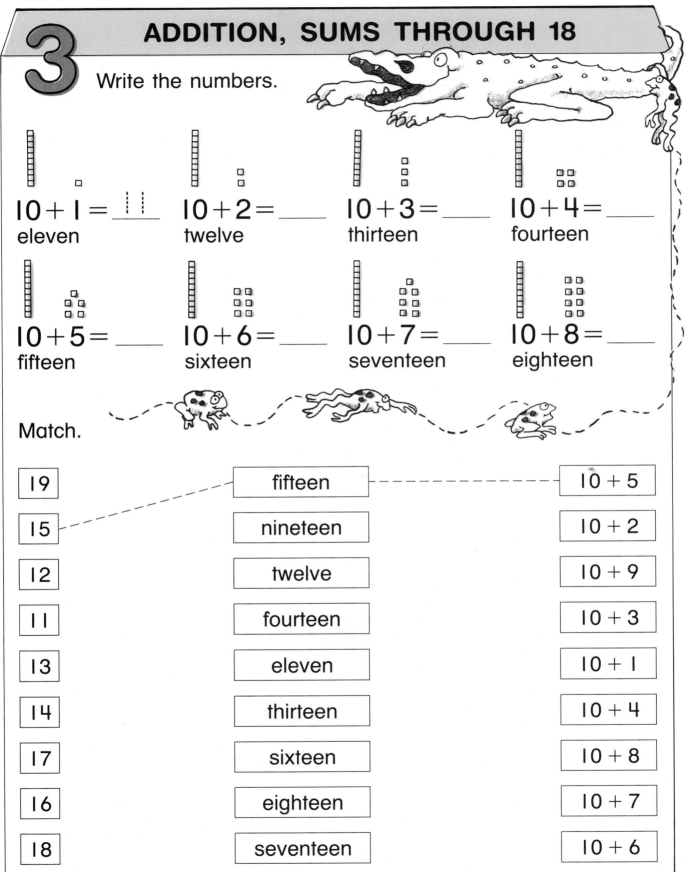

Write the numbers.

1. eleven 11
2. eighteen ____
3. fourteen ____
4. twelve ____
5. ten ____
6. seventeen ____
7. nineteen ____
8. thirteen ____
9. sixteen ____
10. fifteen ____
11. zero ____
12. nine ____

Add. Color by answers.

11	red	12	blue	13	green
14	black	15	orange	16	brown
17	yellow	18	purple	19	pink

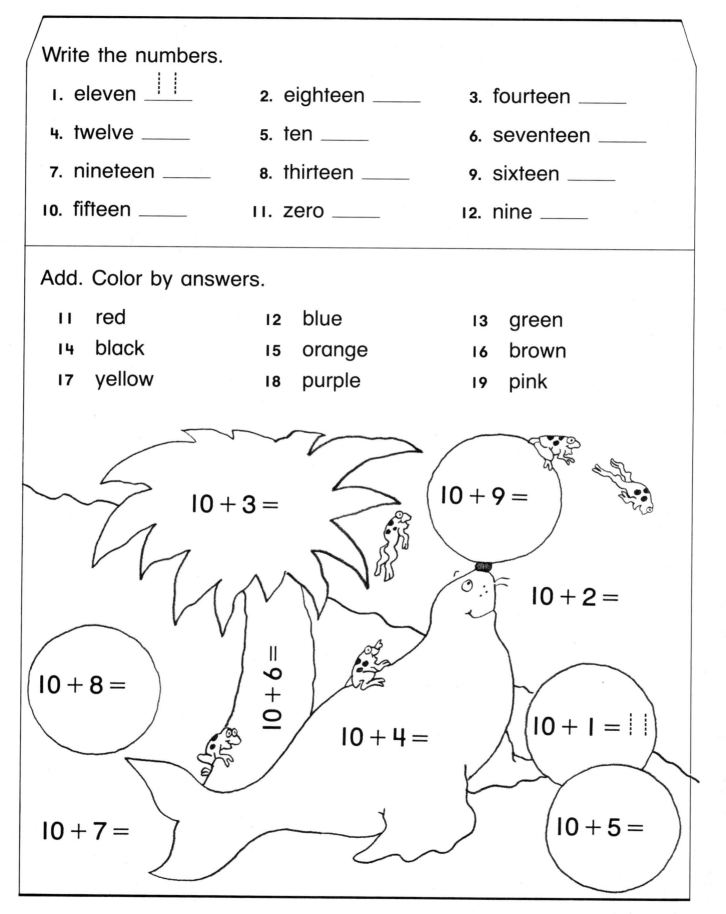

$10 + 3 =$

$10 + 9 =$

$10 + 2 =$

$10 + 8 =$

$10 + 6 =$

$10 + 4 =$

$10 + 1 = 11$

$10 + 7 =$

$10 + 5 =$

Reading and writing numbers through 19

Add.

$8 + 3 = \underline{11}$

$\begin{array}{r} 8 \\ +3 \\ \hline 11 \end{array}$

1.

$\begin{array}{r} 7 \\ +3 \\ \hline 10 \end{array}$

2.

$\begin{array}{r} 6 \\ +6 \\ \hline \end{array}$

3.
$\begin{array}{r} 5 \\ +5 \\ \hline \end{array}$
$\begin{array}{r} 7 \\ +4 \\ \hline \end{array}$
$\begin{array}{r} 1 \\ +9 \\ \hline \end{array}$
$\begin{array}{r} 9 \\ +2 \\ \hline \end{array}$
$\begin{array}{r} 3 \\ +8 \\ \hline \end{array}$
$\begin{array}{r} 5 \\ +7 \\ \hline \end{array}$
$\begin{array}{r} 9 \\ +1 \\ \hline \end{array}$

4.
$\begin{array}{r} 2 \\ +8 \\ \hline \end{array}$
$\begin{array}{r} 5 \\ +6 \\ \hline \end{array}$
$\begin{array}{r} 7 \\ +3 \\ \hline \end{array}$
$\begin{array}{r} 8 \\ +2 \\ \hline \end{array}$
$\begin{array}{r} 9 \\ +3 \\ \hline \end{array}$
$\begin{array}{r} 6 \\ +5 \\ \hline \end{array}$
$\begin{array}{r} 8 \\ +4 \\ \hline \end{array}$

5.
$\begin{array}{r} 3 \\ +7 \\ \hline \end{array}$
$\begin{array}{r} 3 \\ +9 \\ \hline \end{array}$
$\begin{array}{r} 4 \\ +8 \\ \hline \end{array}$
$\begin{array}{r} 6 \\ +4 \\ \hline \end{array}$
$\begin{array}{r} 2 \\ +9 \\ \hline \end{array}$
$\begin{array}{r} 7 \\ +5 \\ \hline \end{array}$
$\begin{array}{r} 4 \\ +7 \\ \hline \end{array}$

Solve.

6. Mitch planted 8 tulips.
Then he planted
3 more.
How many tulips
did Mitch plant?

_____ tulips

7. Tony saw 6 horses.
Karen saw 6 cows.
How many animals
did they see?

_____ animals

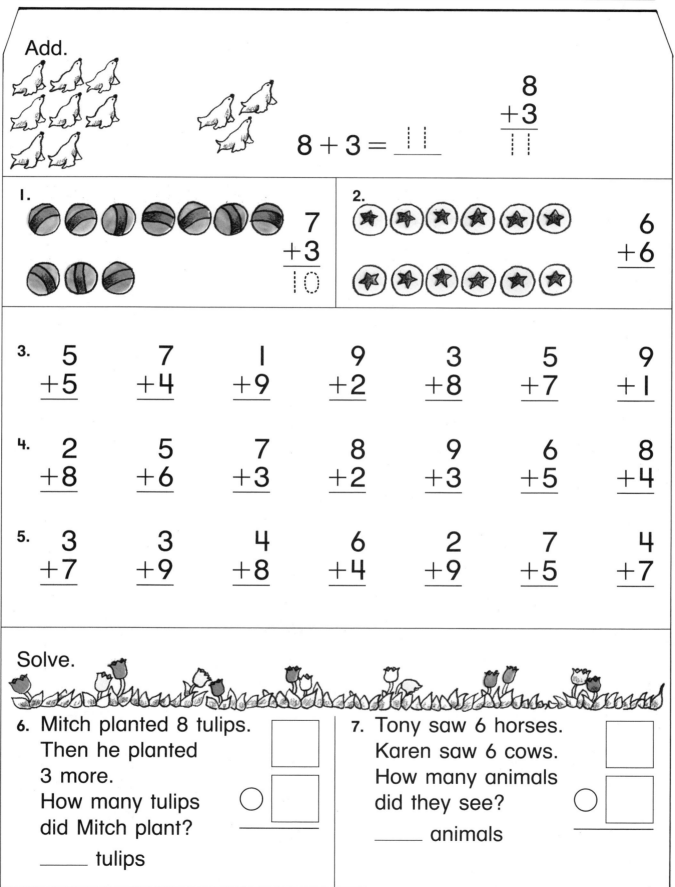

Addition facts, sums through 12

Add.

1.

3	5	3	8	5	9	8
+9	+5	+6	+2	+3	+1	+4

2.

5	1	7	6	4	3	7
+7	+9	+3	+5	+8	+3	+5

3.

3	7	8	4	7	4	2
+4	+4	+3	+5	+2	+4	+9

4.

6	9	4	5	2	9	4
+6	+3	+7	+3	+8	+2	+6

FIELD TRIP

Answer the riddles.

My double is 8.

Who am I?__4__

My double is between

4 and 8. Who am I?_____

My double is 10.

Who am I?_____

When you double me,

you get 12. Who am I?_____

Addition facts, sums through 12

Add.

1.
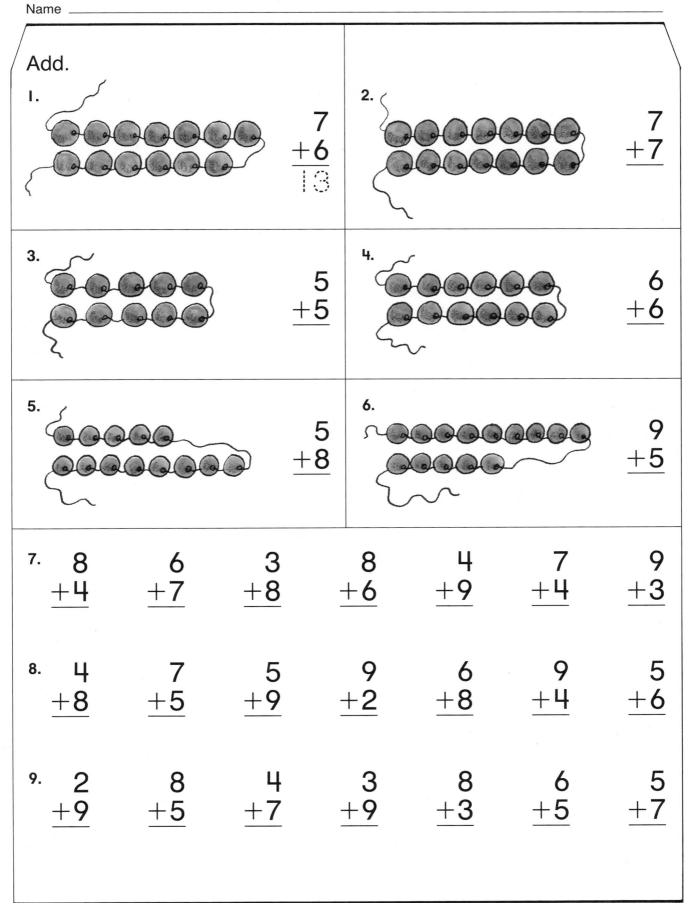

$$\begin{array}{r} 7 \\ +6 \\ \hline 13 \end{array}$$

2.

$$\begin{array}{r} 7 \\ +7 \\ \hline \end{array}$$

3.

$$\begin{array}{r} 5 \\ +5 \\ \hline \end{array}$$

4.

$$\begin{array}{r} 6 \\ +6 \\ \hline \end{array}$$

5.

$$\begin{array}{r} 5 \\ +8 \\ \hline \end{array}$$

6.

$$\begin{array}{r} 9 \\ +5 \\ \hline \end{array}$$

7.

$$\begin{array}{r} 8 \\ +4 \\ \hline \end{array} \qquad \begin{array}{r} 6 \\ +7 \\ \hline \end{array} \qquad \begin{array}{r} 3 \\ +8 \\ \hline \end{array} \qquad \begin{array}{r} 8 \\ +6 \\ \hline \end{array} \qquad \begin{array}{r} 4 \\ +9 \\ \hline \end{array} \qquad \begin{array}{r} 7 \\ +4 \\ \hline \end{array} \qquad \begin{array}{r} 9 \\ +3 \\ \hline \end{array}$$

8.

$$\begin{array}{r} 4 \\ +8 \\ \hline \end{array} \qquad \begin{array}{r} 7 \\ +5 \\ \hline \end{array} \qquad \begin{array}{r} 5 \\ +9 \\ \hline \end{array} \qquad \begin{array}{r} 9 \\ +2 \\ \hline \end{array} \qquad \begin{array}{r} 6 \\ +8 \\ \hline \end{array} \qquad \begin{array}{r} 9 \\ +4 \\ \hline \end{array} \qquad \begin{array}{r} 5 \\ +6 \\ \hline \end{array}$$

9.

$$\begin{array}{r} 2 \\ +9 \\ \hline \end{array} \qquad \begin{array}{r} 8 \\ +5 \\ \hline \end{array} \qquad \begin{array}{r} 4 \\ +7 \\ \hline \end{array} \qquad \begin{array}{r} 3 \\ +9 \\ \hline \end{array} \qquad \begin{array}{r} 8 \\ +3 \\ \hline \end{array} \qquad \begin{array}{r} 6 \\ +5 \\ \hline \end{array} \qquad \begin{array}{r} 5 \\ +7 \\ \hline \end{array}$$

Add.

1. $5 + 5 = \underline{\qquad}$
2. $8 + 2 = \underline{\qquad}$
3. $5 + 6 = \underline{\qquad}$
4. $3 + 7 = \underline{\qquad}$
5. $3 + 9 = \underline{\qquad}$
6. $7 + 4 = \underline{\qquad}$
7. $4 + 7 = \underline{\qquad}$
8. $8 + 6 = \underline{\qquad}$
9. $7 + 5 = \underline{\qquad}$
10. $4 + 6 = \underline{\qquad}$
11. $6 + 6 = \underline{\qquad}$
12. $5 + 9 = \underline{\qquad}$

13.
$\begin{array}{r} 9 \\ +2 \\ \hline \end{array}$
$\begin{array}{r} 3 \\ +8 \\ \hline \end{array}$
$\begin{array}{r} 7 \\ +7 \\ \hline \end{array}$
$\begin{array}{r} 4 \\ +9 \\ \hline \end{array}$

14.
$\begin{array}{r} 5 \\ +7 \\ \hline \end{array}$
$\begin{array}{r} 6 \\ +8 \\ \hline \end{array}$
$\begin{array}{r} 8 \\ +5 \\ \hline \end{array}$
$\begin{array}{r} 9 \\ +3 \\ \hline \end{array}$

15.
$\begin{array}{r} 6 \\ +7 \\ \hline \end{array}$
$\begin{array}{r} 6 \\ +5 \\ \hline \end{array}$
$\begin{array}{r} 8 \\ +3 \\ \hline \end{array}$
$\begin{array}{r} 1 \\ +9 \\ \hline \end{array}$

16.
$\begin{array}{r} 2 \\ +8 \\ \hline \end{array}$
$\begin{array}{r} 9 \\ +5 \\ \hline \end{array}$
$\begin{array}{r} 5 \\ +8 \\ \hline \end{array}$
$\begin{array}{r} 6 \\ +4 \\ \hline \end{array}$

17.
$\begin{array}{r} 8 \\ +4 \\ \hline \end{array}$
$\begin{array}{r} 2 \\ +9 \\ \hline \end{array}$
$\begin{array}{r} 4 \\ +8 \\ \hline \end{array}$
$\begin{array}{r} 9 \\ +4 \\ \hline \end{array}$

FIELD TRIP

Use these numbers to write addition sentences.

1. $\quad$ 8 $\quad$ 6 $\quad$ 4 $\quad$ 2

$\underline{\;6\;} + \underline{\;2\;} = \underline{\;8\;}$

$\underline{\;4\;} + \underline{\quad} = \underline{\quad}$

2. $\quad$ 9 $\quad$ 5 $\quad$ 14 $\quad$ 4

$\underline{\quad} + \underline{\quad} = \underline{\quad}$

$\underline{\quad} + \underline{\quad} = \underline{\quad}$

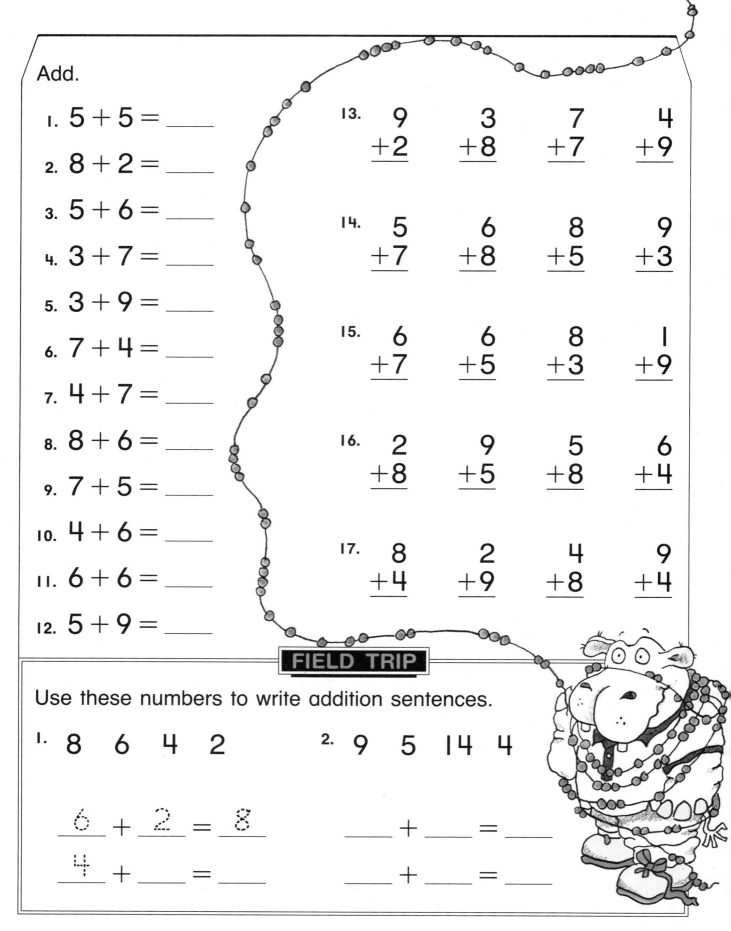

Addition facts, sums through 14

4¢   6¢   8¢   7¢   5¢

Find the total cost.

1. 8 ¢ + 6 ¢ = ____ ¢

2. 4 ¢ + 8 ¢

3. ____ + ____

4. ____ + ____

5. ____ + ____

6. ____ + ____

7. ____ + ____

8. ____ + ____

9. ____ + ____

Fill in the missing word, number and sign.

10. Dean bought 1 pear. He also bought an _____. He spent 12¢.

    8 ¢ ◯ ____ = 12 ¢

11. Carla bought 1 orange. She also bought a _____. She spent 14¢.

    6 ¢ ◯ ____ = 14 ¢

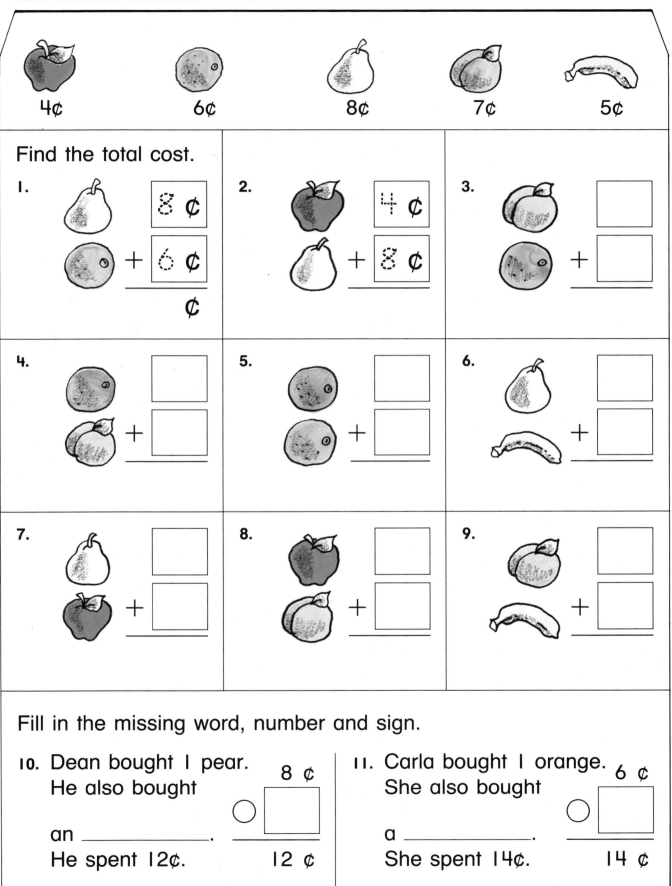

Add.

1. $5¢ + 5¢ = 10¢$ $4¢ + 6¢ = \underline{\hphantom{00}}$ $7¢ + 4¢ = \underline{\hphantom{00}}$

2. $2¢ + 8¢ = \underline{\hphantom{00}}$ $8¢ + 4¢ = \underline{\hphantom{00}}$ $6¢ + 4¢ = \underline{\hphantom{00}}$

3. $5¢ + 4¢ = \underline{\hphantom{00}}$ $1¢ + 9¢ = \underline{\hphantom{00}}$ $5¢ + 6¢ = \underline{\hphantom{00}}$

4. $9¢ + 1¢ = \underline{\hphantom{00}}$ $8¢ + 2¢ = \underline{\hphantom{00}}$ $6¢ + 6¢ = \underline{\hphantom{00}}$

5. $4¢ + 7¢ = \underline{\hphantom{00}}$ $6¢ + 5¢ = \underline{\hphantom{00}}$ $1¢ + 9¢ = \underline{\hphantom{00}}$

6.

$6¢$	$8¢$	$7¢$	$7¢$	$5¢$	$8¢$	$4¢$
$+8¢$	$+3¢$	$+5¢$	$+6¢$	$+7¢$	$+5¢$	$+9¢$

7.

$5¢$	$9¢$	$3¢$	$8¢$	$9¢$	$6¢$	$7¢$
$+9¢$	$+3¢$	$+7¢$	$+6¢$	$+2¢$	$+7¢$	$+3¢$

8.

$4¢$	$9¢$	$3¢$	$5¢$	$9¢$	$7¢$	$3¢$
$+8¢$	$+4¢$	$+9¢$	$+8¢$	$+5¢$	$+7¢$	$+8¢$

Solve.

9. There were 9 children on the playground. 4 more children joined them. How many children are on the playground?

_____ children

10. Eric has 7 aunts. He has 7 uncles. How many aunts and uncles does Eric have?

_____ aunts and uncles.

   Adding money, sums through 14

Name _____

Add.

1.
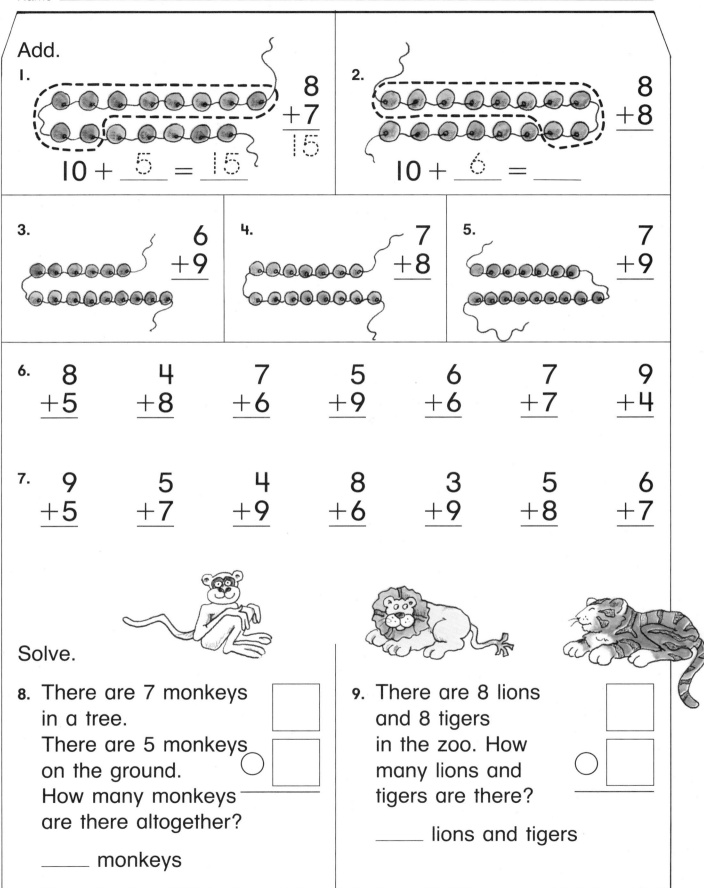

$\begin{array}{r} 8 \\ +7 \\ \hline 15 \end{array}$

$10 + \underline{5} = \underline{15}$

2.

$\begin{array}{r} 8 \\ +8 \\ \hline \end{array}$

$10 + \underline{6} = \underline{}$

3.
$\begin{array}{r} 6 \\ +9 \\ \hline \end{array}$

4.
$\begin{array}{r} 7 \\ +8 \\ \hline \end{array}$

5.
$\begin{array}{r} 7 \\ +9 \\ \hline \end{array}$

6.
$\begin{array}{r} 8 \\ +5 \\ \hline \end{array}$
$\begin{array}{r} 4 \\ +8 \\ \hline \end{array}$
$\begin{array}{r} 7 \\ +6 \\ \hline \end{array}$
$\begin{array}{r} 5 \\ +9 \\ \hline \end{array}$
$\begin{array}{r} 6 \\ +6 \\ \hline \end{array}$
$\begin{array}{r} 7 \\ +7 \\ \hline \end{array}$
$\begin{array}{r} 9 \\ +4 \\ \hline \end{array}$

7.
$\begin{array}{r} 9 \\ +5 \\ \hline \end{array}$
$\begin{array}{r} 5 \\ +7 \\ \hline \end{array}$
$\begin{array}{r} 4 \\ +9 \\ \hline \end{array}$
$\begin{array}{r} 8 \\ +6 \\ \hline \end{array}$
$\begin{array}{r} 3 \\ +9 \\ \hline \end{array}$
$\begin{array}{r} 5 \\ +8 \\ \hline \end{array}$
$\begin{array}{r} 6 \\ +7 \\ \hline \end{array}$

Solve.

8. There are 7 monkeys in a tree.
There are 5 monkeys on the ground.
How many monkeys are there altogether?

_____ monkeys

9. There are 8 lions and 8 tigers in the zoo. How many lions and tigers are there?

_____ lions and tigers

Addition facts, sums through 16

(forty-five) **45**

Add.

1. $9 + 2$ $8 + 3$ $7 + 5$ $9 + 3$ $7 + 7$ $5 + 9$ $5 + 5$

2. $7 + 4$ $6 + 6$ $8 + 5$ $4 + 7$ $3 + 9$ $8 + 8$ $9 + 5$

3. $6 + 5$ $9 + 4$ $4 + 8$ $7 + 6$ $3 + 8$ $7 + 4$ $6 + 9$

4. $8 + 6 = \underline{\quad}$ $7 + 8 = \underline{\quad}$ $6 + 8 = \underline{\quad}$

5. $4 + 9 = \underline{\quad}$ $6 + 5 = \underline{\quad}$ $5 + 7 = \underline{\quad}$

6. $6 + 7 = \underline{\quad}$ $8 + 7 = \underline{\quad}$ $9 + 6 = \underline{\quad}$

7. $8 + 4 = \underline{\quad}$ $5 + 8 = \underline{\quad}$ $7 + 9 = \underline{\quad}$

Solve.

8. There are 9 children playing tag. There are 6 more playing kickball. How many children are playing?

_____ children

9. Luis saw 7 ladybugs. Then he saw 9 more. How many ladybugs did Luis see?

_____ ladybugs

Addition facts, sums through 16

Name _____

Add.

1.

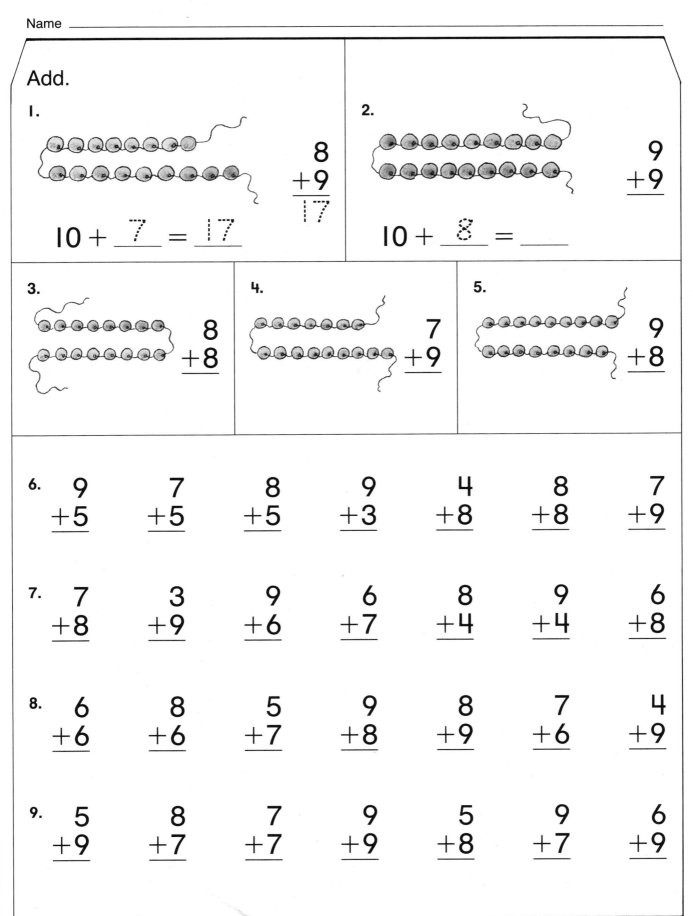

$$\begin{array}{r} 8 \\ +9 \\ \hline 17 \end{array}$$

$10 + \underline{7} = \underline{17}$

2.

$$\begin{array}{r} 9 \\ +9 \\ \hline \end{array}$$

$10 + \underline{8} = \underline{\hphantom{00}}$

3.

$$\begin{array}{r} 8 \\ +8 \\ \hline \end{array}$$

4.

$$\begin{array}{r} 7 \\ +9 \\ \hline \end{array}$$

5.

$$\begin{array}{r} 9 \\ +8 \\ \hline \end{array}$$

6.

$$\begin{array}{r} 9 \\ +5 \\ \hline \end{array} \qquad \begin{array}{r} 7 \\ +5 \\ \hline \end{array} \qquad \begin{array}{r} 8 \\ +5 \\ \hline \end{array} \qquad \begin{array}{r} 9 \\ +3 \\ \hline \end{array} \qquad \begin{array}{r} 4 \\ +8 \\ \hline \end{array} \qquad \begin{array}{r} 8 \\ +8 \\ \hline \end{array} \qquad \begin{array}{r} 7 \\ +9 \\ \hline \end{array}$$

7.

$$\begin{array}{r} 7 \\ +8 \\ \hline \end{array} \qquad \begin{array}{r} 3 \\ +9 \\ \hline \end{array} \qquad \begin{array}{r} 9 \\ +6 \\ \hline \end{array} \qquad \begin{array}{r} 6 \\ +7 \\ \hline \end{array} \qquad \begin{array}{r} 8 \\ +4 \\ \hline \end{array} \qquad \begin{array}{r} 9 \\ +4 \\ \hline \end{array} \qquad \begin{array}{r} 6 \\ +8 \\ \hline \end{array}$$

8.

$$\begin{array}{r} 6 \\ +6 \\ \hline \end{array} \qquad \begin{array}{r} 8 \\ +6 \\ \hline \end{array} \qquad \begin{array}{r} 5 \\ +7 \\ \hline \end{array} \qquad \begin{array}{r} 9 \\ +8 \\ \hline \end{array} \qquad \begin{array}{r} 8 \\ +9 \\ \hline \end{array} \qquad \begin{array}{r} 7 \\ +6 \\ \hline \end{array} \qquad \begin{array}{r} 4 \\ +9 \\ \hline \end{array}$$

9.

$$\begin{array}{r} 5 \\ +9 \\ \hline \end{array} \qquad \begin{array}{r} 8 \\ +7 \\ \hline \end{array} \qquad \begin{array}{r} 7 \\ +7 \\ \hline \end{array} \qquad \begin{array}{r} 9 \\ +9 \\ \hline \end{array} \qquad \begin{array}{r} 5 \\ +8 \\ \hline \end{array} \qquad \begin{array}{r} 9 \\ +7 \\ \hline \end{array} \qquad \begin{array}{r} 6 \\ +9 \\ \hline \end{array}$$

Addition facts, sums through 18

Complete the wheels.

1.

+7 +5
+9 +3
7
+2 +8
+6 +4

10

2.

14

+8 +4
+5 +7
9
+6 +2
+3 +9

Complete the tables.

3.

Add 6	
3	9
7	
4	
9	
2	

4.

Add 5	
3	8
7	
8	
9	
5	

5.

Add 8	
3	11
7	
6	
9	
8	

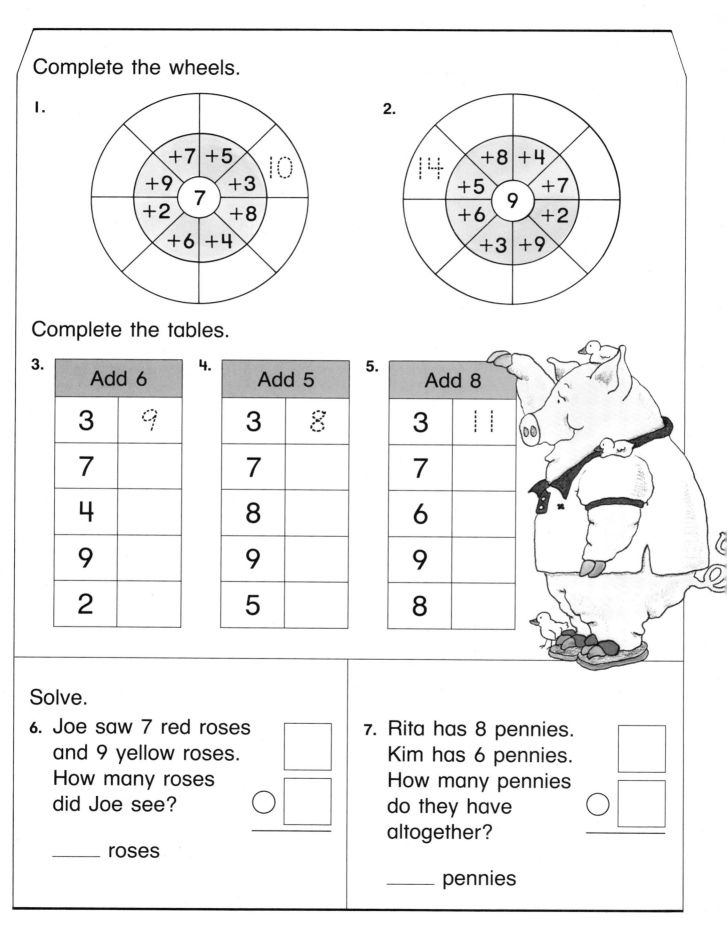

Solve.

6. Joe saw 7 red roses and 9 yellow roses. How many roses did Joe see?

_____ roses

7. Rita has 8 pennies. Kim has 6 pennies. How many pennies do they have altogether?

_____ pennies

Addition facts, sums through 18

This is great!
I can add anyway
I want.

$$\left.\begin{array}{r}3\\4\\+5\end{array}\right\} \boxed{7}$$
$$\overline{12}$$

$$\left.\begin{array}{r}3\\4\\+5\end{array}\right\} \boxed{9}$$
$$\overline{12}$$

$$\begin{array}{r}3\\4\\+5\end{array} \boxed{8}$$
$$\overline{12}$$

Add. Look for a ten.

1.

$$\left.\begin{array}{r}7\\3\\+5\end{array}\right\} \boxed{10}$$
$$\overline{15}$$

2.

$$\left.\begin{array}{r}2\\2\\6\\+4\end{array}\right\} \boxed{}$$

3.

$$\begin{array}{r}5\\4\\+5\end{array}$$

4.

$$\begin{array}{r}8\\2\\4\\+1\end{array}$$

5.

| $\begin{array}{r}9\\1\\+7\end{array}$ | $\begin{array}{r}6\\4\\+4\end{array}$ | $\begin{array}{r}5\\5\\+8\end{array}$ | $\begin{array}{r}1\\9\\+7\end{array}$ | $\begin{array}{r}4\\2\\+4\end{array}$ | $\begin{array}{r}3\\7\\+8\end{array}$ | $\begin{array}{r}2\\2\\+8\end{array}$ |

6.

| $\begin{array}{r}7\\3\\+6\end{array}$ | $\begin{array}{r}8\\2\\+7\end{array}$ | $\begin{array}{r}2\\8\\+6\end{array}$ | $\begin{array}{r}2\\6\\1\\+4\end{array}$ | $\begin{array}{r}2\\4\\4\\+8\end{array}$ | $\begin{array}{r}3\\2\\4\\+8\end{array}$ | $\begin{array}{r}1\\5\\5\\+5\end{array}$ |

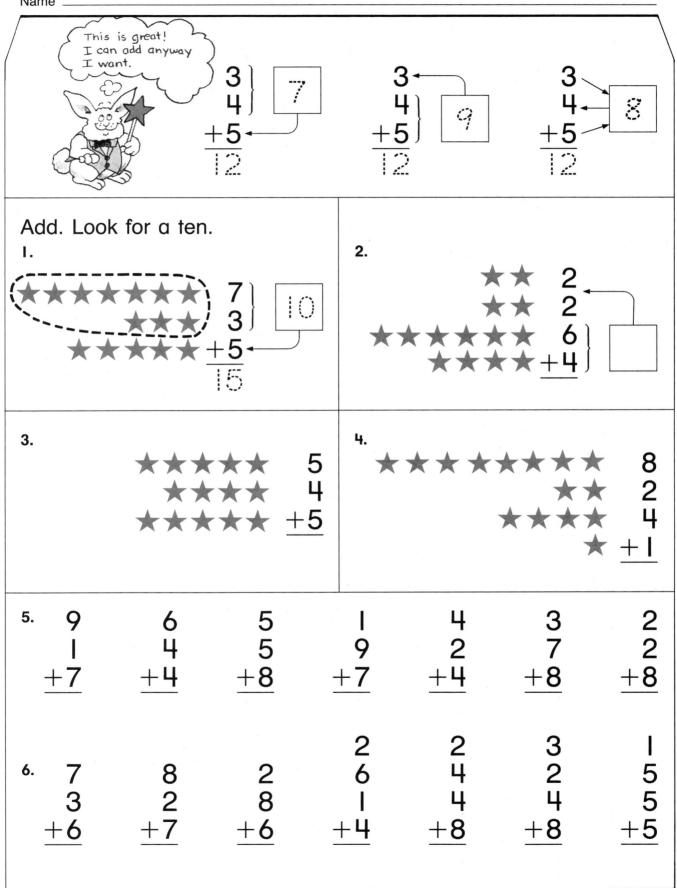

Add. Look for a ten.

1.
2	2	3	3	7	7	1
3	7	2	7	2	3	1
+7	+3	+7	+2	+3	+2	+1

2.
2	3	4	5	6	7	8
2	3	4	5	6	3	2
+2	+3	+4	+5	+4	+7	+8

3.
4	5	2	3	7	6	4
2	1	3	6	1	2	4
3	2	4	1	1	1	1
+7	+6	+8	+5	+6	+7	+3

FIELD TRIP

Write two addition number sentences using each number only once.

1. △1 △2 △3 △4 △5 △7

1 + 3 = 4

2 + ___ = ___

2. ☐2 ☐3 ☐4 ☐5 ☐6 ☐8

___ + ___ = ___

___ + ___ = ___

Column addition, 3 or 4 addends

Name _____

I penny 1¢   I nickel 5¢

$$\begin{array}{r} 1¢ \\ + 5¢ \\ \hline 6¢ \end{array}$$

Count each amount. Then add.

1.

5¢   7¢

$$\begin{array}{r} 5¢ \\ + 7¢ \\ \hline 12¢ \end{array}$$

2.

_____   _____

$$+ $$

3.

_____   _____

$$+ $$

4.

_____   _____   _____

$$+ $$

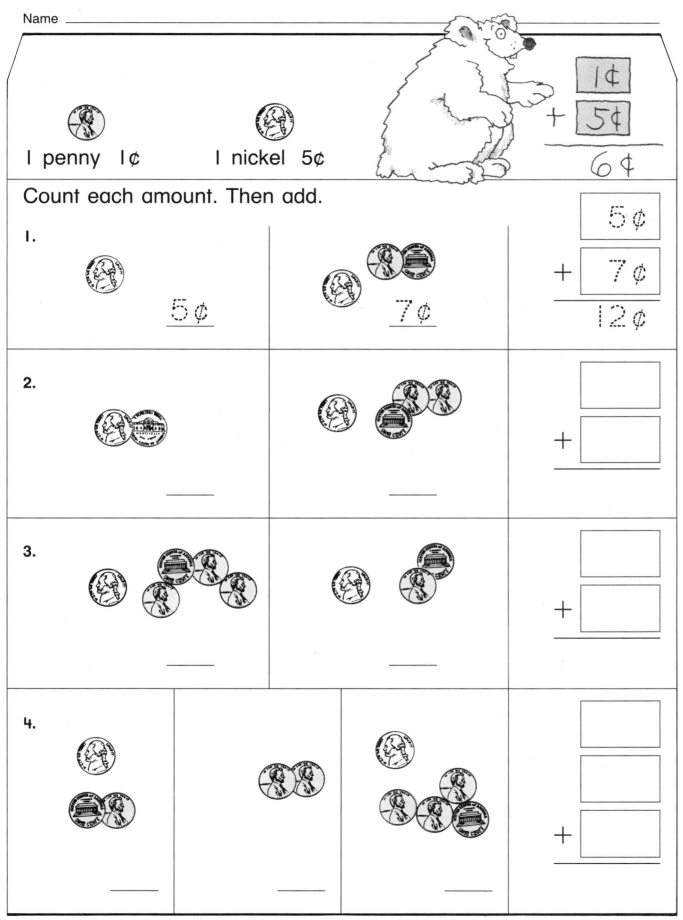

Adding money   (fifty-one) **51**

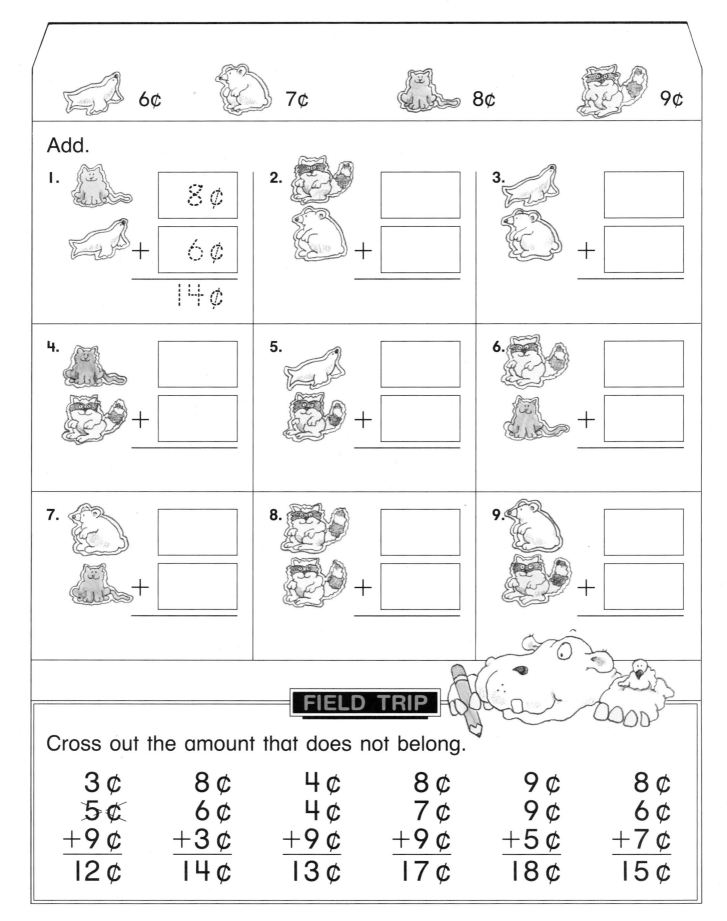

6¢   7¢   8¢   9¢

Add.

1. 8¢ + 6¢ = 14¢

2. ☐ + ☐

3. ☐ + ☐

4. ☐ + ☐

5. ☐ + ☐

6. ☐ + ☐

7. ☐ + ☐

8. ☐ + ☐

9. ☐ + ☐

FIELD TRIP

Cross out the amount that does not belong.

3¢	8¢	4¢	8¢	9¢	8¢
5¢	6¢	4¢	7¢	9¢	6¢
+9¢	+3¢	+9¢	+9¢	+5¢	+7¢
12¢	14¢	13¢	17¢	18¢	15¢

Adding money

Name _____

Solve.

1. There were 8 cars in the parking lot. Then 9 more drove in. How many cars are now in the parking lot?

$\begin{array}{r} 8 \\ + 9 \\ \hline \end{array}$

_____ cars

2. Sally found 8 shells. Trudy found 7 shells. How many shells did they find?

_____ shells

3. There were 6 children playing a video game. 5 more children joined them. Now how many are playing?

_____ children

4. Mike used 5 tickets for the roller coaster. He used 9 tickets for the rocket. How many tickets did he use?

_____ tickets

5. There are 7 dogs on the grass. 5 more dogs join them. How many dogs are on the grass?

_____ dogs

6. Father used 5 apples and 8 bananas in a salad. How many pieces of fruit did he use?

_____ pieces of fruit

7. Kyle ate 9 crackers. Chris ate 7 crackers. How many crackers did they eat?

_____ crackers

8. Doyle counted 4 blue trucks and 8 red trucks. How many trucks did Doyle count?

_____ trucks

Problem solving, addition

(fifty-three) **53**

Solve.

1. Chen built 8 sandcastles. Leo built 8 more. How many sandcastles were built?

   ☐
   ☐ ○
   _____

   _____ sandcastles

2. Larry has 9 keys. He needs 8 more. How many keys does Larry need?

   ☐
   ☐ ○
   _____

   _____ keys

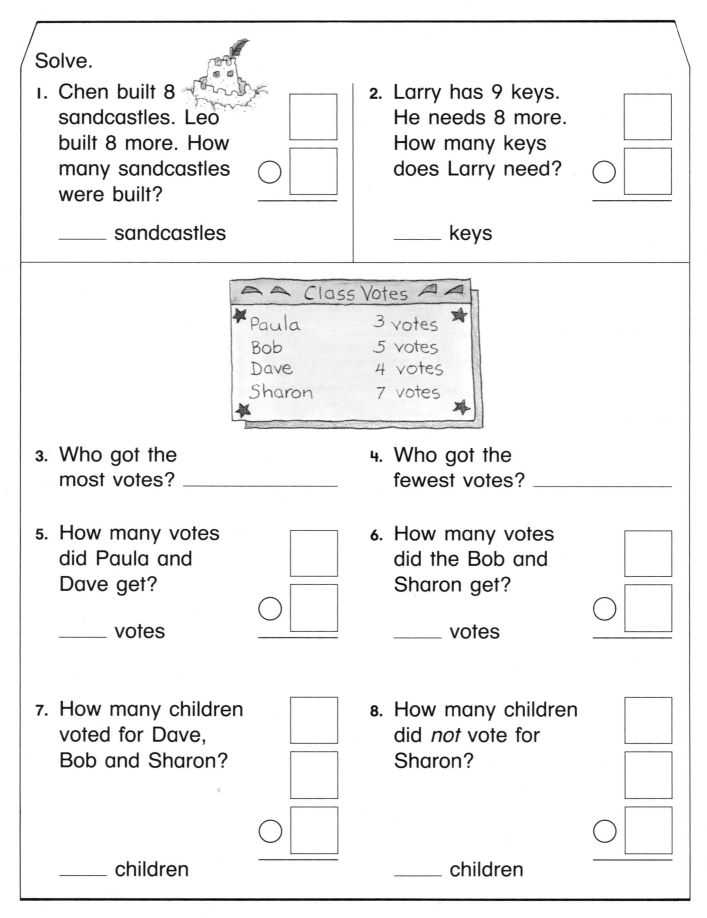

Class Votes

Paula   3 votes
Bob   5 votes
Dave   4 votes
Sharon   7 votes

3. Who got the most votes? _____

4. Who got the fewest votes? _____

5. How many votes did Paula and Dave get?

   ☐
   ☐ ○
   _____

   _____ votes

6. How many votes did the Bob and Sharon get?

   ☐
   ☐ ○
   _____

   _____ votes

7. How many children voted for Dave, Bob and Sharon?

   ☐
   ☐
   ☐ ○
   _____

   _____ children

8. How many children did *not* vote for Sharon?

   ☐
   ☐
   ☐ ○
   _____

   _____ children

Problem solving, addition

CHAPTER CHECKUP

Add.

1.
9	6	7	6	8	6	9
+6	+6	+4	+7	+6	+5	+9

2.
8	2	3	8	7	8	3
+3	+8	+9	+8	+5	+4	+7

3.
8¢	4¢	5¢	7¢	5¢	7¢	9¢
+7¢	+9¢	+8¢	+9¢	+9¢	+7¢	+8¢

Add. Look for a ten.

4.
2	5	8	9	7	6	3
3	4	2	5	3	4	4
+4	+7	+6	+1	+7	+8	+7

Solve.

5. Casey bought one flower for 9¢ and another flower for 7¢. How much did both cost?

____

6. There were 7 girls and 8 boys at Sandy's party. How many children were at the party?

____ children

ROUNDUP REVIEW

Add or subtract.

1. $12 - 3 = $ _____ $12 - 8 = $ _____ $11 - 2 = $ _____

2. $11 - 5 = $ _____ $11 - 4 = $ _____ $8 + 4 = $ _____

3. $5 + 5 = $ _____ $12 - 5 = $ _____ $3 + 8 = $ _____

Add.

4.
$$\begin{array}{r} 7 \\ +7 \\ \hline \end{array} \quad \begin{array}{r} 8 \\ +8 \\ \hline \end{array} \quad \begin{array}{r} 9 \\ +9 \\ \hline \end{array} \quad \begin{array}{r} 6 \\ +7 \\ \hline \end{array} \quad \begin{array}{r} 7 \\ +8 \\ \hline \end{array} \quad \begin{array}{r} 8 \\ +9 \\ \hline \end{array} \quad \begin{array}{r} 7 \\ +6 \\ \hline \end{array}$$

5.
$$\begin{array}{r} 8 \\ +7 \\ \hline \end{array} \quad \begin{array}{r} 9 \\ +8 \\ \hline \end{array} \quad \begin{array}{r} 9 \\ +7 \\ \hline \end{array} \quad \begin{array}{r} 6 \\ +8 \\ \hline \end{array} \quad \begin{array}{r} 8 \\ +5 \\ \hline \end{array} \quad \begin{array}{r} 9 \\ +6 \\ \hline \end{array} \quad \begin{array}{r} 7 \\ +9 \\ \hline \end{array}$$

6.
$$\begin{array}{r} 9 \\ +5 \\ \hline \end{array} \quad \begin{array}{r} 5 \\ +8 \\ \hline \end{array} \quad \begin{array}{r} 6 \\ +9 \\ \hline \end{array} \quad \begin{array}{r} 5 \\ +7 \\ \hline \end{array} \quad \begin{array}{r} 5 \\ 3 \\ +5 \\ \hline \end{array} \quad \begin{array}{r} 3 \\ 2 \\ +7 \\ \hline \end{array} \quad \begin{array}{r} 6 \\ 4 \\ +7 \\ \hline \end{array}$$

Solve.

7. There were 12 frogs. 7 hopped away. How many frogs were left?

_____ frogs

8. Bruce saved 9¢ on Monday and 5¢ on Friday. How much money did he save?

_____

4 SUBTRACTION, MINUENDS THROUGH 18

Subtract.

How many are there in all? _____

How many are crossed out? _____

How many are left? _____ $12 - 4 = $ _____

1. $\begin{array}{r} 10 \\ -5 \\ \hline \end{array}$

2. $\begin{array}{r} 11 \\ -7 \\ \hline \end{array}$

3. $\begin{array}{r} 12 \\ -3 \\ \hline \end{array}$ $\quad \begin{array}{r} 11 \\ -5 \\ \hline \end{array}$ $\quad \begin{array}{r} 10 \\ -1 \\ \hline \end{array}$ $\quad \begin{array}{r} 12 \\ -6 \\ \hline \end{array}$ $\quad \begin{array}{r} 11 \\ -2 \\ \hline \end{array}$ $\quad \begin{array}{r} 10 \\ -5 \\ \hline \end{array}$ $\quad \begin{array}{r} 11 \\ -9 \\ \hline \end{array}$

4. $\begin{array}{r} 11 \\ -6 \\ \hline \end{array}$ $\quad \begin{array}{r} 10 \\ -9 \\ \hline \end{array}$ $\quad \begin{array}{r} 11 \\ -7 \\ \hline \end{array}$ $\quad \begin{array}{r} 9 \\ -5 \\ \hline \end{array}$ $\quad \begin{array}{r} 12 \\ -4 \\ \hline \end{array}$ $\quad \begin{array}{r} 9 \\ -2 \\ \hline \end{array}$ $\quad \begin{array}{r} 10 \\ -7 \\ \hline \end{array}$

5. $\begin{array}{r} 10 \\ -2 \\ \hline \end{array}$ $\quad \begin{array}{r} 12 \\ -7 \\ \hline \end{array}$ $\quad \begin{array}{r} 9 \\ -4 \\ \hline \end{array}$ $\quad \begin{array}{r} 10 \\ -6 \\ \hline \end{array}$ $\quad \begin{array}{r} 11 \\ -3 \\ \hline \end{array}$ $\quad \begin{array}{r} 10 \\ -8 \\ \hline \end{array}$ $\quad \begin{array}{r} 12 \\ -9 \\ \hline \end{array}$

6. $\begin{array}{r} 11 \\ -4 \\ \hline \end{array}$ $\quad \begin{array}{r} 9 \\ -1 \\ \hline \end{array}$ $\quad \begin{array}{r} 10 \\ -4 \\ \hline \end{array}$ $\quad \begin{array}{r} 12 \\ -8 \\ \hline \end{array}$ $\quad \begin{array}{r} 11 \\ -8 \\ \hline \end{array}$ $\quad \begin{array}{r} 12 \\ -5 \\ \hline \end{array}$ $\quad \begin{array}{r} 10 \\ -3 \\ \hline \end{array}$

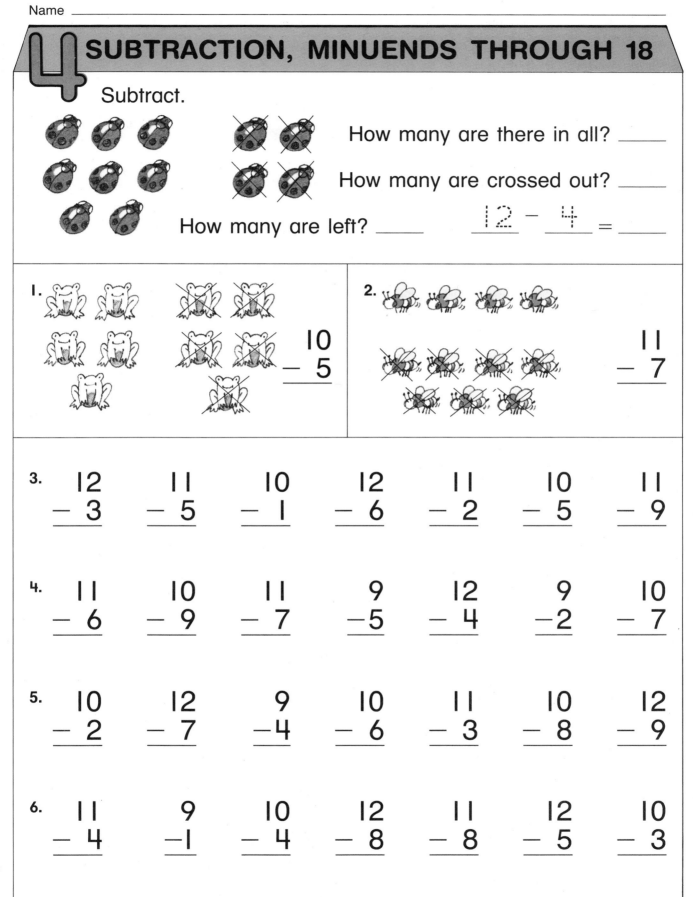

Complete the tables.

1.

Subtract 3	
9	6
7	
12	
10	
8	
11	

2.

Subtract 4	
11	7
8	
4	
10	
12	
9	

3.

Subtract 5	
12	
7	
9	
11	
8	
10	

4.

Subtract 6	
7	
9	
6	
10	
8	
11	

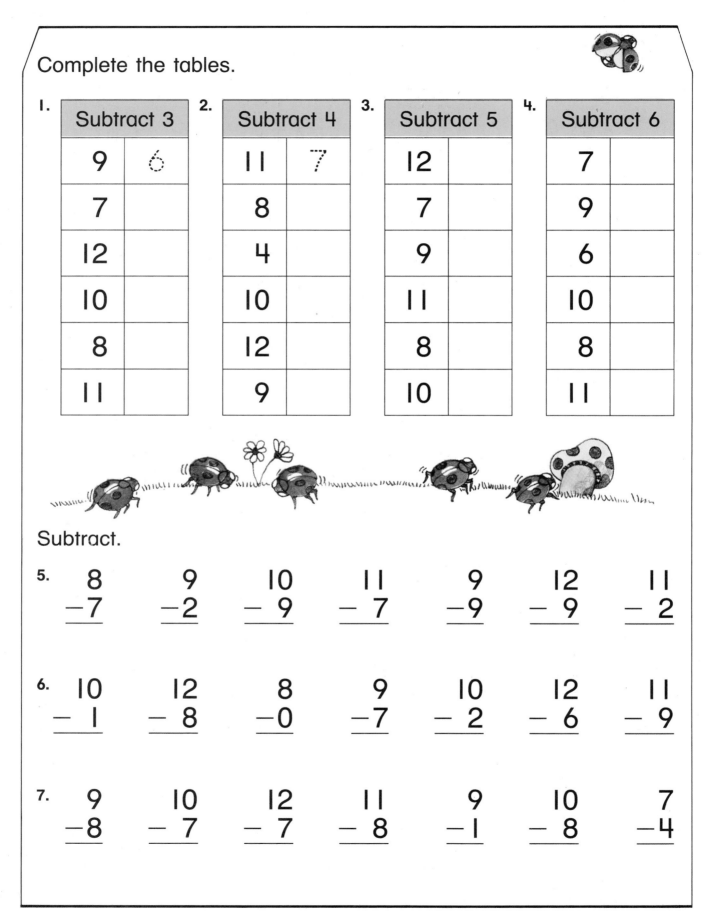

Subtract.

5.
$$\begin{array}{r} 8 \\ -7 \\ \hline \end{array} \qquad \begin{array}{r} 9 \\ -2 \\ \hline \end{array} \qquad \begin{array}{r} 10 \\ -9 \\ \hline \end{array} \qquad \begin{array}{r} 11 \\ -7 \\ \hline \end{array} \qquad \begin{array}{r} 9 \\ -9 \\ \hline \end{array} \qquad \begin{array}{r} 12 \\ -9 \\ \hline \end{array} \qquad \begin{array}{r} 11 \\ -2 \\ \hline \end{array}$$

6.
$$\begin{array}{r} 10 \\ -1 \\ \hline \end{array} \qquad \begin{array}{r} 12 \\ -8 \\ \hline \end{array} \qquad \begin{array}{r} 8 \\ -0 \\ \hline \end{array} \qquad \begin{array}{r} 9 \\ -7 \\ \hline \end{array} \qquad \begin{array}{r} 10 \\ -2 \\ \hline \end{array} \qquad \begin{array}{r} 12 \\ -6 \\ \hline \end{array} \qquad \begin{array}{r} 11 \\ -9 \\ \hline \end{array}$$

7.
$$\begin{array}{r} 9 \\ -8 \\ \hline \end{array} \qquad \begin{array}{r} 10 \\ -7 \\ \hline \end{array} \qquad \begin{array}{r} 12 \\ -7 \\ \hline \end{array} \qquad \begin{array}{r} 11 \\ -8 \\ \hline \end{array} \qquad \begin{array}{r} 9 \\ -1 \\ \hline \end{array} \qquad \begin{array}{r} 10 \\ -8 \\ \hline \end{array} \qquad \begin{array}{r} 7 \\ -4 \\ \hline \end{array}$$

Subtract.

1. How many are there in all? _____

How many are crossed out? _____

How many are left? _____

$$\begin{array}{r} 14 \\ \ominus\ 6 \\ \hline \end{array}$$

2.
$$\begin{array}{r} 12 \\ -\ 5 \\ \hline \end{array}$$

3.
$$\begin{array}{r} 13 \\ -\ 4 \\ \hline \end{array}$$

4.
$$\begin{array}{r} 13 \\ -\ 4 \\ \hline \end{array} \quad \begin{array}{r} 13 \\ -\ 9 \\ \hline \end{array} \quad \begin{array}{r} 14 \\ -\ 6 \\ \hline \end{array} \quad \begin{array}{r} 14 \\ -\ 8 \\ \hline \end{array} \quad \begin{array}{r} 11 \\ -\ 5 \\ \hline \end{array} \quad \begin{array}{r} 13 \\ -\ 8 \\ \hline \end{array} \quad \begin{array}{r} 14 \\ -\ 7 \\ \hline \end{array}$$

5.
$$\begin{array}{r} 13 \\ -\ 6 \\ \hline \end{array} \quad \begin{array}{r} 13 \\ -\ 7 \\ \hline \end{array} \quad \begin{array}{r} 12 \\ -\ 5 \\ \hline \end{array} \quad \begin{array}{r} 12 \\ -\ 7 \\ \hline \end{array} \quad \begin{array}{r} 13 \\ -\ 5 \\ \hline \end{array} \quad \begin{array}{r} 14 \\ -\ 5 \\ \hline \end{array} \quad \begin{array}{r} 14 \\ -\ 9 \\ \hline \end{array}$$

Solve.

6. There were 14 bears asleep. 6 woke up. How many are still asleep?

_____ bears

7. There were 13 deer grazing. 5 go to drink water. How many are still grazing?

_____ deer

Complete the wheels.

1.

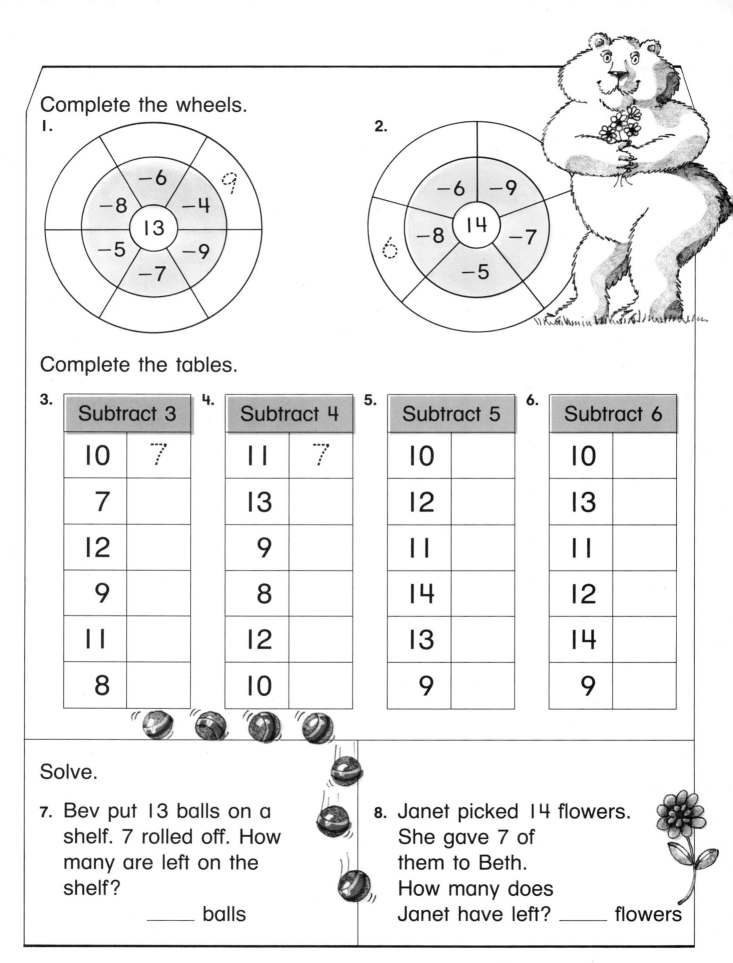

Wheel 1: center 13, with −6, −9, −4, −8, −5, −9, −7

2.

Wheel 2: center 14, with −6, −9, −8, −7, −5, 6

Complete the tables.

3.

Subtract 3	
10	7
7	
12	
9	
11	
8	

4.

Subtract 4	
11	7
13	
9	
8	
12	
10	

5.

Subtract 5	
10	
12	
11	
14	
13	
9	

6.

Subtract 6	
10	
13	
11	
12	
14	
9	

Solve.

7. Bev put 13 balls on a shelf. 7 rolled off. How many are left on the shelf?

_____ balls

8. Janet picked 14 flowers. She gave 7 of them to Beth. How many does Janet have left? _____ flowers

Subtraction facts, minuends through 14

Solve.

1. There are _____ bananas.

   There are _____ monkeys.
   Each monkey ate 1 banana.
   How many bananas are left?

   $\ominus$ 4
   10

   _____ bananas

   How many more
   bananas than monkeys
   are there?

   10 – 4 = _____

   _____ more bananas

2. There are _____ berries.

   There are _____ birds.
   Each bird ate 1 berry.
   How many berries
   are left?

   $\ominus$ 7
   11

   _____ berries

   How many more
   berries than birds
   are there?

   11 – 7 = _____

   _____ more berries

3. There are 13 horses.
   There are 8 saddles.
   How many more
   horses than saddles
   are there?

   _____ more horses

4. There are 13 blue birds.
   There are 7 red birds.
   How many more blue
   birds than red birds
   are there?

   _____ more blue birds

5. Lee has 11 plants.
   He has 8 pots.
   How many more plants
   than pots are there?

   _____ plants

6. There are 14 leaves.
   There are 5 bugs.
   How many more
   leaves than bugs are
   there?

   _____ leaves

Problem solving, comparative subtraction

Solve.

1. There are 12 nuts. The squirrels ate 6 nuts. How many nuts are left?

$$\begin{array}{r} 12 \\ \ominus\ 6 \\ \hline \end{array}$$

_____ nuts

2. There are 12 nuts. There are 6 squirrels. How many more nuts than squirrels are there?

_____ nuts

3. There are 14 flowers in the garden. Chris picked 8 flowers. How many flowers are left in the garden?

_____ flowers

4. There are 8 saucers. There are 10 cups. How many more cups than saucers are there?

_____ cups

5. There are 13 carrots. There are 8 rabbits. How many more carrots than rabbits are there?

_____ carrots

6. There are 12 fish. There are 7 seals. Each seal eats one fish. How many fish are left?

_____ fish

7. There are 14 bones. There are 9 dogs. How many more bones than dogs are there?

_____ bones

8. There are 11 cars parked. There are 8 trucks parked. How many more cars than trucks are parked?

_____ cars

Problem solving, comparative subtraction

Subtract.

1. How many are there in all? _____

How many are crossed out? _____

How many are left? _____

_____ − _____ = _____

2.
$$\begin{array}{r} 15 \\ -\ 7 \\ \hline \end{array}$$

3.
$$\begin{array}{r} 14 \\ -\ 5 \\ \hline \end{array}$$

4.
$$\begin{array}{r} 16 \\ -\ 8 \\ \hline \end{array}$$

5.
$$\begin{array}{r} 14 \\ -\ 9 \\ \hline \end{array}$$

Subtract.

6.

| $\begin{array}{r}15\\-\ 6\\\hline\end{array}$ | $\begin{array}{r}15\\-\ 9\\\hline\end{array}$ | $\begin{array}{r}13\\-\ 6\\\hline\end{array}$ | $\begin{array}{r}13\\-\ 7\\\hline\end{array}$ | $\begin{array}{r}14\\-\ 5\\\hline\end{array}$ | $\begin{array}{r}14\\-\ 9\\\hline\end{array}$ | $\begin{array}{r}16\\-\ 8\\\hline\end{array}$ |

7.

| $\begin{array}{r}15\\-\ 8\\\hline\end{array}$ | $\begin{array}{r}15\\-\ 7\\\hline\end{array}$ | $\begin{array}{r}14\\-\ 6\\\hline\end{array}$ | $\begin{array}{r}14\\-\ 8\\\hline\end{array}$ | $\begin{array}{r}16\\-\ 7\\\hline\end{array}$ | $\begin{array}{r}16\\-\ 9\\\hline\end{array}$ | $\begin{array}{r}14\\-\ 7\\\hline\end{array}$ |

Subtraction facts, minuends through 16

Subtract to fill in the blanks.

1.
-8 -9 -7 16

2.
-6 -9 -8 -7 15

3.
-5 -8 -9 -6 -7 14

4.
-8 -6 -4 -5 -7 13 -9

Circle other names for each number.

5. $\underline{\quad 5 \quad}$
$(12 - 7)$
$14 - 5$
$11 - 6$
$13 - 8$

6. $\underline{\quad 8 \quad}$
$10 - 2$
$(16 - 8)$
$14 - 7$
$13 - 5$

7. $\underline{\quad 4 \quad}$
$14 - 5$
$13 - 9$
$11 - 7$
$12 - 8$

8. $\underline{\quad 7 \quad}$
$14 - 7$
$16 - 8$
$13 - 6$
$15 - 8$

9. $\underline{\quad 9 \quad}$
$14 - 5$
$16 - 7$
$13 - 9$
$11 - 2$

10. $\underline{\quad 6 \quad}$
$12 - 6$
$14 - 8$
$13 - 7$
$15 - 6$

11. $\underline{\quad 3 \quad}$
$12 - 9$
$9 - 5$
$10 - 7$
$11 - 8$

12. $\underline{\quad 8 \quad}$
$16 - 9$
$14 - 6$
$15 - 7$
$13 - 5$

Subtraction facts, minuends through 16

Name _____

Subtract.

1. How many are there in all? _____ [box]

   How many flew away? _____ ○ [box]

   How many are left? _____

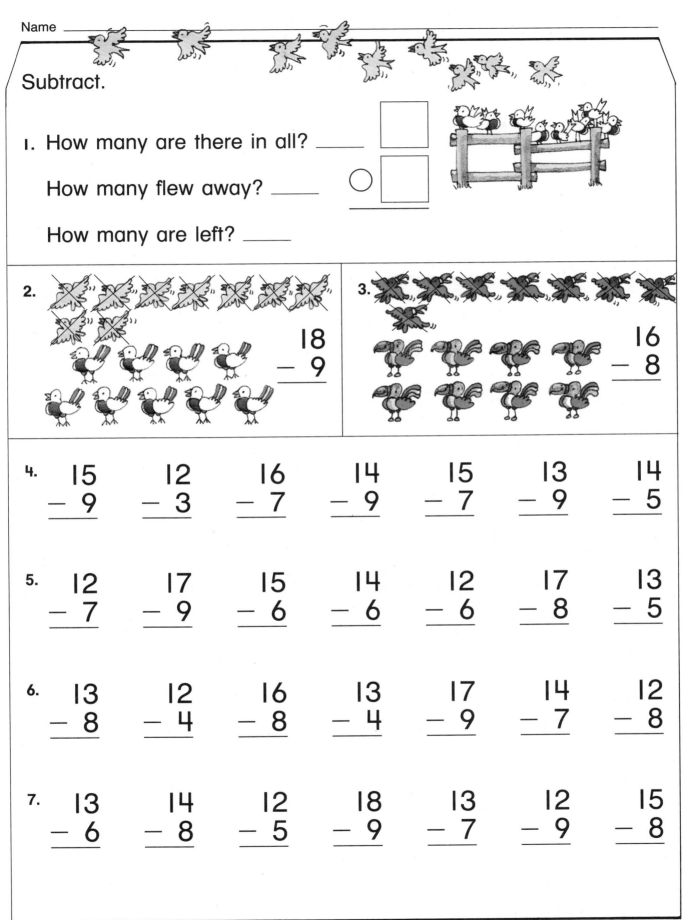

2.
$$\begin{array}{r} 18 \\ -\ 9 \\ \hline \end{array}$$

3.
$$\begin{array}{r} 16 \\ -\ 8 \\ \hline \end{array}$$

4.
$$\begin{array}{r} 15 \\ -\ 9 \\ \hline \end{array} \quad \begin{array}{r} 12 \\ -\ 3 \\ \hline \end{array} \quad \begin{array}{r} 16 \\ -\ 7 \\ \hline \end{array} \quad \begin{array}{r} 14 \\ -\ 9 \\ \hline \end{array} \quad \begin{array}{r} 15 \\ -\ 7 \\ \hline \end{array} \quad \begin{array}{r} 13 \\ -\ 9 \\ \hline \end{array} \quad \begin{array}{r} 14 \\ -\ 5 \\ \hline \end{array}$$

5.
$$\begin{array}{r} 12 \\ -\ 7 \\ \hline \end{array} \quad \begin{array}{r} 17 \\ -\ 9 \\ \hline \end{array} \quad \begin{array}{r} 15 \\ -\ 6 \\ \hline \end{array} \quad \begin{array}{r} 14 \\ -\ 6 \\ \hline \end{array} \quad \begin{array}{r} 12 \\ -\ 6 \\ \hline \end{array} \quad \begin{array}{r} 17 \\ -\ 8 \\ \hline \end{array} \quad \begin{array}{r} 13 \\ -\ 5 \\ \hline \end{array}$$

6.
$$\begin{array}{r} 13 \\ -\ 8 \\ \hline \end{array} \quad \begin{array}{r} 12 \\ -\ 4 \\ \hline \end{array} \quad \begin{array}{r} 16 \\ -\ 8 \\ \hline \end{array} \quad \begin{array}{r} 13 \\ -\ 4 \\ \hline \end{array} \quad \begin{array}{r} 17 \\ -\ 9 \\ \hline \end{array} \quad \begin{array}{r} 14 \\ -\ 7 \\ \hline \end{array} \quad \begin{array}{r} 12 \\ -\ 8 \\ \hline \end{array}$$

7.
$$\begin{array}{r} 13 \\ -\ 6 \\ \hline \end{array} \quad \begin{array}{r} 14 \\ -\ 8 \\ \hline \end{array} \quad \begin{array}{r} 12 \\ -\ 5 \\ \hline \end{array} \quad \begin{array}{r} 18 \\ -\ 9 \\ \hline \end{array} \quad \begin{array}{r} 13 \\ -\ 7 \\ \hline \end{array} \quad \begin{array}{r} 12 \\ -\ 9 \\ \hline \end{array} \quad \begin{array}{r} 15 \\ -\ 8 \\ \hline \end{array}$$

Subtract.

1.
$$15 - 9 \qquad 12 - 5 \qquad 14 - 6 \qquad 9 - 9 \qquad 15 - 6 \qquad 12 - 9 \qquad 13 - 5$$

2.
$$12 - 4 \qquad 17 - 8 \qquad 14 - 9 \qquad 15 - 8 \qquad 12 - 6 \qquad 16 - 9 \qquad 12 - 8$$

3.
$$10 - 6 \qquad 13 - 8 \qquad 17 - 9 \qquad 12 - 3 \qquad 14 - 7 \qquad 12 - 7 \qquad 16 - 7$$

4.
$$16 - 8 \qquad 14 - 5 \qquad 15 - 7 \qquad 18 - 9 \qquad 13 - 7 \qquad 14 - 8 \qquad 13 - 6$$

FIELD TRIP

Answer the riddles.

1. When you add
   me to 5,
   the sum is 11.

   Who am I? _____

2. When you
   double me,
   the sum is 16.

   Who am I? _____

3. When you add
   me to 8,
   the sum is 17.

   Who am I? _____

4. When you double
   me and add 1,
   you get 13.

   Who am I? _____

Name _____

Subtract.

1.
$$14 - 5$$ 　 $$13 - 8$$ 　 $$15 - 6$$ 　 $$12 - 3$$ 　 $$11 - 5$$ 　 $$12 - 7$$ 　 $$13 - 9$$

2.
$$12 - 4$$ 　 $$11 - 6$$ 　 $$16 - 8$$ 　 $$11 - 2$$ 　 $$10 - 7$$ 　 $$12 - 5$$ 　 $$14 - 7$$

3.
$$13 - 4$$ 　 $$10 - 1$$ 　 $$11 - 7$$ 　 $$13 - 5$$ 　 $$10 - 8$$ 　 $$11 - 3$$ 　 $$16 - 7$$

4.
$$17 - 8$$ 　 $$12 - 6$$ 　 $$11 - 4$$ 　 $$15 - 9$$ 　 $$10 - 2$$ 　 $$13 - 6$$ 　 $$14 - 8$$

Complete the tables.

5.
Subtract 9	
11	
15	
18	
13	
17	
14	
16	

6.
Subtract 8	
11	
15	
17	
14	
12	
16	
13	

7.
Subtract 7	
13	
10	
15	
12	
16	
14	
11	

8.
Subtract 6	
9	
14	
11	
12	
13	
10	
15	

Subtract.

1. $11 - 8 =$ _____ $16 - 9 =$ _____ $10 - 6 =$ _____
2. $10 - 3 =$ _____ $10 - 5 =$ _____ $15 - 8 =$ _____
3. $14 - 6 =$ _____ $12 - 8 =$ _____ $9 - 9 =$ _____
4. $18 - 9 =$ _____ $10 - 9 =$ _____ $8 - 5 =$ _____
5. $10 - 4 =$ _____ $13 - 7 =$ _____ $14 - 9 =$ _____
6. $12 - 9 =$ _____ $9 - 3 =$ _____ $9 - 0 =$ _____
7. $15 - 7 =$ _____ $17 - 9 =$ _____ $11 - 9 =$ _____

Complete the wheels.

8.

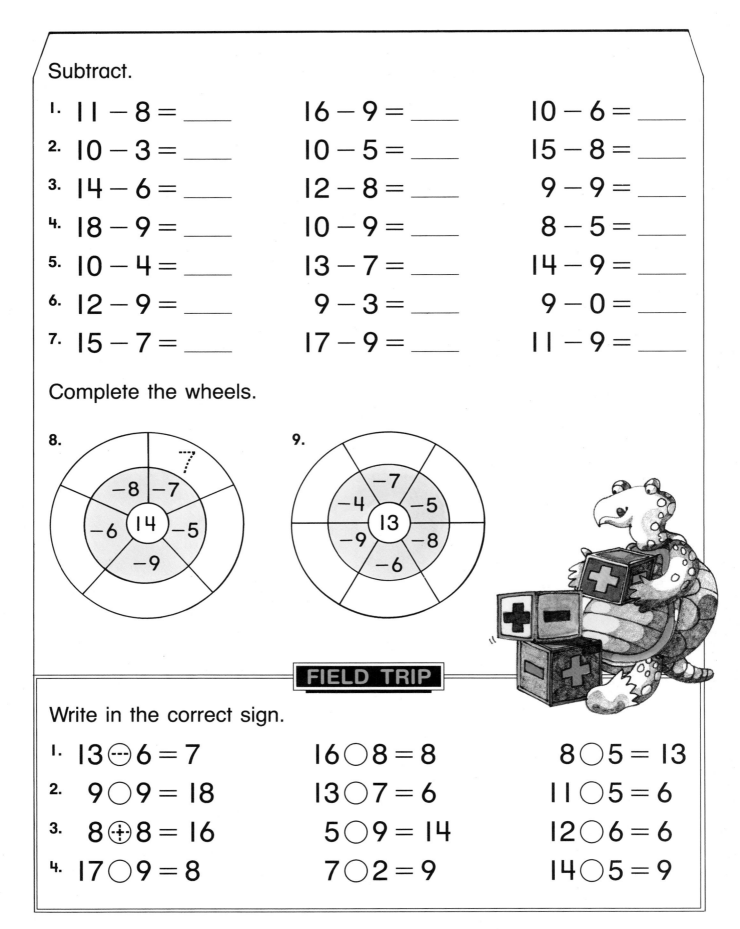

Wheel center: 14; segments: -8 (= 7), -7, -5, -9, -6

9.

Wheel center: 13; segments: -7, -5, -8, -6, -9, -4

FIELD TRIP

Write in the correct sign.

1. $13 \ominus 6 = 7$ $16 \bigcirc 8 = 8$ $8 \bigcirc 5 = 13$
2. $9 \bigcirc 9 = 18$ $13 \bigcirc 7 = 6$ $11 \bigcirc 5 = 6$
3. $8 \oplus 8 = 16$ $5 \bigcirc 9 = 14$ $12 \bigcirc 6 = 6$
4. $17 \bigcirc 9 = 8$ $7 \bigcirc 2 = 9$ $14 \bigcirc 5 = 9$

Name _____

Solve.

1. Carlos had 15¢.
He bought a bear.
How much money
is left?

_____

2. A truck costs _____.

A ring costs _____.
How much more does
the truck cost?

_____

3. Joan had 17¢.
She bought a truck.
How much money
is left?

_____

4. Donna had 15¢.
She bought a train.
How much money
does she have left?

_____

5. Chuck gave the clerk
10¢ to pay for a ring.
How much change did
he get?

_____

6. Marge gave the clerk
10¢ to pay for a car.
How much change did
she get?

_____

7. Dorothy had 18¢.
She bought a truck.
How much does she
have left?

_____

8. How much did Cal pay
for a car and a train?

_____

Problem solving, adding and subtracting money

Circle other names for each amount.

1. _____ 7¢ _____
(16¢ – 9¢)
12¢ – 5¢
13¢ – 8¢
10¢ – 3¢

2. _____ 5¢ _____
12¢ – 7¢
13¢ – 6¢
(14¢ – 9¢)
10¢ – 5¢

3. _____ 4¢ _____
11¢ – 7¢
13¢ – 9¢
10¢ – 6¢
12¢ – 7¢

4. _____ 6¢ _____
11¢ – 6¢
14¢ – 8¢
13¢ – 7¢
12¢ – 6¢

Subtract.

5.
16¢ – 8¢ = 8¢
15¢ – 6¢
14¢ – 7¢
13¢ – 4¢
15¢ – 7¢
17¢ – 9¢

6.
14¢ – 5¢
17¢ – 8¢
13¢ – 5¢
15¢ – 8¢
12¢ – 3¢
14¢ – 6¢

7.
16¢ – 7¢
12¢ – 4¢
11¢ – 5¢
18¢ – 9¢
12¢ – 8¢
15¢ – 9¢

FIELD TRIP

1. How much more do two marbles cost than the ball?

2. Linda wants to buy a fish for 15¢. She has 8¢. How much more money does she need?

_____

_____

Write addition and subtraction sentences.

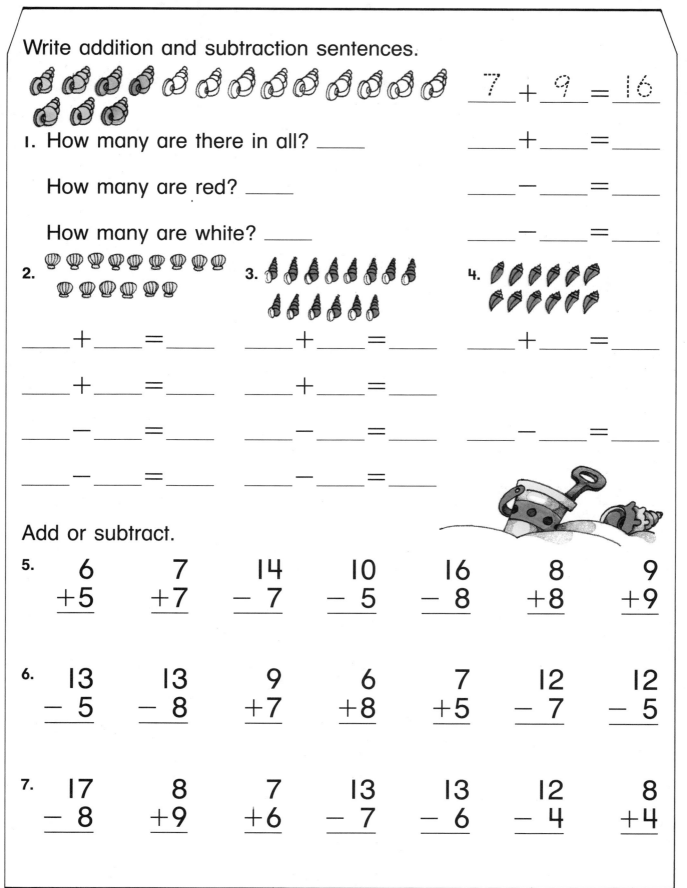

$\underline{7} + \underline{9} = \underline{16}$

1. How many are there in all? _____   _____ + _____ = _____

   How many are red? _____   _____ − _____ = _____

   How many are white? _____   _____ − _____ = _____

2.   _____ + _____ = _____

   _____ + _____ = _____

   _____ − _____ = _____

   _____ − _____ = _____

3.   _____ + _____ = _____

   _____ + _____ = _____

   _____ − _____ = _____

   _____ − _____ = _____

4.   _____ + _____ = _____

   _____ − _____ = _____

Add or subtract.

5.
$$\begin{array}{ccccccc} 6 & 7 & 14 & 10 & 16 & 8 & 9 \\ +5 & +7 & -7 & -5 & -8 & +8 & +9 \end{array}$$

6.
$$\begin{array}{ccccccc} 13 & 13 & 9 & 6 & 7 & 12 & 12 \\ -5 & -8 & +7 & +8 & +5 & -7 & -5 \end{array}$$

7.
$$\begin{array}{ccccccc} 17 & 8 & 7 & 13 & 13 & 12 & 8 \\ -8 & +9 & +6 & -7 & -6 & -4 & +4 \end{array}$$

Add or subtract.

1.
$$2 + 2$$ $$3 + 3$$ $$4 + 4$$ $$5 + 5$$ $$6 + 6$$ $$7 + 7$$ $$8 + 8$$

2.
$$9 + 9$$ $$4 - 2$$ $$6 - 3$$ $$8 - 4$$ $$10 - 5$$ $$12 - 6$$ $$14 - 7$$

3.
$$16 - 8$$ $$18 - 9$$ $$13 - 6$$ $$13 - 7$$ $$6 + 7$$ $$7 + 6$$ $$6 + 5$$

4.
$$11 - 5$$ $$5 + 6$$ $$11 - 6$$ $$15 - 7$$ $$8 + 7$$ $$15 - 8$$ $$7 + 8$$

5.
$$17 - 9$$ $$7 + 9$$ $$12 - 8$$ $$9 + 4$$ $$17 - 8$$ $$6 + 9$$ $$8 + 6$$

FIELD TRIP

Write in the correct sign.

1. $13 \bigcirc 4 = 9$ $6 \bigcirc 9 = 15$ $7 \bigcirc 7 = 14$

2. $7 \bigcirc 2 = 9$ $14 \bigcirc 7 = 7$ $4 \bigcirc 5 = 9$

3. $8 \bigcirc 3 = 5$ $18 \bigcirc 9 = 9$ $11 \bigcirc 5 = 6$

4. $8 \bigcirc 3 = 11$ $7 \bigcirc 3 = 10$ $9 \bigcirc 9 = 0$

    Practice, adding and subtracting

Name _____

Solve.

1. Fido ate 6 dog treats. Then he ate 5 more. How many did he eat in all?

_____ treats

2. Ben saw 16 ladybugs. 8 flew away. How many were left?

_____ ladybugs

3. Lois has 8 bananas and 9 apples. How many pieces of fruit does she have?

_____ pieces of fruit

4. Mario saw 6 frogs on a rock. He saw 8 frogs in the water. How many frogs were there altogether?

_____ frogs

5. There are 16 cherries and 7 strawberries. How many more cherries than strawberries are there?

_____ cherries

6. Jerry counted 15 cows in the field. 6 of them went into the barn. How many cows are left in the field?

_____ cows

7. Allen fed 6 squirrels. Ramona fed 7 squirrels. How many squirrels did they feed?

_____ squirrels

8. There are 16 ducks in the pond. There are 9 ducks on land. How many more ducks are in the pond?

_____ ducks

Problem solving, adding and subtracting

(seventy-three) **73**

Answer the riddles.

1. If you double me, you get 10.

   Who am I? _____

2. If you add 4 to me, you get 12.

   Who am I? _____

3. If you subtract 9 from me, you get 5.

   Who am I? _____

4. If you double me, you get 16.

   Who am I? _____

5. If you add me to myself, you get 14.

   Who am I? _____

6. If you add 2 to me, and then add 3 more, you get 8.

   Who am I? _____

FIELD TRIP

Add or subtract.

Start (15) -8 (7) $+3$ ( ) -5 ( ) $+3$ ( ) $+7$ ( ) -9 ( ) -6 ( ) End

Start (18) -9 (9) -3 ( ) $+8$ ( ) -7 ( ) -7 ( ) $+5$ ( ) -5 ( ) End

Problem solving, adding and subtracting

CHAPTER CHECKUP

Subtract.

1.
10	13	12	15	8	13	14
− 7	− 5	− 3	− 6	−0	− 4	− 7

2.
14	11	13	16	15	13	15
− 6	− 5	− 7	− 8	− 9	− 8	− 7

3.
17	13	9	16	14	11	12
− 8	− 9	−9	− 7	− 8	− 4	− 7

4.
18	14	16	15	13	14	17
− 9	− 5	− 9	− 8	− 6	− 9	− 9

Solve.

5. Brenda saw 14 lightning bugs. Elmer saw 9. How many more lightning bugs did Brenda see?

_____ lightning bugs

6. Matt has 17 marbles. Paul has 9 marbles. How many more marbles does Matt have?

_____ marbles

7. Sonja had 15¢. She bought a balloon for 8¢. How much money does she have left?

_____

8. Roy counted 16 crows. 8 of them flew away. How many are left?

_____ crows

Chapter review

ROUNDUP REVIEW

Add or subtract.

1.
$$7 + 0 \qquad 9 + 1 \qquad 6 - 5 \qquad 7 - 5 \qquad 4 - 0 \qquad 8 + 2 \qquad 9 + 7$$

2.
$$9 - 3 \qquad 10 - 5 \qquad 8 - 7 \qquad 10 - 9 \qquad 7 + 3 \qquad 9 + 5 \qquad 7 + 6$$

3.
$$11 - 4 \qquad 12 - 7 \qquad 8 + 4 \qquad 9 + 3 \qquad 8 + 8 \qquad 13 - 5 \qquad 14 - 7$$

4.
$$15 - 6 \qquad 7 + 9 \qquad 8 + 6 \qquad 9 + 9 \qquad 16 - 7 \qquad 17 - 9 \qquad 15 - 8$$

Solve.

5. Nancy counted 9 deer and 5 wild turkeys. How many animals did she count?

_____ animals

6. Bert picked 11 tulips. Fay picked 8 tulips. How many more tulips did Bert pick?

_____ tulips

7. Bill ran 7 blocks. Then he ran 6 blocks more. How many blocks did Bill run?

_____ blocks

8. There were 12 dogs in the park. 7 dogs ran home. How many dogs are left in the park?

_____ dogs

Name _____

5 3-DIGIT PLACE VALUE

Write the numbers.

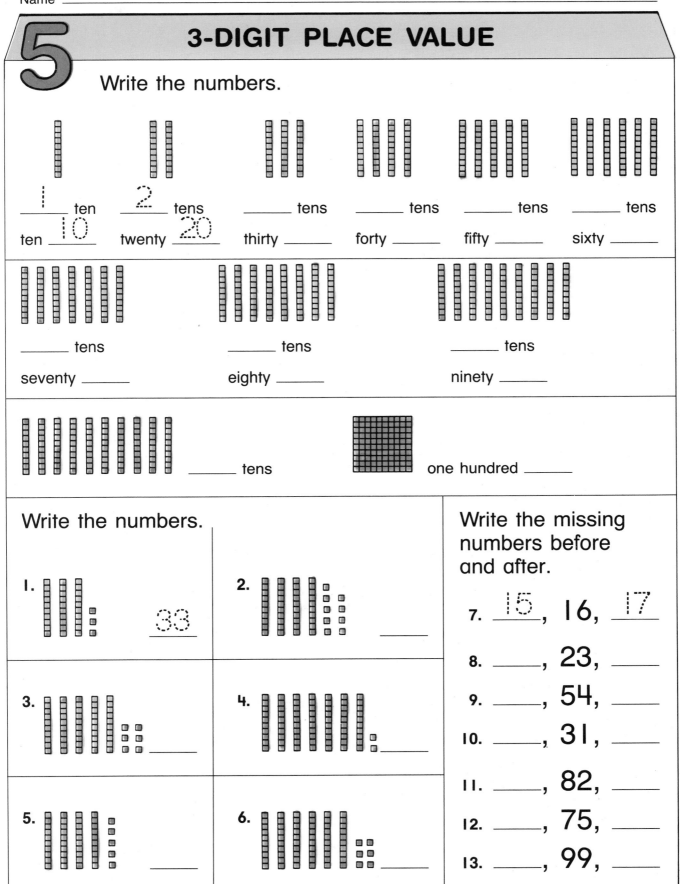

__1__ ten   __2__ tens   _____ tens   _____ tens   _____ tens   _____ tens

ten __10__   twenty __20__   thirty _____   forty _____   fifty _____   sixty _____

_____ tens   _____ tens   _____ tens

seventy _____   eighty _____   ninety _____

_____ tens   one hundred _____

Write the numbers.

1. __33__

2. _____

3. _____

4. _____

5. _____

6. _____

Write the missing numbers before and after.

7. __15__, 16, __17__

8. _____, 23, _____

9. _____, 54, _____

10. _____, 31, _____

11. _____, 82, _____

12. _____, 75, _____

13. _____, 99, _____

Reading and writing numbers through 100   (seventy-seven) **77**

Write the missing numbers.

1. 24, 25, 26, _27_, ____, ____, ____, ____, _32_
2. 37, 38, ____, ____, ____, ____, ____, _44_
3. 56, 57, ____, ____, ____, ____, ____, ____
4. 41, 42, ____, ____, ____, ____, ____, ____

Write the numbers.

5. seventeen _17_

6. fifty-two ____

7. fifteen ____

8. sixty-three ____

9. twelve ____

10. seventy-seven ____

11. fourteen ____

12. eighty-one ____

13. sixteen ____

14. ninety-four ____

15. eighteen ____

16. thirty-five ____

17. twenty-nine ____

18. forty-eight ____

FIELD TRIP

Use these digits to write as many 2-digit numbers as you can.

1. | 2 | 7 | 6 | _27_, _26_, _72_, _76_, ____, ____

2. | 9 | 1 | 5 | ____, ____, ____, ____, ____, ____

How many hundreds, tens and ones are there? Write the numbers.

1.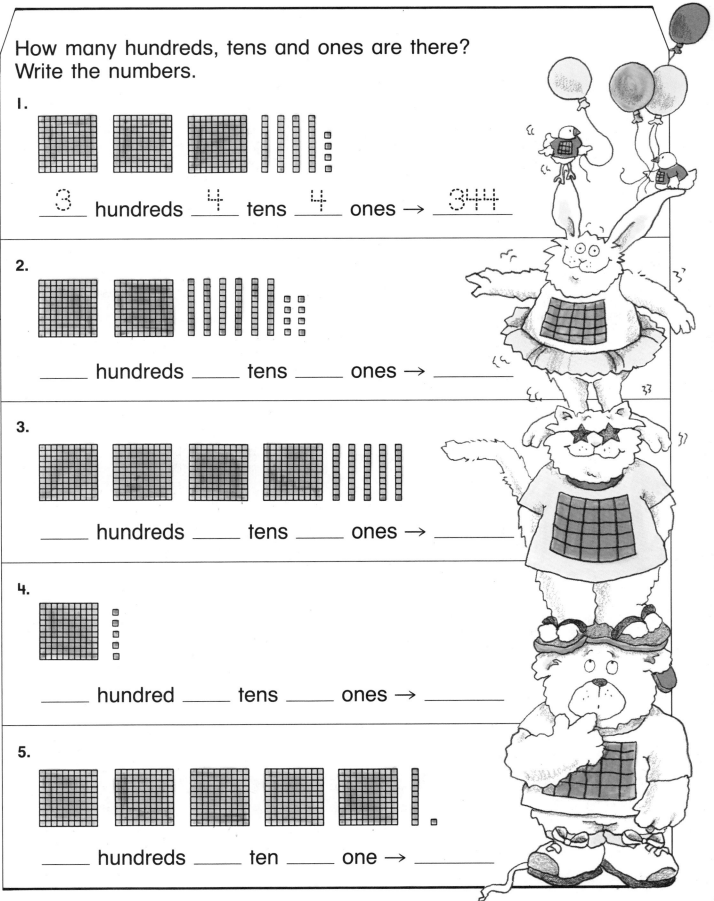

___3___ hundreds ___4___ tens ___4___ ones → ___344___

2.

_____ hundreds _____ tens _____ ones → _____

3.

_____ hundreds _____ tens _____ ones → _____

4.

_____ hundred _____ tens _____ ones → _____

5.

_____ hundreds _____ ten _____ one → _____

How many hundreds, tens and ones are there?
Write the numbers.

1.

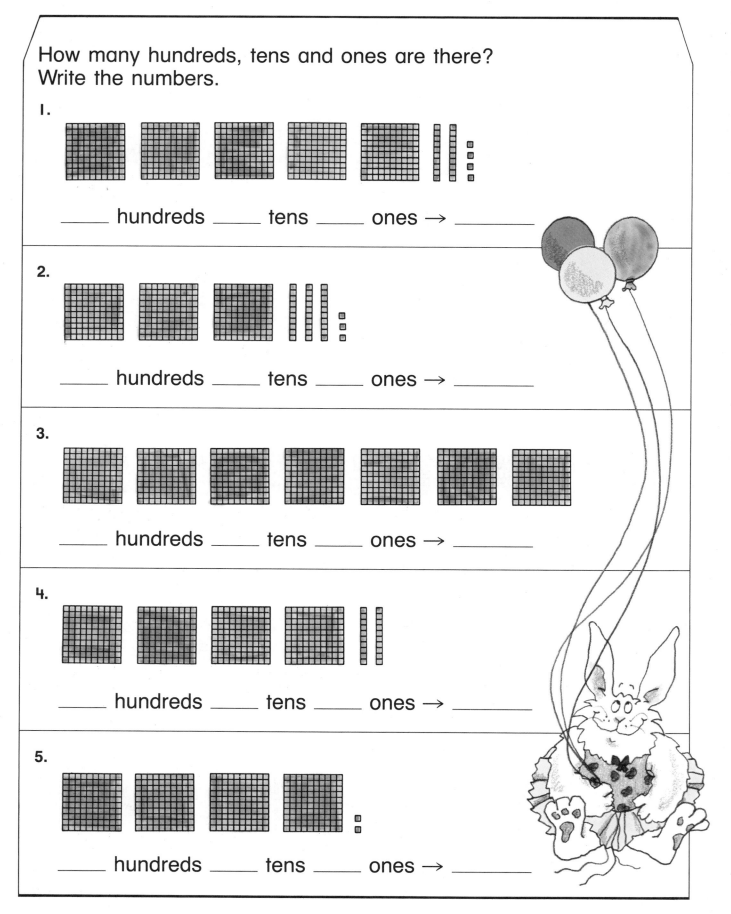

_____ hundreds _____ tens _____ ones → _____

2.

_____ hundreds _____ tens _____ ones → _____

3.

_____ hundreds _____ tens _____ ones → _____

4.

_____ hundreds _____ tens _____ ones → _____

5.

_____ hundreds _____ tens _____ ones → _____

Writing 3-digit numbers

Name _____

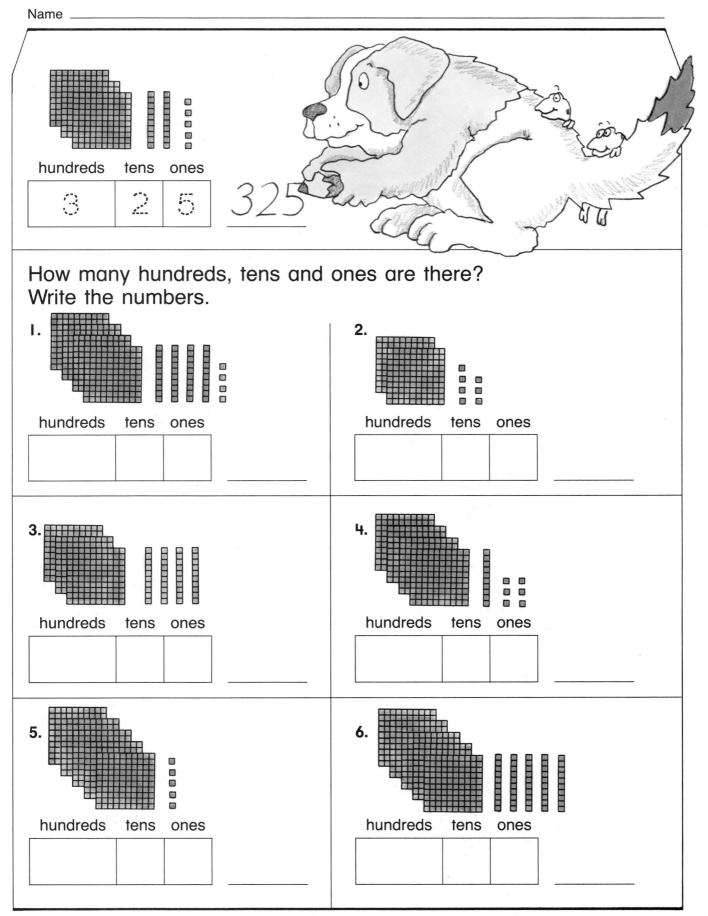

hundreds	tens	ones
3	2	5

325 _____

How many hundreds, tens and ones are there?
Write the numbers.

1.

hundreds	tens	ones

_____

2.

hundreds	tens	ones

_____

3.

hundreds	tens	ones

_____

4.

hundreds	tens	ones

_____

5.

hundreds	tens	ones

_____

6.

hundreds	tens	ones

_____

Writing 3-digit numbers

(eighty-one) **81**

How many hundreds, tens and ones are there?
Write the numbers.

1.

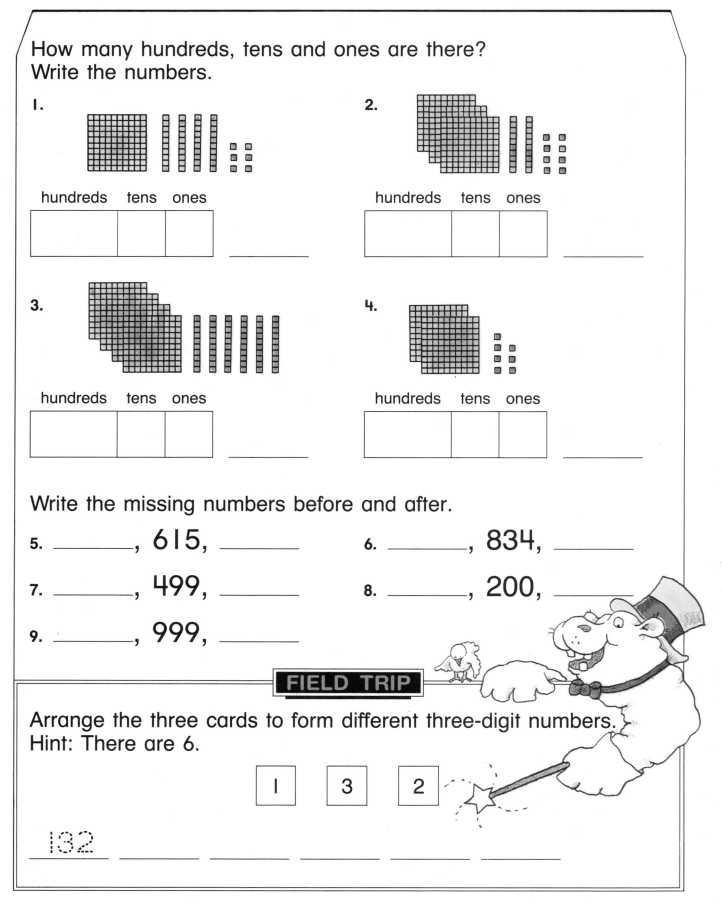

hundreds	tens	ones

_____

2.

hundreds	tens	ones

_____

3.

hundreds	tens	ones

_____

4.

hundreds	tens	ones

_____

Write the missing numbers before and after.

5. _____, 615, _____

6. _____, 834, _____

7. _____, 499, _____

8. _____, 200, _____

9. _____, 999, _____

FIELD TRIP

Arrange the three cards to form different three-digit numbers.
Hint: There are 6.

| 1 | 3 | 2 |

132 _____ _____ _____ _____ _____

Writing 3-digit numbers

This is one dollar.

100¢ $1.00

This is one dollar and thirty cents.

130¢ $1. 3 0

Write the amount in two ways.

1.
	dollars	cents
	2	20

220¢ $2. 2 0

2.
dollars	cents

_____ _____

3.
dollars	cents

_____ _____

4.
dollars	cents

_____ _____

Counting money, dollars and dimes

(eighty-three) **83**

Write the amount in two ways.

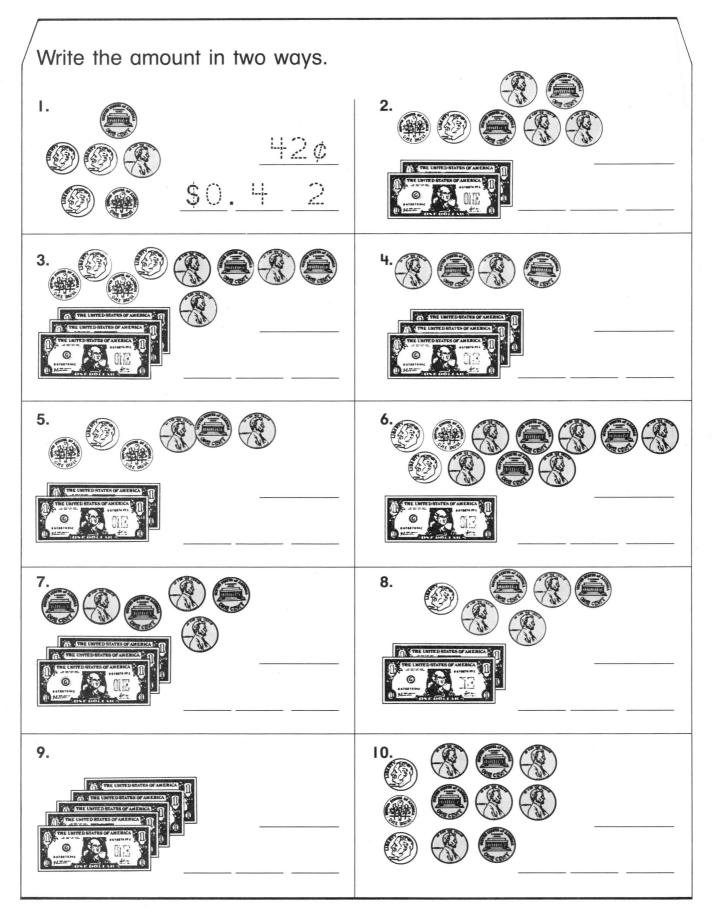

1. $42¢$ $0.4 2

2. _____ _____

3. _____ _____

4. _____ _____

5. _____ _____

6. _____ _____

7. _____ _____

8. _____ _____

9. _____ _____

10. _____ _____

      Counting money, dollars, dimes, and pennies

Name _____

Count by ones. Write the missing numbers.

1. 185, 186, 187, _____, _____, _____, _____, _____

2. 96, 97, 98, _____, _____, _____, _____, _____, _____

3. 396, 397, 398, _____, _____, _____, _____, _____

4. 105, 106, _____, _____, _____, _____, _____, _____

5. 215, 216, 217, _____, _____, _____, _____, _____

Count by fives. Write the missing numbers.

6. 5, 10, 15, _____, _____, _____, _____, _____, _____

7. 105, 110, 115, _____, _____, _____, _____, _____

8. 535, 540, 545, _____, _____, _____, _____, _____

9. 380, 385, 390, _____, _____, _____, _____, _____

Count by tens. Write the missing numbers.

10. 10, 20, 30, _____, _____, _____, _____, _____, _____

11. 110, 120, 130, _____, _____, _____, _____, _____

12. 450, 460, 470, _____, _____, _____, _____, _____

13. 580, 590, _____, _____, _____, _____, _____, _____

Count by hundreds. Write the missing numbers.

14. 100, 200, _____, _____, _____, _____, _____, _____,

_____, _____

Counting by ones, fives, tens, and hundreds through 1,000   (eighty-five) **85**

What does the red digit mean? Circle the correct word.

1. 275	(tens) ones hundreds	2. 341	hundreds tens ones	3. 204	ones tens hundreds
4. 526	tens hundreds ones	5. 973	hundreds ones tens	6. 858	tens ones hundreds

Write the number of hundreds, tens and ones.

7. 732	_7_ hundreds _3_ tens _2_ ones	8. 467	___ tens ___ ones ___ hundreds	9. 618	___ hundreds ___ ones ___ tens
10. 279	___ hundreds ___ ones ___ tens	11. 312	___ tens ___ hundreds ___ ones	12. 103	___ ones ___ tens ___ hundreds

FIELD TRIP

Solve.

1. I am thinking of a number. It has 2 tens, 3 hundreds and 5 ones. What is my number?

_____

2. My number has no ones, two hundreds and no tens. What is my number?

_____

Place value, recognizing ones, tens, and hundreds

Name _____

233 ← 10 less **243** 10 more → 253

Write the missing numbers.

10 less   10 more   10 less   10 more

1. _324_, 334, _344_   2. _____, 771, _____

3. _____, 80, _____   4. _____, 105, _____

5. _____, 262, _____   6. _____, 593, _____

7. _____, 428, _____   8. _____, 322, _____

9. _____, 110, _____   10. _____, 607, _____

11. _____, 549, _____   12. _____, 989, _____

13. _____, 852, _____   14. _____, 400, _____

15. _____, 901, _____   16. _____, 990, _____

17. _____, 309, _____   18. _____, 555, _____

Solve.

19. Diane saves baseball cards. She has 210 cards. Her brother has 10 more cards than Diane. How many cards does Diane's brother have?

   _____ cards

20. Cynthia has 102 shells in her collection. Dino has 10 less shells than Cynthia. How many shells does Dino have?

   _____ shells

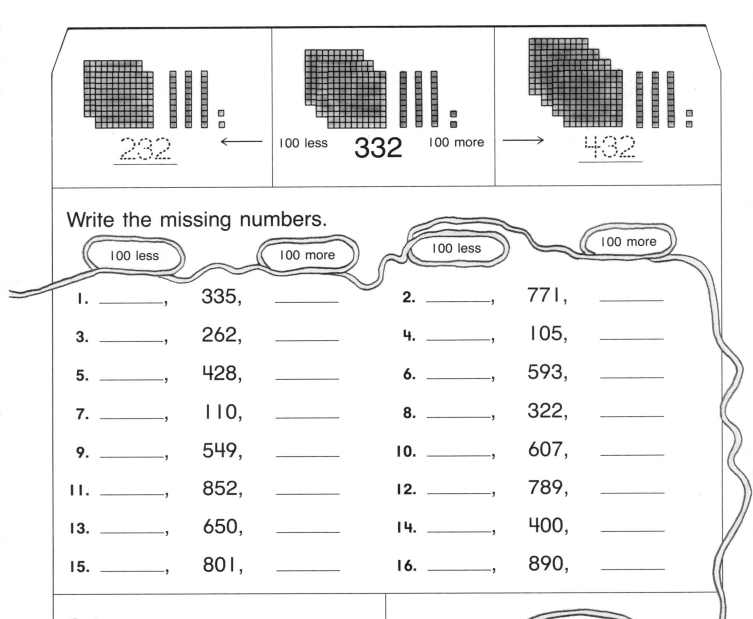

232 ← 100 less **332** 100 more → 432

Write the missing numbers.

100 less   100 more   100 less   100 more

1. _____, 335, _____   2. _____, 771, _____

3. _____, 262, _____   4. _____, 105, _____

5. _____, 428, _____   6. _____, 593, _____

7. _____, 110, _____   8. _____, 322, _____

9. _____, 549, _____   10. _____, 607, _____

11. _____, 852, _____   12. _____, 789, _____

13. _____, 650, _____   14. _____, 400, _____

15. _____, 801, _____   16. _____, 890, _____

Solve.

17. The Perez family took a trip. They drove 183 miles on Thursday. On Friday, they drove 100 miles farther than they did on Thursday. How many miles did they drive on Friday?

_____ miles

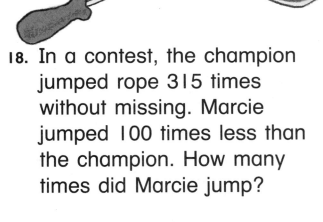

18. In a contest, the champion jumped rope 315 times without missing. Marcie jumped 100 times less than the champion. How many times did Marcie jump?

_____ times

Name _____

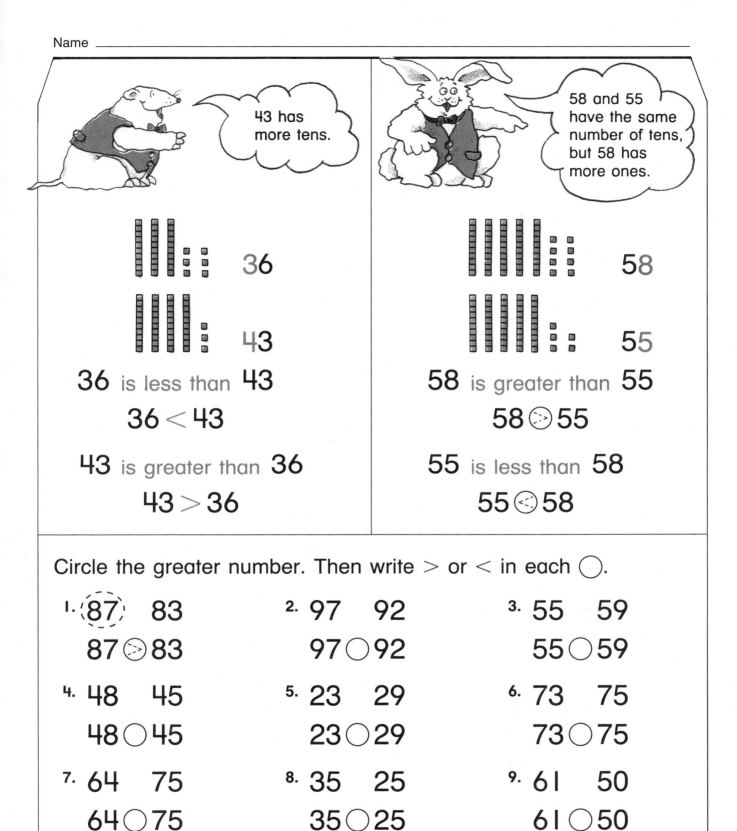

43 has more tens.

58 and 55 have the same number of tens, but 58 has more ones.

36

43

36 is less than 43

36 < 43

43 is greater than 36

43 > 36

58

55

58 is greater than 55

58 > 55

55 is less than 58

55 < 58

Circle the greater number. Then write > or < in each ◯.

1. (87) 83
   87 > 83

2. 97 92
   97 ◯ 92

3. 55 59
   55 ◯ 59

4. 48 45
   48 ◯ 45

5. 23 29
   23 ◯ 29

6. 73 75
   73 ◯ 75

7. 64 75
   64 ◯ 75

8. 35 25
   35 ◯ 25

9. 61 50
   61 ◯ 50

10. 43 28
    43 ◯ 28

11. 49 57
    49 ◯ 57

12. 47 74
    47 ◯ 74

Comparing 2-digit numbers, greater than and less than

(eighty-nine) **89**

Write $>$ or $<$ in each $\bigcirc$.

1. $39 \mathbin{<} 93$
2. $91 \bigcirc 97$
3. $70 \bigcirc 60$
4. $27 \bigcirc 38$
5. $57 \bigcirc 67$
6. $82 \bigcirc 72$
7. $41 \bigcirc 14$
8. $32 \bigcirc 52$
9. $63 \bigcirc 56$
10. $54 \bigcirc 65$
11. $96 \bigcirc 89$
12. $75 \bigcirc 57$
13. $70 \bigcirc 50$
14. $71 \bigcirc 58$
15. $88 \bigcirc 98$

Write the numbers in order from least to greatest.

16. 37 29 61

    29 37 61
    least   greatest

17. 60 80 40

    ___ ___ ___
    least   greatest

18. 85 55 75

    ___ ___ ___
    least   greatest

19. 51 34 19

    ___ ___ ___
    least   greatest

20. 67 50 76

    ___ ___ ___
    least   greatest

21. 39 45 72

    ___ ___ ___
    least   greatest

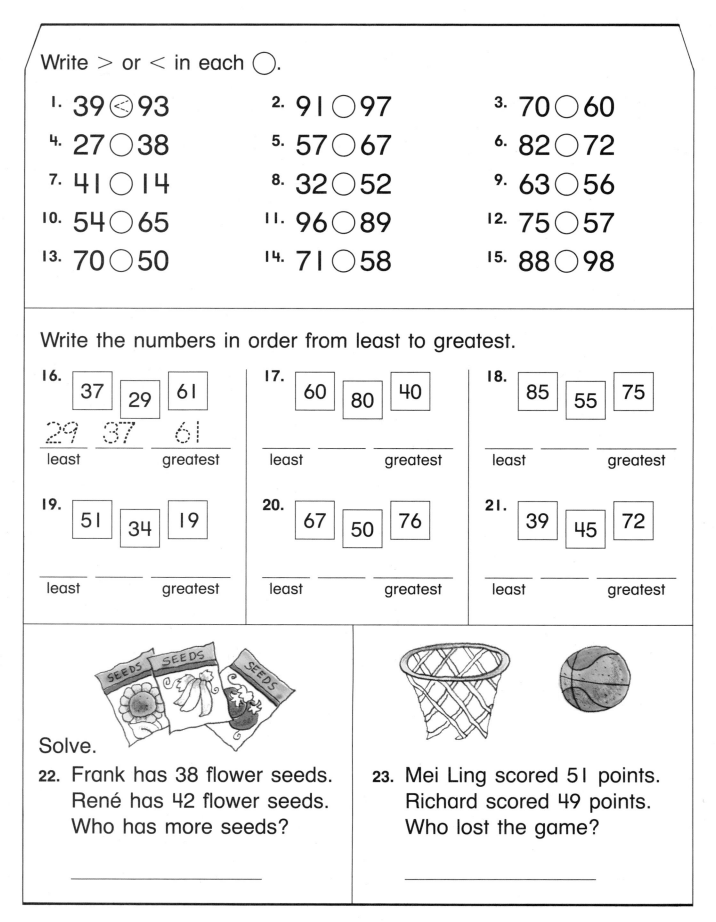

Solve.

22. Frank has 38 flower seeds. René has 42 flower seeds. Who has more seeds?

_____

23. Mei Ling scored 51 points. Richard scored 49 points. Who lost the game?

_____

Comparing 2-digit numbers, greater than and less than

Name _____

123 is greater than 86
123   123 > 86

86 is less than 123
86   86 < 123

123 has more hundreds.

325 is less than 349
325   325 < 349

349 is greater than 325
349   349 > 325

349 and 325 have the same number of hundreds, but 349 has more tens.

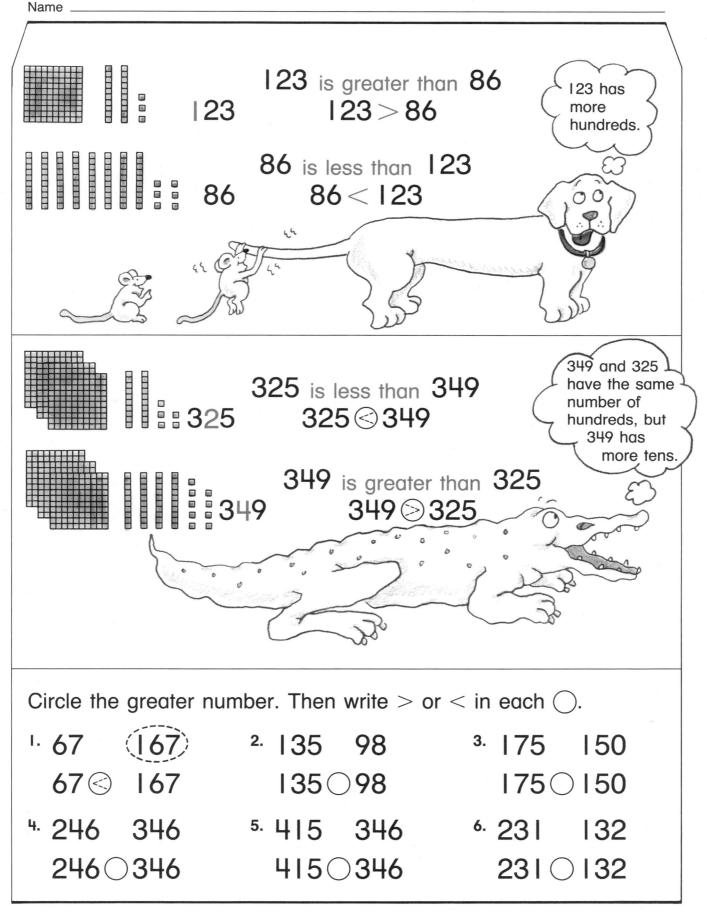

Circle the greater number. Then write > or < in each ◯.

1. 67   (167)
   67 < 167

2. 135   98
   135 ◯ 98

3. 175   150
   175 ◯ 150

4. 246   346
   246 ◯ 346

5. 415   346
   415 ◯ 346

6. 231   132
   231 ◯ 132

Comparing 2- and 3-digit numbers, greater than and less than   (ninety-one) **91**

Write $>$ or $<$ in each $\bigcirc$.

1. $458 \bigcirc> 302$
2. $86 \bigcirc 129$
3. $265 \bigcirc 625$
4. $912 \bigcirc 832$
5. $901 \bigcirc 109$
6. $302 \bigcirc 298$
7. $600 \bigcirc 706$
8. $97 \bigcirc 79$
9. $989 \bigcirc 999$
10. $350 \bigcirc 450$
11. $126 \bigcirc 120$
12. $325 \bigcirc 523$
13. $367 \bigcirc 361$
14. $554 \bigcirc 455$
15. $717 \bigcirc 698$
16. $302 \bigcirc 285$
17. $998 \bigcirc 999$
18. $502 \bigcirc 499$
19. $230 \bigcirc 99$
20. $707 \bigcirc 706$
21. $445 \bigcirc 435$

Write the numbers in order from least to greatest.

22. | 301 | 95 | 102 |

_____ _____ _____
least   greatest

23. | 249 | 234 | 251 |

_____ _____ _____
least   greatest

24. | 9 | 999 | 99 |

_____ _____ _____
least   greatest

25. | 275 | 546 | 489 |

_____ _____ _____
least   greatest

FIELD TRIP

Make the greatest possible number and the least possible number. Use all three number cards each time.

1. | 6 | 3 | 9 |

greatest: _____

least: _____

2. | 2 | 1 | 7 |

greatest: _____

least: _____

Comparing 2- and 3-digit numbers, greater than and less than

Mrs. Jones wants to put her class role in order
for the school party. Write each name in order.

3.	Bill	first	Adam	21.	Mike	seventeenth _____
2.	Beverly	second _____		18.	Linda	eighteenth _____
4.	Chan	third _____		20.	Me Lin	nineteenth _____
1.	Adam	fourth _____		17.	Leah	twentieth _____
6.	Diane	fifth _____		19.	Mary	twenty-first _____
5.	Cheryl	sixth _____		24.	Paul	twenty-second _____
8.	Dorothy	seventh _____		22.	Noah	twenty-third _____
10.	George	eighth _____		26.	Rosa	twenty-fourth _____
7.	Dick	ninth _____		23.	Opal	twenty-fifth _____
13.	Jack	tenth _____		27.	Sarah	twenty-sixth _____
11.	Harry	eleventh _____		25.	Raul	twenty-seventh _____
9.	Emma	twelfth _____		30.	Tom	twenty-eighth _____
14.	Jean	thirteenth _____		28.	Stacey	twenty-ninth _____
12.	Isaac	fourteenth _____		32.	Wade	thirtieth _____
16.	Ken	fifteenth _____		29.	Terry	thirty-first _____
15.	Juan	sixteenth _____		31.	Vera	thirty-second _____

Reading ordinal numbers through thirty-second

January

Sunday	Monday	Tuesday	Wednesday	Thursday	Friday	Saturday
		1	2	3	4	5
6	7	8	9	10	11	12
13	14	15	16	17	18	19
20	21	22	23	24	25	26
27	28	29	30	31		

Use the calendar to write the day of the month.

1. first Monday __7__

2. fourth Saturday _____

3. second Sunday _____

4. fifth Tuesday _____

5. third Wednesday _____

6. second Friday _____

Use the calendar to write the day of the week.

7. January first __Tuesday__

8. January sixteenth _____

9. January tenth _____

10. January twelfth _____

11. January eleventh _____

12. January fifteenth _____

13. January thirteenth _____

14. January twenty-first _____

15. January eighteenth _____

16. January seventh _____

17. January thirty-first _____

18. January twenty-sixth _____

19. January thirtieth _____

20. January twentieth _____

21. January seventeenth

_____

22. January twenty-eighth

_____

Reading ordinal numbers using the calendar

Name _____

Match the number name with the number.

1. two hundred   400
2. six hundred   900
3. nine hundred   200
4. four hundred   700
5. seven hundred   600

6. three hundred seventy   130
7. one hundred thirty   490
8. five hundred ten   860
9. eight hundred sixty   370
10. four hundred ninety   510

11. two hundred fifty-three   255
12. five hundred sixty-six   998
13. nine hundred ninety-eight 566
14. five hundred sixteen   516
15. two hundred fifty-five   253

16. eight hundred seventy-two 344
17. three hundred forty-four   872
18. eight hundred twenty-seven 418
19. three hundred four   827
20. four hundred eighteen   304

Write the numbers.

1. forty-five _____

2. nine hundred ninety _____

3. one hundred forty-five _____

4. four hundred five _____

5. two hundred nineteen

_____

6. seven hundred eighteen

_____

7. five hundred _____

8. ninety-nine _____

9. three hundred ten _____

10. eight hundred eight _____

11. six hundred fifty _____

12. five hundred twenty _____

Solve.

13. I am a number greater than 8 tens and 5 ones. I am less than 8 tens and 7 ones.
Who am I? _____

14. We are two numbers. We are both less than 8 tens. We are both greater than 77.
Who are we? _____ _____

15. We are two numbers. We are both less than 2 hundreds, 5 tens, and 6 ones. We are both greater than 2 hundreds, 5 tens, 3 ones.

Who are we?

_____ _____

16. I am a 3-digit number. All my digits are the number 3.

Who am I? _____

17. I am a number 1 less than 1,000.

Who am I? _____

Reading 3-digit number names, problem solving

Name _____

CHAPTER CHECKUP

How many hundreds, tens and ones are there?
Write the numbers.

1.

_____ hundreds _____ tens _____ ones ⟶ _____

Write the amount in two ways.

2.

_____

_____ . _____

Write the missing numbers.

3. 125, 126, 127, _____, _____, _____, _____

4. 70, 80, 90, _____, _____, _____, _____

Write the number of hundreds, tens and ones.

5. 971

___ hundreds ___ tens
___ ones

6. 804

___ hundreds ___ tens
___ ones

Write the missing numbers before and after.

7. _____, 998, _____

8. _____, 400, _____

Write > or < in each ◯.

9. 342 ◯ 415

10. 625 ◯ 605

11. 773 ◯ 737

12. 899 ◯ 900

ROUNDUP REVIEW

Add or subtract.

1.
$$2 + 7$$ $$5 + 5$$ $$8 + 3$$ $$3 + 6$$ $$11 - 7$$ $$14 - 6$$ $$15 - 8$$

2.
$$12 - 5$$ $$17 - 8$$ $$2 + 9$$ $$9 + 7$$ $$8 + 8$$ $$11 - 5$$ $$15 - 6$$

3.
$$11 - 8$$ $$13 - 7$$ $$10 - 6$$ $$7 + 7$$ $$9 + 3$$ $$8 + 5$$ $$16 - 7$$

4.
$$18 - 9$$ $$14 - 8$$ $$16 - 9$$ $$2 + 8$$ $$7 + 7$$ $$9 + 9$$ $$5 + 7$$

Solve.

5.

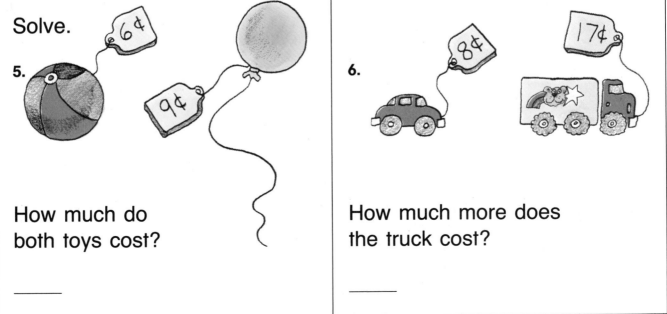

How much do both toys cost?

_____

6.

How much more does the truck cost?

_____

TIME AND MONEY

There are 12 hour marks on a clock. Write the hour numbers on the clock.

It is 3 o'clock. We can also write 3:00.

The minute hand is on 12.

The hour hand is on 3.

Color the minute hand blue.

Color the hour hand red.

Match the clocks that show the same time.

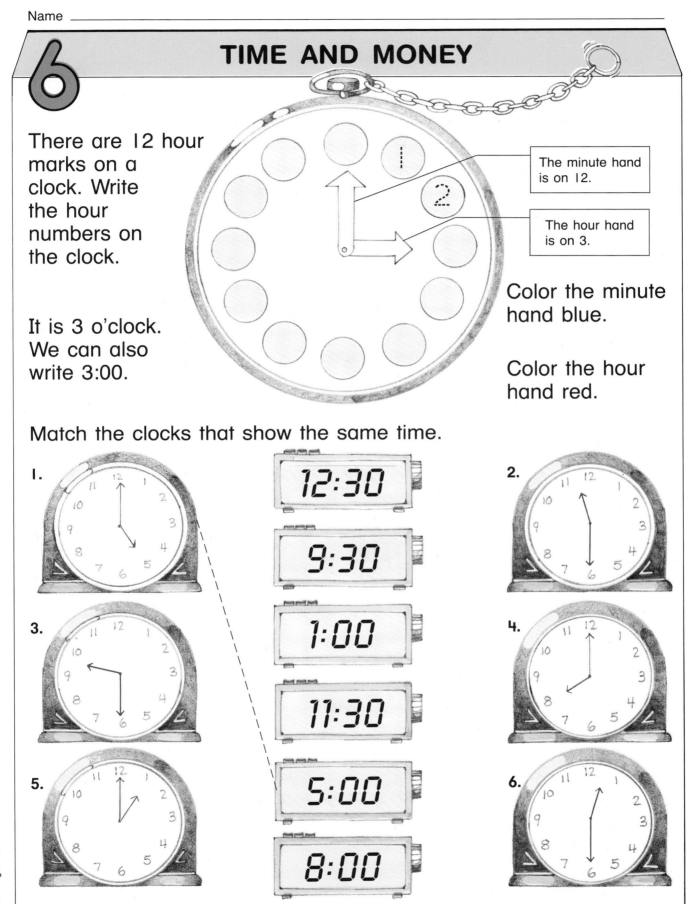

1.

12:30

9:30

1:00

11:30

5:00

8:00

2.

3.

4.

5.

6.

Telling time to the hour and half-hour

(ninety-nine) **99**

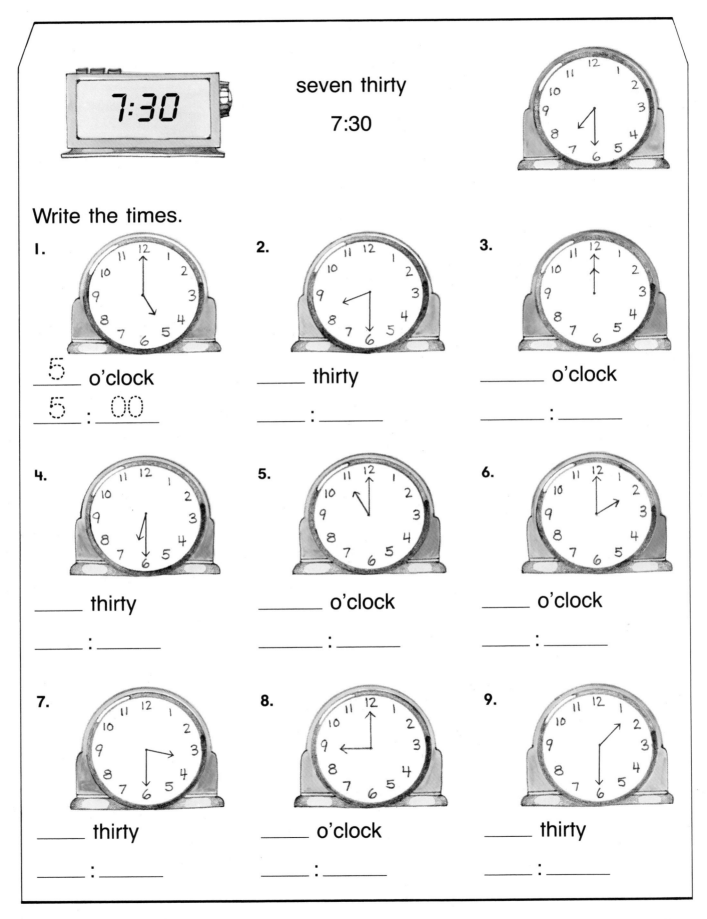

7:30

seven thirty

7:30

Write the times.

1. ___5___ o'clock

___5___ : __00__

2. _____ thirty

_____ : _____

3. _____ o'clock

_____ : _____

4. _____ thirty

_____ : _____

5. _____ o'clock

_____ : _____

6. _____ o'clock

_____ : _____

7. _____ thirty

_____ : _____

8. _____ o'clock

_____ : _____

9. _____ thirty

_____ : _____

Telling time to the hour and half-hour

There are _____ minutes in each hour. As the minute hand moves around the clock face, the hour hand gets closer to the next hour number. Count by fives. Write the minute numbers on the clock.

It is 25 minutes after 3.

The hour hand is between the 3 and the 4.

We can also write 3:25.

The minute hand is on the 5.

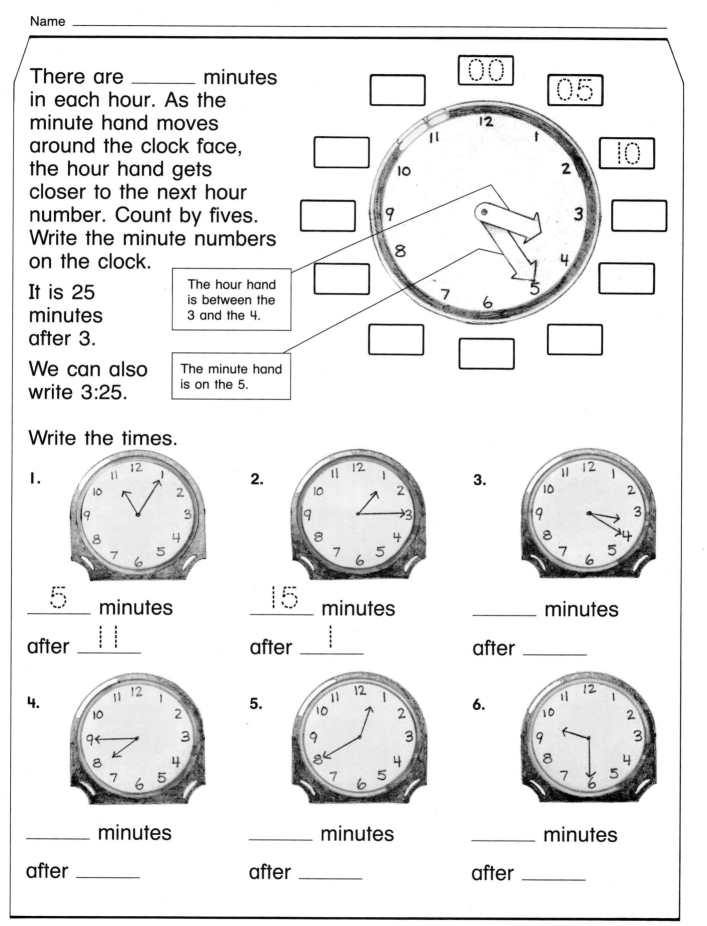

Write the times.

1. _____ minutes after _____

2. _____ minutes after _____

3. _____ minutes after _____

4. _____ minutes after _____

5. _____ minutes after _____

6. _____ minutes after _____

10 minutes after 5

5:10

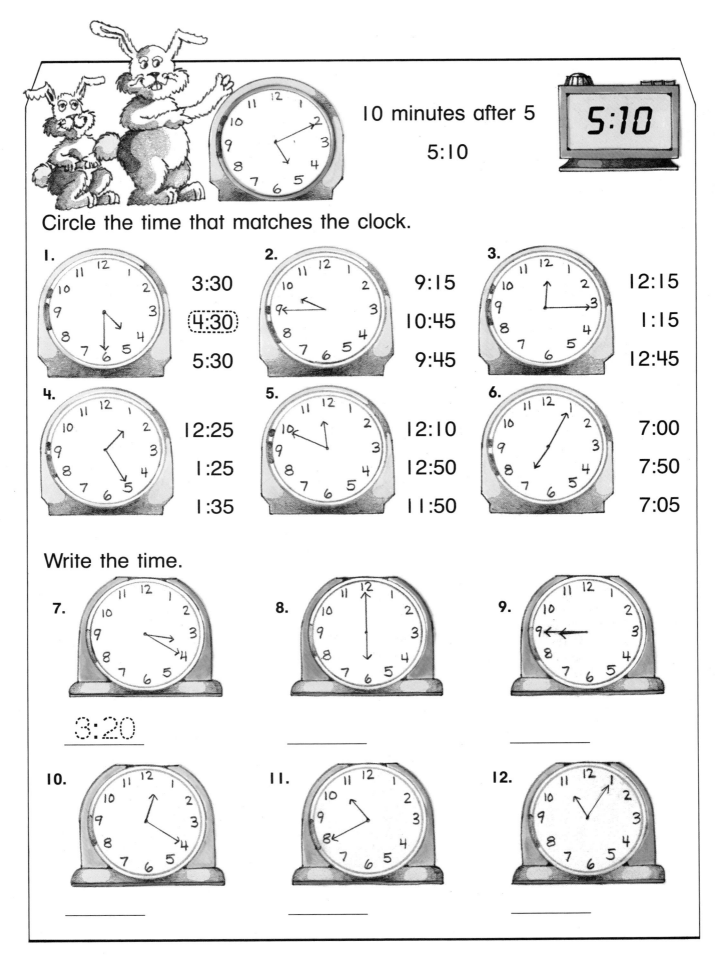

Circle the time that matches the clock.

1.
3:30
(4:30)
5:30

2.
9:15
10:45
9:45

3.
12:15
1:15
12:45

4.
12:25
1:25
1:35

5.
12:10
12:50
11:50

6.
7:00
7:50
7:05

Write the time.

7. 3:20

8. _____

9. _____

10. _____

11. _____

12. _____

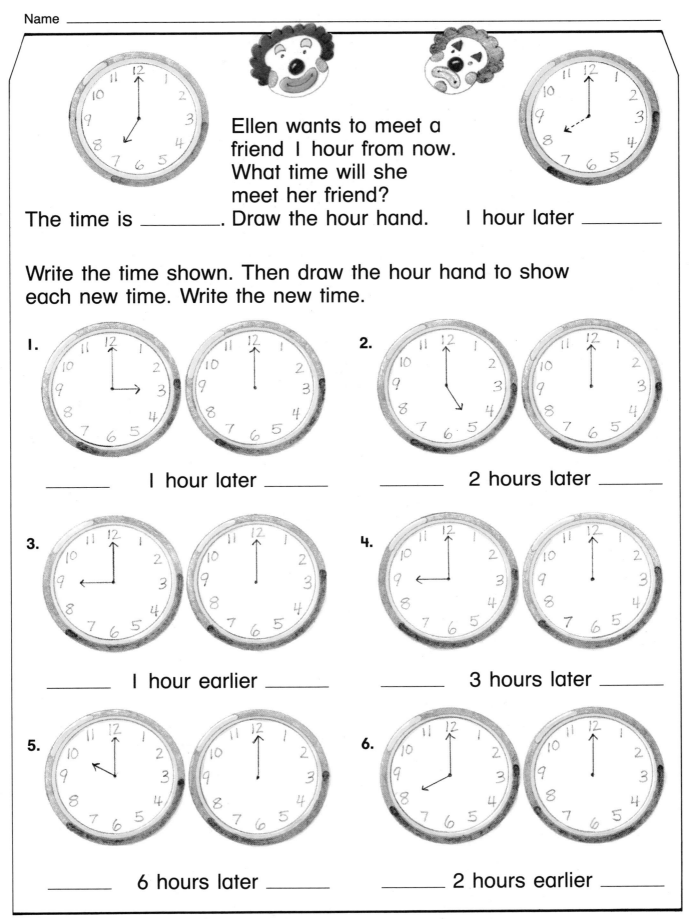

Ellen wants to meet a friend I hour from now. What time will she meet her friend?

The time is _____. Draw the hour hand.   I hour later _____

Write the time shown. Then draw the hour hand to show each new time. Write the new time.

1. _____ I hour later _____

2. _____ 2 hours later _____

3. _____ I hour earlier _____

4. _____ 3 hours later _____

5. _____ 6 hours later _____

6. _____ 2 hours earlier _____

Telling time, problem solving   (one hundred three) **103**

Solve.

1.

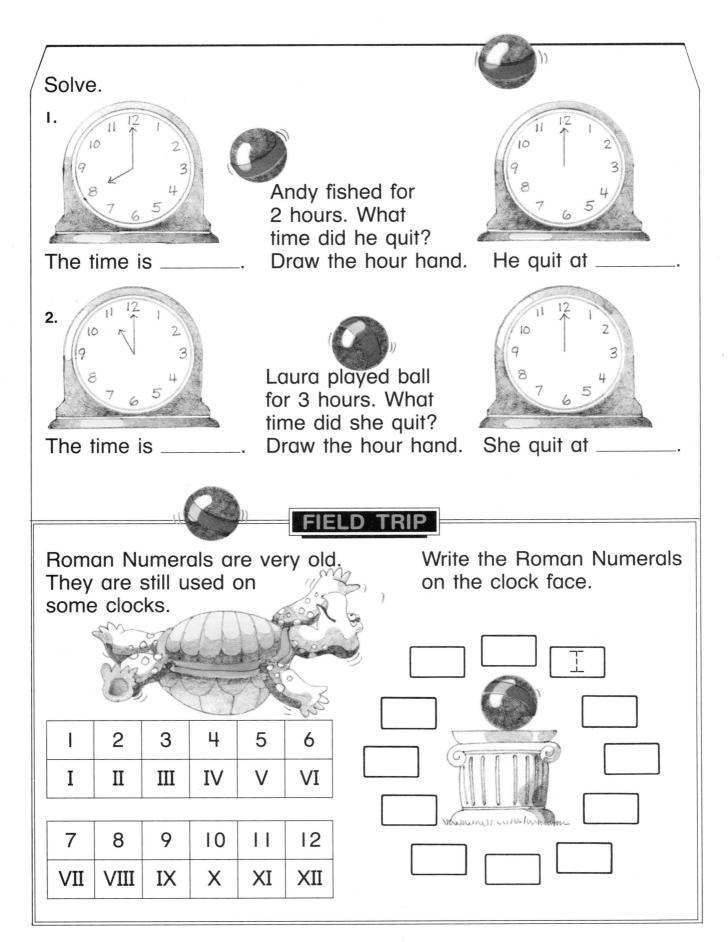

The time is _____.

Andy fished for 2 hours. What time did he quit? Draw the hour hand.

He quit at _____.

2.

The time is _____.

Laura played ball for 3 hours. What time did she quit? Draw the hour hand.

She quit at _____.

FIELD TRIP

Roman Numerals are very old. They are still used on some clocks.

Write the Roman Numerals on the clock face.

1	2	3	4	5	6
I	II	III	IV	V	VI

7	8	9	10	11	12
VII	VIII	IX	X	XI	XII

Telling time, problem solving

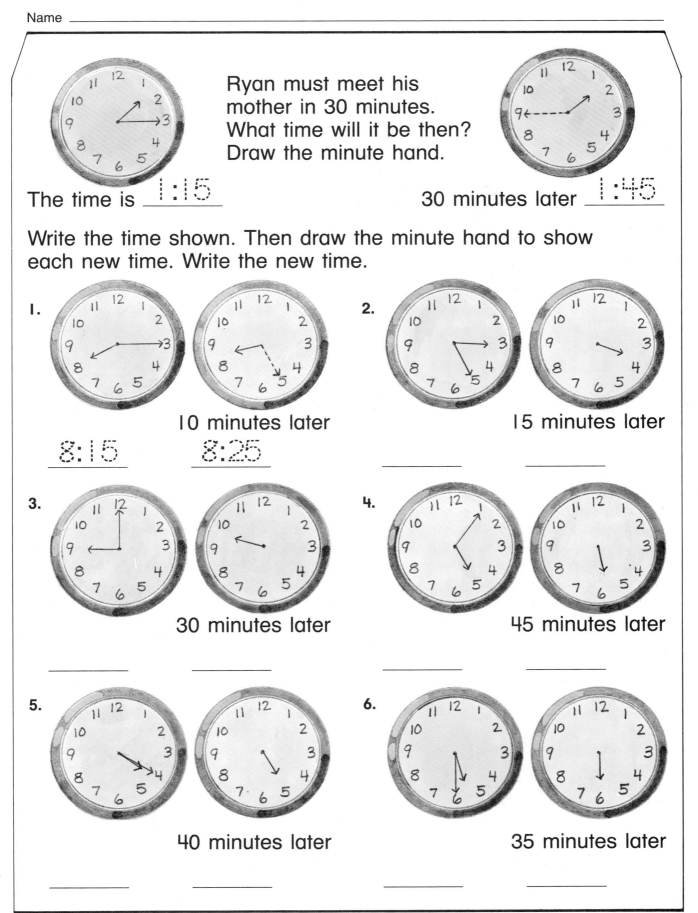

Ryan must meet his mother in 30 minutes. What time will it be then? Draw the minute hand.

The time is __1:15__   30 minutes later __1:45__

Write the time shown. Then draw the minute hand to show each new time. Write the new time.

1.   10 minutes later

__8:15__   __8:25__

2.   15 minutes later

_____   _____

3.   30 minutes later

_____   _____

4.   45 minutes later

_____   _____

5.   40 minutes later

_____   _____

6.   35 minutes later

_____   _____

Solve.

1.

Alan started at
3:15.

Alan quit at
3:30.

How long did
Alan jump rope?
15 minutes

2.

Amanda started at
_____.

Amanda quit at
_____.

How long did
Amanda jog?
_____ minutes

3.

Becky started at
_____.

Becky quit at
_____.

How long did
Becky play
tennis?
_____ minutes

4.

Royce started at
_____.

Royce quit at
_____.

How long did
Royce ride?
_____ minutes

Telling time, problem solving

There are

__60__ minutes in each hour.

There are

__5__ minutes between each hour number.

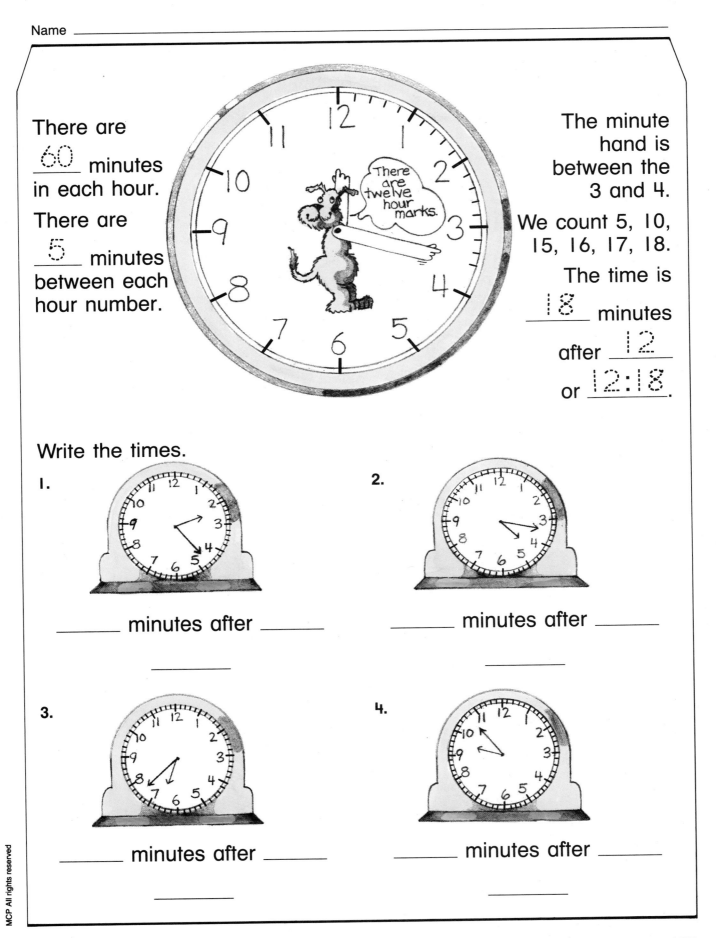

There are twelve hour marks.

The minute hand is between the 3 and 4.

We count 5, 10, 15, 16, 17, 18.

The time is

__18__ minutes

after __12__

or __12:18__.

Write the times.

1. _____ minutes after _____

_____

2. _____ minutes after _____

_____

3. _____ minutes after _____

_____

4. _____ minutes after _____

_____

Telling time to the minute

Match the clocks that show the same time.

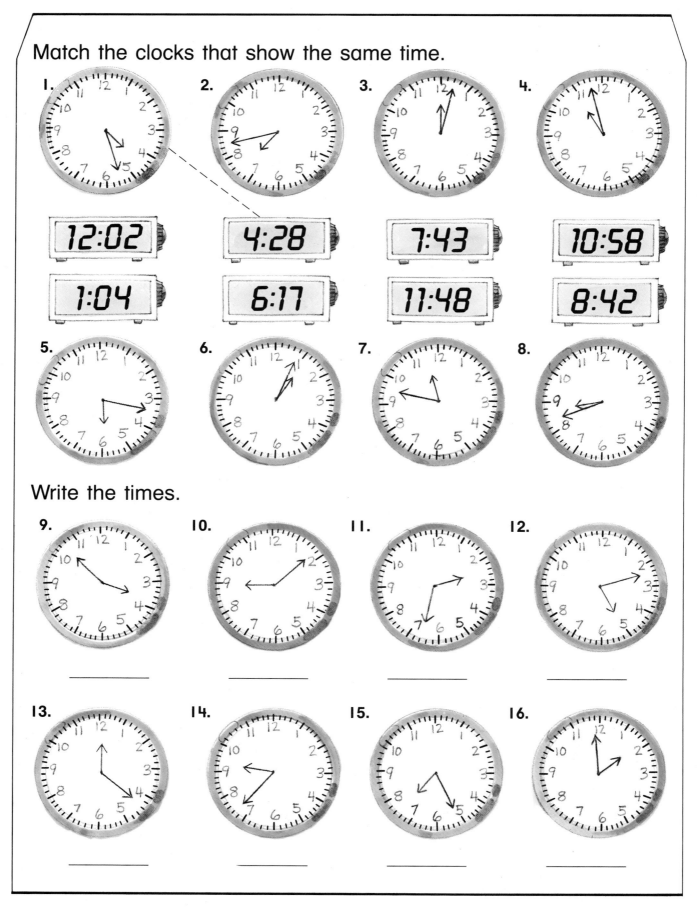

1.

2.

3.

4.

12:02

4:28

7:43

10:58

1:04

6:17

11:48

8:42

5.

6.

7.

8.

Write the times.

9.

10.

11.

12.

_____

_____

_____

_____

13.

14.

15.

16.

_____

_____

_____

_____

Name _____

Sunday	Monday	Tuesday	Wednesday	Thursday	Friday	Saturday

1. There are _____ days in a week.

Write the days of the week in order.

2. Sunday, _____, _____, _____,

_____, _____, _____

Write the day that follows:

3. Thursday, _____   4. Wednesday, _____

5. Monday, _____   6. Sunday, _____

Write the day that comes before:

7. _____, Friday   8. _____, Monday

9. _____, Wednesday   10. _____, Saturday

January	February	March	April
May	June	July	August
September	October	November	December

Write the correct month or number on the line.

1. There are _____ months in one year.

2. The first month of the year is _____.

3. The last month of the year is _____.

4. The fourth month of the year is _____.

5. Which month comes before June? _____

6. Which month comes before November? _____

7. Which month comes before March? _____

8. Which month comes after April? _____

9. Which month comes after February? _____

10. Which month comes after December? _____

Writing months of the year

January

Sunday	Monday	Tuesday	Wednesday	Thursday	Friday	Saturday
				1	2	3
4	5	6	7	8	9	10
11	12	13	14	15	16	17
18	19	20	21	22	23	24
25	26	27	28	29	30	31

1. January has _____ days.

Write the dates for each day of the week.

2. Monday: __5__, __12__, _____, _____

3. Friday: __2__, _____, _____, _____, _____

4. Saturday: _____, _____, _____, _____, _____

5. What day of the week does this month begin with? _____

Write the day of the week for each of the following.

6. January fourth: _____

7. January twelfth: _____

8. January nineteenth: _____

9. January thirtieth: _____

10. January twenty-third: _____

11. January fifteenth: _____

Complete the calendar for this month.

_____ Month					_____ Year	
Sunday	Monday	Tuesday	Wednesday	Thursday	Friday	Saturday

1. How many days are in this month? _____

2. _____ is the first day of the month.

3. _____ is the last day of the month.

4. There are _____ holidays in this month.

How many of each of the following days are there in this month?

5. Sundays _____

6. Mondays _____

7. Tuesdays _____

8. Wednesdays _____

9. Thursdays _____

10. Fridays _____

11. Saturdays _____

Making a calendar

Name _____

I penny	I nickel	I dime
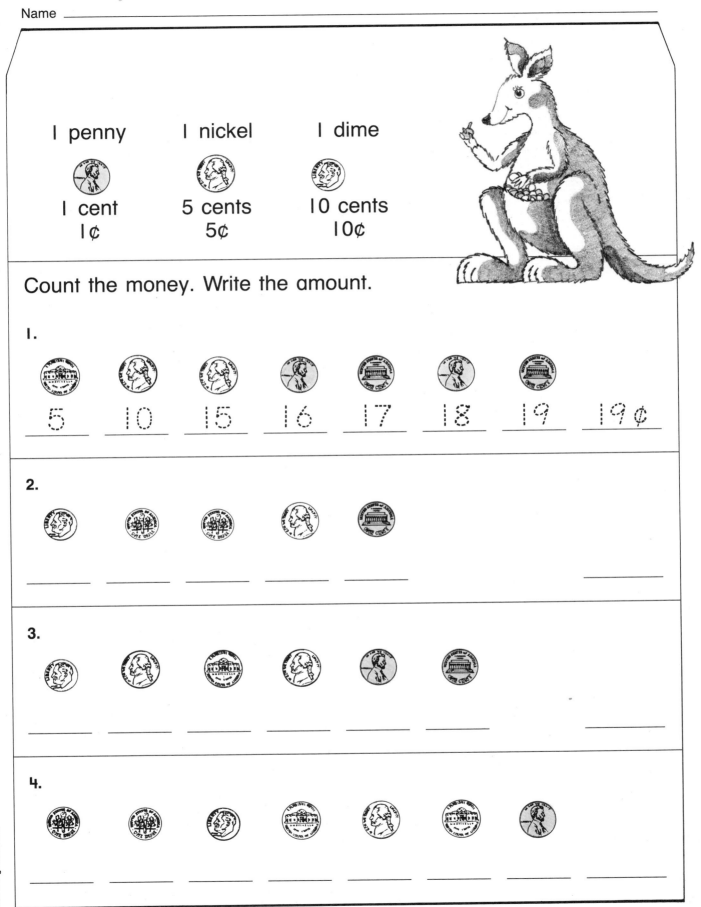		
I cent	5 cents	10 cents
I¢	5¢	10¢

Count the money. Write the amount.

1.

5   10   15   16   17   18   19   19¢

2.

_____

3.

_____

4.

_____

Check the coins needed to buy each item.

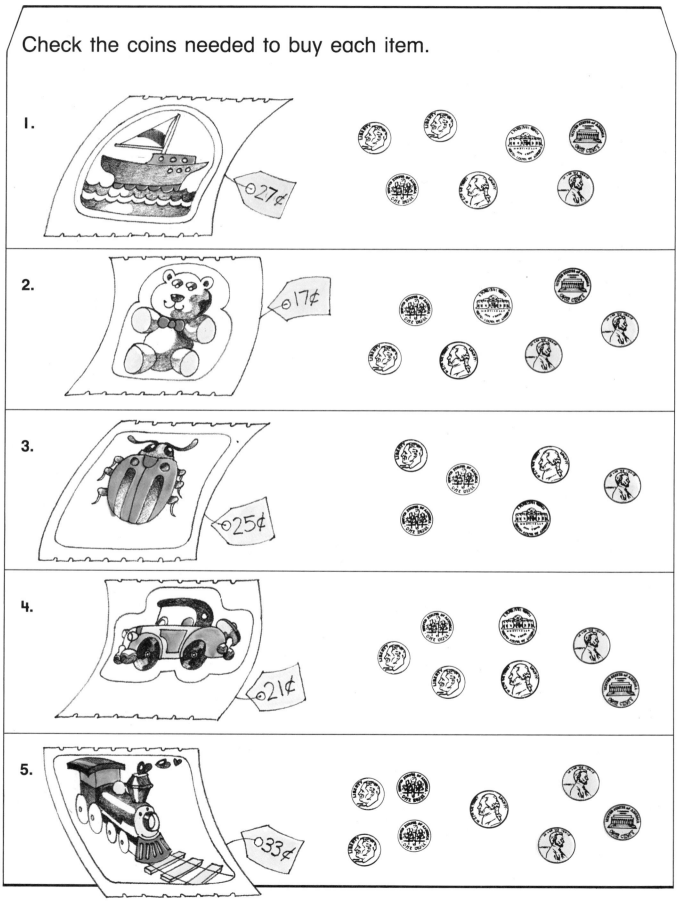

1. 27¢

2. 17¢

3. 25¢

4. 21¢

5. 33¢

Counting money, problem solving

Name _____

1 quarter   5 nickels   2 dimes
                                              1 nickel

25 cents   25 cents   25 cents
  25¢   25¢   25¢

Count the money. Write the amount.

1.

25 35 45 55 60 65 66 67   *67 ¢*

2.

_____

_____

3.

_____

_____

4.

_____

_____

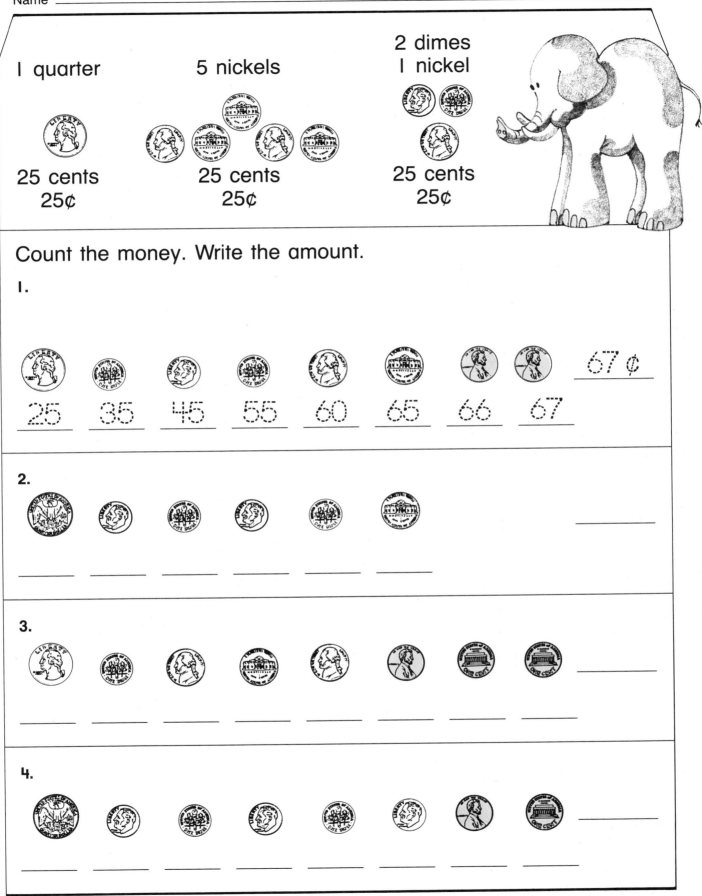

Counting money, pennies, nickels, dimes, quarters   (one hundred fifteen) **115**

Is there enough money to buy the item? Circle yes or no.

1. 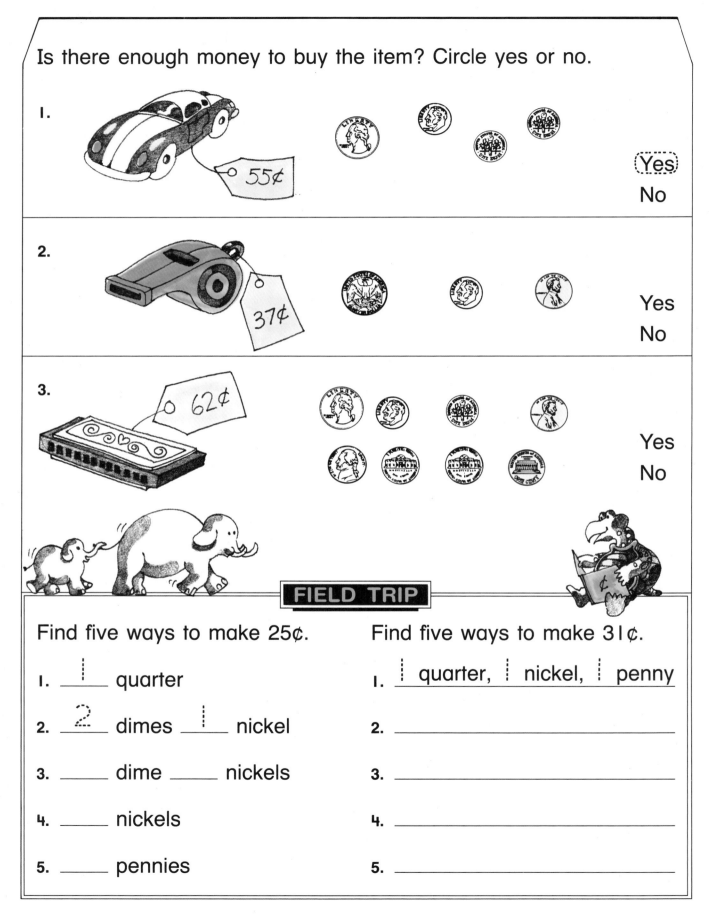 55¢   (Yes) No

2. 37¢   Yes No

3. 62¢   Yes No

FIELD TRIP

Find five ways to make 25¢.

1. ___1___ quarter

2. ___2___ dimes ___1___ nickel

3. _____ dime _____ nickels

4. _____ nickels

5. _____ pennies

Find five ways to make 31¢.

1. ___1___ quarter, ___1___ nickel, ___1___ penny

2. _____

3. _____

4. _____

5. _____

Counting money, problem solving

1 half dollar

50 cents
50¢

2 quarters

50 cents
50¢

5 dimes

50 cents
50¢

Count the money. Write the amount.

1.

10   20   25   25 ¢

2.

_____

3.

___ ___ ___ ___

4.

_____

5.

_____

_____ quarters = _____ half dollar

6.

_____

7.

_____

_____ nickels = _____ half dollar

Count the money. Write the amount.
Is there enough money to buy the item? Circle yes or no.

1. 60¢ _____ Yes No

2. 57¢ _____ Yes No

3. 83¢ _____ Yes No

4. 75¢ _____ Yes No

5. 68¢ _____ Yes No

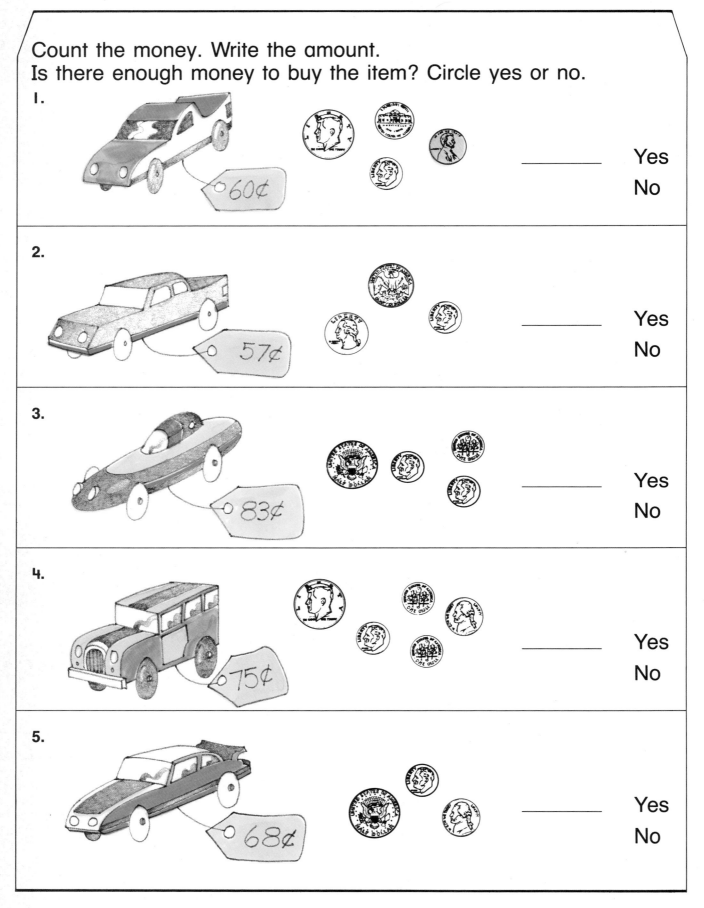

Counting money, problem solving

Name _____

1¢	5¢	10¢	25¢	50¢	100¢
$0.01	$0.05	$0.10	$0.25	$0.50	$1.00

Count the money. Write the amount in two ways.

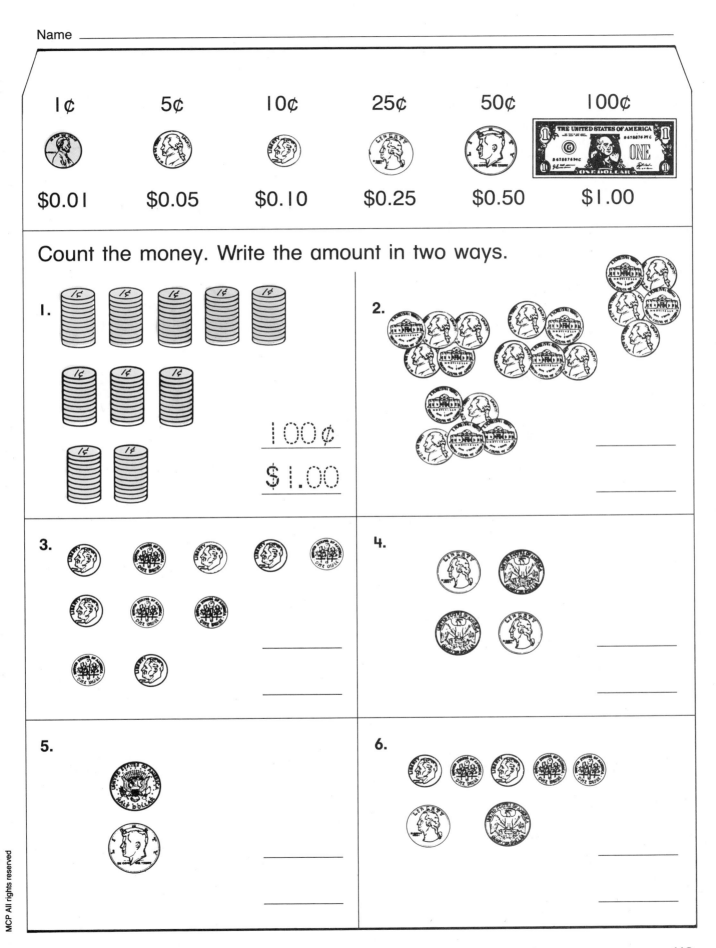

1. 100¢
   $1.00

2. _____ _____

3. _____ _____

4. _____ _____

5. _____ _____

6. _____ _____

Count the money. Write the amount in two ways.

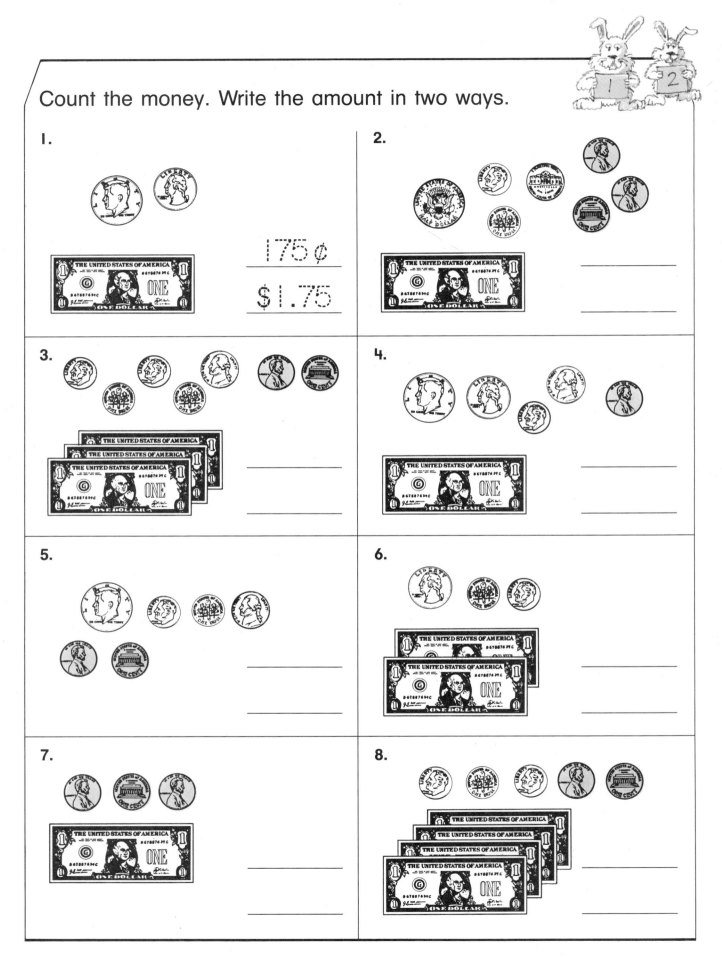

1.

175 ¢

$1.75

2.

3.

4.

5.

6.

7.

8.

Counting money, $1.00, 50¢, 25¢, 10¢, 5¢, 1¢

Count the money. Check the coins spent. Solve.

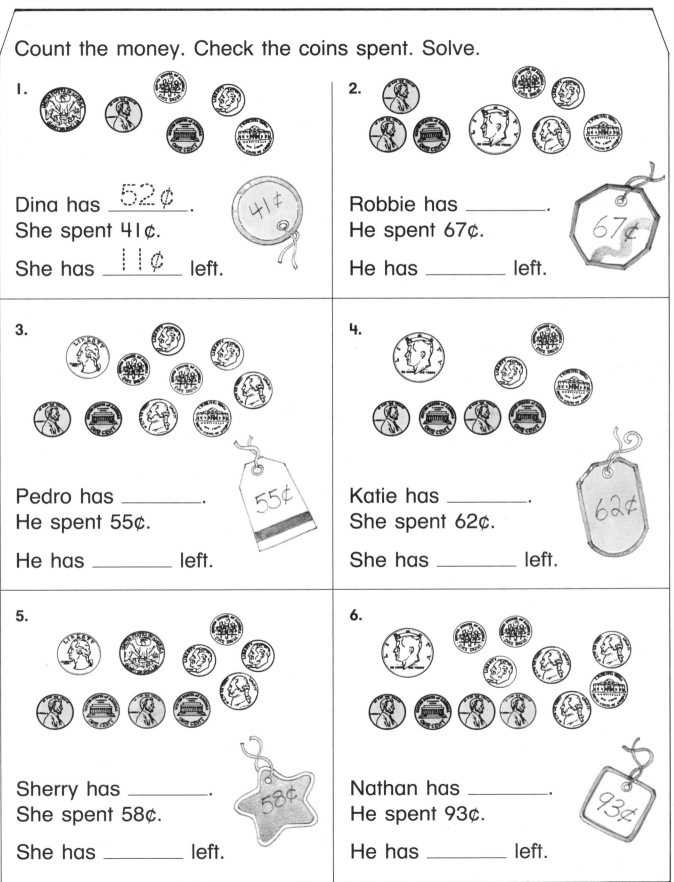

1. Dina has __52¢__.
She spent 41¢.
She has __11¢__ left.

2. Robbie has _____.
He spent 67¢.
He has _____ left.

3. Pedro has _____.
He spent 55¢.
He has _____ left.

4. Katie has _____.
She spent 62¢.
She has _____ left.

5. Sherry has _____.
She spent 58¢.
She has _____ left.

6. Nathan has _____.
He spent 93¢.
He has _____ left.

Problem solving, money

Count the money. Check the money spent. Solve.

1.

Chan has $ 1.28 .
He spent $1.02.

He has 26¢ left.

$1.02

2.

Julie has _____ .
She spent $2.32.

She has _____ left.

$2.32

3.

Lory has _____ .
She spent $1.16.

She has _____ left.

$1.16

4.

Sam has _____ .
He spent 17¢.

He has _____ left.

17¢

FIELD TRIP

1. 50¢ is the same as:

_____ half-dollar

_____ quarters

_____ dimes

_____ nickels

_____ pennies

2. $1.00 is the same as:

_____ half-dollars

_____ quarters

_____ dimes

_____ nickels

_____ pennies

Problem solving, money

CHAPTER CHECKUP

Write the times.

1. 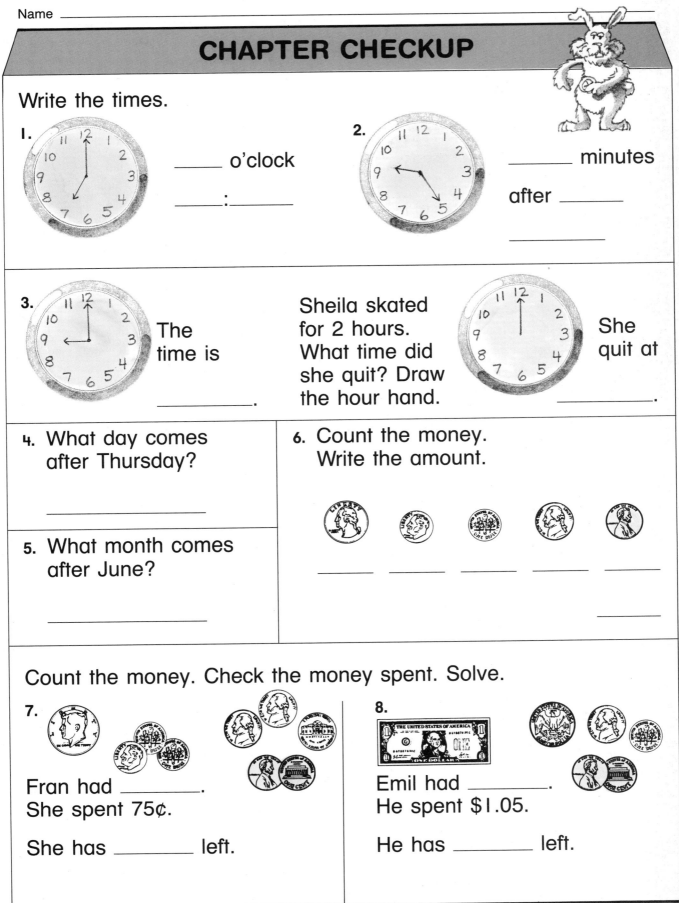 _____ o'clock

_____ : _____

2. _____ minutes

after _____

_____

3. The time is _____ .

Sheila skated for 2 hours. What time did she quit? Draw the hour hand.

She quit at _____ .

4. What day comes after Thursday?

_____

5. What month comes after June?

_____

6. Count the money. Write the amount.

_____ _____ _____ _____

Count the money. Check the money spent. Solve.

7.

Fran had _____ .
She spent 75¢.

She has _____ left.

8.

Emil had _____ .
He spent $1.05.

He has _____ left.

ROUNDUP REVIEW

Add or subtract.

1.
$$7 + 4 \qquad 8 + 7 \qquad 5 + 5 \qquad 14 - 6 \qquad 10 - 9 \qquad 15 - 6 \qquad 12 - 5$$

2.
$$11 - 6 \qquad 13 - 5 \qquad 6 + 6 \qquad 8 + 5 \qquad 16 - 8 \qquad 8 + 6 \qquad 9 + 9$$

Write the number.

3. 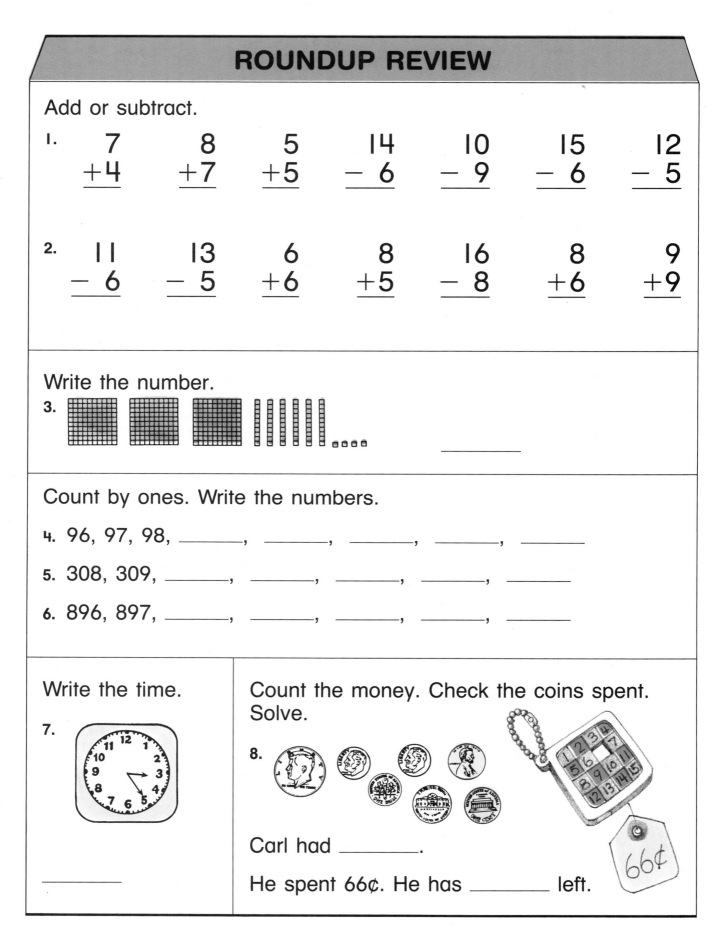 _____

Count by ones. Write the numbers.

4. 96, 97, 98, _____, _____, _____, _____, _____

5. 308, 309, _____, _____, _____, _____, _____

6. 896, 897, _____, _____, _____, _____, _____

Write the time.

7.

_____

Count the money. Check the coins spent. Solve.

8.

Carl had _____.

He spent 66¢. He has _____ left.

MATH AWARD

Certificate of Completion

This is to certify that

_____
Student

has completed Chapters 1 through 6
of Modern Curriculum Press
Mathematics, Level B.

_____
Teacher

125

GET READY, GET SET, GO ON . . .

WATCH FOR . . .

MODEL PROBLEM
Work through the problem with your teacher.

GETTING STARTED
Try the new math skill. Ask questions.

PRACTICE
Complete the problems to practice the new skill.

APPLY
Solve word problems using the math skills you have learned.

FIELD TRIP
Have fun with mathematics.

7 ADDITION, 2-DIGIT NUMBERS

Adding 2-digit Numbers

Anita took 32 pictures on Monday.
She took 4 pictures on Tuesday.
How many pictures did Anita take?

We are looking for the total number
of pictures that Anita took.

Anita took _____ pictures on Monday.

She took _____ pictures on Tuesday.

To find the total, we add _____ and _____.

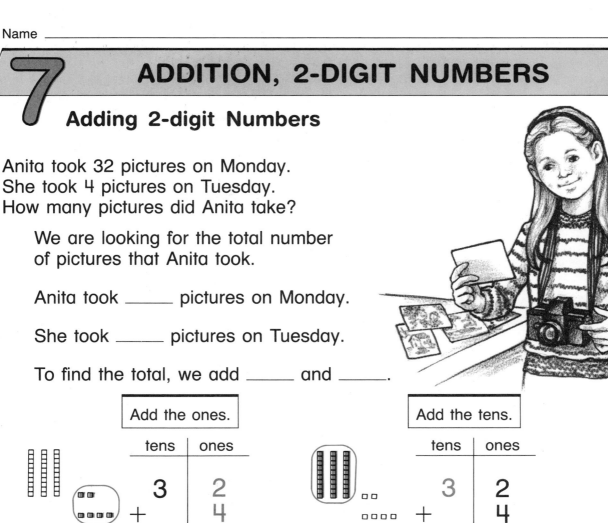

Add the ones.

tens	ones
3	2
+	4
	6

Add the tens.

tens	ones
3	2
+	4
3	6

Anita took _____ pictures.

Getting Started

Add.

1.

tens	ones
4	4
+	3

2.

tens	ones
7	3
+	5

3.

tens	ones
2	1
+	6

4. 83
   + 1

5. 13
   + 2

6. 57
   + 2

7. 95
   + 1

8. 64
   + 4

9. 33
   + 2

Practice

Add.

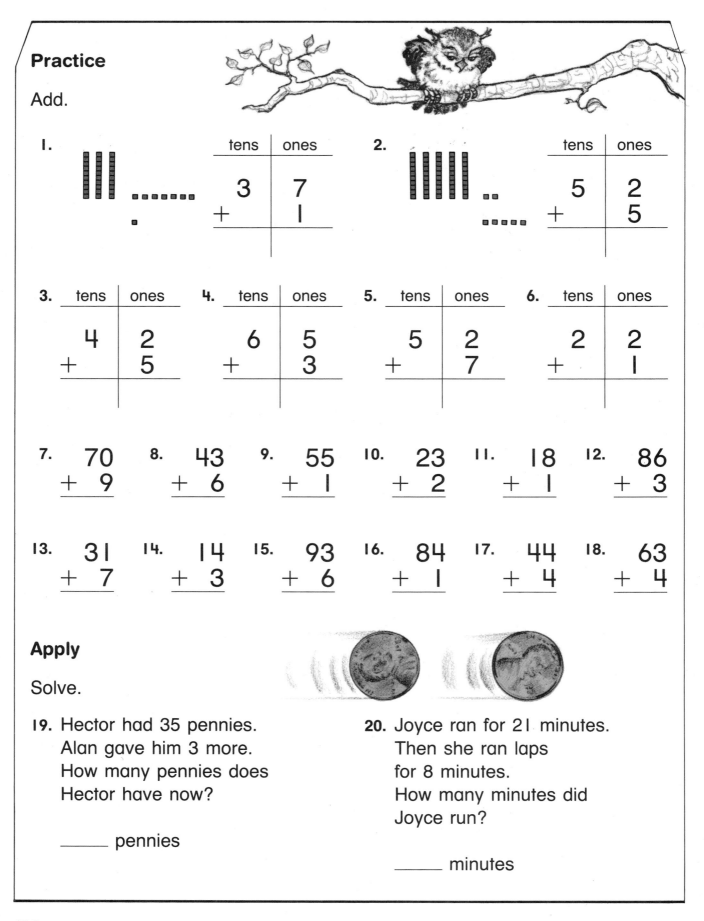

1.
tens	ones
3	7
+	1

2.
tens	ones
5	2
+	5

3.
tens	ones
4	2
+	5

4.
tens	ones
6	5
+	3

5.
tens	ones
5	2
+	7

6.
tens	ones
2	2
+	1

7. 70
   + 9

8. 43
   + 6

9. 55
   + 1

10. 23
   + 2

11. 18
   + 1

12. 86
   + 3

13. 31
   + 7

14. 14
   + 3

15. 93
   + 6

16. 84
   + 1

17. 44
   + 4

18. 63
   + 4

Apply

Solve.

19. Hector had 35 pennies.
    Alan gave him 3 more.
    How many pennies does
    Hector have now?

    _____ pennies

20. Joyce ran for 21 minutes.
    Then she ran laps
    for 8 minutes.
    How many minutes did
    Joyce run?

    _____ minutes

Adding 1-digit to 2-digit numbers, no trading

Addition with Trading

Andrew hopped 26 times on his left foot and 8 times on his right foot. How many times did Andrew hop?

We want to find out how many times Andrew hopped.

Andrew hopped _____ times on his left foot.

He hopped _____ times on his right foot. To find the total number of hops,

we add _____ and _____.

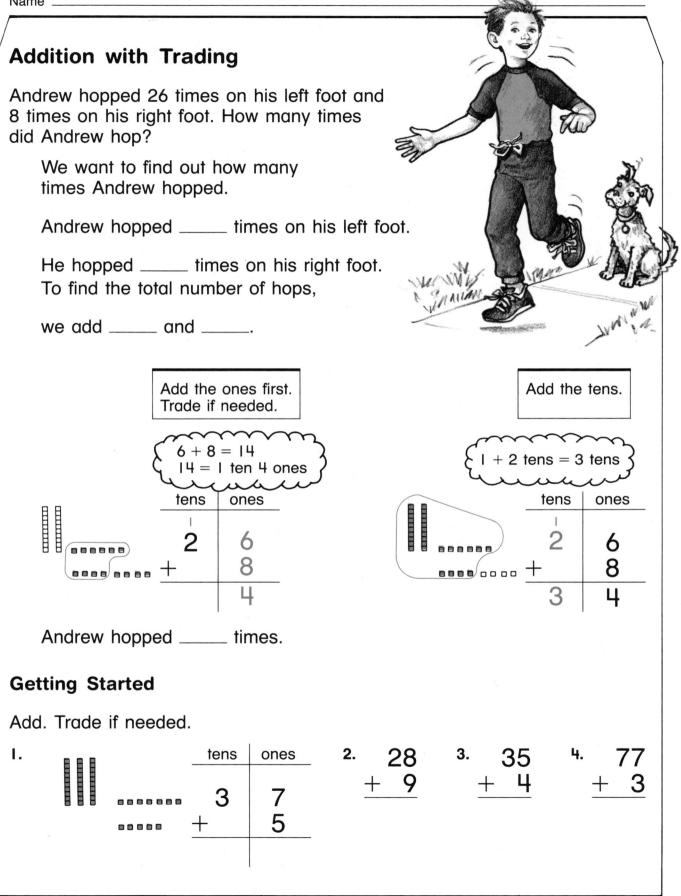

| Add the ones first. Trade if needed. | | Add the tens. | |

$6 + 8 = 14$
$14 = 1$ ten 4 ones

$1 + 2$ tens $= 3$ tens

tens	ones
^{1} 2	6
+	8
	4

tens	ones
^{1} 2	6
+	8
3	4

Andrew hopped _____ times.

Getting Started

Add. Trade if needed.

1.

tens	ones
3	7
+	5

2. 28
  + 9

3. 35
  + 4

4. 77
  + 3

Practice

Add. Trade if needed.

1.

	tens	ones
	3	7
+		6

2.

	tens	ones
	5	3
+		9

3. 34
+ 5

4. 65
+ 6

5. 83
+ 9

6. 62
+ 7

7. 29
+ 5

8. 56
+ 8

9. 23
+ 6

10. 39
+ 3

11. 28
+ 6

12. 61
+ 8

13. 75
+ 9

14. 57
+ 4

FIELD TRIP

Write the missing numbers.

1. 3 4
+ ☐
3 6

2. 1 7
+ ☐
1 9

3. 1 6
+ ☐
2 0

4. 3 1
+ ☐
3 9

5. 6 2
+ ☐
6 7

6. 2 3
+ ☐
3 0

7. 3 5
+ ☐
4 1

8. 6 3
+ ☐
7 2

9. 4 6
+ ☐
5 3

10. 5 7
+ ☐
6 5

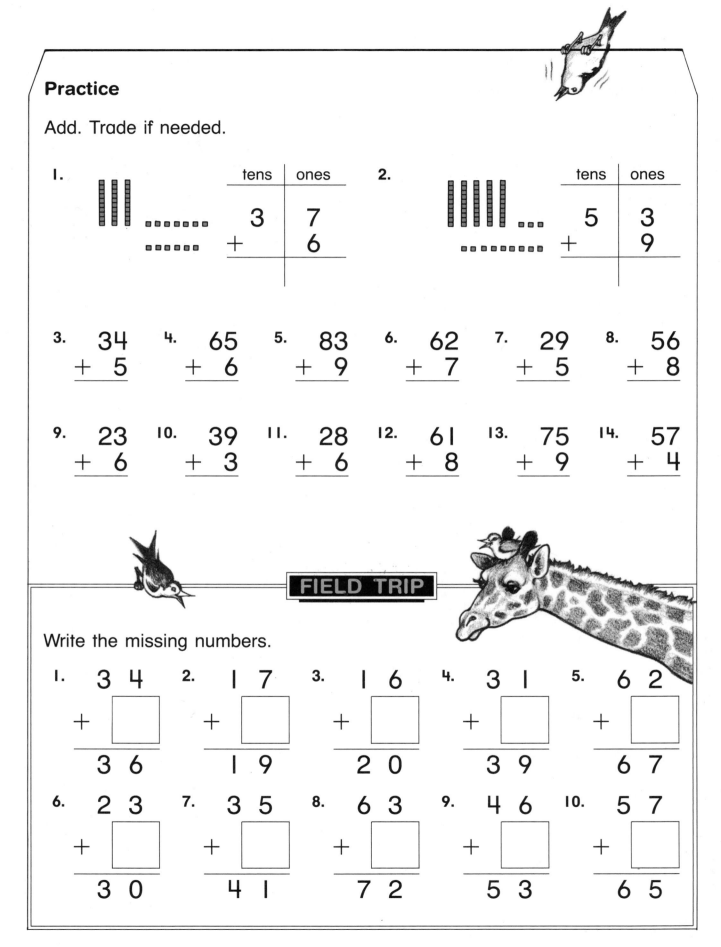

Adding 1-digit to 2-digit numbers with trading

Adding 2-Digit Numbers

The Bowsers took a vacation. They drove from Boneville to Pooch City on Monday. On Tuesday they drove from Pooch City to Wagtown. How many miles did they drive?

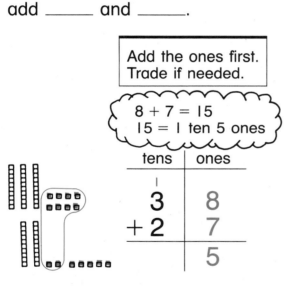

We want to find out the total number of miles they drove.

On Monday they drove _____ miles.

On Tuesday they drove _____ miles. To find how far they drove, we

add _____ and _____.

Add the ones first. Trade if needed.		Add the tens.	

$8 + 7 = 15$
$15 = 1$ ten 5 ones

$1 + 3 + 2$ tens $= 6$ tens

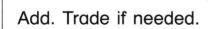

	tens	ones
	3	8
+	2	7
		5

	tens	ones
	3	8
+	2	7
	6	5

The Bowsers drove _____ miles.

Getting Started

Add. Trade if needed.

1.

	tens	ones
	2	9
+	4	3

2. $\begin{array}{r} 27 \\ + 64 \\ \hline \end{array}$

3. $\begin{array}{r} 14 \\ + 73 \\ \hline \end{array}$

4. $\begin{array}{r} 61 \\ + 19 \\ \hline \end{array}$

Practice

Add. Trade if needed.

1.

tens	ones
4	6
+1	6

2.

tens	ones
3	5
+4	9

3.
$$36 + 47$$

4.
$$52 + 45$$

5.
$$35 + 16$$

6.
$$53 + 46$$

7.
$$37 + 48$$

8.
$$52 + 18$$

9.
$$60 + 25$$

10.
$$16 + 17$$

11.
$$29 + 44$$

12.
$$48 + 23$$

13.
$$56 + 39$$

14.
$$19 + 31$$

15.
$$28 + 37$$

16.
$$46 + 45$$

17.
$$18 + 68$$

18.
$$25 + 14$$

19.
$$73 + 17$$

20.
$$49 + 38$$

Apply

Solve.

21. The cafeteria sold 35 ham sandwiches and 25 cheese sandwiches. How many sandwiches were sold?

_____ sandwiches

22. The cafeteria sold 45 cartons of milk and 29 cartons of orange juice. How many cartons were sold?

_____ cartons

Adding 2-digit numbers with trading

Adding Multiples of 10

Manuel and Chris wanted to see how many times they could bounce a basketball without missing. What is the total number of times they bounced the ball?

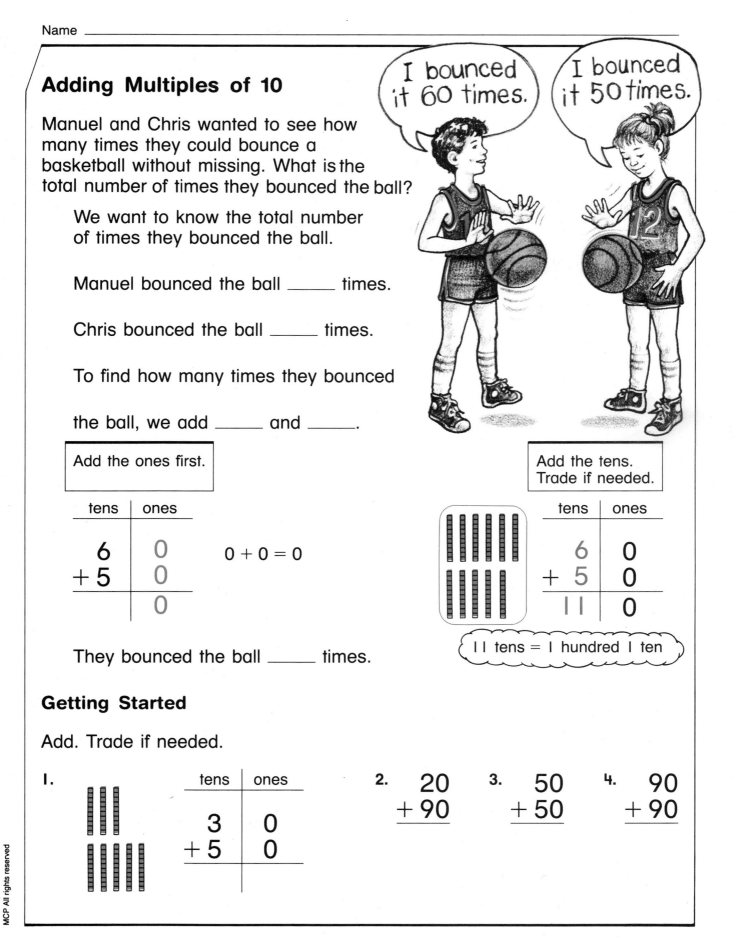

I bounced it 60 times.

I bounced it 50 times.

We want to know the total number of times they bounced the ball.

Manuel bounced the ball _____ times.

Chris bounced the ball _____ times.

To find how many times they bounced

the ball, we add _____ and _____.

Add the ones first.

tens	ones
6	0
+ 5	0
	0

$0 + 0 = 0$

They bounced the ball _____ times.

Add the tens.
Trade if needed.

tens	ones
6	0
+ 5	0
1 1	0

11 tens = 1 hundred 1 ten

Getting Started

Add. Trade if needed.

1.

tens	ones
3	0
+ 5	0

2. 20
  + 90

3. 50
  + 50

4. 90
  + 90

Practice

Add. Trade if needed.

1.

tens	ones
7	0
+ 6	0

2.

tens	ones
2	0
+ 9	0

3. 40
  + 30

4. 60
  + 60

5. 80
  + 80

6. 30
  + 50

7. 90
  + 90

8. 50
  + 50

9. 50
  + 40

10. 90
  + 50

11. 70
  + 80

12. 10
  + 90

13. 80
  + 40

14. 70
  + 50

15. 80
  + 90

16. 90
  + 70

17. 20
  + 30

18. 70
  + 60

19. 20
  + 80

20. 60
  + 50

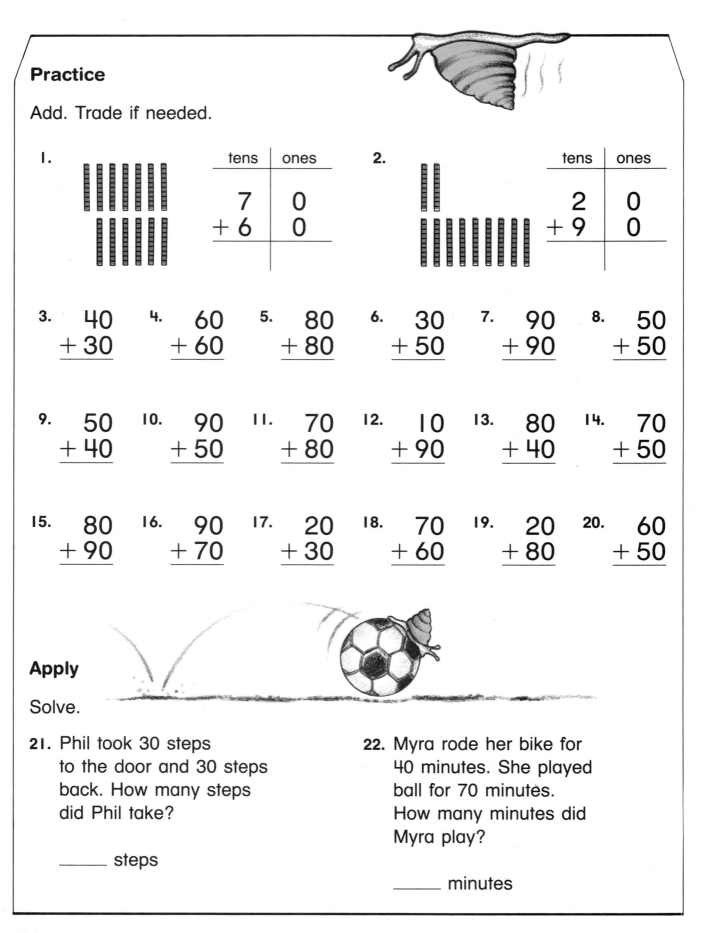

Apply

Solve.

21. Phil took 30 steps to the door and 30 steps back. How many steps did Phil take?

_____ steps

22. Myra rode her bike for 40 minutes. She played ball for 70 minutes. How many minutes did Myra play?

_____ minutes

Adding Any 2-Digit Numbers

Some children collect baseball cards. How many cards did Morris and Sandi collect together?

Baseball Cards Collected	
Morris	58 cards
Sandi	67 cards
Del	51 cards

We are looking for the total number of cards collected by Morris and Sandi.

Morris has _____ cards.

Sandi has _____ cards.
To find how many cards Morris and

Sandi have, we add _____ and _____.

Add the ones. Trade if needed.

$8 + 7 = 15$
$15 = 1$ ten 5 ones

tens	ones
5	8
+ 6	7
	5

Add the tens. Trade if needed.

12 tens = 1 hundred 2 tens

tens	ones
5	8
+ 6	7
12	5

Morris and Sandi have _____ cards.

Getting Started

Add. Trade if needed.

1.
tens	ones
5	7
+ 8	5

2.
```
  38
+ 85
```

3.
```
  27
+ 58
```

4.
```
  79
+ 65
```

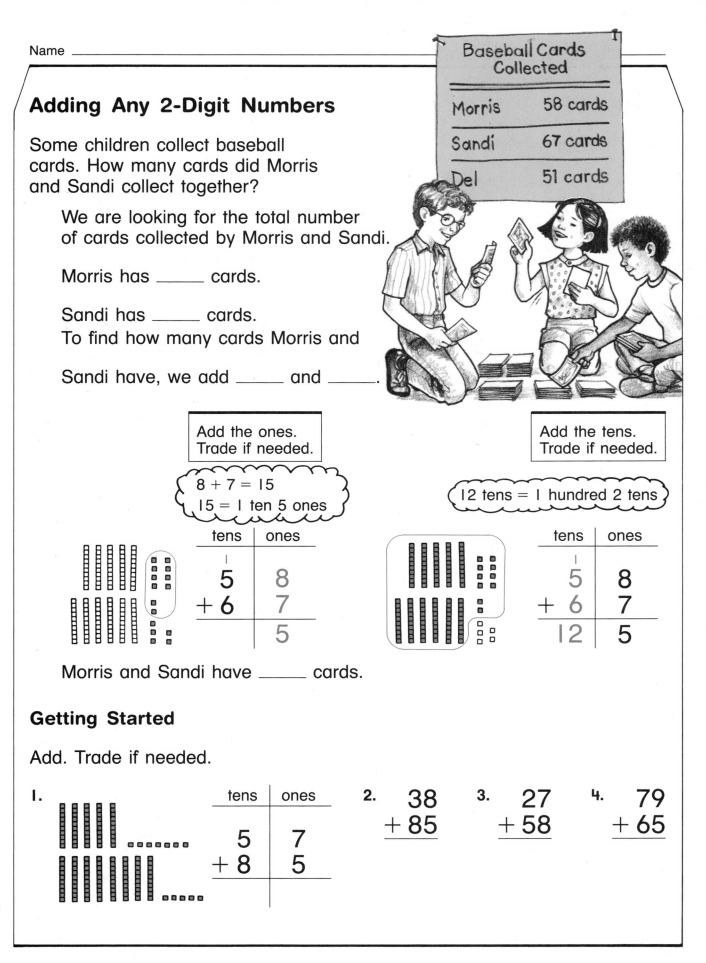

Practice

Add. Trade if needed.

1.

tens	ones
2	9
+ 7	4

2.

tens	ones
8	8
+ 7	7

3. 34
  + 23

4. 85
  + 57

5. 29
  + 76

6. 16
  + 37

7. 43
  + 44

8. 91
  + 26

9. 35
  + 45

10. 67
   + 78

11. 38
   + 38

12. 75
   + 75

13. 41
   + 99

14. 27
   + 98

15. 57
   + 23

16. 56
   + 65

17. 99
   + 99

18. 65
   + 85

19. 36
   + 55

20. 43
   + 75

21. 25
   + 63

22. 69
   + 32

23. 47
   + 77

24. 38
   + 95

25. 67
   + 27

26. 83
   + 79

Adding 2-digit numbers with trading, 3-digit answers

Problem Solving

There are 58 girls and 57 boys going on a field trip. How many children are going on the field trip?

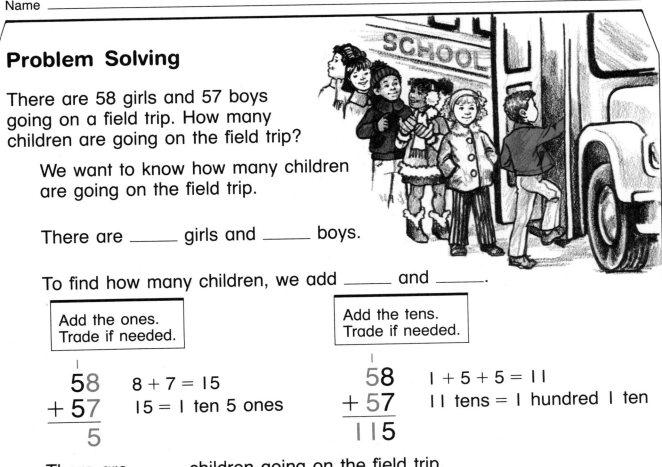

We want to know how many children are going on the field trip.

There are _____ girls and _____ boys.

To find how many children, we add _____ and _____.

Add the ones. Trade if needed.		Add the tens. Trade if needed.	
$\begin{array}{r} \overset{1}{5}8 \\ +\ 57 \\ \hline 5 \end{array}$	$8 + 7 = 15$ $15 = 1$ ten 5 ones	$\begin{array}{r} \overset{1}{5}8 \\ +\ 57 \\ \hline 115 \end{array}$	$1 + 5 + 5 = 11$ 11 tens $= 1$ hundred 1 ten

There are _____ children going on the field trip.

Getting Started

Solve.

1. The Sport Shop had a sale. They sold 89 baseballs and 35 basketballs. How many balls were sold?

   _____ balls

2. The shop sold 53 large warm-up suits and 49 small warm-up suits. How many suits did they sell?

   _____ suits

3. The shop sold 85 T-shirts and 75 sweat shirts. How many shirts were sold?

   _____ shirts

4. The shop sold 83 ten-speed bikes and 57 three-speed bikes. How many bikes did they sell?

   _____ bikes

Problem solving, addition

Solve.

1. The Jackson Ranch has 98 cows and 67 horses. How many cows and horses do they have?

_____ cows and horses

2. The ranch has 65 wild turkeys and 89 wild pigs. How many pigs and turkeys do they have?

_____ pigs and turkeys

3. Read exercise 1 again. What if the Jacksons sell 23 of their horses? Then how many cows and horses will they have?

_____ cows and horses

4. Read exercise 2 again. What if the ranch got 21 more wild turkeys? Then how many pigs and turkeys would they have?

_____ pigs and turkeys

FIELD TRIP

Add. Then write the answers in the puzzle.

Across:

1. $47 + 44$

3. $76 + 85$

5. $37 + 47$

6. $15 + 16$

8. $93 + 79$

9. $52 + 25$

Down:

2. $98 + 16$

4. $79 + 58$

7. $40 + 82$

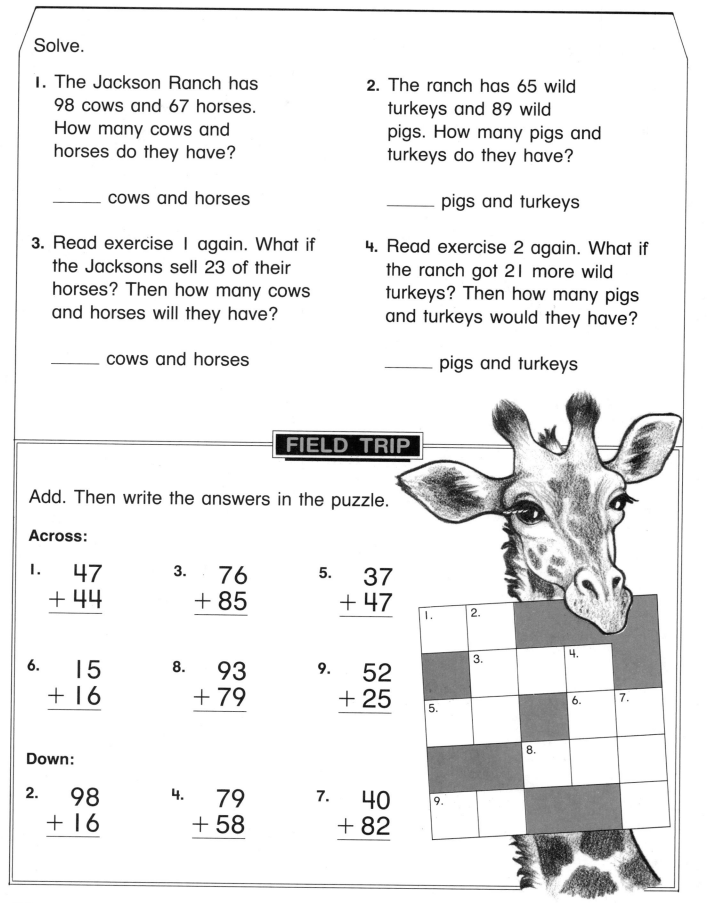

Problem solving, addition

Adding Money

Gene went shopping for gifts. He bought a bag of marbles and a yoyo. How much did he pay?

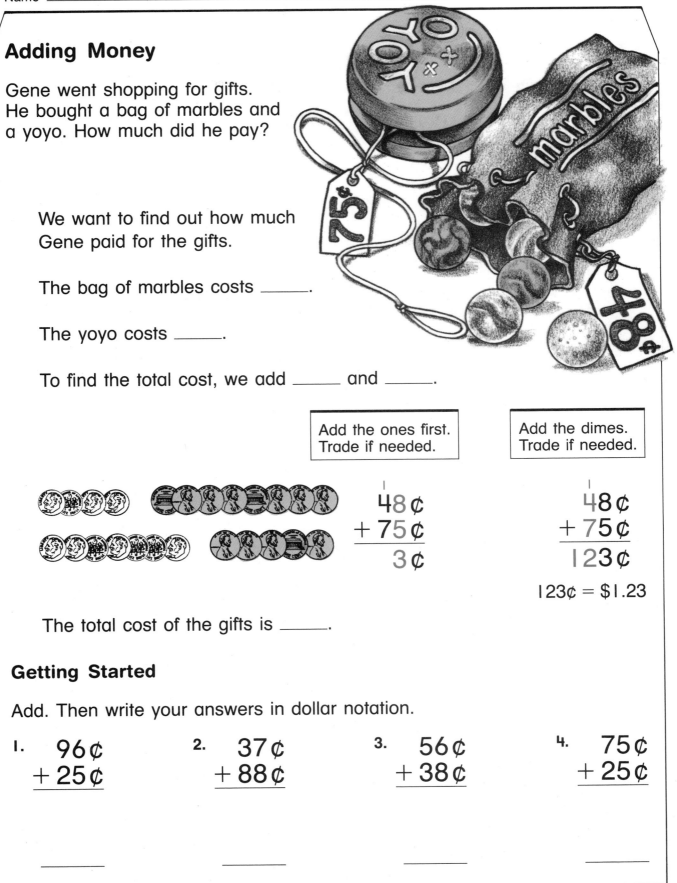

We want to find out how much Gene paid for the gifts.

The bag of marbles costs _____.

The yoyo costs _____.

To find the total cost, we add _____ and _____.

Add the ones first. Trade if needed.	Add the dimes. Trade if needed.

$$\begin{array}{r} \overset{1}{4}8\cent \\ +\,75\cent \\ \hline 3\cent \end{array} \qquad \begin{array}{r} \overset{1}{4}8\cent \\ +\,75\cent \\ \hline 123\cent \end{array}$$

$123\cent = \$1.23$

The total cost of the gifts is _____.

Getting Started

Add. Then write your answers in dollar notation.

1. $\begin{array}{r} 96\cent \\ +25\cent \\ \hline \end{array}$
2. $\begin{array}{r} 37\cent \\ +88\cent \\ \hline \end{array}$
3. $\begin{array}{r} 56\cent \\ +38\cent \\ \hline \end{array}$
4. $\begin{array}{r} 75\cent \\ +25\cent \\ \hline \end{array}$

_____ _____ _____ _____

Practice

Add. Then write your answers in dollar notation.

1. $30¢ + 30¢$
2. $45¢ + 56¢$
3. $62¢ + 76¢$
4. $79¢ + 75¢$
5. $8¢ + 99¢$

6. $81¢ + 93¢$
7. $84¢ + 68¢$
8. $91¢ + 65¢$
9. $87¢ + 26¢$
10. $58¢ + 82¢$

11. $40¢ + 87¢$
12. $55¢ + 98¢$
13. $90¢ + 71¢$
14. $73¢ + 68¢$
15. $64¢ + 63¢$

Apply

Solve. Then write your answers in dollar notation.

16. Lu had 50¢. She earned 75¢ raking leaves. How much money does she have now?

17. Walt bought one book for 89¢ and another book for 95¢. How much money did he spend?

Adding money

Problem Solving

Solve.

1. 65 girls and 72 boys attended Fun Day. How many children attended Fun Day?

   _____ children

2. Tim rode the Roller Coaster for 75¢ and the Ferris Wheel for 80¢. How much did he spend?

   _____

3. Wendy rode the Tilt-A-Whirl for 65¢ and the Hammer for 85¢. How much did both rides cost?

   _____

4. Bill rode the Merry-Go-Round for 95¢ and the Snake for 55¢. How much money did he spend?

   _____

5. Read exercise 3 again. What if Wendy rode the Hammer twice? How much would both rides cost?

   _____

6. Read exercise 4 again. Which would cost more, a ride on the Merry-Go-Round or two rides on the Snake?

   _____

Solve.

1. Willie spent 72¢. Stan spent 68¢. Who spent more money?

_____

2. Kiyo rode the Ferris Wheel for 80¢ and the Tilt-A-Whirl for 65¢. How much money did she pay for both?

_____

3. Read exercise 1 again. Decide if both boys together spent more or less than $1.50.

_____

4. Read exercises 1 and 2 again. Decide who spent more money, Kiyo or the two boys.

_____

FIELD TRIP

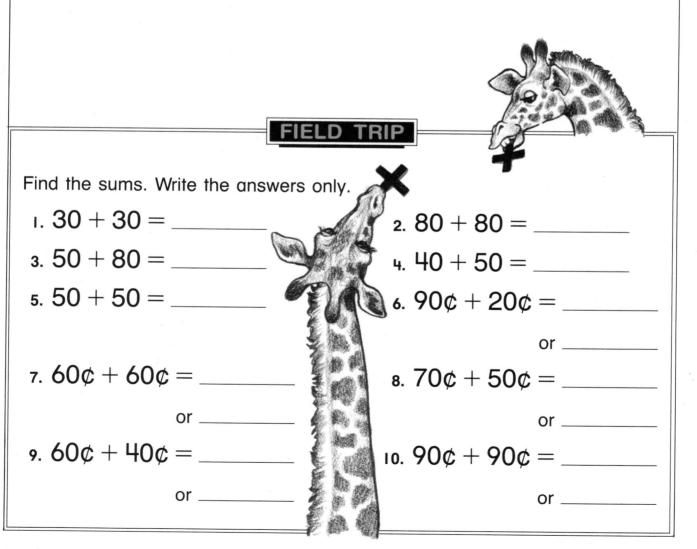

Find the sums. Write the answers only.

1. $30 + 30 =$ _____

2. $80 + 80 =$ _____

3. $50 + 80 =$ _____

4. $40 + 50 =$ _____

5. $50 + 50 =$ _____

6. $90¢ + 20¢ =$ _____

or _____

7. $60¢ + 60¢ =$ _____

or _____

8. $70¢ + 50¢ =$ _____

or _____

9. $60¢ + 40¢ =$ _____

or _____

10. $90¢ + 90¢ =$ _____

or _____

Problem solving

Name _____

CHAPTER CHECKUP

Add. Trade if needed.

1. $83 + 5$
2. $35 + 9$
3. $86 + 7$
4. $80 + 50$
5. $30 + 70$
6. $90 + 40$

7. $57 + 31$
8. $65 + 29$
9. $34 + 82$
10. $76 + 77$
11. $99 + 99$
12. $42 + 38$

13. $16 + 7$
14. $56 + 68$
15. $30 + 80$
16. $76 + 21$
17. $64 + 4$
18. $43 + 17$

19. $45 + 45$
20. $59 + 84$
21. $38 + 37$
22. $27 + 9$
23. $98 + 3$
24. $75 + 83$

Add. Then write your answers in dollar notation.

25. $68¢ + 7¢$
26. $70¢ + 50¢$
27. $64¢ + 24¢$
28. $75¢ + 18¢$
29. $96¢ + 89¢$

_____   _____   _____   _____   _____

Solve.

30. There were 65 girls and 77 boys on the skating rink. How many children were skating?

_____ children

31. Cleve has 85¢. Lu Ann has 98¢. How much money do they have in all?

_____

Chapter review   (one hundred forty-three) **143**

ROUNDUP REVIEW

Fill in the oval next to the correct answer.

1.
$$\begin{array}{r} 8 \\ + 7 \\ \hline \end{array}$$
- ○ 16
- ○ 15
- ○ 14
- ○ NG

2. $9 + 3$
- ○ 10
- ○ 16
- ○ 12
- ○ NG

3.
$$\begin{array}{r} 15 \\ - 6 \\ \hline \end{array}$$
- ○ 9
- ○ 7
- ○ 6
- ○ NG

4.
$$\begin{array}{r} 13 \\ - 7 \\ \hline \end{array}$$
- ○ 5
- ○ 7
- ○ 6
- ○ NG

5.
- ○ 3:10
- ○ 2:15
- ○ 2:03
- ○ NG

6.
- ○ $3.45
- ○ $3.35
- ○ $3.40
- ○ NG

7. What is the value of the 6 in 2**6**7?
- ○ hundreds
- ○ tens
- ○ ones
- ○ NG

8. What is the value of the 7 in **7**50?
- ○ hundreds
- ○ tens
- ○ ones
- ○ NG

9. $364 \bigcirc 446$
- ○ >
- ○ <

10.
$$\begin{array}{r} 37 \\ + 58 \\ \hline \end{array}$$
- ○ 94
- ○ 85
- ○ 95
- ○ NG

11.
$$\begin{array}{r} 60 \\ + 60 \\ \hline \end{array}$$
- ○ 12
- ○ 102
- ○ 130
- ○ NG

12.
$$\begin{array}{r} 35 \\ + 7 \\ \hline \end{array}$$
- ○ 42
- ○ 32
- ○ 47
- ○ NG

13.
$$\begin{array}{r} 75 \\ + 88 \\ \hline \end{array}$$
- ○ 153
- ○ 165
- ○ 163
- ○ NG

☐ score

8 SUBTRACTION, 2-DIGIT NUMBERS

Subtracting 2-digit Numbers

Gary had 47 fish in his aquarium.
He gave 15 fish to Sun Li.
How many fish does he have left?

We want to know how many fish Gary has left.

Gary had _____ fish.

He gave _____ fish to Sun Li.
To find the number of fish he has left,

we subtract _____ from _____.

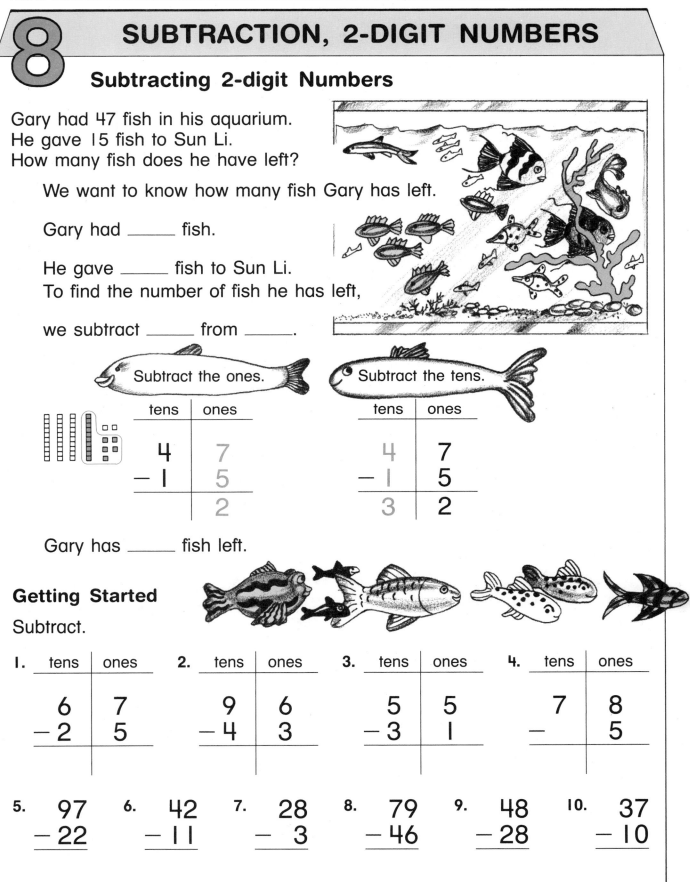

Subtract the ones.

tens	ones
4	7
− 1	5
2	

Subtract the tens.

tens	ones
4	7
− 1	5
3	2

Gary has _____ fish left.

Getting Started

Subtract.

1. tens	ones
6	7
− 2	5

2. tens	ones
9	6
− 4	3

3. tens	ones
5	5
− 3	1

4. tens	ones
7	8
−	5

5. 97
  − 22

6. 42
  − 11

7. 28
  − 3

8. 79
  − 46

9. 48
  − 28

10. 37
  − 10

Practice

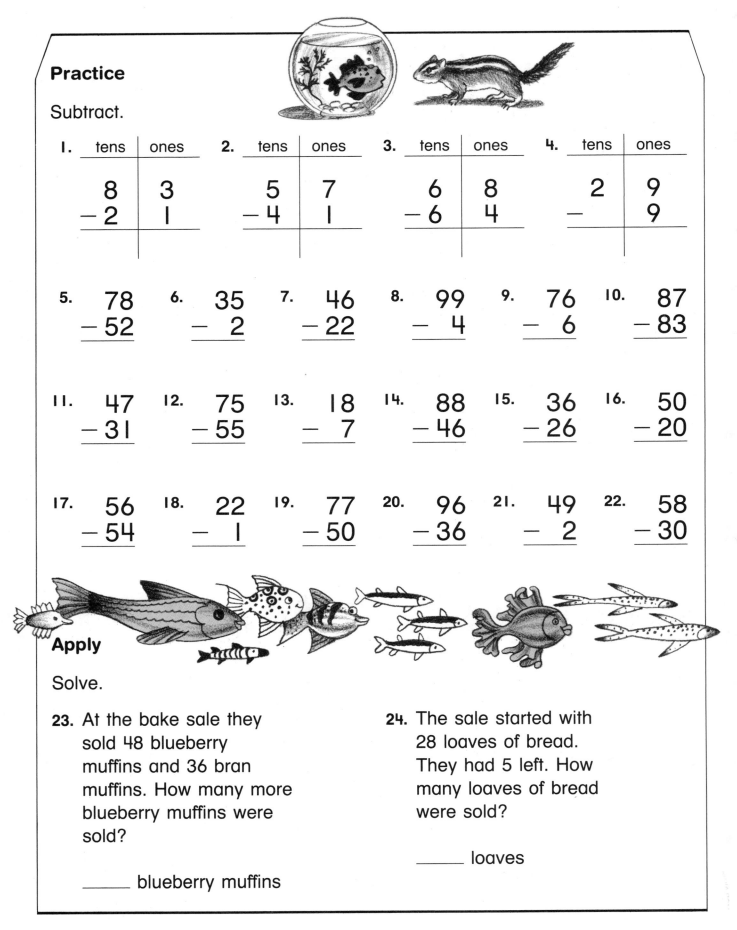

Subtract.

1.	tens	ones		2.	tens	ones		3.	tens	ones		4.	tens	ones
	8	3			5	7			6	8			2	9
	−2	1			−4	1			−6	4			−	9

5. $\begin{array}{r} 78 \\ -52 \\ \hline \end{array}$ 6. $\begin{array}{r} 35 \\ -2 \\ \hline \end{array}$ 7. $\begin{array}{r} 46 \\ -22 \\ \hline \end{array}$ 8. $\begin{array}{r} 99 \\ -4 \\ \hline \end{array}$ 9. $\begin{array}{r} 76 \\ -6 \\ \hline \end{array}$ 10. $\begin{array}{r} 87 \\ -83 \\ \hline \end{array}$

11. $\begin{array}{r} 47 \\ -31 \\ \hline \end{array}$ 12. $\begin{array}{r} 75 \\ -55 \\ \hline \end{array}$ 13. $\begin{array}{r} 18 \\ -7 \\ \hline \end{array}$ 14. $\begin{array}{r} 88 \\ -46 \\ \hline \end{array}$ 15. $\begin{array}{r} 36 \\ -26 \\ \hline \end{array}$ 16. $\begin{array}{r} 50 \\ -20 \\ \hline \end{array}$

17. $\begin{array}{r} 56 \\ -54 \\ \hline \end{array}$ 18. $\begin{array}{r} 22 \\ -1 \\ \hline \end{array}$ 19. $\begin{array}{r} 77 \\ -50 \\ \hline \end{array}$ 20. $\begin{array}{r} 96 \\ -36 \\ \hline \end{array}$ 21. $\begin{array}{r} 49 \\ -2 \\ \hline \end{array}$ 22. $\begin{array}{r} 58 \\ -30 \\ \hline \end{array}$

Apply

Solve.

23. At the bake sale they sold 48 blueberry muffins and 36 bran muffins. How many more blueberry muffins were sold?

_____ blueberry muffins

24. The sale started with 28 loaves of bread. They had 5 left. How many loaves of bread were sold?

_____ loaves

Subtracting 2-digit numbers, no trading

Trading a Ten to Subtract

The pet store had 34 puppies for sale.
They sold 8 puppies. How many are left?

We want to know how many puppies are left?

There are _____ puppies for sale.

The store sold _____ puppies.
To find out how many are left,

we subtract _____ from _____.

✔ Subtract the ones first.

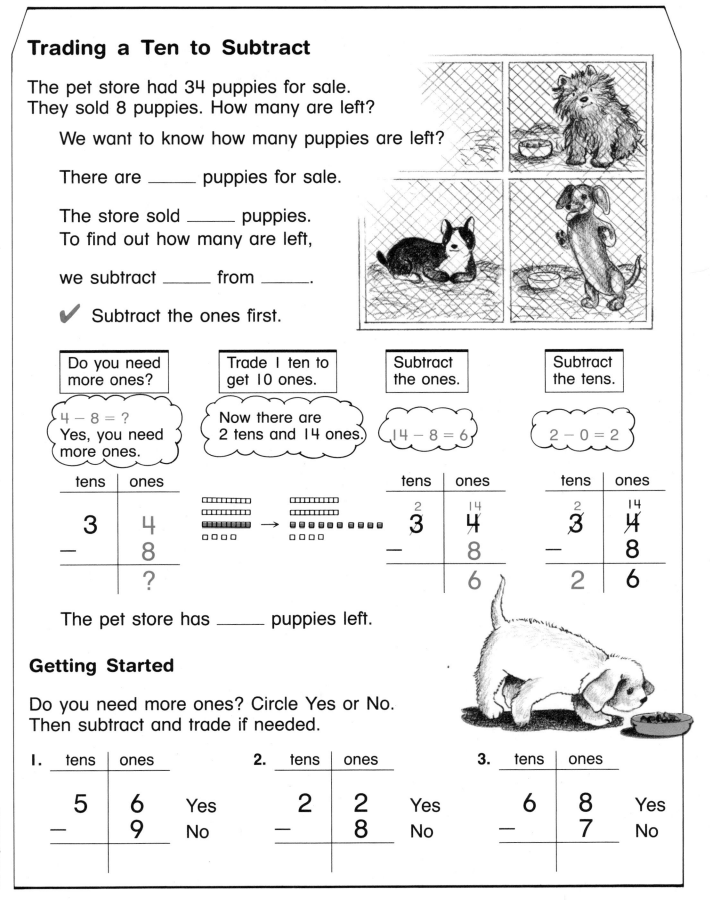

Do you need more ones?	Trade 1 ten to get 10 ones.	Subtract the ones.	Subtract the tens.
$4 - 8 = ?$ Yes, you need more ones.	Now there are 2 tens and 14 ones.	$14 - 8 = 6$	$2 - 0 = 2$

tens	ones
3	4
−	8
	?

tens	ones
$\overset{2}{3}$	$\overset{14}{4}$
−	8
	6

tens	ones
$\overset{2}{3}$	$\overset{14}{4}$
−	8
2	6

The pet store has _____ puppies left.

Getting Started

Do you need more ones? Circle Yes or No.
Then subtract and trade if needed.

1.
tens	ones	
5	6	Yes
−	9	No

2.
tens	ones	
2	2	Yes
−	8	No

3.
tens	ones	
6	8	Yes
−	7	No

Practice

Do you need more ones? Circle Yes or No.
Then subtract and trade if needed.

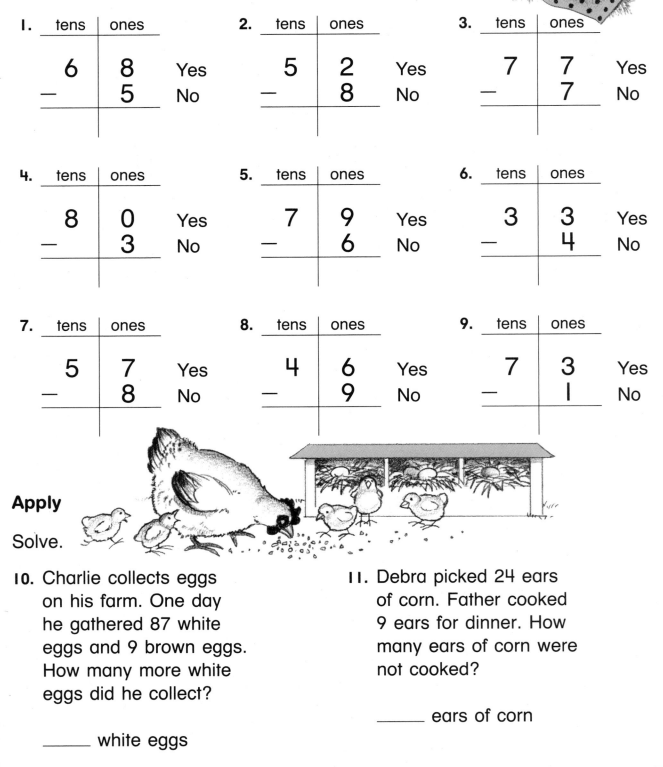

1.

tens	ones	
6	8	Yes
−	5	No

2.

tens	ones	
5	2	Yes
−	8	No

3.

tens	ones	
7	7	Yes
−	7	No

4.

tens	ones	
8	0	Yes
−	3	No

5.

tens	ones	
7	9	Yes
−	6	No

6.

tens	ones	
3	3	Yes
−	4	No

7.

tens	ones	
5	7	Yes
−	8	No

8.

tens	ones	
4	6	Yes
−	9	No

9.

tens	ones	
7	3	Yes
−	1	No

Apply

Solve.

10. Charlie collects eggs on his farm. One day he gathered 87 white eggs and 9 brown eggs. How many more white eggs did he collect?

_____ white eggs

11. Debra picked 24 ears of corn. Father cooked 9 ears for dinner. How many ears of corn were not cooked?

_____ ears of corn

Trading 1 ten for 10 ones to subtract

Subtracting 2-digit Numbers

Annie collects stuffed animals. She must take 17 of them to school for a display. How many are left at home?

We want to know how many animals she left at home.

Annie has _____ stuffed animals.

She is taking _____ animals to school. To find how many animals she left at

home, we subtract _____ from _____.

✔ Subtract the ones first.

Do you need more ones?

$6 - 7 = ?$
Yes, you need more ones.

tens	ones
3	6
− 1	7
	?

Trade 1 ten to get 10 ones.

Now there are 2 tens and 16 ones.

Subtract the ones.

$16 - 7 = 9$

tens	ones
$\overset{2}{\cancel{3}}$	$\overset{16}{\cancel{6}}$
− 1	7
	9

Subtract the tens.

$2 - 1 = 1$

tens	ones
$\overset{2}{\cancel{3}}$	$\overset{16}{\cancel{6}}$
− 1	7
1	9

Annie left _____ stuffed animals at home.

Getting Started

Subtract. Trade if needed.

1. tens	ones		2. tens	ones		3. tens	ones		4. tens	ones
9	3		6	2		8	4		8	8
− 5	9		− 3	6		− 2	9		− 1	8

Practice

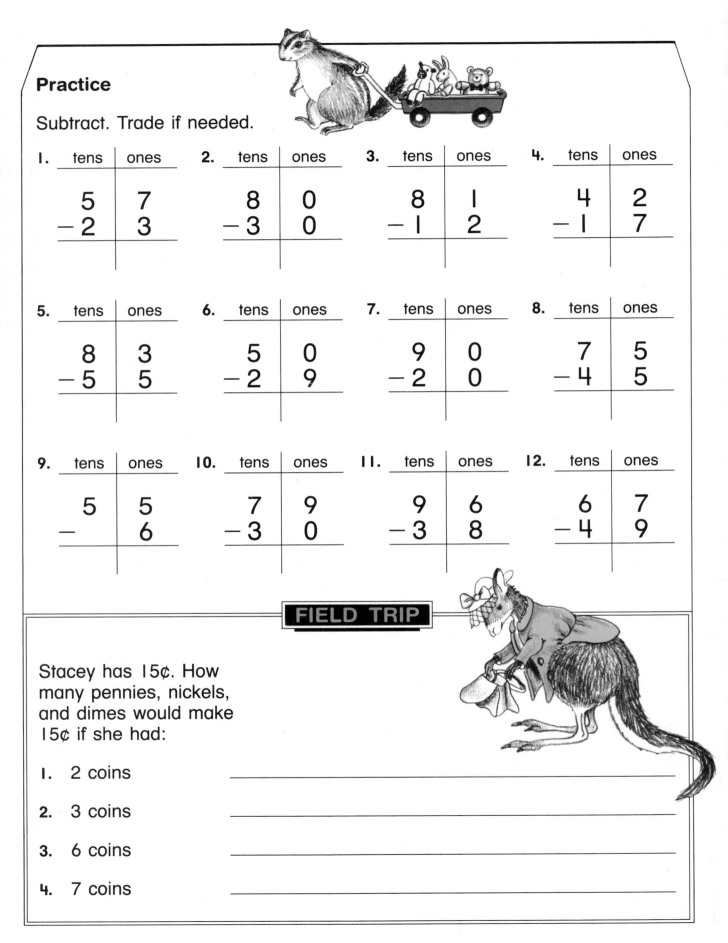

Subtract. Trade if needed.

1.
tens	ones
5	7
−2	3

2.
tens	ones
8	0
−3	0

3.
tens	ones
8	1
−1	2

4.
tens	ones
4	2
−1	7

5.
tens	ones
8	3
−5	5

6.
tens	ones
5	0
−2	9

7.
tens	ones
9	0
−2	0

8.
tens	ones
7	5
−4	5

9.
tens	ones
5	5
−	6

10.
tens	ones
7	9
−3	0

11.
tens	ones
9	6
−3	8

12.
tens	ones
6	7
−4	9

FIELD TRIP

Stacey has 15¢. How many pennies, nickels, and dimes would make 15¢ if she had:

1. 2 coins _____

2. 3 coins _____

3. 6 coins _____

4. 7 coins _____

Subtracting 2-digit Numbers

Rhoda collected 55 shells.
Diana collected 39 shells.
How many more shells did Rhoda collect?

We want to know how many more shells Rhoda has.

Rhoda has _____ shells.

Diana has _____ shells.
To find how many more shells Rhoda has,

we subtract _____ from _____.

✔ Subtract the ones first.

Do you need more ones?	Trade 1 ten to get 10 ones.	Subtract the ones.	Subtract the tens.
$5 - 9 = ?$ Yes, you need more ones.	Now there are 4 tens and 15 ones.	$15 - 9 = 6$	$4 - 3 = 1$

tens	ones
5	5
−3	9
	?

tens	ones
4	15
5	5
−3	9
	6

tens	ones
4	15
5	5
−3	9
1	6

Rhoda has _____ more shells than Diana.

Getting Started

Subtract. Trade if needed.

1.
tens	ones
6	3
−2	8

2.
tens	ones
8	7
−3	4

3.
$$\begin{array}{r} 75 \\ -12 \\ \hline \end{array}$$

4.
$$\begin{array}{r} 52 \\ -25 \\ \hline \end{array}$$

5.
$$\begin{array}{r} 90 \\ -52 \\ \hline \end{array}$$

Practice

Subtract. Trade if needed.

1.	tens	ones		2.	tens	ones		3.	tens	ones		4.	tens	ones
	6	8			7	1			5	2			8	5
	−2	3			−3	9			−2	6			−2	5

5. $57 - 23$

6. $75 - 29$

7. $53 - 46$

8. $79 - 30$

9. $50 - 8$

10. $32 - 18$

11. $73 - 50$

12. $57 - 45$

13. $81 - 15$

14. $77 - 39$

15. $31 - 17$

16. $64 - 9$

17. $83 - 33$

18. $61 - 34$

19. $60 - 20$

20. $77 - 18$

21. $82 - 55$

22. $53 - 47$

Apply

Solve.

23. Martha had 80¢.
She lost 35¢.
How much was left?

_____

24. Allan earned 68¢ on
Friday. He earned 25¢ on
Saturday. How much
money does
he have now?

_____

Subtracting 2-digit numbers, with trading

Subtracting 2-digit Numbers

Chip has fun riding his bike.
How many more blocks did he ride the
first week than the second week?

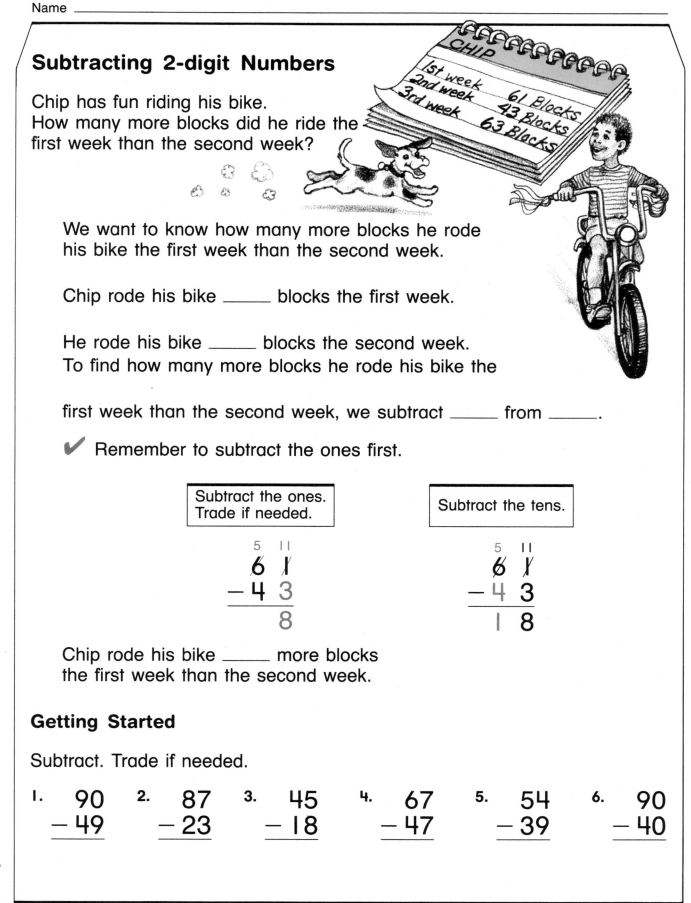

CHIP
1st week   61 Blocks
2nd week   43 Blocks
3rd week   63 Blocks

We want to know how many more blocks he rode
his bike the first week than the second week.

Chip rode his bike _____ blocks the first week.

He rode his bike _____ blocks the second week.
To find how many more blocks he rode his bike the

first week than the second week, we subtract _____ from _____.

✔ Remember to subtract the ones first.

Subtract the ones. Trade if needed.	Subtract the tens.

$$\begin{array}{r} \overset{5}{\cancel{6}}\ \overset{11}{\cancel{1}} \\ -\ 4\ \ 3 \\ \hline 8 \end{array}$$

$$\begin{array}{r} \overset{5}{\cancel{6}}\ \overset{11}{\cancel{1}} \\ -\ 4\ \ 3 \\ \hline 1\ 8 \end{array}$$

Chip rode his bike _____ more blocks
the first week than the second week.

Getting Started

Subtract. Trade if needed.

1. $\begin{array}{r} 90 \\ -49 \\ \hline \end{array}$	2. $\begin{array}{r} 87 \\ -23 \\ \hline \end{array}$	3. $\begin{array}{r} 45 \\ -18 \\ \hline \end{array}$	4. $\begin{array}{r} 67 \\ -47 \\ \hline \end{array}$	5. $\begin{array}{r} 54 \\ -39 \\ \hline \end{array}$	6. $\begin{array}{r} 90 \\ -40 \\ \hline \end{array}$

Practice

Subtract. Trade if needed.

1. $90 - 50$
2. $65 - 35$
3. $73 - 40$
4. $65 - 9$
5. $51 - 27$
6. $86 - 28$

7. $75 - 41$
8. $48 - 24$
9. $34 - 17$
10. $56 - 37$
11. $83 - 55$
12. $51 - 19$

13. $62 - 28$
14. $97 - 65$
15. $80 - 52$
16. $45 - 25$
17. $37 - 18$
18. $64 - 57$

19. $83 - 48$
20. $77 - 56$
21. $44 - 14$
22. $32 - 16$
23. $58 - 25$
24. $33 - 18$

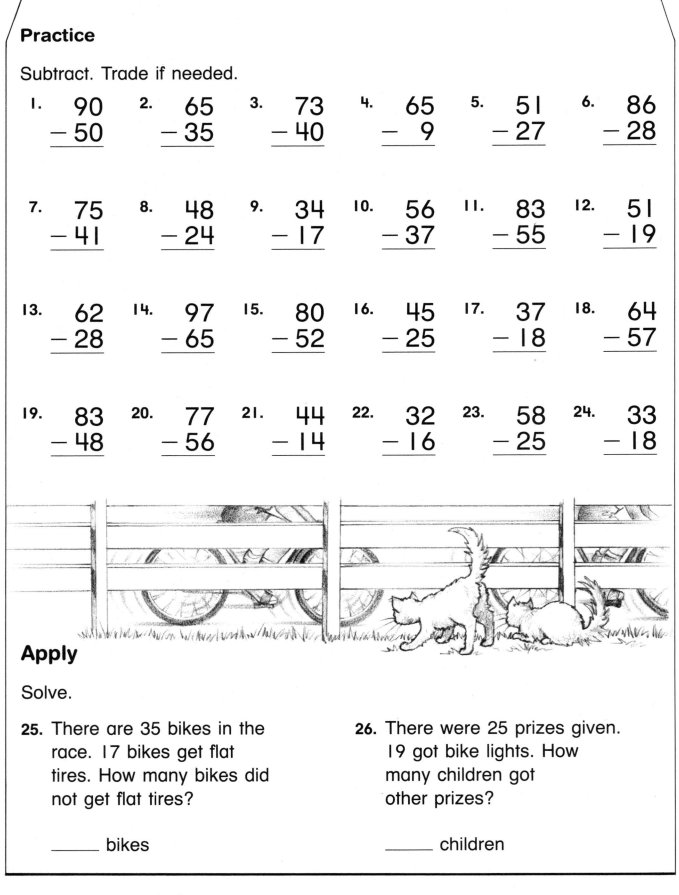

Apply

Solve.

25. There are 35 bikes in the race. 17 bikes get flat tires. How many bikes did not get flat tires?

    _____ bikes

26. There were 25 prizes given. 19 got bike lights. How many children got other prizes?

    _____ children

Subtracting 2-digit numbers, with trading

Checking Subtraction

The Pet Shoppe had 55 birds.
They sold 27 of them.
How many birds are left?

We want to know how many birds are left?

The store had _____ birds.

They sold _____ birds.

To find how many are left, we subtract _____ from _____.

Subtract the ones first. Trade if needed.

Subtract the tens.

Check by adding.

$$\begin{array}{r} \overset{4}{\cancel{5}}\,\overset{15}{\cancel{5}} \\ -\ 2\ 7 \\ \hline 8 \end{array}$$

$$\begin{array}{r} \overset{4}{\cancel{5}}\,\overset{15}{\cancel{5}} \\ -\ 2\ 7 \\ \hline 2\ 8 \end{array}$$

These should be the same.

$$\begin{array}{r} 2\ 8 \\ +\ 2\ 7 \\ \hline 5\ 5 \end{array}$$

The Pet Shoppe has _____ birds left.

Getting Started

Subtract. Trade if needed. Check your answers.

1. $\begin{array}{r} 37 \\ -15 \\ \hline 22 \end{array}$ → $\begin{array}{r} 22 \\ +15 \\ \hline 37 \end{array}$

2. $\begin{array}{r} 81 \\ -43 \\ \hline \end{array}$

3. $\begin{array}{r} 75 \\ -39 \\ \hline \end{array}$

4. $\begin{array}{r} 43 \\ -17 \\ \hline \end{array}$

5. $\begin{array}{r} 64 \\ -41 \\ \hline \end{array}$

6. $\begin{array}{r} 57 \\ -28 \\ \hline \end{array}$

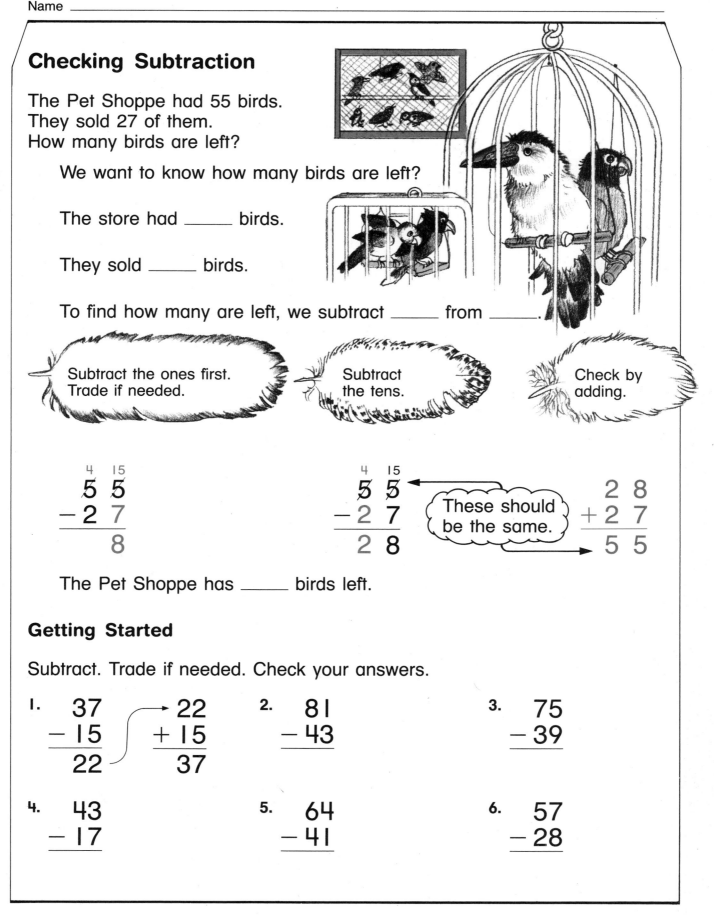

Practice

Subtract. Trade if needed. Check your answers.

1. $\begin{array}{r} 75 \\ -25 \\ \hline \end{array}$

2. $\begin{array}{r} 61 \\ -27 \\ \hline \end{array}$

3. $\begin{array}{r} 38 \\ -13 \\ \hline \end{array}$

4. $\begin{array}{r} 53 \\ -36 \\ \hline \end{array}$

5. $\begin{array}{r} 85 \\ -59 \\ \hline \end{array}$

6. $\begin{array}{r} 67 \\ -39 \\ \hline \end{array}$

7. $\begin{array}{r} 42 \\ -15 \\ \hline \end{array}$

8. $\begin{array}{r} 95 \\ -58 \\ \hline \end{array}$

9. $\begin{array}{r} 51 \\ -43 \\ \hline \end{array}$

10. $\begin{array}{r} 99 \\ -69 \\ \hline \end{array}$

11. $\begin{array}{r} 64 \\ -25 \\ \hline \end{array}$

12. $\begin{array}{r} 77 \\ -48 \\ \hline \end{array}$

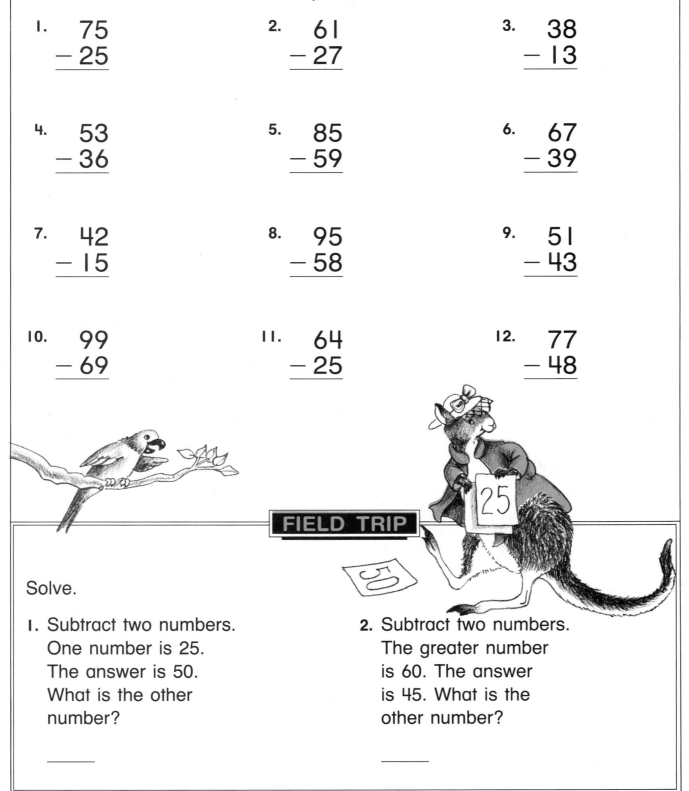

FIELD TRIP

Solve.

1. Subtract two numbers. One number is 25. The answer is 50. What is the other number?

_____

2. Subtract two numbers. The greater number is 60. The answer is 45. What is the other number?

_____

Checking subtraction

Subtracting Money

Alice saved 85¢ to buy a kite.
After buying one kite, how
much money does she have left?

We want to know how much money she has left.

Alice saved _____.

She spends _____.

To find how much money she has left,

we subtract _____ from _____.

Subtract the pennies first.
Trade if needed.

10¢	1¢
7 8	15 5¢
−5	9¢
	6¢

Subtract the dimes.

10¢	1¢
7 8	15 5¢
−5	9¢
2	6¢

Alice has _____ left.

Getting Started

Subtract. Trade if needed.

1. 36¢
   − 15¢

2. 47¢
   − 19¢

3. 75¢
   − 38¢

4. 78¢
   − 56¢

5. 91¢
   − 73¢

6. 83¢
   − 42¢

7. 90¢
   − 53¢

8. 84¢
   − 58¢

9. 97¢
   − 57¢

10. 46¢
    − 28¢

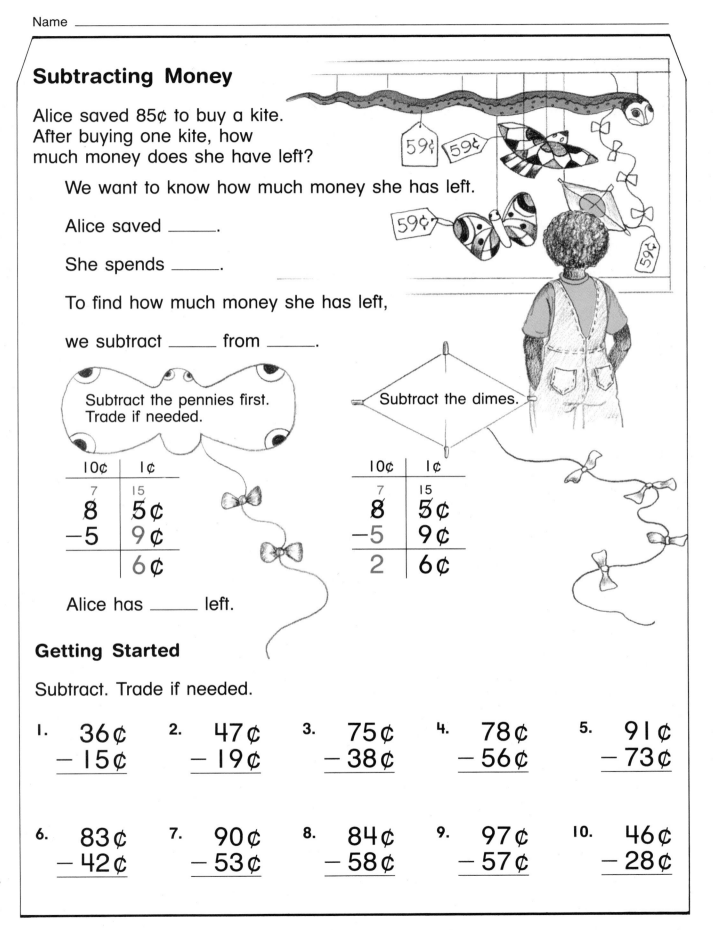

Practice

Subtract. Trade if needed.

1. 70¢ − 30¢
2. 90¢ − 21¢
3. 84¢ − 27¢
4. 99¢ − 66¢
5. 51¢ − 23¢

6. 98¢ − 29¢
7. 45¢ − 22¢
8. 57¢ − 39¢
9. 75¢ − 50¢
10. 60¢ − 41¢

11. 27¢ − 9¢
12. 65¢ − 35¢
13. 80¢ − 50¢
14. 52¢ − 7¢
15. 45¢ − 36¢

16. 48¢ − 15¢
17. 73¢ − 55¢
18. 64¢ − 17¢
19. 35¢ − 15¢
20. 96¢ − 77¢

Apply

Solve.

21. Li saved 95¢. She bought some crayons for 75¢. How much money does she have left?

22. Lonnie saved 45¢. His mother gave him 35¢. How much does he have now?

Subtracting using money notation

Problem Solving

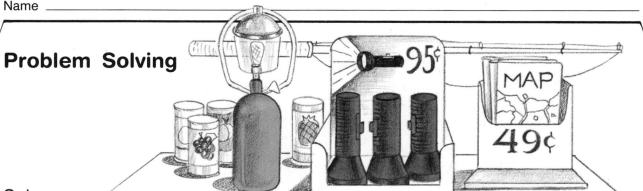

Solve.

1. There were 87 maps
of hiking trails.
Lannie sold 25 maps.
How many maps are left?

_____ maps

2. Jo bought a flashlight
and a map. How much
more did she pay
for the flashlight?

_____

3. The Taylor family drove
40 miles to Jackson
and 28 miles on to the
park. How many miles
did they drive in all?

_____ miles

4. There were
75 flashlights.
Wayne sold 46 of them.
How many were not
sold?

_____ flashlights

5. There were
53 rowboats for
rent at the lake.
25 boats were
rented. How many
were not rented?

_____ boats

6. There are 35 cans
of orange juice and
29 cans of apple
juice. How many
cans of juice are
there in all?

_____ cans of juice

7. Jo has $2.00. Decide if she has
enough money to buy 2
flashlights.

_____

8. Decide if Jo could buy a
flashlight and a map with her
$2.00.

_____

(one hundred fifty-nine) **159**

Maria showed a list of four pets
to her friends at school. She
asked each friend to pick their
favorite pet and then made
a graph of their choices.

Use her graph to find the answers.

1. _____ children chose a cat.

2. _____ children chose a dog.

3. _____ children chose a bird.

4. _____ children chose a rabbit.

5. How many children
chose a cat or a dog?

_____

6. How many more children
chose a dog than a cat?

_____

7. How many children
chose a bird or a rabbit?

_____

8. How many children
chose a dog or a rabbit?

_____

9. How many more children
chose a cat than a rabbit?

_____

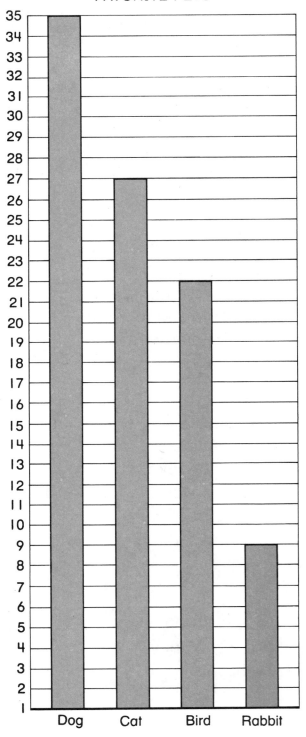

FAVORITE PETS

Using information from a graph

Name _____

CHAPTER CHECKUP

Subtract. Trade if needed.

1. $25 - 3$

2. $35 - 8$

3. $71 - 5$

4. $55 - 9$

5. $80 - 30$

6. $90 - 30$

7. $60 - 20$

8. $85 - 31$

9. $45 - 17$

10. $71 - 53$

11. $64 - 19$

12. $97 - 29$

13. $83 - 15$

14. $98 - 75$

15. $81 - 67$

16. $35 - 19$

17. $75¢ - 25¢$

18. $65¢ - 48¢$

19. $92¢ - 55¢$

20. $73¢ - 15¢$

Solve.

21. Pat saved 35 marbles. She gave Dino 16 of them. How many marbles did she have left?

_____ marbles

22. The pet store had 75 goldfish. They sold 39 of them. How many did they have left?

_____ goldfish

ROUNDUP REVIEW

Fill in the oval next to the correct answer.

1. $\begin{array}{r} 15 \\ -\ 9 \\ \hline \end{array}$
    - ○ 24
    - ○ 6
    - ○ 14
    - ○ NG

2. $\begin{array}{r} 7 \\ +\ 4 \\ \hline \end{array}$
    - ○ 11
    - ○ 3
    - ○ 4
    - ○ NG

3. (coins)
    - ○ 81¢
    - ○ 80¢
    - ○ 76¢
    - ○ NG

4. (clock)
    - ○ 4:25
    - ○ 3:25
    - ○ 5:15
    - ○ NG

5. (base-ten blocks)
    - ○ 135
    - ○ 55
    - ○ 145
    - ○ NG

6. $\begin{array}{r} 51 \\ +\ 37 \\ \hline \end{array}$
    - ○ 14
    - ○ 98
    - ○ 89
    - ○ NG

7. $\begin{array}{r} 29¢ \\ +\ 34¢ \\ \hline \end{array}$
    - ○ 63¢
    - ○ 53¢
    - ○ 513
    - ○ NG

8. $\begin{array}{r} 80 \\ +\ 70 \\ \hline \end{array}$
    - ○ 160
    - ○ 150
    - ○ 10
    - ○ NG

9. $\begin{array}{r} 76 \\ +\ 97 \\ \hline \end{array}$
    - ○ 163
    - ○ 1,613
    - ○ 173
    - ○ NG

10. $\begin{array}{r} 80 \\ -\ 30 \\ \hline \end{array}$
    - ○ 50
    - ○ 110
    - ○ 40
    - ○ NG

11. $\begin{array}{r} 59 \\ -\ 15 \\ \hline \end{array}$
    - ○ 44
    - ○ 74
    - ○ 54
    - ○ NG

12. $\begin{array}{r} 98¢ \\ -\ 35¢ \\ \hline \end{array}$
    - ○ 133¢
    - ○ 36¢
    - ○ 63¢
    - ○ NG

13. $\begin{array}{r} 71¢ \\ -\ 23¢ \\ \hline \end{array}$
    - ○ 52¢
    - ○ 48¢
    - ○ 94¢
    - ○ NG

☐ score

9 ADDITION AND SUBTRACTION, 2-DIGITS

Finding 2- or 3-digit Sums

The Walkers planted 75 tomato plants and 49 pepper plants in their garden. How many plants are there in all?

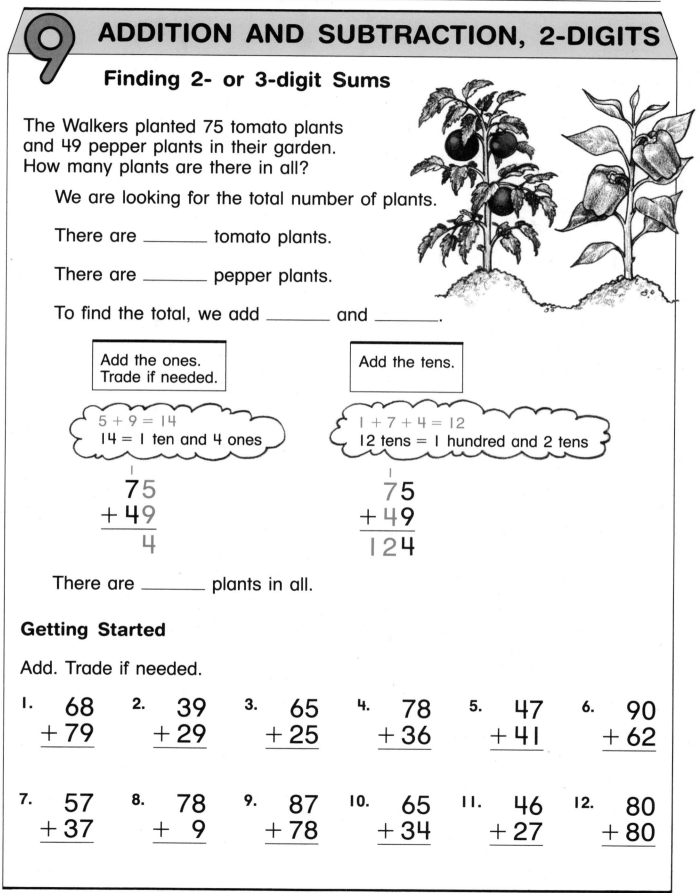

We are looking for the total number of plants.

There are _____ tomato plants.

There are _____ pepper plants.

To find the total, we add _____ and _____.

Add the ones. Trade if needed.	Add the tens.

$5 + 9 = 14$
$14 = 1$ ten and 4 ones

$$\begin{array}{r} \overset{1}{7}5 \\ +49 \\ \hline 4 \end{array}$$

$1 + 7 + 4 = 12$
12 tens $= 1$ hundred and 2 tens

$$\begin{array}{r} \overset{1}{7}5 \\ +49 \\ \hline 124 \end{array}$$

There are _____ plants in all.

Getting Started

Add. Trade if needed.

1. $\begin{array}{r} 68 \\ +79 \\ \hline \end{array}$
2. $\begin{array}{r} 39 \\ +29 \\ \hline \end{array}$
3. $\begin{array}{r} 65 \\ +25 \\ \hline \end{array}$
4. $\begin{array}{r} 78 \\ +36 \\ \hline \end{array}$
5. $\begin{array}{r} 47 \\ +41 \\ \hline \end{array}$
6. $\begin{array}{r} 90 \\ +62 \\ \hline \end{array}$

7. $\begin{array}{r} 57 \\ +37 \\ \hline \end{array}$
8. $\begin{array}{r} 78 \\ +\ 9 \\ \hline \end{array}$
9. $\begin{array}{r} 87 \\ +78 \\ \hline \end{array}$
10. $\begin{array}{r} 65 \\ +34 \\ \hline \end{array}$
11. $\begin{array}{r} 46 \\ +27 \\ \hline \end{array}$
12. $\begin{array}{r} 80 \\ +80 \\ \hline \end{array}$

Practice

Add. Trade if needed.

1. $11 + 46$
2. $80 + 44$
3. $49 + 6$
4. $18 + 44$
5. $99 + 33$
6. $18 + 15$

7. $36 + 64$
8. $19 + 22$
9. $23 + 39$
10. $96 + 32$
11. $8 + 48$
12. $45 + 74$

13. $79 + 89$
14. $72 + 77$
15. $27 + 17$
16. $88 + 33$
17. $28 + 45$
18. $67 + 70$

19. $49 + 9$
20. $63 + 48$
21. $48 + 86$
22. $82 + 12$
23. $67 + 23$
24. $85 + 12$

25. $56 + 84$
26. $37 + 28$
27. $44 + 37$
28. $62 + 17$
29. $59 + 98$
30. $26 + 6$

Apply

Solve.

31. Ellie picked 50 tomatoes in the morning and 80 in the afternoon. How many tomatoes did she pick?

_____ tomatoes

32. Charley picked 75 green peppers and 65 yellow peppers. How many peppers did he pick?

_____ peppers

Adding 2-digit numbers, 3-digit sums

Adding 2-digit Numbers

The students in Garden School sold cookies for charity. How many boxes of cookies did Holly, Keith and Gloria sell altogether?

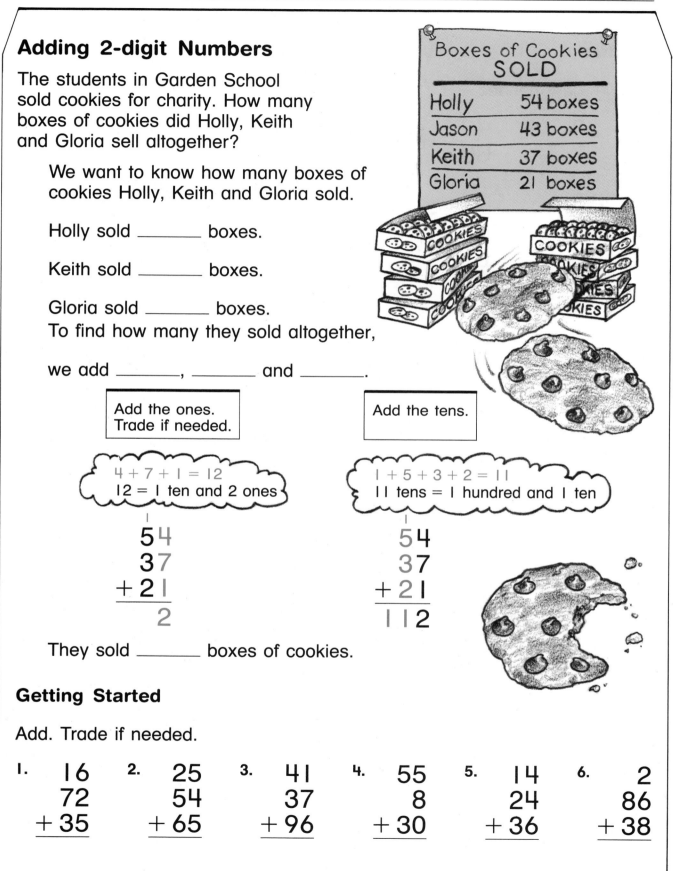

Boxes of Cookies
SOLD

Holly	54 boxes
Jason	43 boxes
Keith	37 boxes
Gloria	21 boxes

We want to know how many boxes of cookies Holly, Keith and Gloria sold.

Holly sold _____ boxes.

Keith sold _____ boxes.

Gloria sold _____ boxes.

To find how many they sold altogether,

we add _____, _____ and _____.

| Add the ones. Trade if needed. | | Add the tens. |

$4 + 7 + 1 = 12$
$12 = 1$ ten and 2 ones

$$\begin{array}{r} 5\overset{1}{4} \\ 37 \\ +21 \\ \hline 2 \end{array}$$

$1 + 5 + 3 + 2 = 11$
11 tens $= 1$ hundred and 1 ten

$$\begin{array}{r} 5\overset{1}{4} \\ 37 \\ +21 \\ \hline 112 \end{array}$$

They sold _____ boxes of cookies.

Getting Started

Add. Trade if needed.

1.	2.	3.	4.	5.	6.
$\begin{array}{r} 16 \\ 72 \\ +35 \\ \hline \end{array}$	$\begin{array}{r} 25 \\ 54 \\ +65 \\ \hline \end{array}$	$\begin{array}{r} 41 \\ 37 \\ +96 \\ \hline \end{array}$	$\begin{array}{r} 55 \\ 8 \\ +30 \\ \hline \end{array}$	$\begin{array}{r} 14 \\ 24 \\ +36 \\ \hline \end{array}$	$\begin{array}{r} 2 \\ 86 \\ +38 \\ \hline \end{array}$

Practice

Add. Trade if needed.

1.
$$\begin{array}{r} 23 \\ 37 \\ +90 \\ \hline \end{array}$$

2.
$$\begin{array}{r} 40 \\ 30 \\ +70 \\ \hline \end{array}$$

3.
$$\begin{array}{r} 6 \\ 70 \\ +58 \\ \hline \end{array}$$

4.
$$\begin{array}{r} 13 \\ 33 \\ +76 \\ \hline \end{array}$$

5.
$$\begin{array}{r} 11 \\ 37 \\ +59 \\ \hline \end{array}$$

6.
$$\begin{array}{r} 49 \\ 10 \\ +68 \\ \hline \end{array}$$

7.
$$\begin{array}{r} 10 \\ 69 \\ +18 \\ \hline \end{array}$$

8.
$$\begin{array}{r} 59 \\ 61 \\ + 3 \\ \hline \end{array}$$

9.
$$\begin{array}{r} 51 \\ 39 \\ +97 \\ \hline \end{array}$$

10.
$$\begin{array}{r} 31 \\ 6 \\ +52 \\ \hline \end{array}$$

11.
$$\begin{array}{r} 10 \\ 70 \\ +80 \\ \hline \end{array}$$

12.
$$\begin{array}{r} 54 \\ 34 \\ +25 \\ \hline \end{array}$$

13.
$$\begin{array}{r} 86 \\ 1 \\ + 8 \\ \hline \end{array}$$

14.
$$\begin{array}{r} 35 \\ 30 \\ +35 \\ \hline \end{array}$$

15.
$$\begin{array}{r} 83 \\ 6 \\ +54 \\ \hline \end{array}$$

16.
$$\begin{array}{r} 30 \\ 19 \\ +88 \\ \hline \end{array}$$

17.
$$\begin{array}{r} 82 \\ 14 \\ +18 \\ \hline \end{array}$$

18.
$$\begin{array}{r} 72 \\ 23 \\ +98 \\ \hline \end{array}$$

FIELD TRIP

If you toss a coin 30 times, guess how many times it will land tail up?

_____ times

Try it.

Toss a coin 30 times.

How many tails did you get?

_____

How many heads did you get?

_____

Was your guess close? _____

166 (one hundred sixty-six)

Subtracting 2-digit Numbers

Greg sold 75 adult tickets to
the school play. He sold 48
student tickets. How many
more adult tickets did Greg sell?

We want to know how many more
adult tickets were sold.

Greg sold _____ adult tickets.

He sold _____ student tickets.

To find how many more adult tickets were sold,

we subtract _____ from _____.

✔ Remember to subtract the ones first.

Subtract the ones.
Trade if needed.

$15 - 8 = 7$

$$\begin{array}{r} \overset{6\ 15}{7\!\!\!/5} \\ -\ 4\,8 \\ \hline 7 \end{array}$$

Subtract the tens.

$6 - 4 = 2$

$$\begin{array}{r} \overset{6\ 15}{7\!\!\!/5} \\ -\ 4\,8 \\ \hline 2\,7 \end{array}$$

Greg sold _____ more adult tickets.

Getting Started

Subtract. Trade if needed.

1. $\begin{array}{r} 74 \\ -26 \\ \hline \end{array}$
2. $\begin{array}{r} 47 \\ -33 \\ \hline \end{array}$
3. $\begin{array}{r} 71 \\ -51 \\ \hline \end{array}$
4. $\begin{array}{r} 89 \\ -76 \\ \hline \end{array}$
5. $\begin{array}{r} 80 \\ -52 \\ \hline \end{array}$
6. $\begin{array}{r} 91 \\ -27 \\ \hline \end{array}$

Practice

Subtract. Trade if needed.

1. $\begin{array}{r} 47 \\ -36 \end{array}$
2. $\begin{array}{r} 66 \\ -34 \end{array}$
3. $\begin{array}{r} 38 \\ -14 \end{array}$
4. $\begin{array}{r} 75 \\ -68 \end{array}$
5. $\begin{array}{r} 70 \\ -57 \end{array}$
6. $\begin{array}{r} 61 \\ -44 \end{array}$

7. $\begin{array}{r} 93 \\ -13 \end{array}$
8. $\begin{array}{r} 32 \\ -15 \end{array}$
9. $\begin{array}{r} 78 \\ -29 \end{array}$
10. $\begin{array}{r} 61 \\ -28 \end{array}$
11. $\begin{array}{r} 54 \\ -37 \end{array}$
12. $\begin{array}{r} 63 \\ -29 \end{array}$

13. $\begin{array}{r} 80 \\ -65 \end{array}$
14. $\begin{array}{r} 52 \\ -30 \end{array}$
15. $\begin{array}{r} 93 \\ -87 \end{array}$
16. $\begin{array}{r} 17 \\ -11 \end{array}$
17. $\begin{array}{r} 95 \\ -76 \end{array}$
18. $\begin{array}{r} 75 \\ -59 \end{array}$

19. $\begin{array}{r} 72 \\ -29 \end{array}$
20. $\begin{array}{r} 87 \\ -42 \end{array}$
21. $\begin{array}{r} 54 \\ -18 \end{array}$
22. $\begin{array}{r} 31 \\ -29 \end{array}$
23. $\begin{array}{r} 60 \\ -34 \end{array}$
24. $\begin{array}{r} 82 \\ -20 \end{array}$

25. $\begin{array}{r} 60 \\ -19 \end{array}$
26. $\begin{array}{r} 55 \\ -23 \end{array}$
27. $\begin{array}{r} 94 \\ -75 \end{array}$
28. $\begin{array}{r} 27 \\ -20 \end{array}$
29. $\begin{array}{r} 50 \\ -46 \end{array}$
30. $\begin{array}{r} 37 \\ -11 \end{array}$

Apply

Solve.

31. Martin found 37 shells. He gave 18 shells to Nell. How many shells does Martin have left?

_____ shells

32. Rona poured 65 cups of juice. She sold 28 cups. How many cups of juice were not sold?

_____ cups of juice

Subtracting 2-digit numbers, with trading

Mixed Practice

Add or subtract. Trade if needed.

1. $35 + 23$
2. $74 + 96$
3. $90 + 57$
4. $54 + 29$
5. $58 + 36$
6. $32 + 99$

7. $49 - 15$
8. $86 - 34$
9. $90 - 25$
10. $41 - 28$
11. $72 - 33$
12. $91 - 59$

13. $63 + 33$
14. $86 + 46$
15. $57 - 50$
16. $90 - 67$
17. $75 + 95$
18. $51 - 26$

19. $53 + 24 + 87$
20. $65 + 4 + 38$
21. $40 + 21 + 30$
22. $7 + 52 + 73$
23. $32 + 14 + 94$
24. $74 + 44 + 4$

Solve.

25. There are 33 puppies in the pet store. There are 17 kittens. How many more puppies than kittens are there?

_____ puppies

26. There are 75 goldfish and 85 guppies. How many fish are there altogether?

_____ fish

27. There are 18 canaries and 26 parakeets. How many birds are there altogether?

_____ birds

28. The pet store had 34 turtles. They sold 19. How many were not sold?

_____ turtles

More Mixed Practice

Add or subtract. Trade if needed.

1. $\begin{array}{r} 66 \\ +40 \\ \hline \end{array}$
2. $\begin{array}{r} 97 \\ +41 \\ \hline \end{array}$
3. $\begin{array}{r} 95 \\ -20 \\ \hline \end{array}$
4. $\begin{array}{r} 91 \\ -59 \\ \hline \end{array}$
5. $\begin{array}{r} 35 \\ +44 \\ \hline \end{array}$
6. $\begin{array}{r} 79 \\ +44 \\ \hline \end{array}$

7. $\begin{array}{r} 95 \\ -70 \\ \hline \end{array}$
8. $\begin{array}{r} 73 \\ -26 \\ \hline \end{array}$
9. $\begin{array}{r} 64 \\ -17 \\ \hline \end{array}$
10. $\begin{array}{r} 79 \\ +74 \\ \hline \end{array}$
11. $\begin{array}{r} 56 \\ +40 \\ \hline \end{array}$
12. $\begin{array}{r} 69 \\ +64 \\ \hline \end{array}$

13. $\begin{array}{r} 65 \\ -52 \\ \hline \end{array}$
14. $\begin{array}{r} 95 \\ +74 \\ \hline \end{array}$
15. $\begin{array}{r} 82 \\ -27 \\ \hline \end{array}$
16. $\begin{array}{r} 77 \\ -49 \\ \hline \end{array}$
17. $\begin{array}{r} 63 \\ +99 \\ \hline \end{array}$
18. $\begin{array}{r} 95 \\ -74 \\ \hline \end{array}$

Solve.

19. Clown School has 61 happy clowns and 45 sad clowns. How many more happy clowns are there?

_____ happy clowns

20. The circus needs 23 horses, 14 lions and 18 dogs. How many animals do they need?

_____ animals

21. 89 girls and 94 boys went to the circus. How many children went to the circus?

_____ children

22. Jumbo, the elephant, is 53 years old. Atlas, the elephant, is 38 years old. How many years older is Jumbo?

_____ years

Mixed addition and subtraction practice

Addition and Subtraction Sentences

Adding and subtracting problems are sometimes written across as number sentences. To work the problems, you need to copy them as shown below. Then you can add or subtract.

$23 + 42 = \underline{\qquad}$

$$\begin{array}{r} 23 \\ +42 \\ \hline \end{array}$$

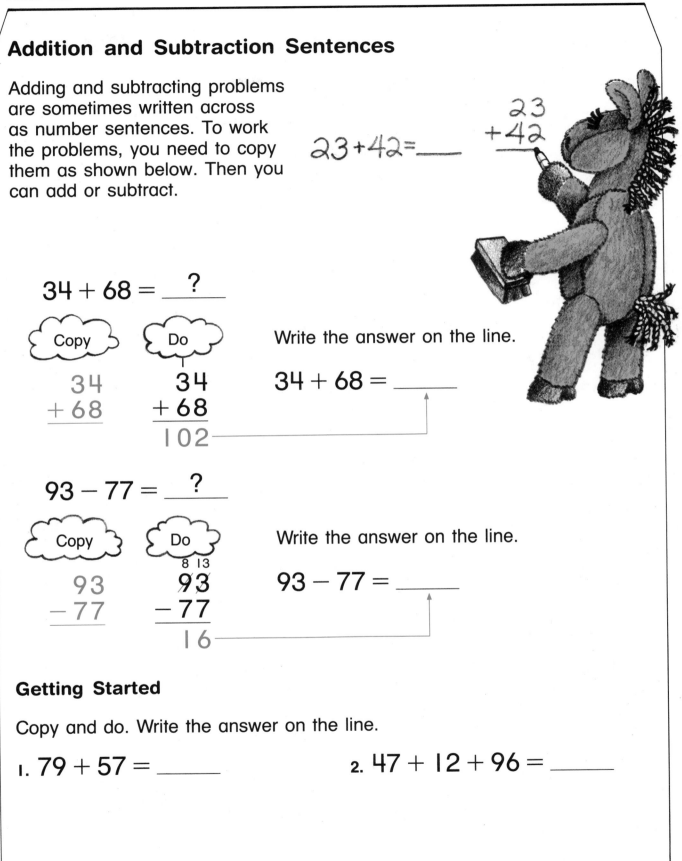

$34 + 68 = \underline{\quad ? \quad}$

Copy
$$\begin{array}{r} 34 \\ +68 \\ \hline \end{array}$$

Do
$$\begin{array}{r} 34 \\ +68 \\ \hline 102 \end{array}$$

Write the answer on the line.

$34 + 68 = \underline{\qquad}$

$93 - 77 = \underline{\quad ? \quad}$

Copy
$$\begin{array}{r} 93 \\ -77 \\ \hline \end{array}$$

Do
$$\begin{array}{r} {}^{8}\!\!\not{9}\,{}^{13}\!\!\not{3} \\ -77 \\ \hline 16 \end{array}$$

Write the answer on the line.

$93 - 77 = \underline{\qquad}$

Getting Started

Copy and do. Write the answer on the line.

1. $79 + 57 = \underline{\qquad}$

2. $47 + 12 + 96 = \underline{\qquad}$

Practice

Copy and do. Write the answer on the line.

1. $38 - 13 =$ _____

2. $80 - 5 =$ _____

3. $63 - 7 =$ _____

4. $62 + 14 =$ _____

5. $23 + 4 + 32 =$ _____

6. $99 + 99 =$ _____

FIELD TRIP

Complete the tables.

Add 5	
37	
22	
43	
55	

Add 7	
21	
52	
43	
67	

Subtract 4	
41	
35	
60	
23	

Adding and subtracting sentences

Subtracting Money

Mel had 85¢.
He bought a balloon.
How much does he have left?

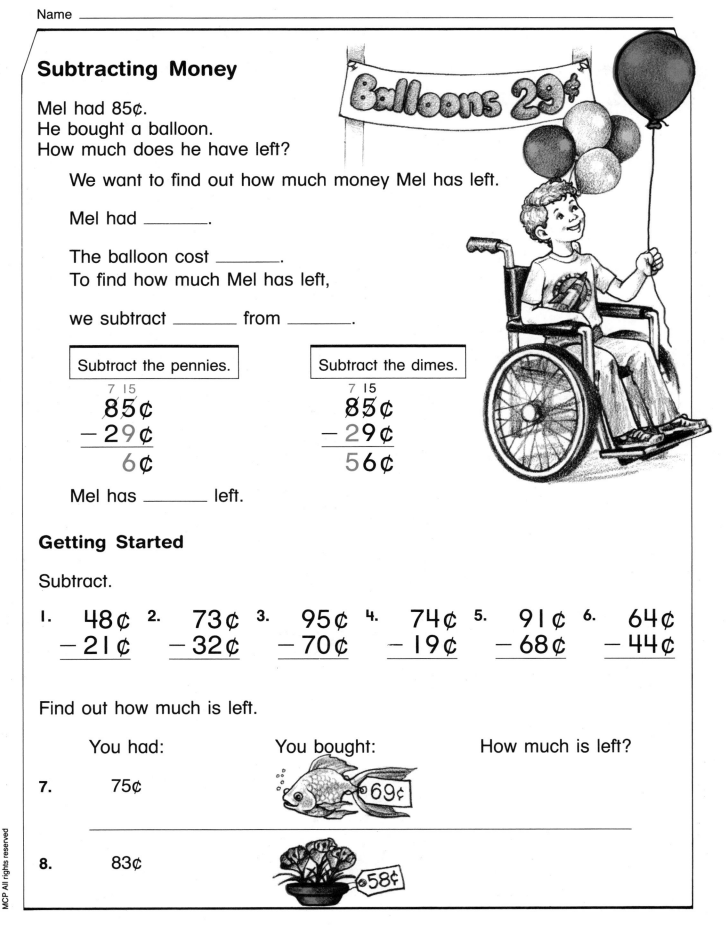

We want to find out how much money Mel has left.

Mel had _____.

The balloon cost _____.
To find how much Mel has left,

we subtract _____ from _____.

Subtract the pennies.		Subtract the dimes.

$$\begin{array}{r} {\scriptstyle 7\ 15} \\ 8\!\!\!/5¢ \\ -29¢ \\ \hline 6¢ \end{array}$$

$$\begin{array}{r} {\scriptstyle 7\ 15} \\ 8\!\!\!/5¢ \\ -29¢ \\ \hline 56¢ \end{array}$$

Mel has _____ left.

Getting Started

Subtract.

1. $\begin{array}{r} 48¢ \\ -21¢ \\ \hline \end{array}$
2. $\begin{array}{r} 73¢ \\ -32¢ \\ \hline \end{array}$
3. $\begin{array}{r} 95¢ \\ -70¢ \\ \hline \end{array}$
4. $\begin{array}{r} 74¢ \\ -19¢ \\ \hline \end{array}$
5. $\begin{array}{r} 91¢ \\ -68¢ \\ \hline \end{array}$
6. $\begin{array}{r} 64¢ \\ -44¢ \\ \hline \end{array}$

Find out how much is left.

You had:	You bought:	How much is left?
7. 75¢	69¢	
8. 83¢	58¢	

Practice

Subtract.

1.	2.	3.	4.	5.	6.
$90¢$	$50¢$	$87¢$	$33¢$	$96¢$	$70¢$
$-30¢$	$-36¢$	$-82¢$	$-\ 9¢$	$-49¢$	$-17¢$

7.	8.	9.	10.	11.	12.
$61¢$	$93¢$	$62¢$	$28¢$	$74¢$	$44¢$
$-24¢$	$-78¢$	$-\ 6¢$	$-16¢$	$-39¢$	$-18¢$

Find out how much is left.

	You had:	You bought:	How much is left?
13.	45¢	18¢	
14.	88¢	45¢	
15.	67¢	38¢	
16.	50¢	18¢	
17.	91¢	55¢	

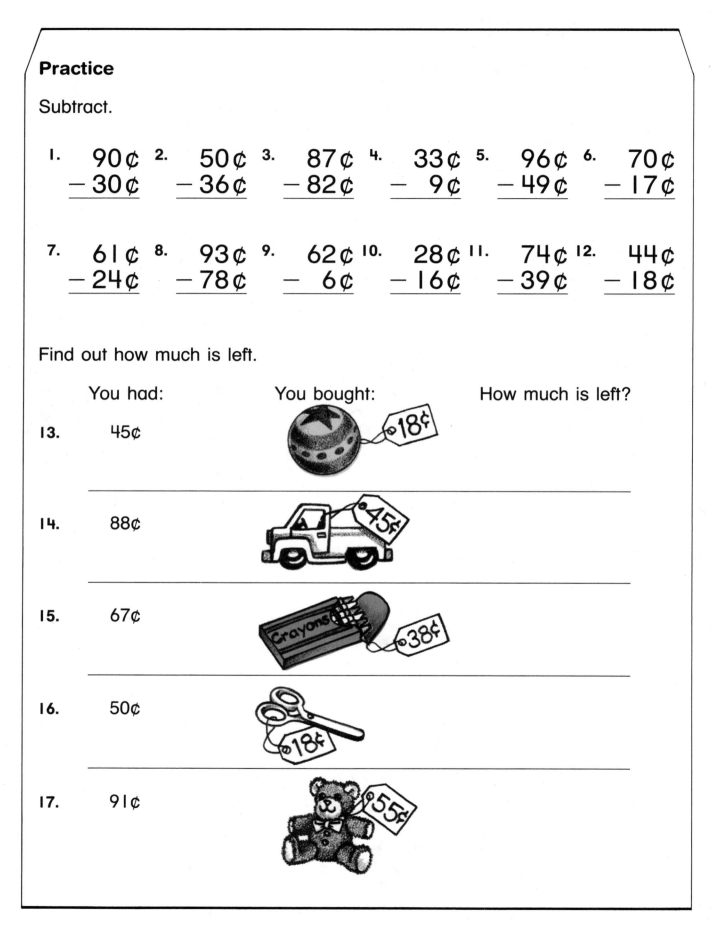

Subtracting money

Adding Money

Bear and Lion are
putting their money
together to buy a game.
How much money do they
have altogether?

I have 57¢.

I have 95¢.

We want to know how much money
they have altogether.

Bear has _____.

Lion has _____.
To find how much they have altogether,

we add _____ and _____.

Add the pennies.	Add the dimes.

$$57¢$$
$$+95¢$$
$$\overline{2¢}$$

$$57¢$$
$$+95¢$$
$$\overline{152¢}$$

$$152¢ = \$1.52$$

Bear and Lion have _____.

Getting Started

Add. Then write the answers in dollar notation.

1. $$15¢$$
    $$+85¢$$

2. $$63¢$$
    $$+25¢$$

3. $$57¢$$
    $$32¢$$
    $$+57¢$$

4. $$25¢$$
    $$3¢$$
    $$+75¢$$

5. $$58¢$$
    $$20¢$$
    $$+49¢$$

_____ _____   _____ _____ _____

(one hundred seventy-five) **175**

Practice

Add. Then write the answers in dollar notation.

1. $75¢$ $+52¢$ _____

2. $98¢$ $+95¢$ _____

3. $61¢$ $+89¢$ _____

4. $50¢$ $+41¢$ _____

5. $83¢$ $+42¢$ _____

6. $92¢$ $+69¢$ _____

7. $88¢$ $+63¢$ _____

8. $12¢$ $+98¢$ _____

9. $55¢$ $+45¢$ _____

10. $77¢$ $+37¢$ _____

11. $87¢$ $+62¢$ _____

12. $56¢$ $+39¢$ _____

13. $86¢$ $3¢$ $+46¢$ _____

14. $14¢$ $34¢$ $+26¢$ _____

15. $55¢$ $11¢$ $+45¢$ _____

Apply

Write the answers on the lines.

☆ Lana has $1.25.
☆ Craig has 37¢.
☆ José has 75¢.

16. Who has the most money? _____

17. Who has the least money? _____

18. How much money do Craig and José have together?

_____

19. How much more money does José have than Craig?

_____

Problem Solving

Solve.

1. Melissa has 75¢. She bought a beach ball. How much does she have left?

_____

43¢

2. How much did Yong pay for both toys?

_____

89¢   55¢

3. Circle the toy that costs more. How much more does it cost?

_____

75¢   98¢

4. Ashley bought a yo-yo. She gave the clerk 50¢. How much change did she get?

_____

34¢

5. Steven had 95¢. He bought a top. How much does he have left?

_____

68¢

6. Mr. Jon took his daughter to a movie. How much did he spend for the tickets?

_____

ADULT 25¢   CHILD 45¢

7. What is the cost of a bat and a ball together?

_____

85¢   67¢

8. Kiku and Cathy each bought a glove. How much did they pay altogether?

_____

98¢

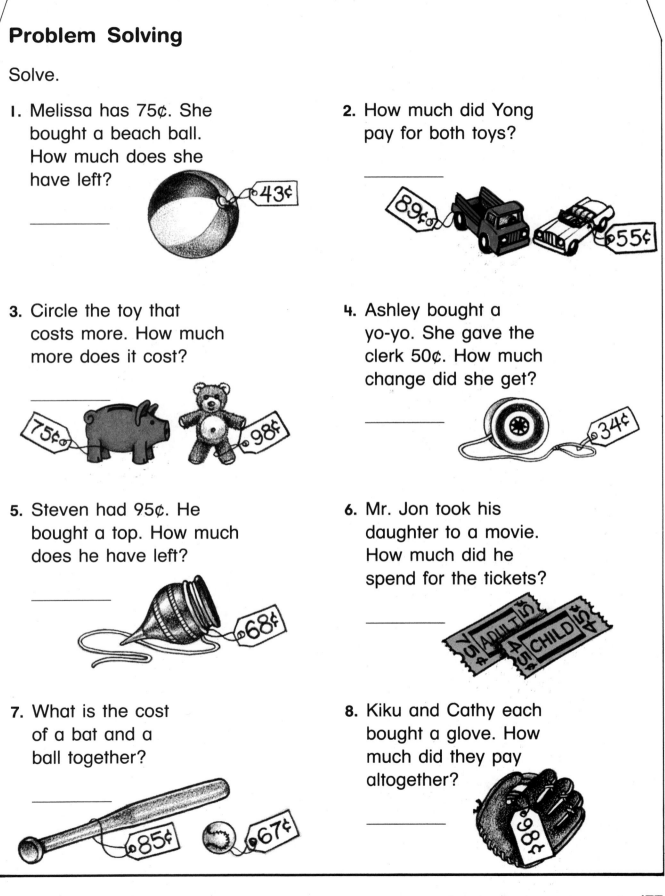

Solve.

1. How much more did Cary pay for the teddy bear?

2. How much did Dino pay for the scissors and crayons?

3. How much did Al pay for the hammer and pliers?

4. Kasey had 85¢. She bought a top. How much does she have left?

5. How much more did Rhea pay for the truck?

6. What is the cost for all three toys?

7. How much did Bart pay for all three toys?

8. How much do the three toys cost altogether?

178 (one hundred seventy-eight)

Problem solving, money

Name _____

CHAPTER CHECKUP

Add or subtract.

1. $38 + 9$ 2. $46 + 21$ 3. $15 + 83$ 4. $24 + 63$ 5. $25 + 38$ 6. $46 + 26$

7. $87 + 62$ 8. $32 + 77$ 9. $77 + 43$ 10. $69 + 66$ 11. $83 + 58$ 12. $67 + 63$

13. $86 - 23$ 14. $75 - 14$ 15. $67 - 17$ 16. $93 - 24$ 17. $51 - 39$ 18. $75 - 48$

19. $23 + 14 + 42$ 20. $10 + 50 + 70$ 21. $13 + 65 + 63$ 22. $43 + 73 + 6$ 23. $45 + 50 + 55$ 24. $32 + 27 + 93$

25. $34 + 21 + 22$ 26. $53 + 72 + 8$ 27. $32 + 42 + 26$ 28. $20 + 60 + 40$ 29. $40 + 51 + 69$ 30. $16 + 75 + 60$

Add or subtract. Then write the answers in dollar notation.

31. $35¢ + 75¢$ 32. $57¢ + 98¢$ 33. $97¢ - 65¢$ 34. $75¢ + 50¢$ 35. $83¢ - 25¢$

_____   _____   _____   _____   _____

ROUNDUP REVIEW

Fill in the oval next to the correct answer.

1.
$$\begin{array}{r} 7 \\ + 6 \\ \hline \end{array}$$
- ◯ 12
- ◯ 13
- ◯ 14
- ◯ NG

8.
$$\begin{array}{r} 25 \\ 34 \\ + 17 \\ \hline \end{array}$$
- ◯ 66
- ◯ 77
- ◯ 76
- ◯ NG

2. $8 + 9$
- ◯ 17
- ◯ 16
- ◯ 18
- ◯ NG

9.
$$\begin{array}{r} 78 \\ - 45 \\ \hline \end{array}$$
- ◯ 123
- ◯ 33
- ◯ 113
- ◯ NG

3.
$$\begin{array}{r} 12 \\ - 5 \\ \hline \end{array}$$
- ◯ 17
- ◯ 15
- ◯ 7
- ◯ NG

10.
$$\begin{array}{r} 91 \\ - 25 \\ \hline \end{array}$$
- ◯ 66
- ◯ 74
- ◯ 76
- ◯ NG

4. $15 - 6$
- ◯ 8
- ◯ 21
- ◯ 11
- ◯ NG

11. $48 + 35$
- ◯ 82
- ◯ 83
- ◯ 73
- ◯ NG

5.
- ◯ 76
- ◯ 57
- ◯ 67
- ◯ NG

12.
$$\begin{array}{r} 57 \\ + 6 \\ \hline \end{array}$$
- ◯ 51
- ◯ 53
- ◯ 63
- ◯ NG

6. $39 \bigcirc 41$
- ◯ >
- ◯ <

13. $71 - 29$
- ◯ 58
- ◯ 42
- ◯ 52
- ◯ NG

7.
$$\begin{array}{r} 69 \\ + 89 \\ \hline \end{array}$$
- ◯ 158
- ◯ 20
- ◯ 148
- ◯ NG

◻ score

10 ADDITION, 3-DIGIT NUMBERS

Place Value

_____ ones = _____ ten

_____ tens = _____ hundred

_____ hundreds = _____ thousand

Count by tens. Write the missing numbers.

10   20   _____ _____ _____ _____ _____ _____ _____

Count by hundreds. Write the missing numbers.

100   200   _____ _____ _____ _____ _____ _____ _____

Getting Started

How many hundreds, tens and ones are there? Write the numbers.

_____ hundreds _____ tens _____ ones

_____

Practice

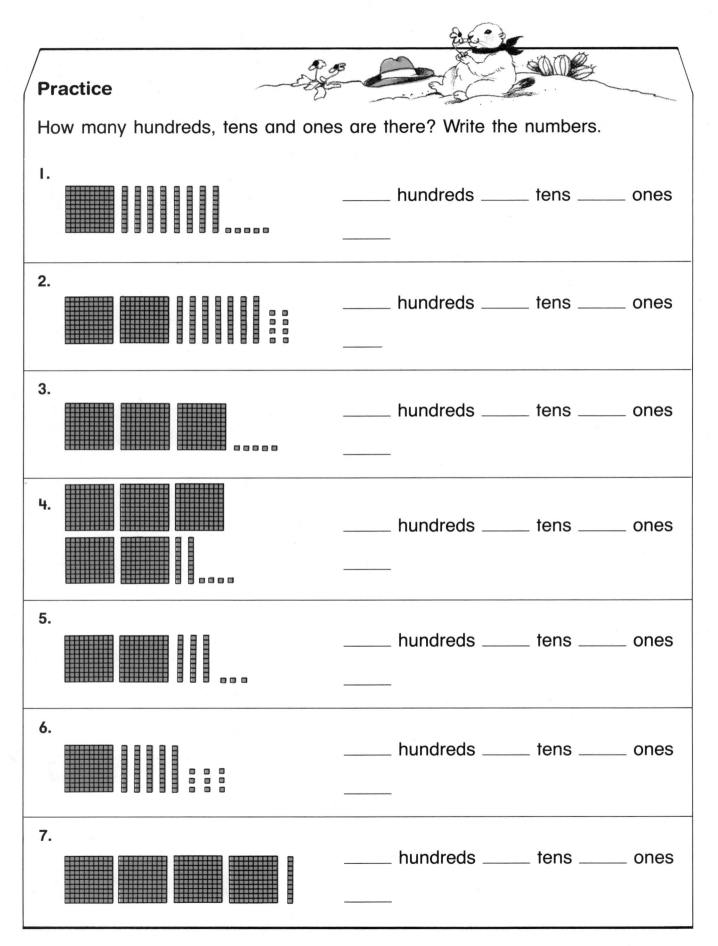

How many hundreds, tens and ones are there? Write the numbers.

1.

_____ hundreds _____ tens _____ ones

_____

2.

_____ hundreds _____ tens _____ ones

_____

3.

_____ hundreds _____ tens _____ ones

_____

4.

_____ hundreds _____ tens _____ ones

_____

5.

_____ hundreds _____ tens _____ ones

_____

6.

_____ hundreds _____ tens _____ ones

_____

7.

_____ hundreds _____ tens _____ ones

_____

Adding 2-digit Numbers

The hardware store had a sale.
How many tools were for sale?

Tools For Sale

75 Hammers
88 Saws

We want to know the number of tools for sale.

The store had _____ hammers.

They had _____ saws.
To find how many tools were for

sale, we add _____ and _____.

Add the ones.
Trade if needed.

$$\begin{array}{r} 7\,5 \\ +\,8\,8 \\ \hline 3 \end{array}$$

Add the tens.

$$\begin{array}{r} 7\,5 \\ +\,8\,8 \\ \hline 1\,6\,3 \end{array}$$

The store had _____ tools for sale.

Getting Started

Add. Trade if needed.

1.	2.	3.	4.	5.
$\begin{array}{r}37\\+82\\\hline\end{array}$	$\begin{array}{r}96\\+44\\\hline\end{array}$	$\begin{array}{r}39\\+99\\\hline\end{array}$	$\begin{array}{r}81\\+85\\\hline\end{array}$	$\begin{array}{r}27\\+73\\\hline\end{array}$

6.	7.	8.	9.	10.
$\begin{array}{r}14\\+96\\\hline\end{array}$	$\begin{array}{r}75\\+50\\\hline\end{array}$	$\begin{array}{r}49\\+98\\\hline\end{array}$	$\begin{array}{r}52\\+77\\\hline\end{array}$	$\begin{array}{r}63\\+58\\\hline\end{array}$

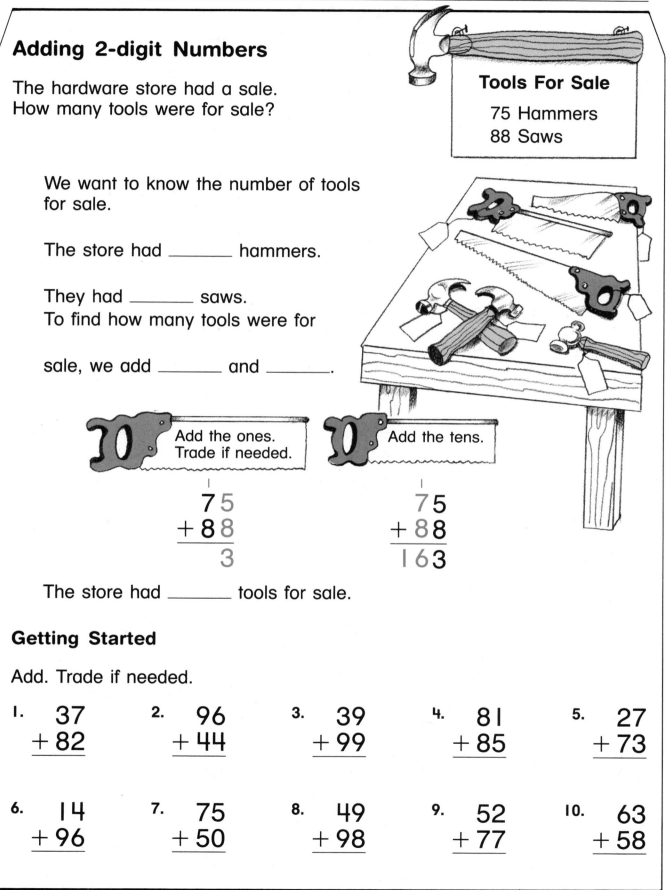

Practice

Add. Trade if needed.

1. $42 + 83$
2. $95 + 70$
3. $84 + 29$
4. $39 + 57$
5. $79 + 83$
6. $18 + 67$

7. $68 + 54$
8. $86 + 76$
9. $22 + 54$
10. $82 + 68$
11. $56 + 55$
12. $90 + 53$

13. $63 + 82$
14. $97 + 85$
15. $78 + 79$
16. $51 + 84$
17. $68 + 24$
18. $77 + 89$

FIELD TRIP

Solve.

1. Add two numbers.
   The sum is 96.
   One number is 35.
   What is the other number?

   _____

2. Subtract two numbers.
   The answer is 38.
   The larger number is 96.
   What is the other number?

   _____

3. Add two numbers.
   The sum is 91.
   One number is 36.
   What is the other number?

   _____

4. Subtract two numbers.
   The answer is 57.
   The smaller number is 19.
   What is the larger number?

   _____

Review adding two 2-digit numbers

Name _____

Adding a 3-digit and a 1-digit Number

Some students and parents from Allen School went to Clown School. How many people studied clowning?

Clown School!
- 154 students
- 8 parents

We want to know how many went to Clown School.

There were _____ students and

_____ parents attending Clown School.

To find how many people were attending,

we add _____ and _____.

Add the ones. Trade if needed.	Add the tens.	Add the hundreds.

$$\begin{array}{r} 1\overset{1}{5}4 \\ +\ \ 8 \\ \hline 2 \end{array} \qquad \begin{array}{r} 1\overset{1}{5}4 \\ +\ \ 8 \\ \hline 62 \end{array} \qquad \begin{array}{r} 1\overset{1}{5}4 \\ +\ \ 8 \\ \hline 162 \end{array}$$

There were _____ people attending Clown School.

Getting Started

Add. Trade if needed.

1. $\begin{array}{r} 237 \\ +\ \ 5 \\ \hline \end{array}$
2. $\begin{array}{r} 374 \\ +\ \ 7 \\ \hline \end{array}$
3. $\begin{array}{r} 964 \\ +\ \ 6 \\ \hline \end{array}$
4. $\begin{array}{r} 555 \\ +\ \ 5 \\ \hline \end{array}$
5. $\begin{array}{r} 423 \\ +\ \ 9 \\ \hline \end{array}$

6. $\begin{array}{r} 105 \\ +\ \ 8 \\ \hline \end{array}$
7. $\begin{array}{r} 675 \\ +\ \ 6 \\ \hline \end{array}$
8. $\begin{array}{r} 815 \\ +\ \ 7 \\ \hline \end{array}$
9. $\begin{array}{r} 276 \\ +\ \ 2 \\ \hline \end{array}$
10. $\begin{array}{r} 349 \\ +\ \ 8 \\ \hline \end{array}$

Practice

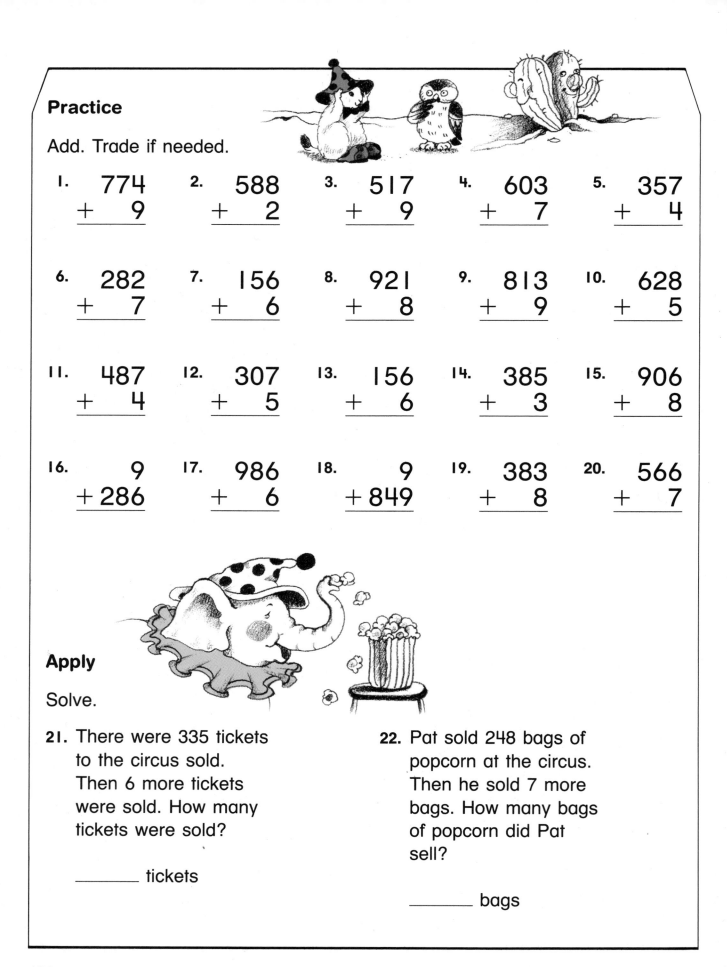

Add. Trade if needed.

1. $774 + 9$
2. $588 + 2$
3. $517 + 9$
4. $603 + 7$
5. $357 + 4$

6. $282 + 7$
7. $156 + 6$
8. $921 + 8$
9. $813 + 9$
10. $628 + 5$

11. $487 + 4$
12. $307 + 5$
13. $156 + 6$
14. $385 + 3$
15. $906 + 8$

16. $9 + 286$
17. $986 + 6$
18. $9 + 849$
19. $383 + 8$
20. $566 + 7$

Apply

Solve.

21. There were 335 tickets to the circus sold. Then 6 more tickets were sold. How many tickets were sold?

_____ tickets

22. Pat sold 248 bags of popcorn at the circus. Then he sold 7 more bags. How many bags of popcorn did Pat sell?

_____ bags

Adding 3-digit numbers to 1-digit numbers

Adding a 3-digit and a 2-digit Number

Both students and parents bought tickets to the school carnival. How many tickets were sold?

There were _____ student tickets sold.

There were _____ adult tickets sold.

To find how many tickets were sold,

we add _____ and _____.

I sold 257 student tickets.

I sold 82 adult tickets.

Add the ones. Trade if needed.	Add the tens. Trade if needed.	Add the hundreds.
7 + 2 = 9 ones No trade needed.	5 + 8 = 13 tens 13 tens = 1 hundred and 3 tens	1 + 2 = 3 hundreds

$$\begin{array}{r} 257 \\ +\ 82 \\ \hline 9 \end{array} \qquad \begin{array}{r} 2\overset{1}{5}7 \\ +\ 82 \\ \hline 39 \end{array} \qquad \begin{array}{r} \overset{1}{2}\overset{1}{5}7 \\ +\ 82 \\ \hline 339 \end{array}$$

There were _____ carnival tickets sold.

Getting Started

Add. Trade if needed.

1. $\begin{array}{r} 580 \\ +\ 87 \\ \hline \end{array}$
2. $\begin{array}{r} 317 \\ +\ 51 \\ \hline \end{array}$
3. $\begin{array}{r} 271 \\ +\ 46 \\ \hline \end{array}$
4. $\begin{array}{r} 450 \\ +\ 92 \\ \hline \end{array}$
5. $\begin{array}{r} 694 \\ +\ 32 \\ \hline \end{array}$

6. $\begin{array}{r} 474 \\ +\ 21 \\ \hline \end{array}$
7. $\begin{array}{r} 425 \\ +\ 84 \\ \hline \end{array}$
8. $\begin{array}{r} 132 \\ +\ 59 \\ \hline \end{array}$
9. $\begin{array}{r} 230 \\ +\ 87 \\ \hline \end{array}$
10. $\begin{array}{r} 488 \\ +\ 70 \\ \hline \end{array}$

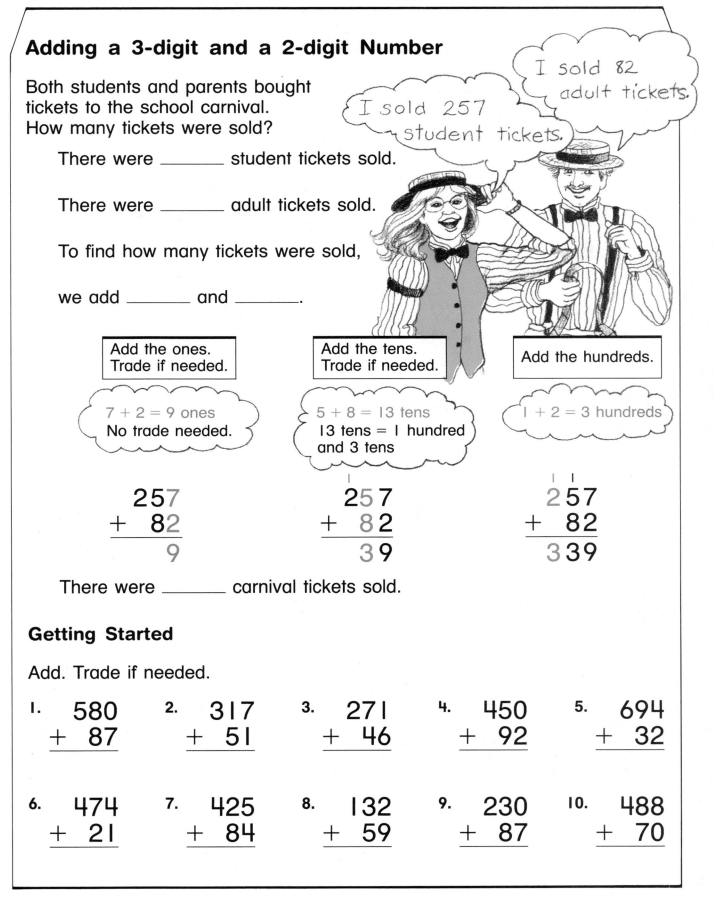

(one hundred eighty-seven) **187**

Practice

Add. Trade if needed.

1. $\begin{array}{r} 279 \\ + \ 12 \\ \hline \end{array}$
2. $\begin{array}{r} 478 \\ + \ 14 \\ \hline \end{array}$
3. $\begin{array}{r} 265 \\ + \ 23 \\ \hline \end{array}$
4. $\begin{array}{r} 343 \\ + \ 49 \\ \hline \end{array}$
5. $\begin{array}{r} 279 \\ + \ 80 \\ \hline \end{array}$

6. $\begin{array}{r} 189 \\ + \ 80 \\ \hline \end{array}$
7. $\begin{array}{r} 191 \\ + \ 53 \\ \hline \end{array}$
8. $\begin{array}{r} 149 \\ + \ 20 \\ \hline \end{array}$
9. $\begin{array}{r} 367 \\ + \ 51 \\ \hline \end{array}$
10. $\begin{array}{r} 186 \\ + \ 21 \\ \hline \end{array}$

11. $\begin{array}{r} 234 \\ + \ 75 \\ \hline \end{array}$
12. $\begin{array}{r} 339 \\ + \ 53 \\ \hline \end{array}$
13. $\begin{array}{r} 322 \\ + \ 74 \\ \hline \end{array}$
14. $\begin{array}{r} 407 \\ + \ 54 \\ \hline \end{array}$
15. $\begin{array}{r} 803 \\ + \ 27 \\ \hline \end{array}$

16. $\begin{array}{r} 725 \\ + \ 15 \\ \hline \end{array}$
17. $\begin{array}{r} 457 \\ + \ 92 \\ \hline \end{array}$
18. $\begin{array}{r} 559 \\ + \ 24 \\ \hline \end{array}$
19. $\begin{array}{r} 753 \\ + \ 38 \\ \hline \end{array}$
20. $\begin{array}{r} 442 \\ + \ 93 \\ \hline \end{array}$

Apply

Solve.

21. Erin saved 276 marbles. Devin gave her 70 more marbles. How many marbles does Erin have now?

   _____ marbles

22. Jason saved 358 stamps. His sister gave him 27 more stamps. How many stamps does Jason have now?

   _____ stamps

Adding a 3-digit and a 2-digit number with one trade

Adding with 2 Trades

The school book store has
275 red pencils and 86 blue pencils.
How many pencils do they have?

We are looking for the total number of pencils.

There are _____ red pencils and _____ blue pencils.

To find the total number of pencils,

we add _____ and _____.

Add the ones. Trade if needed.	Add the tens. Trade if needed.	Add the hundreds.
$5 + 6 = 11$ ones 11 ones = 1 ten and 1 one	$1 + 7 + 8 = 16$ tens 16 tens = 1 hundred and 6 tens	$1 + 2 = 3$ hundreds

$$\begin{array}{r} \overset{1}{2}7\,5 \\ +\ \ 8\,6 \\ \hline 1 \end{array}$$

$$\begin{array}{r} \overset{1}{2}\overset{1}{7}\,5 \\ +\ \ 8\,6 \\ \hline 6\,1 \end{array}$$

$$\begin{array}{r} \overset{1}{2}\overset{1}{7}\,5 \\ +\ \ 8\,6 \\ \hline 3\,6\,1 \end{array}$$

The school book store has _____ pencils.

Getting Started

Add. Trade if needed.

1. $\begin{array}{r} 326 \\ +\ 79 \end{array}$
2. $\begin{array}{r} 542 \\ +\ 88 \end{array}$
3. $\begin{array}{r} 384 \\ +\ 16 \end{array}$
4. $\begin{array}{r} 794 \\ +\ 59 \end{array}$
5. $\begin{array}{r} 453 \\ +\ 98 \end{array}$

6. $\begin{array}{r} 919 \\ +\ 67 \end{array}$
7. $\begin{array}{r} 68 \\ +496 \end{array}$
8. $\begin{array}{r} 154 \\ +\ 96 \end{array}$
9. $\begin{array}{r} 643 \\ +\ 46 \end{array}$
10. $\begin{array}{r} 643 \\ +\ 57 \end{array}$

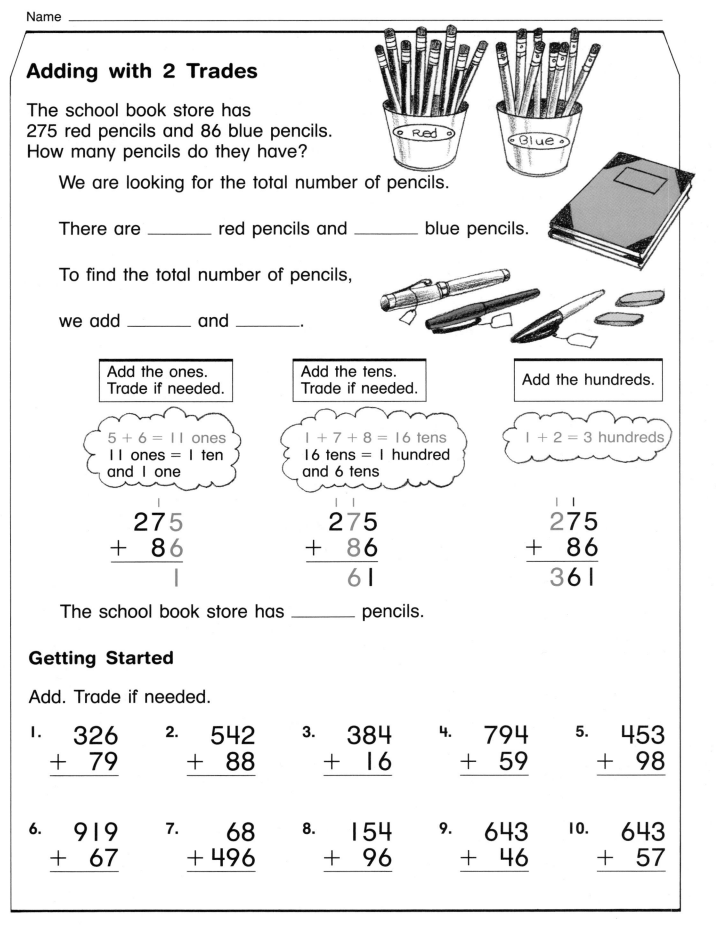

Practice

Add. Trade if needed.

1. $264 + 53$

2. $486 + 45$

3. $332 + 79$

4. $517 + 98$

5. $726 + 75$

6. $154 + 95$

7. $781 + 38$

8. $857 + 69$

9. $695 + 98$

10. $201 + 99$

11. $386 + 76$

12. $850 + 92$

13. $468 + 73$

14. $729 + 58$

15. $596 + 65$

16. $271 + 27$

17. $621 + 84$

18. $586 + 76$

19. $901 + 65$

20. $153 + 73$

21. $615 + 85$

22. $723 + 68$

23. $265 + 39$

24. $37 + 685$

25. $89 + 527$

FIELD TRIP

Complete each Magic Square.

		6
3	5	7
	9	

	0	
2	4	6
	8	1

9	2	7
	10	3

Adding with 0, 1, or 2 trades

Practice Adding with 1 or 2 Trades

There were 355 books and 97 tapes checked out of the school library last week. How many books and tapes were checked out altogether?

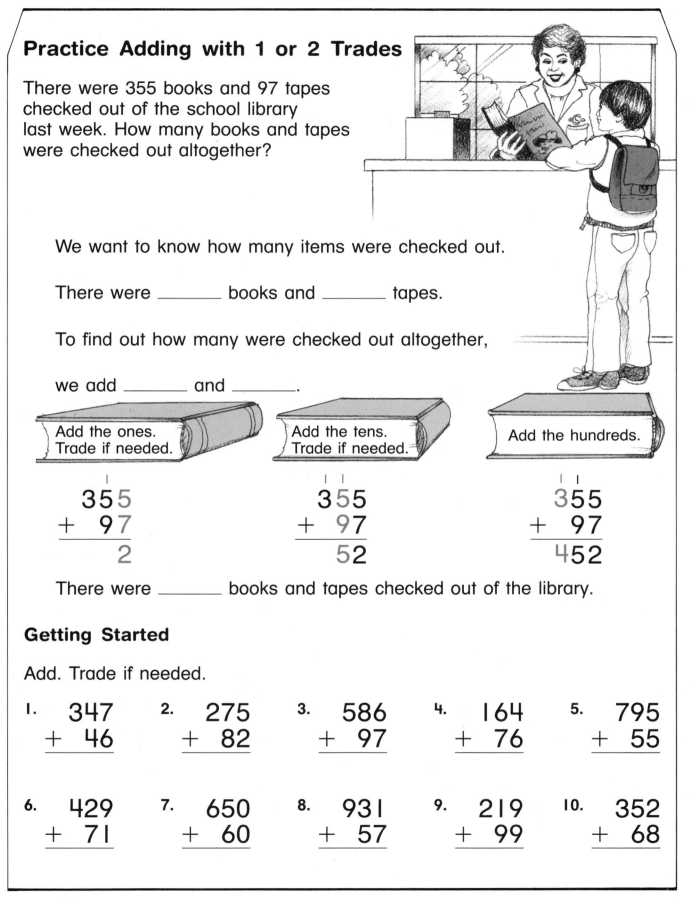

We want to know how many items were checked out.

There were _____ books and _____ tapes.

To find out how many were checked out altogether,

we add _____ and _____.

Add the ones. Trade if needed.

$$\begin{array}{r} 3\,5\,5 \\ +\ \ 9\,7 \\ \hline 2 \end{array}$$

Add the tens. Trade if needed.

$$\begin{array}{r} 3\,5\,5 \\ +\ \ 9\,7 \\ \hline 5\,2 \end{array}$$

Add the hundreds.

$$\begin{array}{r} 3\,5\,5 \\ +\ \ 9\,7 \\ \hline 4\,5\,2 \end{array}$$

There were _____ books and tapes checked out of the library.

Getting Started

Add. Trade if needed.

1. $\begin{array}{r} 347 \\ +\ 46 \\ \hline \end{array}$
2. $\begin{array}{r} 275 \\ +\ 82 \\ \hline \end{array}$
3. $\begin{array}{r} 586 \\ +\ 97 \\ \hline \end{array}$
4. $\begin{array}{r} 164 \\ +\ 76 \\ \hline \end{array}$
5. $\begin{array}{r} 795 \\ +\ 55 \\ \hline \end{array}$

6. $\begin{array}{r} 429 \\ +\ 71 \\ \hline \end{array}$
7. $\begin{array}{r} 650 \\ +\ 60 \\ \hline \end{array}$
8. $\begin{array}{r} 931 \\ +\ 57 \\ \hline \end{array}$
9. $\begin{array}{r} 219 \\ +\ 99 \\ \hline \end{array}$
10. $\begin{array}{r} 352 \\ +\ 68 \\ \hline \end{array}$

Practice

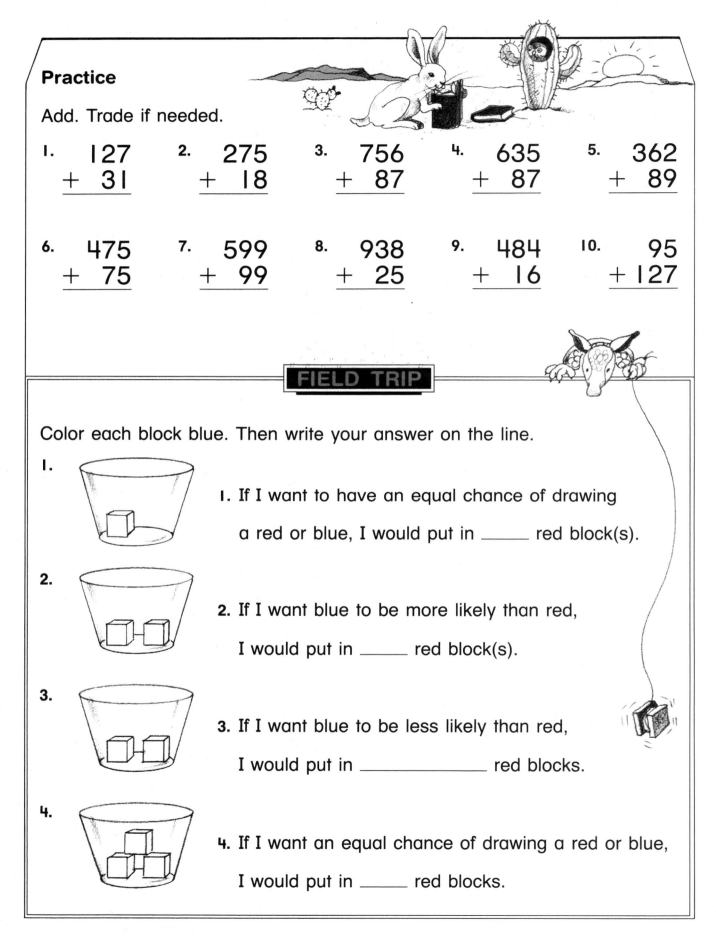

Add. Trade if needed.

1. 127
    + 31

2. 275
    + 18

3. 756
    + 87

4. 635
    + 87

5. 362
    + 89

6. 475
    + 75

7. 599
    + 99

8. 938
    + 25

9. 484
    + 16

10. 95
    +127

FIELD TRIP

Color each block blue. Then write your answer on the line.

1.

1. If I want to have an equal chance of drawing a red or blue, I would put in _____ red block(s).

2.

2. If I want blue to be more likely than red, I would put in _____ red block(s).

3.

3. If I want blue to be less likely than red, I would put in _____ red blocks.

4.

4. If I want an equal chance of drawing a red or blue, I would put in _____ red blocks.

Adding with 1 or 2 trades

Name _____

Adding Two 3-digit Numbers

Plans were made by 128 parents at Lincoln School for a spring picnic. 375 children signed up to go. How many children and parents went to the picnic?

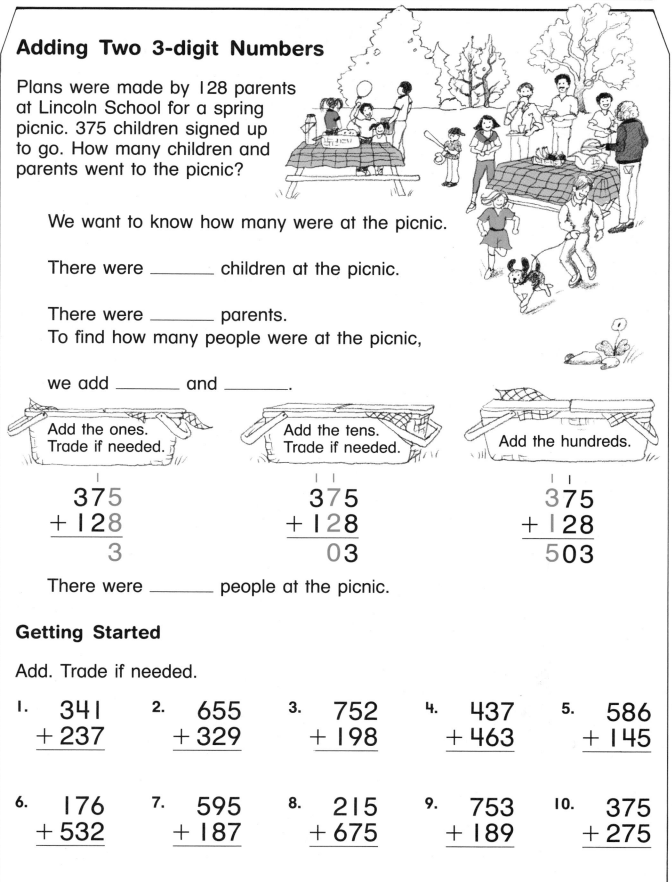

We want to know how many were at the picnic.

There were _____ children at the picnic.

There were _____ parents.
To find how many people were at the picnic,

we add _____ and _____ .

Add the ones.
Trade if needed.

$$\begin{array}{r} 375 \\ +\ 128 \\ \hline 3 \end{array}$$

Add the tens.
Trade if needed.

$$\begin{array}{r} 375 \\ +\ 128 \\ \hline 03 \end{array}$$

Add the hundreds.

$$\begin{array}{r} 375 \\ +\ 128 \\ \hline 503 \end{array}$$

There were _____ people at the picnic.

Getting Started

Add. Trade if needed.

1. $\begin{array}{r} 341 \\ +237 \end{array}$
2. $\begin{array}{r} 655 \\ +329 \end{array}$
3. $\begin{array}{r} 752 \\ +198 \end{array}$
4. $\begin{array}{r} 437 \\ +463 \end{array}$
5. $\begin{array}{r} 586 \\ +145 \end{array}$

6. $\begin{array}{r} 176 \\ +532 \end{array}$
7. $\begin{array}{r} 595 \\ +187 \end{array}$
8. $\begin{array}{r} 215 \\ +675 \end{array}$
9. $\begin{array}{r} 753 \\ +189 \end{array}$
10. $\begin{array}{r} 375 \\ +275 \end{array}$

Practice

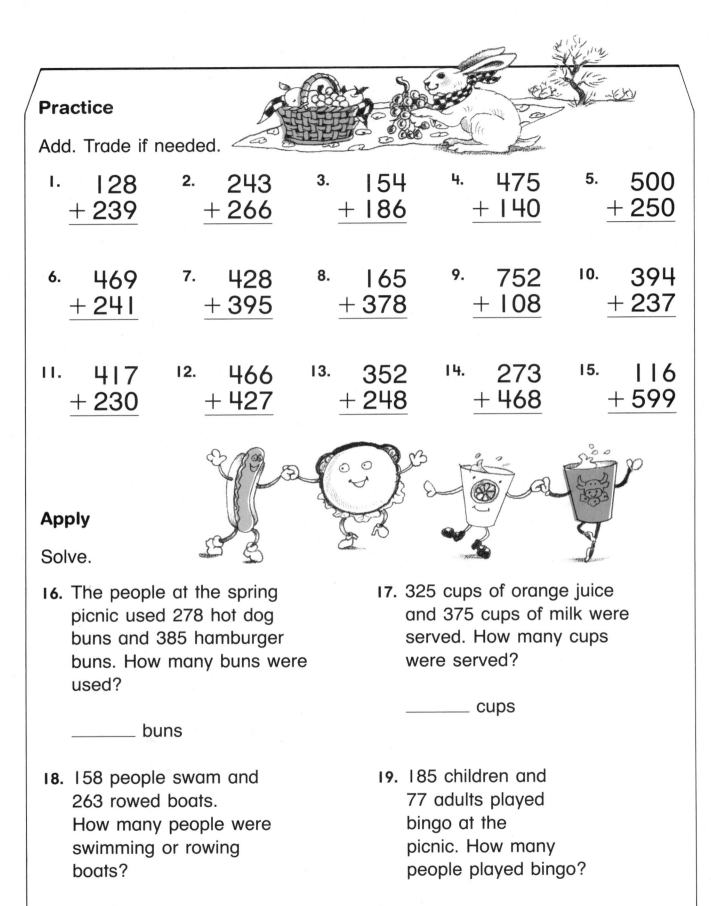

Add. Trade if needed.

1.	128 +239	2.	243 +266	3.	154 +186	4.	475 +140	5.	500 +250
6.	469 +241	7.	428 +395	8.	165 +378	9.	752 +108	10.	394 +237
11.	417 +230	12.	466 +427	13.	352 +248	14.	273 +468	15.	116 +599

Apply

Solve.

16. The people at the spring picnic used 278 hot dog buns and 385 hamburger buns. How many buns were used?

_____ buns

17. 325 cups of orange juice and 375 cups of milk were served. How many cups were served?

_____ cups

18. 158 people swam and 263 rowed boats. How many people were swimming or rowing boats?

_____ people

19. 185 children and 77 adults played bingo at the picnic. How many people played bingo?

_____ people

Adding two 3-digit numbers

Adding 3-digit Numbers

Roger's grandfather works in a bakery. Each day he bakes 228 loaves of white bread and 198 loaves of wheat bread. How many loaves does he bake each day?

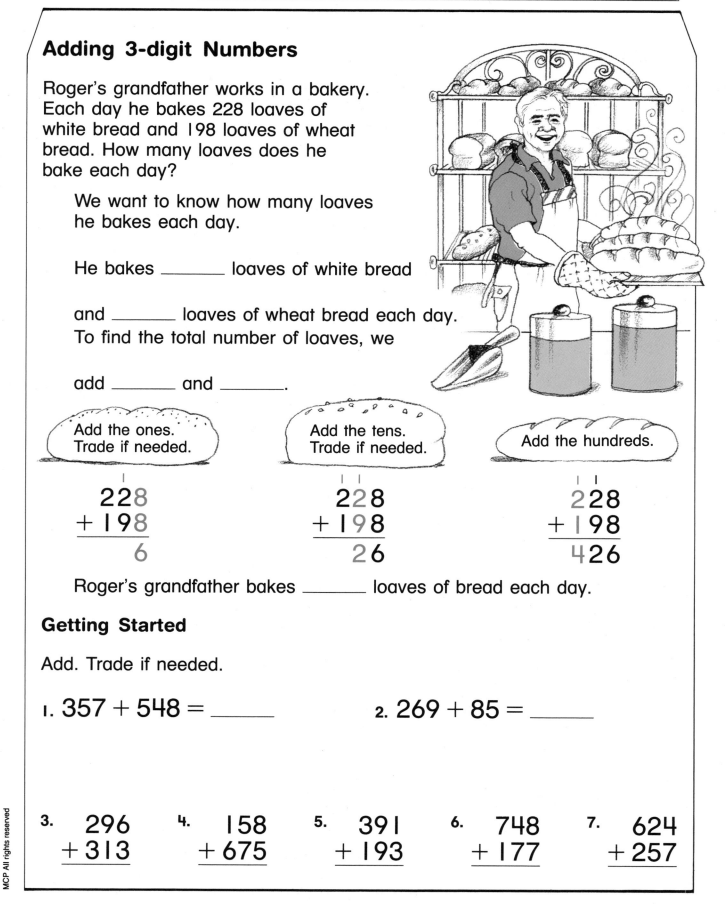

We want to know how many loaves he bakes each day.

He bakes _____ loaves of white bread

and _____ loaves of wheat bread each day. To find the total number of loaves, we

add _____ and _____.

Add the ones. Trade if needed.

$$\begin{array}{r} 228 \\ +198 \\ \hline 6 \end{array}$$

Add the tens. Trade if needed.

$$\begin{array}{r} 228 \\ +198 \\ \hline 26 \end{array}$$

Add the hundreds.

$$\begin{array}{r} 228 \\ +198 \\ \hline 426 \end{array}$$

Roger's grandfather bakes _____ loaves of bread each day.

Getting Started

Add. Trade if needed.

1. $357 + 548 =$ _____

2. $269 + 85 =$ _____

3. $\begin{array}{r} 296 \\ +313 \\ \hline \end{array}$

4. $\begin{array}{r} 158 \\ +675 \\ \hline \end{array}$

5. $\begin{array}{r} 391 \\ +193 \\ \hline \end{array}$

6. $\begin{array}{r} 748 \\ +177 \\ \hline \end{array}$

7. $\begin{array}{r} 624 \\ +257 \\ \hline \end{array}$

Practice

Add. Trade if needed.

1. $166 + 351 =$ _____

2. $449 + 276 =$ _____

3. $256 + 68 =$ _____

4. $159 + 681 =$ _____

5. $\begin{array}{r} 275 \\ + 323 \\ \hline \end{array}$

6. $\begin{array}{r} 384 \\ + 119 \\ \hline \end{array}$

7. $\begin{array}{r} 525 \\ + 195 \\ \hline \end{array}$

8. $\begin{array}{r} 436 \\ + 297 \\ \hline \end{array}$

9. $\begin{array}{r} 523 \\ + 288 \\ \hline \end{array}$

10. $\begin{array}{r} 35 \\ + 265 \\ \hline \end{array}$

11. $\begin{array}{r} 96 \\ + 875 \\ \hline \end{array}$

12. $\begin{array}{r} 105 \\ + 196 \\ \hline \end{array}$

13. $\begin{array}{r} 57 \\ + 288 \\ \hline \end{array}$

14. $\begin{array}{r} 441 \\ + 82 \\ \hline \end{array}$

15. $\begin{array}{r} 73 \\ + 580 \\ \hline \end{array}$

16. $\begin{array}{r} 394 \\ + 262 \\ \hline \end{array}$

17. $\begin{array}{r} 546 \\ + 254 \\ \hline \end{array}$

18. $\begin{array}{r} 9 \\ + 215 \\ \hline \end{array}$

19. $\begin{array}{r} 751 \\ + 163 \\ \hline \end{array}$

20. $\begin{array}{r} 95 \\ + 438 \\ \hline \end{array}$

21. $\begin{array}{r} 526 \\ + 175 \\ \hline \end{array}$

22. $\begin{array}{r} 253 \\ + 288 \\ \hline \end{array}$

23. $\begin{array}{r} 615 \\ + 173 \\ \hline \end{array}$

24. $\begin{array}{r} 252 \\ + 308 \\ \hline \end{array}$

Practice adding 3-digit numbers with trading

Adding Money

Dino went to the store for his Mother.
How much did he spend for bread and meat?

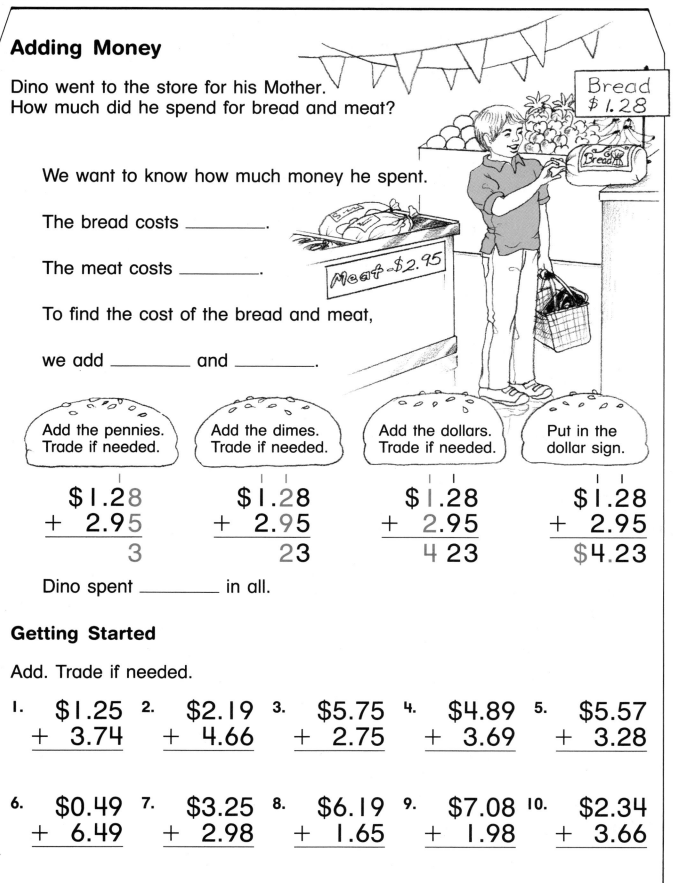

Bread
$1.28

Meat-$2.95

We want to know how much money he spent.

The bread costs _____.

The meat costs _____.

To find the cost of the bread and meat,

we add _____ and _____.

Add the pennies. Trade if needed.	Add the dimes. Trade if needed.	Add the dollars. Trade if needed.	Put in the dollar sign.
$1.28 + 2.95 ___ 3	$1.28 + 2.95 ___ 23	$1.28 + 2.95 ___ 4 23	$1.28 + 2.95 ___ $4.23

Dino spent _____ in all.

Getting Started

Add. Trade if needed.

1. $1.25
   + 3.74

2. $2.19
   + 4.66

3. $5.75
   + 2.75

4. $4.89
   + 3.69

5. $5.57
   + 3.28

6. $0.49
   + 6.49

7. $3.25
   + 2.98

8. $6.19
   + 1.65

9. $7.08
   + 1.98

10. $2.34
   + 3.66

Practice

Add. Trade if needed.

1.	2.	3.	4.	5.
$\begin{array}{r} \$4.38 \\ +\ 1.28 \\ \hline \end{array}$	$\begin{array}{r} \$3.15 \\ +\ 3.42 \\ \hline \end{array}$	$\begin{array}{r} \$4.87 \\ +\ 3.76 \\ \hline \end{array}$	$\begin{array}{r} \$2.65 \\ +\ 0.65 \\ \hline \end{array}$	$\begin{array}{r} \$7.09 \\ +\ 1.95 \\ \hline \end{array}$

Apply

Add to find the total cost.

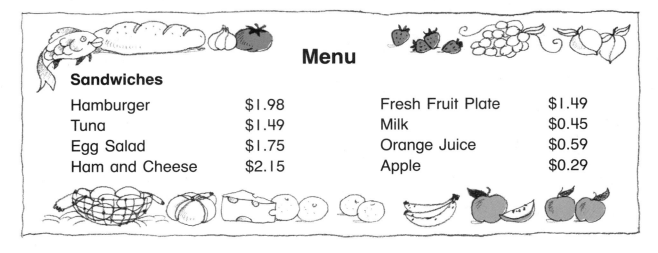

Menu

Sandwiches

Hamburger	$1.98	Fresh Fruit Plate	$1.49
Tuna	$1.49	Milk	$0.45
Egg Salad	$1.75	Orange Juice	$0.59
Ham and Cheese	$2.15	Apple	$0.29

6. Hamburger
   Milk

7. Fresh Fruit Plate
   Milk

8. Tuna Sandwich
   Orange Juice

9. Ham and Cheese Sandwich
   Apple

10. Hamburger
    Fresh Fruit Plate

11. Tuna Sandwich
    Fresh Fruit Plate

12. Egg Salad Sandwich
    Milk

13. Ham and Cheese Sandwich
    Orange Juice

Adding money using dollar notation

Problem Solving

Ticket Prices

Adults $2.75
Children $1.50

COUNTY FAIR

Attendance

Saturday 465
Sunday 298
Monday 320
Tuesday 267

Use the signs above to solve these problems.

1. Mr. Brooks took his eight-year-old daughter to the county fair. How much did he pay for two tickets?

   _____

2. Mr. and Mrs. Velez went to the fair. How much did they pay for two adult tickets?

   _____

3. Robin and Peter are going to the fair. How much did they pay for two children's tickets?

   _____

4. How many people went to the fair on Sunday and Monday?

   _____ people

5. If Robin and Peter in exercise 3 had $5.00, could they have bought one more children's ticket to the fair?

   _____

6. Were there more people at the fair on Saturday and Sunday or on Monday and Tuesday?

   _____

More Problem Solving

County Fair Animals

87 horses
256 cows
107 pigs
127 sheep
148 rabbits

Use the sign to solve these problems.

1. How many horses and cows are shown at the fair?

   _____ horses and cows

2. How many sheep and rabbits are shown at the fair?

   _____ sheep and rabbits

3. How many horses and rabbits are shown at the fair?

   _____ horses and rabbits

4. How many pigs and sheep are shown at the fair?

   _____ pigs and sheep

5. How many pigs and rabbits are shown at the fair?

   _____ pigs and rabbits

6. How many cows and sheep are shown at the fair?

   _____ cows and sheep

Problem solving

CHAPTER CHECKUP

Add. Trade if needed.

1. $341 + 7$

2. $188 + 6$

3. $259 + 4$

4. $525 + 5$

5. $707 + 9$

6. $218 + 81$

7. $175 + 16$

8. $387 + 57$

9. $696 + 73$

10. $575 + 25$

11. $27 + 365$

12. $56 + 128$

13. $75 + 250$

14. $126 + 109$

15. $361 + 278$

16. $613 + 274$

17. $338 + 255$

18. $459 + 382$

19. $175 + 328$

20. $524 + 176$

21. $\$2.25 + 0.31$

22. $\$3.36 + 1.47$

23. $\$5.23 + 1.95$

24. $\$3.37 + 5.63$

Solve.

25. Jaime spent $2.75. Mona spent $3.65. How much did they spend altogether?

_____

26. The Browns drove 245 miles on Saturday. They drove 188 miles on Sunday. How many miles did they drive altogether?

_____ miles

ROUNDUP REVIEW

Fill in the oval next to the correct answer.

1.
   - ○ 1:25
   - ○ 2:25
   - ○ 3:25
   - ○ NG

2.
   - ○ 36
   - ○ 64
   - ○ 46
   - ○ NG

3.
   - ○ 204
   - ○ 240
   - ○ 402
   - ○ NG

4. 38 ○ 52
   - ○ >
   - ○ <

5.
   - ○ $1.66
   - ○ 60¢
   - ○ $1.56
   - ○ NG

6. $\begin{array}{r} 98 \\ -\ 26 \\ \hline \end{array}$
   - ○ 124
   - ○ 72
   - ○ 36
   - ○ NG

7. $\begin{array}{r} 84 \\ -\ 47 \\ \hline \end{array}$
   - ○ 47
   - ○ 131
   - ○ 43
   - ○ NG

8. $\begin{array}{r} 91 \\ -\ 27 \\ \hline \end{array}$
   - ○ 74
   - ○ 64
   - ○ 76
   - ○ NG

9. 38 + 99
   - ○ 127
   - ○ 1217
   - ○ 137
   - ○ NG

10. $\begin{array}{r} 75 \\ +\ 85 \\ \hline \end{array}$
    - ○ 150
    - ○ 170
    - ○ 160
    - ○ NG

11. $\begin{array}{r} 346 \\ +\ 73 \\ \hline \end{array}$
    - ○ 319
    - ○ 419
    - ○ 429
    - ○ NG

12. $\begin{array}{r} 638 \\ +\ 267 \\ \hline \end{array}$
    - ○ 905
    - ○ 895
    - ○ 805
    - ○ NG

13. $\begin{array}{r} 135 \\ +\ 396 \\ \hline \end{array}$
    - ○ 421
    - ○ 531
    - ○ 431
    - ○ NG

☐ score

202 (two hundred two)

Cumulative review

11 SUBTRACTION, 3-DIGIT NUMBERS

Subtracting 1 Digit from 2 Digits

The Tidy Pet Shop had 33 turtles.
Some were sold. How many are left?

We're looking for the number not sold.

The pet shop had _____ turtles.

They sold _____ turtles.

To find how many are left,

we subtract _____ from _____.

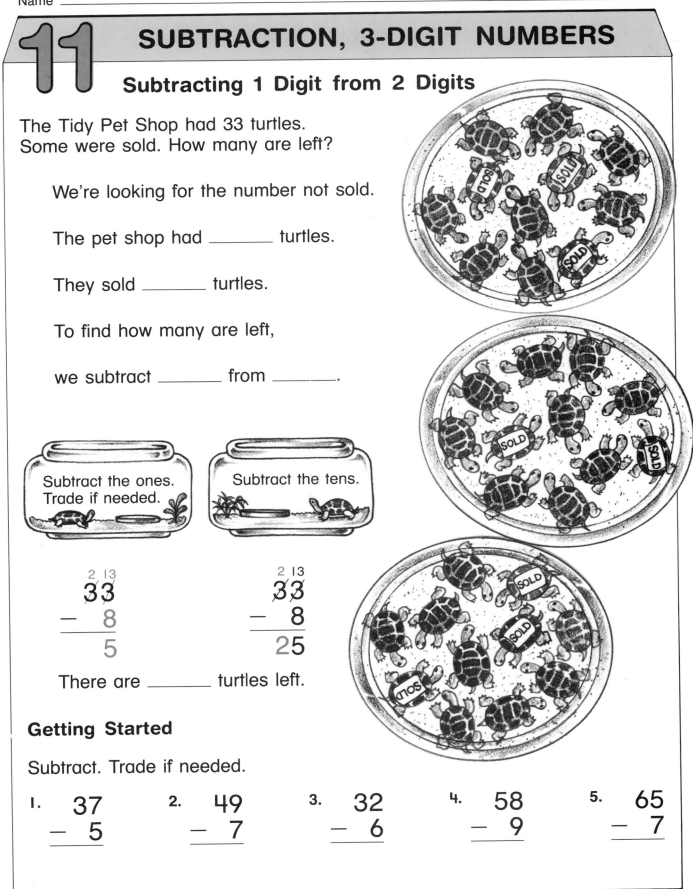

Subtract the ones.
Trade if needed.

Subtract the tens.

$$\begin{array}{r} {\scriptstyle 2\;13} \\ \cancel{33} \\ -\;\;8 \\ \hline 5 \end{array} \qquad \begin{array}{r} {\scriptstyle 2\;13} \\ \cancel{33} \\ -\;\;8 \\ \hline 25 \end{array}$$

There are _____ turtles left.

Getting Started

Subtract. Trade if needed.

1.	2.	3.	4.	5.
$\begin{array}{r} 37 \\ -\;5 \\ \hline \end{array}$	$\begin{array}{r} 49 \\ -\;7 \\ \hline \end{array}$	$\begin{array}{r} 32 \\ -\;6 \\ \hline \end{array}$	$\begin{array}{r} 58 \\ -\;9 \\ \hline \end{array}$	$\begin{array}{r} 65 \\ -\;7 \\ \hline \end{array}$

Practice

Subtract. Trade if needed.

1. $\begin{array}{r} 18 \\ -\ 5 \\ \hline \end{array}$
2. $\begin{array}{r} 27 \\ -\ 3 \\ \hline \end{array}$
3. $\begin{array}{r} 13 \\ -\ 4 \\ \hline \end{array}$
4. $\begin{array}{r} 57 \\ -\ 6 \\ \hline \end{array}$
5. $\begin{array}{r} 41 \\ -\ 8 \\ \hline \end{array}$

6. $\begin{array}{r} 63 \\ -\ 6 \\ \hline \end{array}$
7. $\begin{array}{r} 45 \\ -\ 2 \\ \hline \end{array}$
8. $\begin{array}{r} 77 \\ -\ 8 \\ \hline \end{array}$
9. $\begin{array}{r} 88 \\ -\ 6 \\ \hline \end{array}$
10. $\begin{array}{r} 93 \\ -\ 4 \\ \hline \end{array}$

11. $\begin{array}{r} 25 \\ -\ 5 \\ \hline \end{array}$
12. $\begin{array}{r} 38 \\ -\ 1 \\ \hline \end{array}$
13. $\begin{array}{r} 57 \\ -\ 9 \\ \hline \end{array}$
14. $\begin{array}{r} 47 \\ -\ 3 \\ \hline \end{array}$
15. $\begin{array}{r} 63 \\ -\ 7 \\ \hline \end{array}$

16. $\begin{array}{r} 31 \\ -\ 7 \\ \hline \end{array}$
17. $\begin{array}{r} 87 \\ -\ 8 \\ \hline \end{array}$
18. $\begin{array}{r} 68 \\ -\ 3 \\ \hline \end{array}$
19. $\begin{array}{r} 44 \\ -\ 8 \\ \hline \end{array}$
20. $\begin{array}{r} 55 \\ -\ 7 \\ \hline \end{array}$

Apply

Solve.

21. The pet shop had 42 kittens for sale. They sold 9 kittens. How many kittens are left?

_____ kittens

22. The pet shop had 61 dog collars for sale. Sal sold 7 collars. How many collars are left?

_____ collars

23. There were 55 fish. Trish bought 9. How many fish are left?

_____ fish

24. There were 75 puppies for sale. Walter sold 6. How many puppies are left?

_____ puppies

Subtracting a 1-digit from a 2-digit number

Name _____

Subtracting 2 Digits from 2 Digits

Dana School had a roller skating party. There were 65 children and 27 adults skating. How many more children than adults were skating?

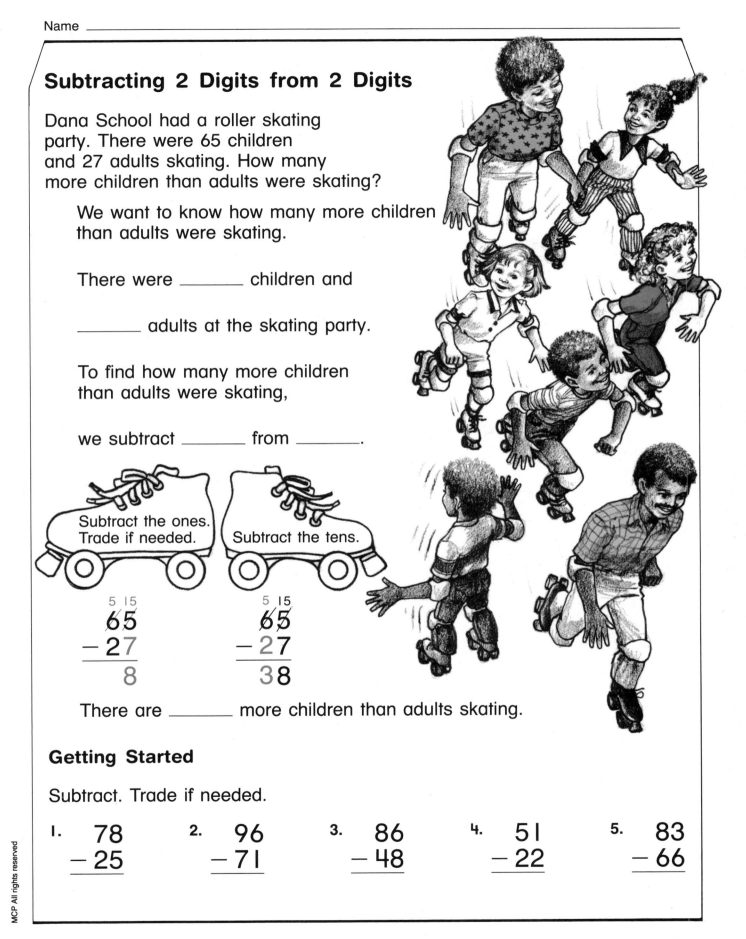

We want to know how many more children than adults were skating.

There were _____ children and

_____ adults at the skating party.

To find how many more children than adults were skating,

we subtract _____ from _____.

Subtract the ones. Trade if needed.

$$\begin{array}{r} \overset{5\;\;15}{\cancel{6}\cancel{5}} \\ -\;2\;7 \\ \hline 8 \end{array}$$

Subtract the tens.

$$\begin{array}{r} \overset{5\;\;15}{\cancel{6}\cancel{5}} \\ -\;2\;7 \\ \hline 3\;8 \end{array}$$

There are _____ more children than adults skating.

Getting Started

Subtract. Trade if needed.

1.	2.	3.	4.	5.
$\begin{array}{r} 78 \\ -25 \\ \hline \end{array}$	$\begin{array}{r} 96 \\ -71 \\ \hline \end{array}$	$\begin{array}{r} 86 \\ -48 \\ \hline \end{array}$	$\begin{array}{r} 51 \\ -22 \\ \hline \end{array}$	$\begin{array}{r} 83 \\ -66 \\ \hline \end{array}$

Practice

Subtract. Trade if needed.

1. $\begin{array}{r} 47 \\ -41 \\ \hline \end{array}$
2. $\begin{array}{r} 67 \\ -17 \\ \hline \end{array}$
3. $\begin{array}{r} 92 \\ -60 \\ \hline \end{array}$
4. $\begin{array}{r} 96 \\ -89 \\ \hline \end{array}$
5. $\begin{array}{r} 63 \\ -59 \\ \hline \end{array}$

6. $\begin{array}{r} 73 \\ -26 \\ \hline \end{array}$
7. $\begin{array}{r} 61 \\ -45 \\ \hline \end{array}$
8. $\begin{array}{r} 96 \\ -78 \\ \hline \end{array}$
9. $\begin{array}{r} 81 \\ -43 \\ \hline \end{array}$
10. $\begin{array}{r} 65 \\ -47 \\ \hline \end{array}$

11. $\begin{array}{r} 95 \\ -87 \\ \hline \end{array}$
12. $\begin{array}{r} 88 \\ -83 \\ \hline \end{array}$
13. $\begin{array}{r} 92 \\ -63 \\ \hline \end{array}$
14. $\begin{array}{r} 49 \\ -25 \\ \hline \end{array}$
15. $\begin{array}{r} 38 \\ -16 \\ \hline \end{array}$

16. $\begin{array}{r} 62 \\ -14 \\ \hline \end{array}$
17. $\begin{array}{r} 71 \\ -31 \\ \hline \end{array}$
18. $\begin{array}{r} 66 \\ -49 \\ \hline \end{array}$
19. $\begin{array}{r} 87 \\ -36 \\ \hline \end{array}$
20. $\begin{array}{r} 64 \\ -16 \\ \hline \end{array}$

21. $\begin{array}{r} 72 \\ -43 \\ \hline \end{array}$
22. $\begin{array}{r} 52 \\ -30 \\ \hline \end{array}$
23. $\begin{array}{r} 47 \\ -21 \\ \hline \end{array}$
24. $\begin{array}{r} 63 \\ -39 \\ \hline \end{array}$
25. $\begin{array}{r} 81 \\ -56 \\ \hline \end{array}$

Apply

Solve.

26. There were 41 girls and 24 boys skating. How many more girls than boys were skating?

_____ more girls

27. Art skated around the rink 75 times. Ro skated around the rink 57 times. How many more times did Art skate around the rink?

_____ times

Subtracting a 2-digit from a 2-digit number

Subtracting 1 Digit from 3 Digits

341 children went to the zoo.
9 parents went to the zoo.
How many more children than
parents went to the zoo?

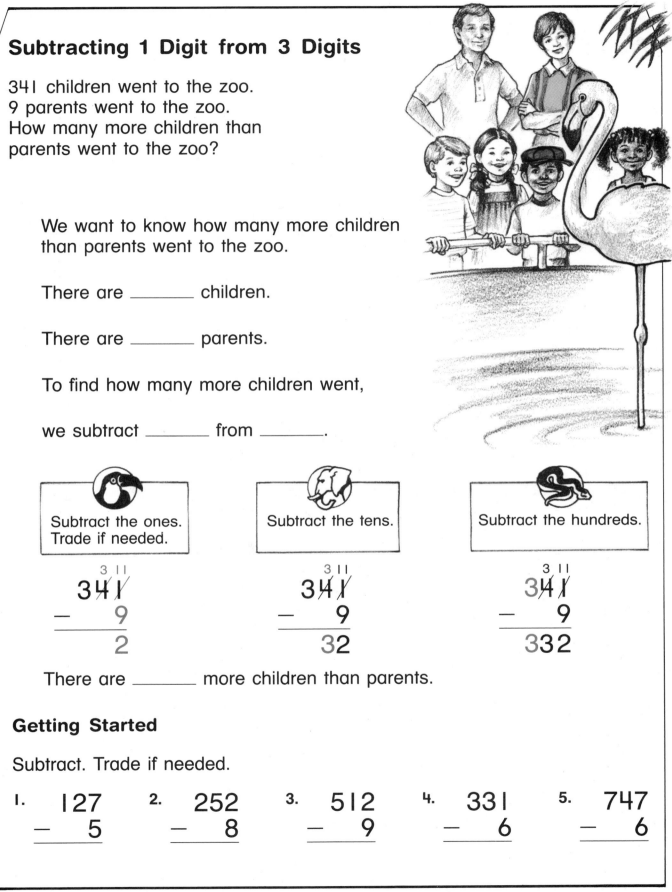

We want to know how many more children
than parents went to the zoo.

There are _____ children.

There are _____ parents.

To find how many more children went,

we subtract _____ from _____.

Subtract the ones. Trade if needed.	Subtract the tens.	Subtract the hundreds.

$$\begin{array}{r} \overset{3\ 11}{3\cancel{4}\cancel{1}} \\ -\ \ \ 9 \\ \hline 2 \end{array}$$

$$\begin{array}{r} \overset{3\ 11}{3\cancel{4}\cancel{1}} \\ -\ \ \ 9 \\ \hline 32 \end{array}$$

$$\begin{array}{r} \overset{3\ 11}{3\cancel{4}\cancel{1}} \\ -\ \ \ 9 \\ \hline 332 \end{array}$$

There are _____ more children than parents.

Getting Started

Subtract. Trade if needed.

1. $\begin{array}{r} 127 \\ -\ \ 5 \\ \hline \end{array}$	2. $\begin{array}{r} 252 \\ -\ \ 8 \\ \hline \end{array}$	3. $\begin{array}{r} 512 \\ -\ \ 9 \\ \hline \end{array}$	4. $\begin{array}{r} 331 \\ -\ \ 6 \\ \hline \end{array}$	5. $\begin{array}{r} 747 \\ -\ \ 6 \\ \hline \end{array}$

Practice

Subtract. Trade if needed.

1. $229 - 4$
2. $636 - 8$
3. $399 - 9$
4. $851 - 7$
5. $233 - 4$

6. $137 - 5$
7. $141 - 7$
8. $725 - 6$
9. $911 - 3$
10. $673 - 5$

11. $252 - 6$
12. $341 - 9$
13. $585 - 7$
14. $463 - 9$
15. $224 - 6$

FIELD TRIP

	4th inning
Blue Sox	5
Green Sox	7

Final Score: 9 to 6

Which team won? _____

How do you know? _____

_____

_____

_____

	5th inning
Red Caps	6
Gold Caps	5

Final Score: 8 to 7

Which team won? _____

How do you know? _____

_____

_____

_____

Subtracting a 1-digit from a 3-digit number

Subtracting Multiples of 10

Morgan's Car Sales sold
256 cars in June and 80 cars
in July. How many more cars
were sold in June?

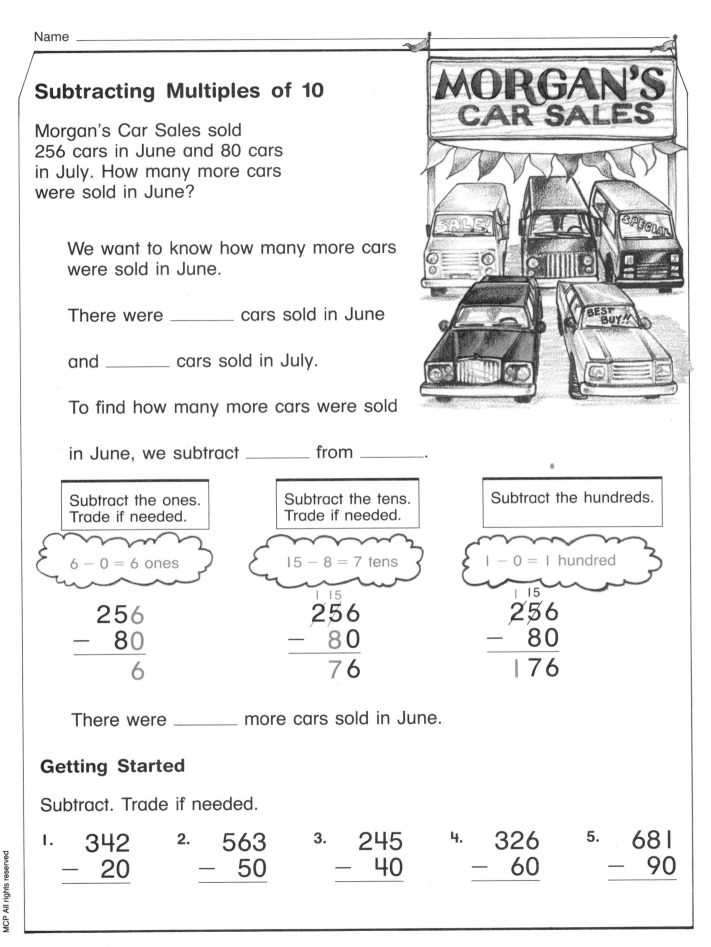

We want to know how many more cars
were sold in June.

There were _____ cars sold in June

and _____ cars sold in July.

To find how many more cars were sold

in June, we subtract _____ from _____.

Subtract the ones. Trade if needed.	Subtract the tens. Trade if needed.	Subtract the hundreds.
$6 - 0 = 6$ ones	$15 - 8 = 7$ tens	$1 - 0 = 1$ hundred
$$\begin{array}{r} 256 \\ -\ 80 \\ \hline 6 \end{array}$$	$$\begin{array}{r} 2\overset{1\ 15}{\cancel{5}}6 \\ -\ 80 \\ \hline 76 \end{array}$$	$$\begin{array}{r} \overset{1\ 15}{2\cancel{5}}6 \\ -\ 80 \\ \hline 176 \end{array}$$

There were _____ more cars sold in June.

Getting Started

Subtract. Trade if needed.

1. $$\begin{array}{r} 342 \\ -\ 20 \\ \hline \end{array}$$
2. $$\begin{array}{r} 563 \\ -\ 50 \\ \hline \end{array}$$
3. $$\begin{array}{r} 245 \\ -\ 40 \\ \hline \end{array}$$
4. $$\begin{array}{r} 326 \\ -\ 60 \\ \hline \end{array}$$
5. $$\begin{array}{r} 681 \\ -\ 90 \\ \hline \end{array}$$

Practice

Subtract. Trade if needed.

1. $636 - 80$
2. $521 - 20$
3. $561 - 80$
4. $327 - 50$
5. $613 - 20$

6. $399 - 30$
7. $229 - 50$
8. $168 - 70$
9. $852 - 90$
10. $355 - 50$

11. $512 - 70$
12. $303 - 50$
13. $756 - 30$
14. $230 - 30$
15. $646 - 60$

16. $116 - 20$
17. $663 - 80$
18. $550 - 70$
19. $909 - 40$
20. $855 - 60$

21. $532 - 50$
22. $763 - 40$
23. $877 - 90$
24. $145 - 30$
25. $315 - 70$

Apply

Solve.

26. During July there were 325 cars and 70 vans sold. How many more cars than vans were sold?

_____ more cars

27. There were 257 used cars on the lot. They sold 80. How many cars were left?

_____ cars

Subtracting a 2-digit multiple of 10

Subtracting 2 Digits from 3 Digits

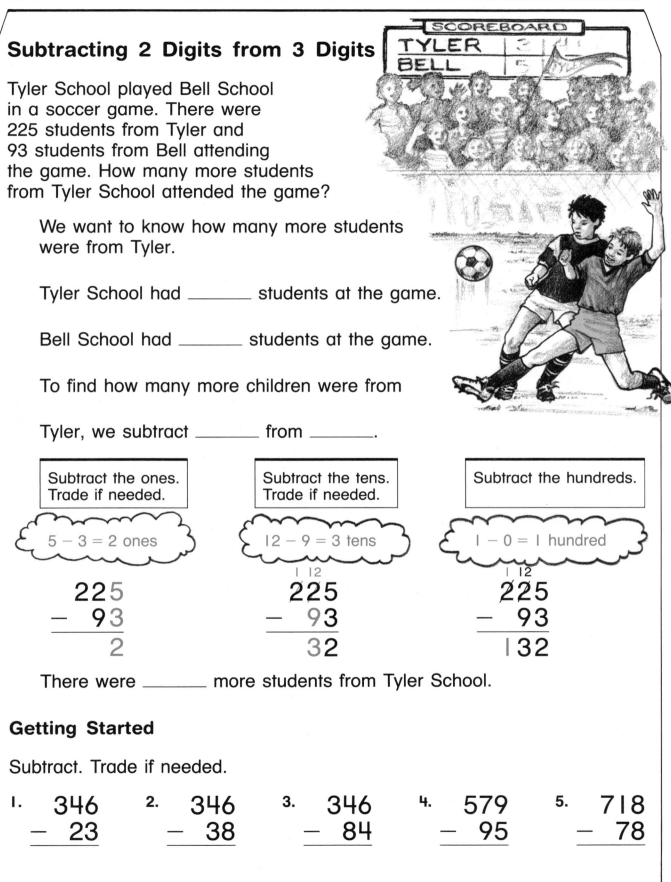

Tyler School played Bell School in a soccer game. There were 225 students from Tyler and 93 students from Bell attending the game. How many more students from Tyler School attended the game?

We want to know how many more students were from Tyler.

Tyler School had _____ students at the game.

Bell School had _____ students at the game.

To find how many more children were from

Tyler, we subtract _____ from _____.

Subtract the ones. Trade if needed.	Subtract the tens. Trade if needed.	Subtract the hundreds.

$5 - 3 = 2$ ones $12 - 9 = 3$ tens $1 - 0 = 1$ hundred

$$
\begin{array}{r}
22\,5 \\
-\ 9\,3 \\
\hline
2
\end{array}
\qquad
\begin{array}{r}
2\overset{1\ 12}{2}5 \\
-\ \ 9\,3 \\
\hline
3\,2
\end{array}
\qquad
\begin{array}{r}
2\overset{1\ 12}{2}5 \\
-\ \ 9\,3 \\
\hline
1\,3\,2
\end{array}
$$

There were _____ more students from Tyler School.

Getting Started

Subtract. Trade if needed.

$$
\begin{array}{lll}
\text{1.} & 346 \\
& -\ 23 \\
\hline
\end{array}
\quad
\begin{array}{lll}
\text{2.} & 346 \\
& -\ 38 \\
\hline
\end{array}
\quad
\begin{array}{lll}
\text{3.} & 346 \\
& -\ 84 \\
\hline
\end{array}
\quad
\begin{array}{lll}
\text{4.} & 579 \\
& -\ 95 \\
\hline
\end{array}
\quad
\begin{array}{lll}
\text{5.} & 718 \\
& -\ 78 \\
\hline
\end{array}
$$

Practice

Subtract. Trade if needed.

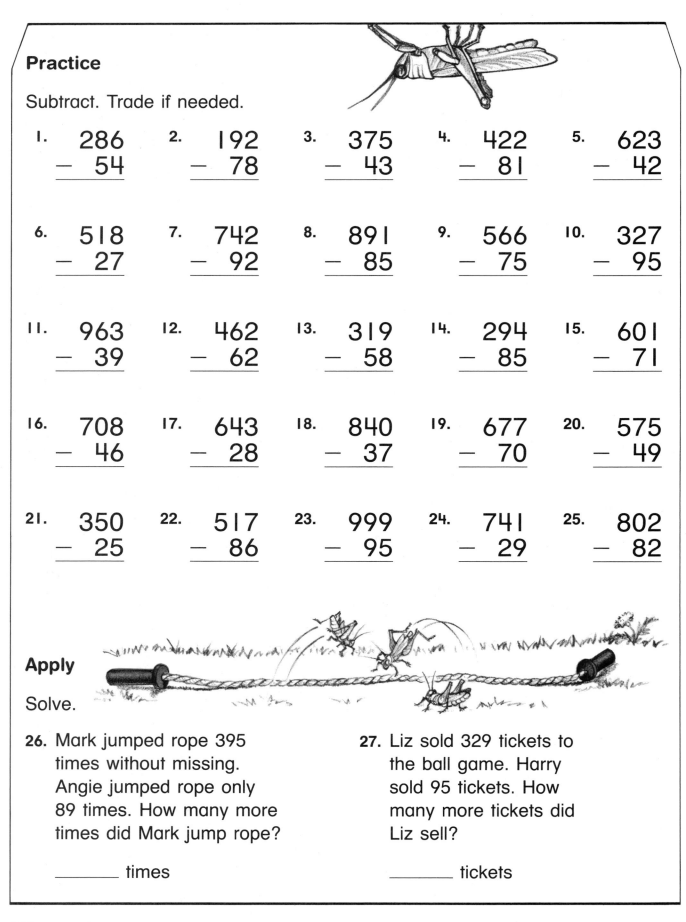

1. $286 - 54$
2. $192 - 78$
3. $375 - 43$
4. $422 - 81$
5. $623 - 42$

6. $518 - 27$
7. $742 - 92$
8. $891 - 85$
9. $566 - 75$
10. $327 - 95$

11. $963 - 39$
12. $462 - 62$
13. $319 - 58$
14. $294 - 85$
15. $601 - 71$

16. $708 - 46$
17. $643 - 28$
18. $840 - 37$
19. $677 - 70$
20. $575 - 49$

21. $350 - 25$
22. $517 - 86$
23. $999 - 95$
24. $741 - 29$
25. $802 - 82$

Apply

Solve.

26. Mark jumped rope 395 times without missing. Angie jumped rope only 89 times. How many more times did Mark jump rope?

_____ times

27. Liz sold 329 tickets to the ball game. Harry sold 95 tickets. How many more tickets did Liz sell?

_____ tickets

Subtracting a 2-digit from a 3-digit number

Subtracting 3-digit Numbers

The Green River adventure store rents rafts, kayaks and canoes. How many more rafts than canoes were rented during August?

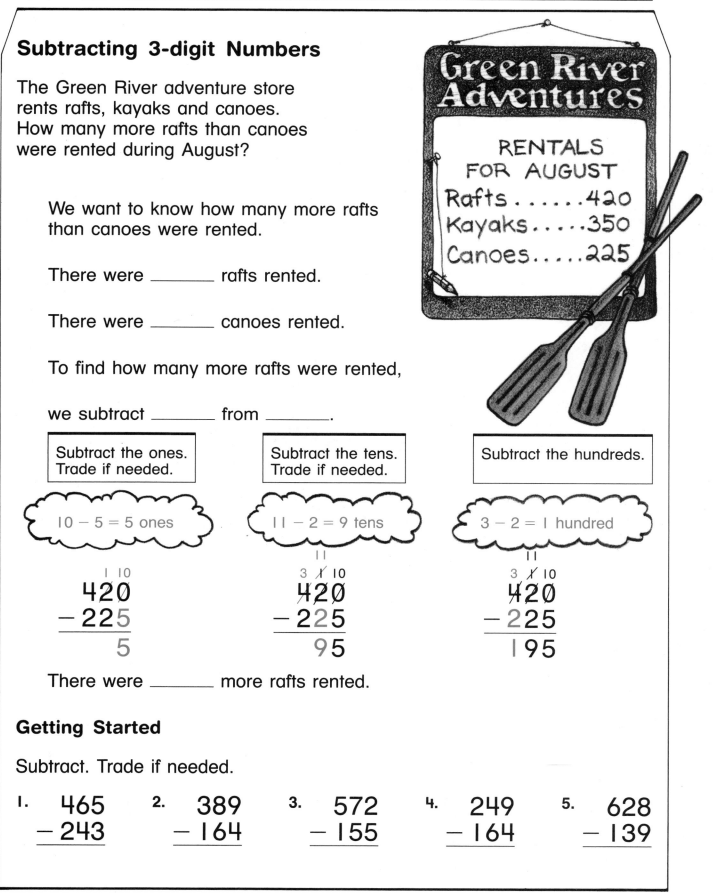

Green River Adventures

RENTALS FOR AUGUST
Rafts......420
Kayaks.....350
Canoes.....225

We want to know how many more rafts than canoes were rented.

There were _____ rafts rented.

There were _____ canoes rented.

To find how many more rafts were rented,

we subtract _____ from _____.

Subtract the ones. Trade if needed.	Subtract the tens. Trade if needed.	Subtract the hundreds.

$10 - 5 = 5$ ones

$$\begin{array}{r} \overset{\scriptstyle 1\ 10}{42\cancel{0}} \\ -225 \\ \hline 5 \end{array}$$

$11 - 2 = 9$ tens

$$\begin{array}{r} \overset{\scriptstyle 3\ \cancel{1}\ 10}{4\cancel{2}\cancel{0}} \\ -225 \\ \hline 95 \end{array}$$

$3 - 2 = 1$ hundred

$$\begin{array}{r} \overset{\scriptstyle 3\ \cancel{1}\ 10}{\cancel{4}\cancel{2}\cancel{0}} \\ -225 \\ \hline 195 \end{array}$$

There were _____ more rafts rented.

Getting Started

Subtract. Trade if needed.

1. $\begin{array}{r} 465 \\ -243 \\ \hline \end{array}$
2. $\begin{array}{r} 389 \\ -164 \\ \hline \end{array}$
3. $\begin{array}{r} 572 \\ -155 \\ \hline \end{array}$
4. $\begin{array}{r} 249 \\ -164 \\ \hline \end{array}$
5. $\begin{array}{r} 628 \\ -139 \\ \hline \end{array}$

Practice

Subtract. Trade if needed.

1. $965 - 234$
2. $782 - 357$
3. $359 - 165$
4. $417 - 186$
5. $531 - 167$

6. $361 - 172$
7. $619 - 285$
8. $999 - 578$
9. $843 - 357$
10. $775 - 298$

11. $375 - 185$
12. $658 - 459$
13. $583 - 196$
14. $417 - 208$
15. $625 - 357$

FIELD TRIP

Complete.

1 hundred = __10__ tens

$104 =$ __10__ tens __4__ ones

$307 =$ _____ tens _____ ones

$208 =$ _____ tens _____ ones

$701 =$ _____ tens _____ ones

Trade 1 ten for 10 ones.

tens	ones
69 70	11 1

tens	ones
50	8

tens	ones
30	2

tens	ones
80	0

Subtract.

tens	ones
80	6
−34	7

tens	ones
50	7
−15	8

tens	ones
60	0
−25	5

tens	ones
80	5
−59	8

Subtracting 3-digit numbers

Subtraction Practice

In the holiday parade there were 452 people marching in bands and 298 in drill teams. How many more people were marching in bands?

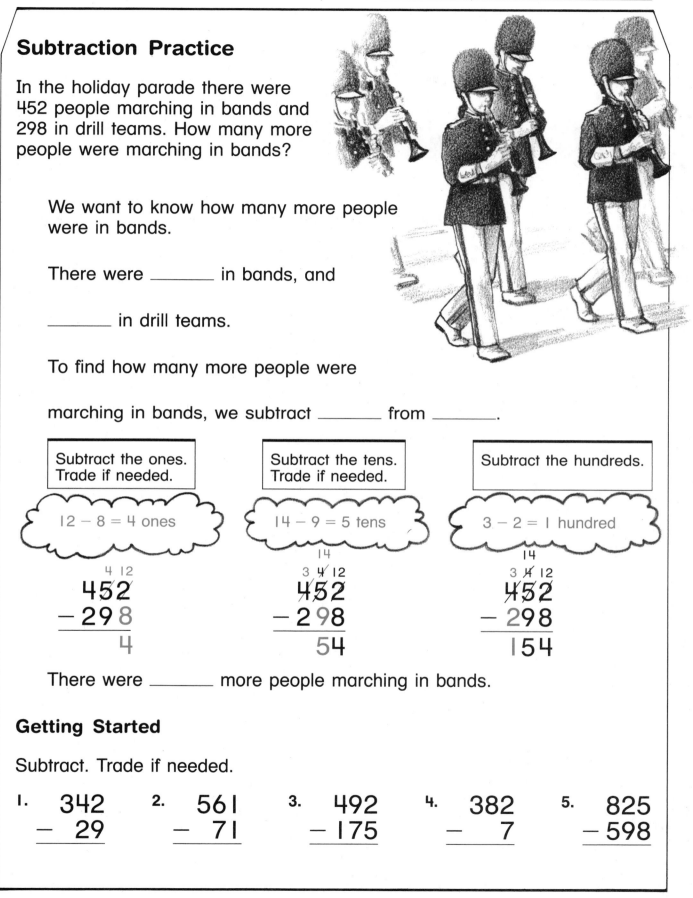

We want to know how many more people were in bands.

There were _____ in bands, and

_____ in drill teams.

To find how many more people were

marching in bands, we subtract _____ from _____.

Subtract the ones. Trade if needed.	Subtract the tens. Trade if needed.	Subtract the hundreds.

$12 - 8 = 4$ ones $\qquad$ $14 - 9 = 5$ tens $\qquad$ $3 - 2 = 1$ hundred

$$
\begin{array}{r} 4\;12 \\ 4\cancel{5}\cancel{2} \\ -\;29\,8 \\ \hline 4 \end{array}
\qquad
\begin{array}{r} 14 \\ 3\;\cancel{4}\;12 \\ \cancel{4}\cancel{5}\cancel{2} \\ -\;298 \\ \hline 54 \end{array}
\qquad
\begin{array}{r} 14 \\ 3\;\cancel{4}\;12 \\ \cancel{4}\cancel{5}\cancel{2} \\ -\;298 \\ \hline 154 \end{array}
$$

There were _____ more people marching in bands.

Getting Started

Subtract. Trade if needed.

1. 342 $-\ 29$	2. 561 $-\ 71$	3. 492 -175	4. 382 $-\ 7$	5. 825 -598

Practice

Subtract. Trade if needed.

1. $342 - 8$
2. $561 - 80$
3. $478 - 96$
4. $658 - 167$
5. $725 - 286$

6. $786 - 451$
7. $892 - 355$
8. $669 - 278$
9. $315 - 192$
10. $669 - 580$

11. $419 - 269$
12. $915 - 400$
13. $643 - 258$
14. $695 - 555$
15. $947 - 589$

16. $456 - 8$
17. $316 - 93$
18. $695 - 636$
19. $721 - 345$
20. $926 - 387$

21. $350 - 75$
22. $736 - 258$
23. $840 - 375$
24. $624 - 398$
25. $261 - 243$

FIELD TRIP

Put in the missing digits.

1.
$$
\begin{array}{r}
3\ 5\ \square \\
-\ 1\ \square\ 2 \\
\hline
2\ 3\ 2
\end{array}
$$

2.
$$
\begin{array}{r}
4\ \square\ 6 \\
-\ \square\ 4\ \square \\
\hline
2\ 3\ 5
\end{array}
$$

3.
$$
\begin{array}{r}
7\ \square\ 7 \\
-\ 3\ 8\ \square \\
\hline
\square\ 7\ 3
\end{array}
$$

Subtraction practice

Subtracting Money

Teresa saved $5.46.
She bought a paint set.
How much money does she have left?

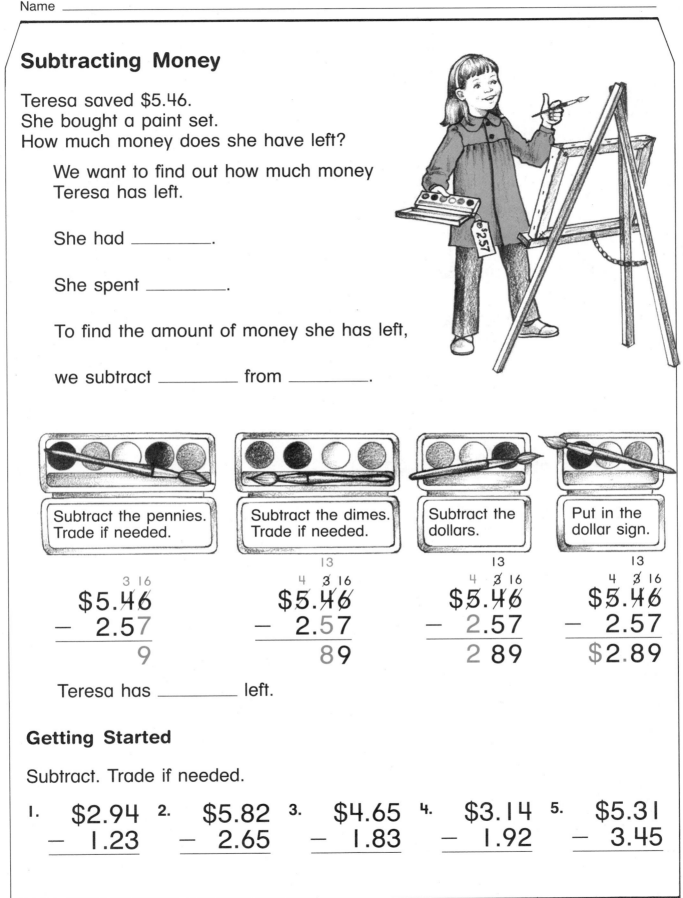

We want to find out how much money Teresa has left.

She had _____.

She spent _____.

To find the amount of money she has left,

we subtract _____ from _____.

Subtract the pennies. Trade if needed.	Subtract the dimes. Trade if needed.	Subtract the dollars.	Put in the dollar sign.
$$\begin{array}{r} \overset{3\ 16}{\$5.4\!\!\!/6} \\ -\ 2.57 \\ \hline 9 \end{array}$$	$$\begin{array}{r} \overset{\ \ \ 13}{\underset{4}{\$5.4\!\!\!/6\!\!\!/}} \\ -\ 2.57 \\ \hline 89 \end{array}$$	$$\begin{array}{r} \overset{\ \ \ 13}{\underset{4}{\$5.4\!\!\!/6\!\!\!/}} \\ -\ 2.57 \\ \hline 2\ 89 \end{array}$$	$$\begin{array}{r} \overset{\ \ \ 13}{\underset{4}{\$5.4\!\!\!/6\!\!\!/}} \\ -\ 2.57 \\ \hline \$2.89 \end{array}$$

Teresa has _____ left.

Getting Started

Subtract. Trade if needed.

1. $$\begin{array}{r} \$2.94 \\ -\ 1.23 \\ \hline \end{array}$$
2. $$\begin{array}{r} \$5.82 \\ -\ 2.65 \\ \hline \end{array}$$
3. $$\begin{array}{r} \$4.65 \\ -\ 1.83 \\ \hline \end{array}$$
4. $$\begin{array}{r} \$3.14 \\ -\ 1.92 \\ \hline \end{array}$$
5. $$\begin{array}{r} \$5.31 \\ -\ 3.45 \\ \hline \end{array}$$

Practice

Subtract. Trade if needed.

1. $1.07
  − 0.75

2. $4.71
  − 1.89

3. $6.35
  − 2.75

4. $1.98
  − 0.98

5. $7.45
  − 1.49

Apply

PAT'S DINER

Hamburger.............$2.95	Salad Plate.......$3.49
Ham Sandwich.........$3.25	Milk..............$0.65
Egg Salad Sandwich.... $1.88	Chocolate Milk....$0.75
Tuna Sandwich.........$2.59	Iced Tea.........$0.49

Solve.

6. How much more did Jack pay for a hamburger than an egg salad sandwich?

_____

7. How much more is a chocolate milk than iced tea?

_____

8. How much did Joe pay for a hamburger and a glass of milk?

_____

9. How much less is a tuna sandwich than a ham sandwich?

_____

10. How much more is a ham sandwich than an egg salad sandwich?

_____

11. How much is a salad plate and a chocolate milk?

_____

Subtracting money using dollar notation

Name _____

CHAPTER CHECKUP

Subtract. Trade if needed.

1. $348 - 9$
2. $273 - 6$
3. $781 - 50$
4. $528 - 70$
5. $417 - 60$

6. $465 - 81$
7. $278 - 90$
8. $847 - 35$
9. $750 - 23$
10. $641 - 78$

11. $687 - 55$
12. $566 - 59$
13. $318 - 135$
14. $628 - 435$
15. $919 - 378$

16. $475 - 149$
17. $721 - 254$
18. $833 - 126$
19. $715 - 359$
20. $454 - 168$

21. $\$3.18 - 0.15$
22. $\$2.75 - 1.50$
23. $\$5.75 - 1.56$
24. $\$7.15 - 4.91$
25. $\$6.35 - 2.98$

Solve.

26. The pet store had 251 goldfish. Alison sold 163 of them. How many goldfish are left?

_____ goldfish

27. Kiel had $7.35. He bought a toy boat for $2.45. How much money does he have left?

_____

ROUNDUP REVIEW

Fill in the oval next to the correct answer.

1.
$$7$$
$$+ 8$$
- ○ 16
- ○ 14
- ○ 15
- ○ NG

7.
$$57$$
$$+ 38$$
- ○ 21
- ○ 95
- ○ 85
- ○ NG

2. $13 - 6$
- ○ 7
- ○ 3
- ○ 19
- ○ NG

8.
$$35$$
$$+ 68$$
- ○ 915
- ○ 33
- ○ 103
- ○ NG

3.
- ○ 55
- ○ 145
- ○ 154
- ○ NG

9.
$$275$$
$$+ 465$$
- ○ 630
- ○ 740
- ○ 730
- ○ NG

4.
- ○ 2:18
- ○ 2:08
- ○ 3:18
- ○ NG

10.
$$71$$
$$- 24$$
- ○ 47
- ○ 53
- ○ 57
- ○ NG

5.
- ○ 42¢
- ○ 57¢
- ○ 47¢
- ○ NG

11.
$$93$$
$$- 27$$
- ○ 74
- ○ 76
- ○ 66
- ○ NG

6.
- ○ $1.51
- ○ $1.76
- ○ $1.71
- ○ NG

12.
$$435$$
$$- 162$$
- ○ 333
- ○ 273
- ○ 373
- ○ NG

☐ score

12 ADDING AND SUBTRACTING LARGE NUMBERS

Adding Large Numbers

Marilyn and Thomas helped collect paper for the senior citizens' paper drive. How much paper did they collect?

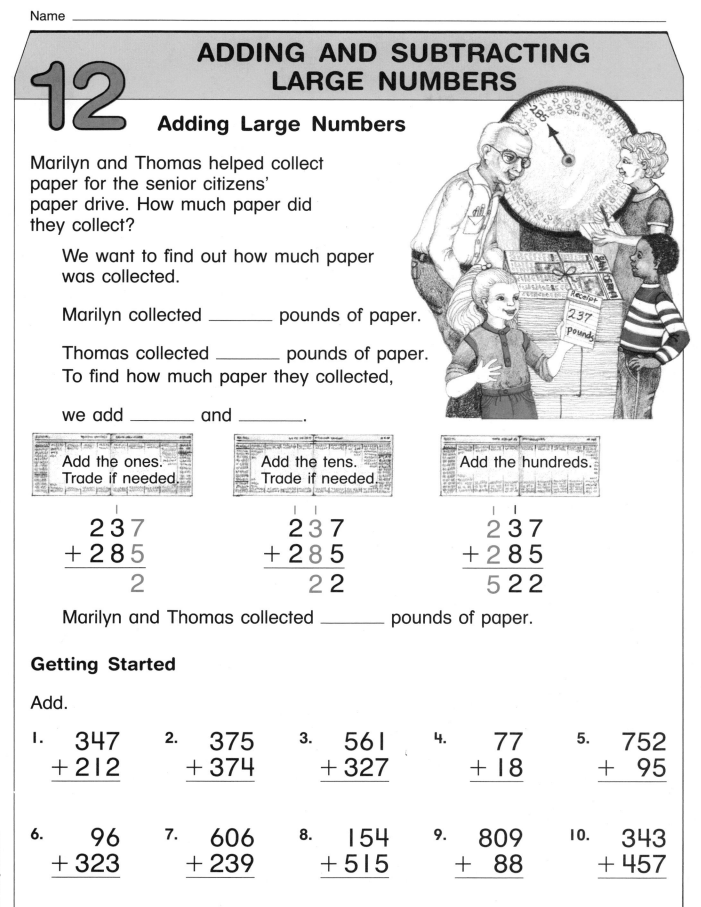

We want to find out how much paper was collected.

Marilyn collected _____ pounds of paper.

Thomas collected _____ pounds of paper. To find how much paper they collected,

we add _____ and _____.

Add the ones. Trade if needed.	Add the tens. Trade if needed.	Add the hundreds.
$\begin{array}{r} 2\,3\,7 \\ +2\,8\,5 \\ \hline 2 \end{array}$	$\begin{array}{r} 2\,3\,7 \\ +2\,8\,5 \\ \hline 2\,2 \end{array}$	$\begin{array}{r} 2\,3\,7 \\ +2\,8\,5 \\ \hline 5\,2\,2 \end{array}$

Marilyn and Thomas collected _____ pounds of paper.

Getting Started

Add.

1. $\begin{array}{r} 347 \\ +212 \end{array}$
2. $\begin{array}{r} 375 \\ +374 \end{array}$
3. $\begin{array}{r} 561 \\ +327 \end{array}$
4. $\begin{array}{r} 77 \\ +18 \end{array}$
5. $\begin{array}{r} 752 \\ +\ 95 \end{array}$

6. $\begin{array}{r} 96 \\ +323 \end{array}$
7. $\begin{array}{r} 606 \\ +239 \end{array}$
8. $\begin{array}{r} 154 \\ +515 \end{array}$
9. $\begin{array}{r} 809 \\ +\ 88 \end{array}$
10. $\begin{array}{r} 343 \\ +457 \end{array}$

Practice

Add.

1. $618 + 135$
2. $515 + 87$
3. $156 + 372$
4. $612 + 279$
5. $350 + 350$

6. $175 + 175$
7. $149 + 289$
8. $649 + 329$
9. $233 + 565$
10. $578 + 9$

11. $219 + 356$
12. $317 + 483$
13. $86 + 75$
14. $529 + 91$
15. $490 + 390$

16. $96 + 78$
17. $775 + 189$
18. $89 + 367$
19. $455 + 224$
20. $496 + 287$

21. $634 + 275$
22. $398 + 198$
23. $758 + 163$
24. $239 + 467$
25. $683 + 192$

Apply

Solve.

26. Clark School has 345 students. Polk School has 488 students. What is the total number of students at both schools?

_____ students

27. Bonnie collected 159 stickers. Her sister collected 258 stickers. How many stickers did they collect together?

_____ stickers

Adding 2- and 3-digit numbers

Adding Three Numbers

How many baseball cards did Bobby, Cathleen and Keith collect together?

We want to know how many cards were collected.

Bobby collected _____ cards.

Cathleen collected _____ cards.

Keith collected _____ cards.
To find how many cards in all,

we add _____, _____ and _____.

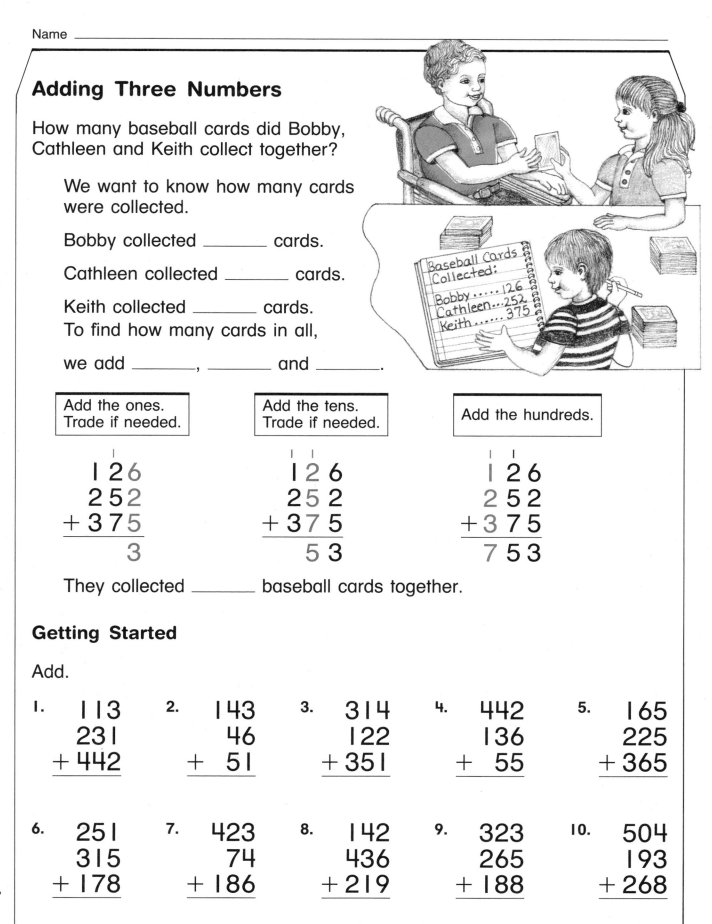

Baseball Cards Collected:
Bobby.....126
Cathleen...252
Keith......375

Add the ones. Trade if needed.	Add the tens. Trade if needed.	Add the hundreds.
$\begin{array}{r} 1\ 2\ 6 \\ 2\ 5\ 2 \\ +\ 3\ 7\ 5 \\ \hline 3 \end{array}$	$\begin{array}{r} 1\ 2\ 6 \\ 2\ 5\ 2 \\ +\ 3\ 7\ 5 \\ \hline 5\ 3 \end{array}$	$\begin{array}{r} 1\ 2\ 6 \\ 2\ 5\ 2 \\ +\ 3\ 7\ 5 \\ \hline 7\ 5\ 3 \end{array}$

They collected _____ baseball cards together.

Getting Started

Add.

1. $\begin{array}{r} 113 \\ 231 \\ +442 \\ \hline \end{array}$
2. $\begin{array}{r} 143 \\ 46 \\ +\ 51 \\ \hline \end{array}$
3. $\begin{array}{r} 314 \\ 122 \\ +351 \\ \hline \end{array}$
4. $\begin{array}{r} 442 \\ 136 \\ +\ 55 \\ \hline \end{array}$
5. $\begin{array}{r} 165 \\ 225 \\ +365 \\ \hline \end{array}$

6. $\begin{array}{r} 251 \\ 315 \\ +178 \\ \hline \end{array}$
7. $\begin{array}{r} 423 \\ 74 \\ +186 \\ \hline \end{array}$
8. $\begin{array}{r} 142 \\ 436 \\ +219 \\ \hline \end{array}$
9. $\begin{array}{r} 323 \\ 265 \\ +188 \\ \hline \end{array}$
10. $\begin{array}{r} 504 \\ 193 \\ +268 \\ \hline \end{array}$

Practice

Add.

1. 511
    330
    + 145

2. 232
    27
    + 47

3. 314
    85
    + 200

4. 125
    54
    + 397

5. 325
    132
    + 538

6. 534
    134
    + 237

7. 415
    162
    + 244

8. 241
    367
    + 179

9. 321
    465
    + 212

10. 165
    316
    + 273

11. 923
    56
    + 19

12. 86
    202
    + 658

13. 192
    505
    + 247

14. 434
    143
    + 309

15. 107
    581
    + 270

FIELD TRIP

Fill in the missing numbers.

1.   3 4 6
   + ☐ ☐ ☐
     7 9 8

2.   2 ☐ 5
   + ☐ 6 ☐
     8 8 8

3.   3 2 7
   + ☐ 5 ☐
     8 8 3

4.   ☐ 9 ☐
   + 3 4 2
     7 3 9

Adding three 3-digit numbers

Subtracting Large Numbers

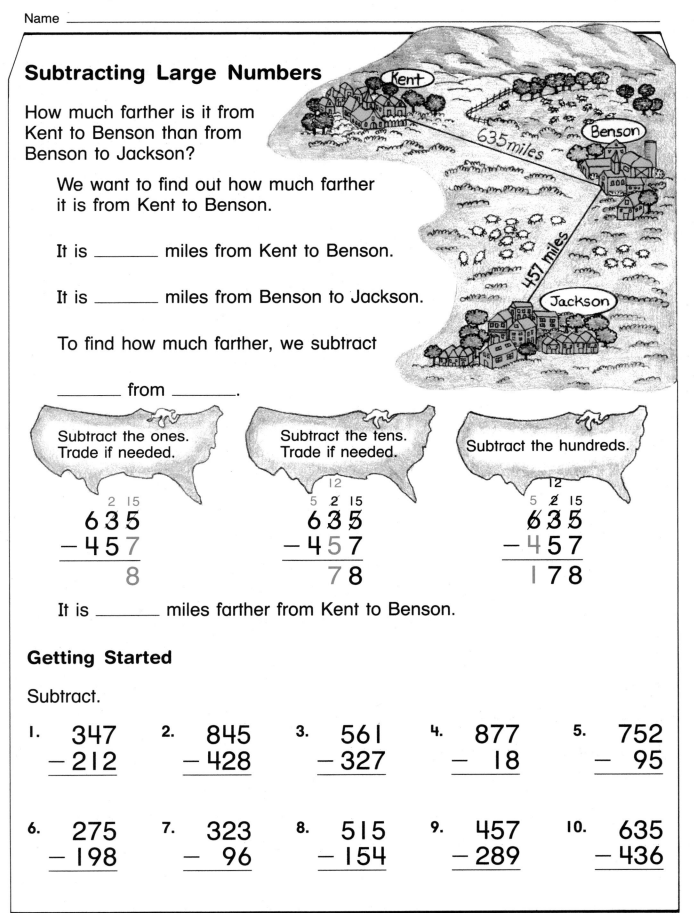

How much farther is it from Kent to Benson than from Benson to Jackson?

We want to find out how much farther it is from Kent to Benson.

It is _____ miles from Kent to Benson.

It is _____ miles from Benson to Jackson.

To find how much farther, we subtract

_____ from _____.

Subtract the ones. Trade if needed.

$$\begin{array}{r} \overset{2}{\cancel{6}}\overset{15}{\cancel{3}}5 \\ -457 \\ \hline 8 \end{array}$$

Subtract the tens. Trade if needed.

$$\begin{array}{r} \overset{5}{\cancel{6}}\overset{12}{\cancel{3}}\overset{15}{\cancel{5}} \\ -457 \\ \hline 78 \end{array}$$

Subtract the hundreds.

$$\begin{array}{r} \overset{5}{\cancel{6}}\overset{12}{\cancel{3}}\overset{15}{\cancel{5}} \\ -457 \\ \hline 178 \end{array}$$

It is _____ miles farther from Kent to Benson.

Getting Started

Subtract.

1.	2.	3.	4.	5.
347 −212	845 −428	561 −327	877 − 18	752 − 95

6.	7.	8.	9.	10.
275 −198	323 − 96	515 −154	457 −289	635 −436

Practice

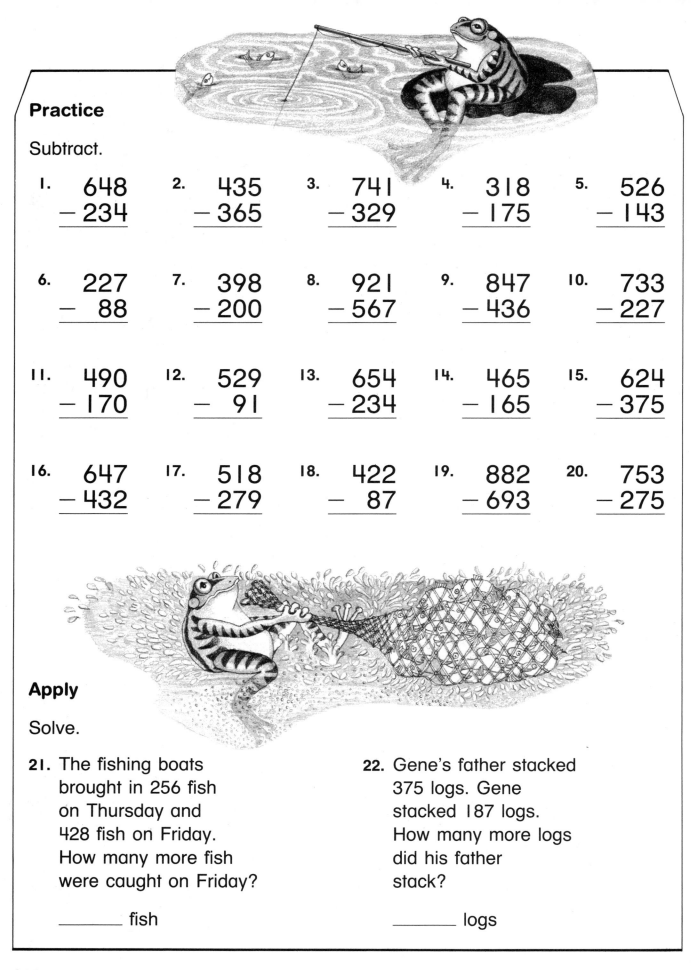

Subtract.

1. 648 -234	2. 435 -365	3. 741 -329	4. 318 -175	5. 526 -143
6. 227 $-\ \ 88$	7. 398 -200	8. 921 -567	9. 847 -436	10. 733 -227
11. 490 -170	12. 529 $-\ \ 91$	13. 654 -234	14. 465 -165	15. 624 -375
16. 647 -432	17. 518 -279	18. 422 $-\ \ 87$	19. 882 -693	20. 753 -275

Apply

Solve.

21. The fishing boats brought in 256 fish on Thursday and 428 fish on Friday. How many more fish were caught on Friday?

_____ fish

22. Gene's father stacked 375 logs. Gene stacked 187 logs. How many more logs did his father stack?

_____ logs

More Subtracting Large Numbers

During the spring sale, the Sports Store sold 325 baseballs and 179 footballs. How many more baseballs were sold?

We want to know how many more baseballs were sold.

There were _____ baseballs sold.

There were _____ footballs sold.

To find how many more baseballs were sold,

we subtract _____ from _____.

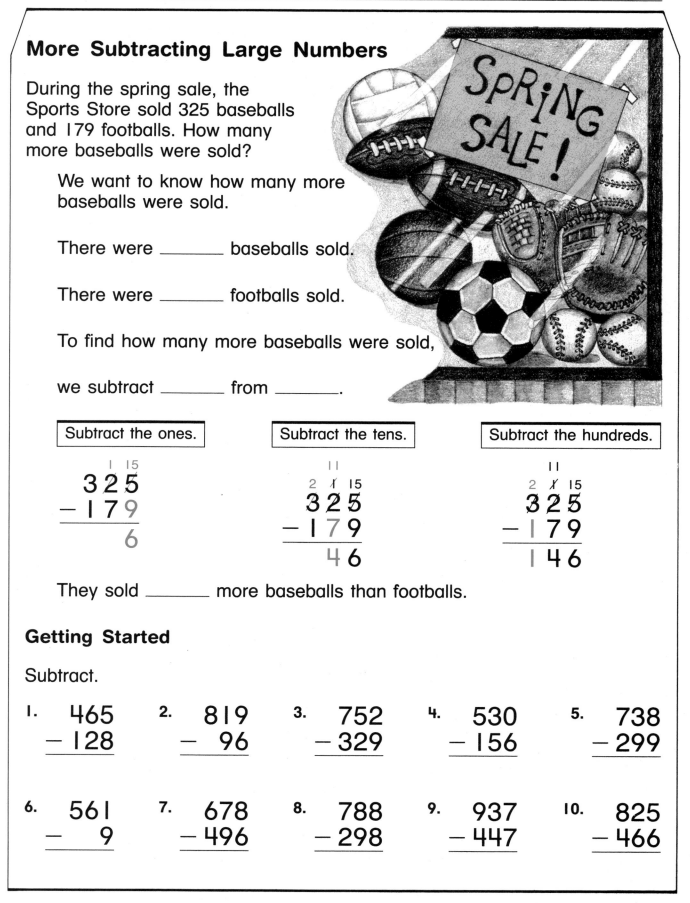

Subtract the ones.	Subtract the tens.	Subtract the hundreds.
$\begin{array}{r} 115 \\ 3\,2\,\cancel{5} \\ -\,1\,7\,9 \\ \hline 6 \end{array}$	$\begin{array}{r} 1\,1 \\ 2\,\cancel{1}\,15 \\ 3\,\cancel{2}\,\cancel{5} \\ -\,1\,7\,9 \\ \hline 4\,6 \end{array}$	$\begin{array}{r} 1\,1 \\ 2\,\cancel{1}\,15 \\ \cancel{3}\,\cancel{2}\,\cancel{5} \\ -\,1\,7\,9 \\ \hline 1\,4\,6 \end{array}$

They sold _____ more baseballs than footballs.

Getting Started

Subtract.

1. $\begin{array}{r} 465 \\ -128 \\ \hline \end{array}$
2. $\begin{array}{r} 819 \\ -96 \\ \hline \end{array}$
3. $\begin{array}{r} 752 \\ -329 \\ \hline \end{array}$
4. $\begin{array}{r} 530 \\ -156 \\ \hline \end{array}$
5. $\begin{array}{r} 738 \\ -299 \\ \hline \end{array}$

6. $\begin{array}{r} 561 \\ -9 \\ \hline \end{array}$
7. $\begin{array}{r} 678 \\ -496 \\ \hline \end{array}$
8. $\begin{array}{r} 788 \\ -298 \\ \hline \end{array}$
9. $\begin{array}{r} 937 \\ -447 \\ \hline \end{array}$
10. $\begin{array}{r} 825 \\ -466 \\ \hline \end{array}$

Practice

Subtract.

1. 578
  − 294

2. 428
  − 183

3. 687
  − 269

4. 824
  − 470

5. 633
  − 156

6. 258
  − 85

7. 755
  − 255

8. 515
  − 347

9. 786
  − 395

10. 678
   − 493

11. 714
   − 529

12. 337
   − 165

13. 758
   − 132

14. 621
   − 279

15. 582
   − 298

FIELD TRIP

Solve the following problems.

Start with	225	Start with	396
Add 126	+ 126	Add 275	
	351		
Subtract 38		Subtract 385	
Add 87		Add 214	

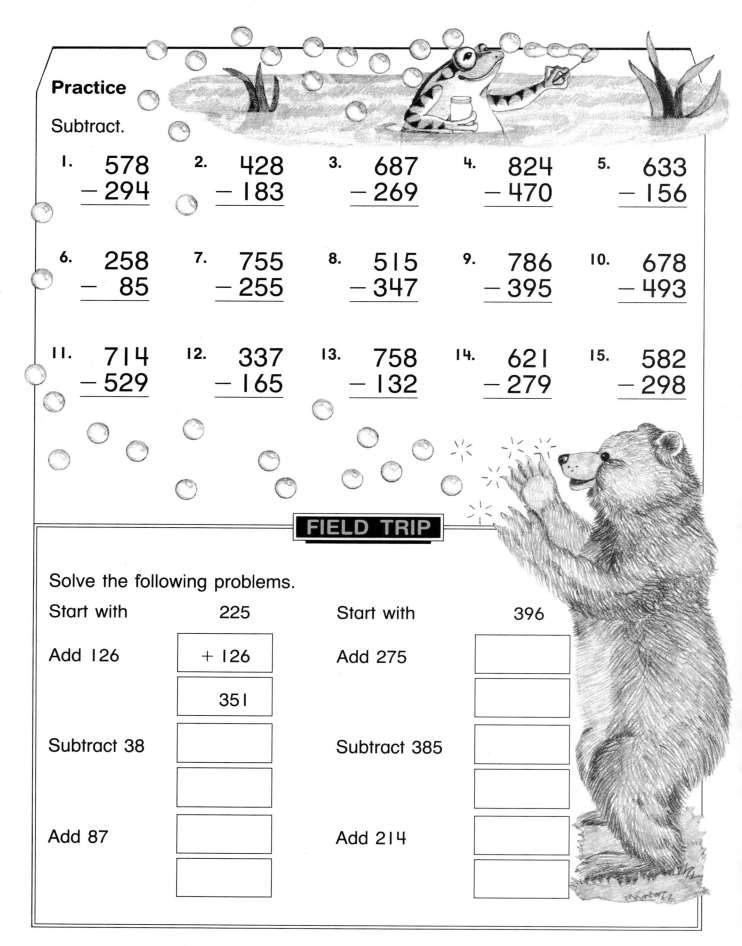

Practice subtracting 2- and 3-digit numbers

Checking Subtraction

You can check subtraction by adding.

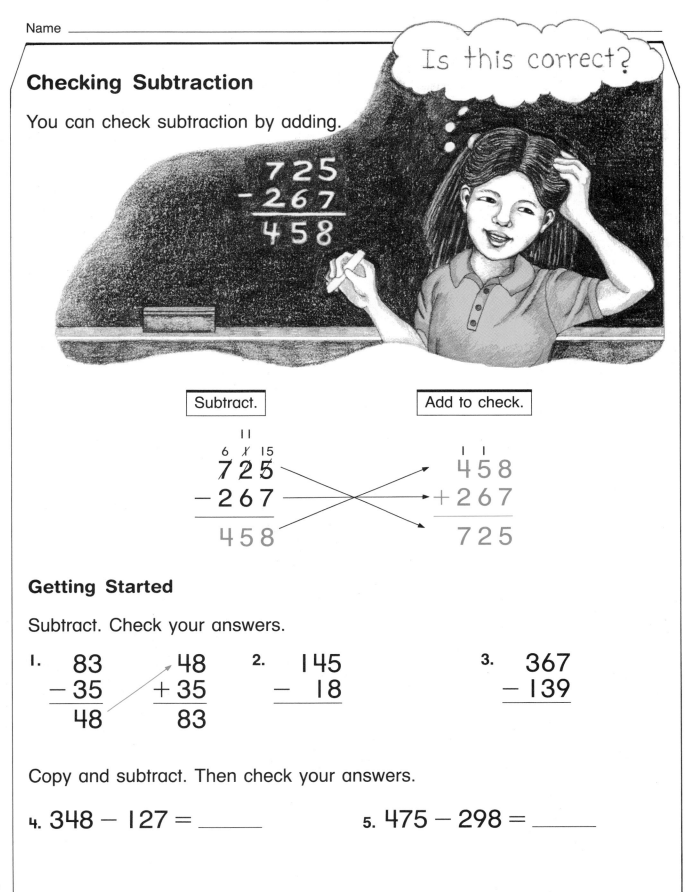

Is this correct?

$$\begin{array}{r} 725 \\ -267 \\ \hline 458 \end{array}$$

Subtract.		Add to check.

$$\begin{array}{r} {\overset{11}{}} \\ 7\overset{6}{2}\overset{\cancel{1}}{5}{}^{15} \\ -267 \\ \hline 458 \end{array} \qquad \begin{array}{r} {}^{1\ \ 1} \\ 458 \\ +267 \\ \hline 725 \end{array}$$

Getting Started

Subtract. Check your answers.

1.
$$\begin{array}{r} 83 \\ -35 \\ \hline 48 \end{array} \qquad \begin{array}{r} 48 \\ +35 \\ \hline 83 \end{array}$$

2.
$$\begin{array}{r} 145 \\ -\ 18 \\ \hline \end{array}$$

3.
$$\begin{array}{r} 367 \\ -139 \\ \hline \end{array}$$

Copy and subtract. Then check your answers.

4. $348 - 127 = $ _____

5. $475 - 298 = $ _____

Practice

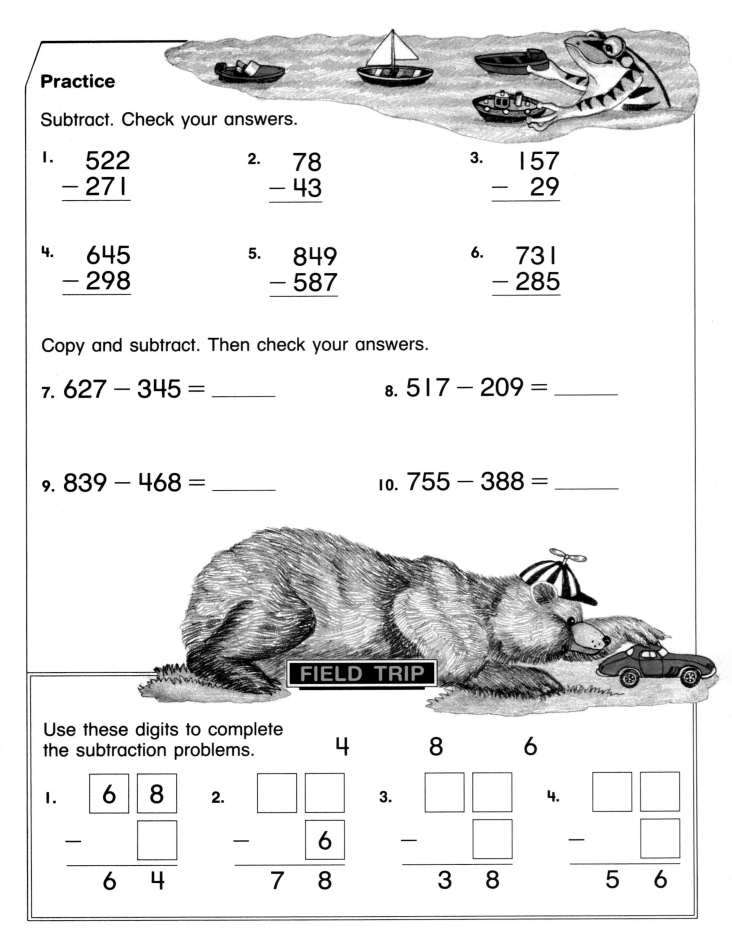

Subtract. Check your answers.

1. $\begin{array}{r} 522 \\ -271 \\ \hline \end{array}$

2. $\begin{array}{r} 78 \\ -43 \\ \hline \end{array}$

3. $\begin{array}{r} 157 \\ -29 \\ \hline \end{array}$

4. $\begin{array}{r} 645 \\ -298 \\ \hline \end{array}$

5. $\begin{array}{r} 849 \\ -587 \\ \hline \end{array}$

6. $\begin{array}{r} 731 \\ -285 \\ \hline \end{array}$

Copy and subtract. Then check your answers.

7. $627 - 345 = $ _____

8. $517 - 209 = $ _____

9. $839 - 468 = $ _____

10. $755 - 388 = $ _____

FIELD TRIP

Use these digits to complete the subtraction problems.

4   8   6

1. $\begin{array}{r} 6\ 8 \\ -\ \square \\ \hline 6\ 4 \end{array}$

2. $\begin{array}{r} \square\ \square \\ -\ 6 \\ \hline 7\ 8 \end{array}$

3. $\begin{array}{r} \square\ \square \\ -\ \square \\ \hline 3\ 8 \end{array}$

4. $\begin{array}{r} \square\ \square \\ -\ \square \\ \hline 5\ 6 \end{array}$

Checking subtraction problems by adding

Working with Money

How much more does the car cost than the boat?

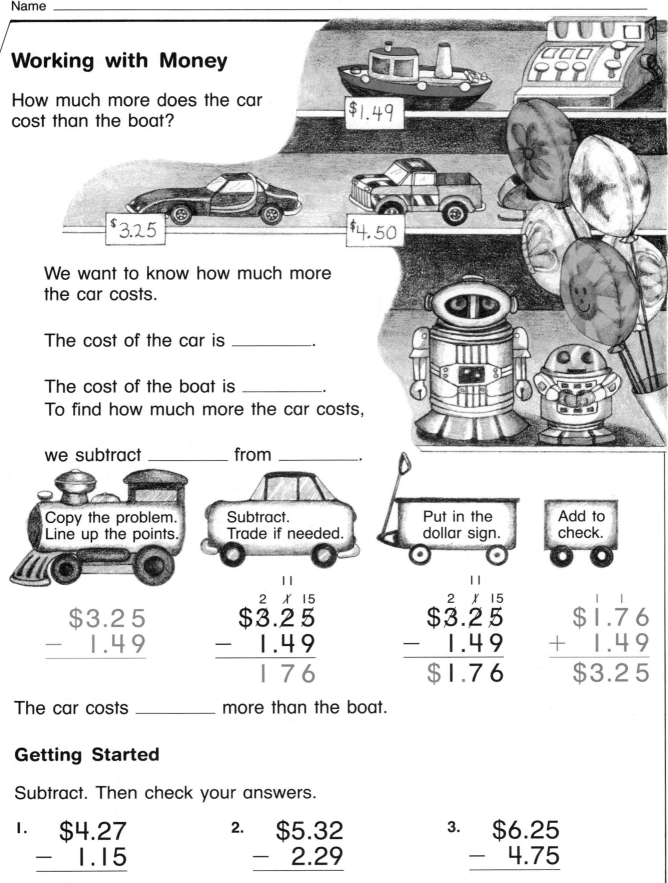

$1.49

$3.25

$4.50

We want to know how much more the car costs.

The cost of the car is _____.

The cost of the boat is _____.
To find how much more the car costs,

we subtract _____ from _____.

Copy the problem. Line up the points.

Subtract. Trade if needed.

Put in the dollar sign.

Add to check.

$$\$3.25 - 1.49$$

$$\$3.\overset{2}{\cancel{3}}\overset{15}{\cancel{2}5} - 1.49 = 176$$

$$\$3.\overset{2}{\cancel{3}}\overset{15}{\cancel{2}5} - 1.49 = \$1.76$$

$$\$1.76 + 1.49 = \$3.25$$

The car costs _____ more than the boat.

Getting Started

Subtract. Then check your answers.

1. $$\$4.27 - 1.15$$

2. $$\$5.32 - 2.29$$

3. $$\$6.25 - 4.75$$

Practice

Subtract. Then check your answers.

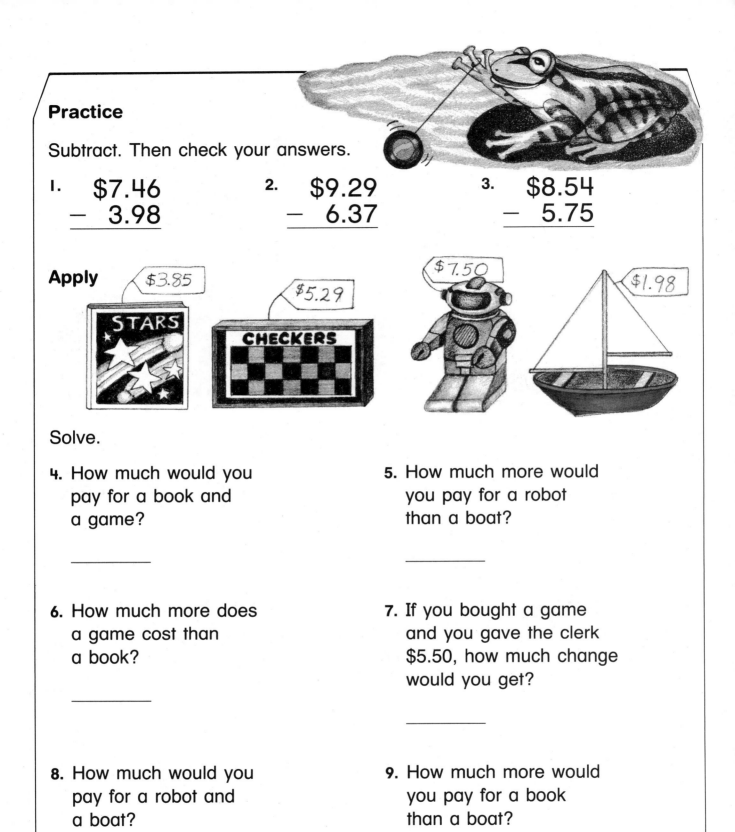

1. $7.46
 − 3.98

2. $9.29
 − 6.37

3. $8.54
 − 5.75

Apply

$3.85 (STARS)
$5.29 (CHECKERS)
$7.50 (robot)
$1.98 (boat)

Solve.

4. How much would you pay for a book and a game?

_____

5. How much more would you pay for a robot than a boat?

_____

6. How much more does a game cost than a book?

_____

7. If you bought a game and you gave the clerk $5.50, how much change would you get?

_____

8. How much would you pay for a robot and a boat?

_____

9. How much more would you pay for a book than a boat?

_____

Adding and subtracting money

Problem Solving

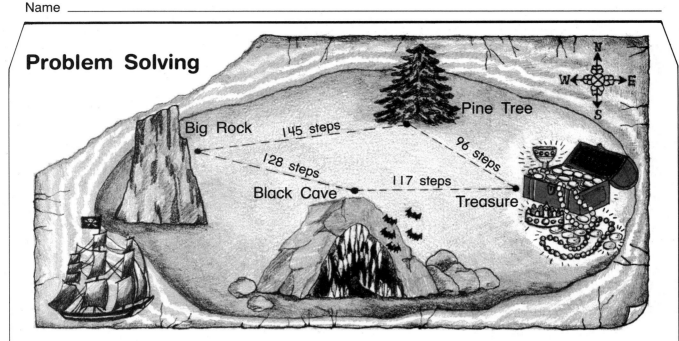

Solve.

1. How many steps would you walk from Big Rock to Pine Tree to the Treasure?

   _____ steps

2. How many steps is it from Big Rock to Black Cave to the Treasure?

   _____ steps

3. How much further is it from Big Rock to Pine Tree than from Pine Tree to the Treasure?

   _____ steps

4. How much further is it from Big Rock to Black Cave than from Black Cave to the Treasure?

   _____ steps

5. How much further is it from Big Rock to Pine Tree than from Big Rock to Black Cave?

   _____ steps

6. How much further is it from Black Cave to the Treasure than from Pine Tree to the Treasure?

   _____ steps

(two hundred thirty-three) **233**

Solve.

1. How much more is
   936 than 375?

   936 is _____ more than 375.

2. How much less is
   562 than 821?

   562 is _____ less than 821.

3. How much is
   456 and 279?

   The sum is _____.

4. How much is
   312 and 395?

   The sum is _____.

5. Betsy had $6.35.
   She spent $2.98.
   How much money
   is left?

   Betsy has _____ left.

6. John has $4.50.
   He earned $2.75.
   How much money
   does John have now?

   John has _____.

7. Gary has $3.80.
   He earned $2.90
   babysitting. How
   much money does
   he have now?

   Gary has _____.

8. Bre had $8.15.
   She spent $3.69.
   How much money
   does Bre have left?

   Bre has _____ left.

9. What if Gary in exercise 7
   spends $1.55 of his money?
   How much will he have left?

   _____

10. Read exercise 8 again. How
    much more does Bre need to
    have $5.00?

    _____

Name _____

CHAPTER CHECKUP

Add or subtract.

1. $276 + 23$ 2. $357 + 28$ 3. $515 - 48$ 4. $148 + 347$ 5. $259 + 620$

6. 468
132
$+375$

7. 206
280
$+214$

8. 383
115
$+129$

9. $685 + 133$ 10. $767 - 258$ 11. $873 - 395$ 12. $931 - 567$ 13. $472 - 274$

14. $\$3.95 + \$1.22$ 15. $\$5.25 + \$3.29$ 16. $\$8.34 - \$2.49$ 17. $\$6.15 - \$2.37$

Subtract. Then check your answers.

18. $\$5.69 - 2.87$ 19. $346 - 157$ 20. $\$7.53 - 2.75$

Solve.

21. Ling had $\$5.75$.
He spent $\$1.89$.
How much money does
he have left?

Ling has _____ left.

22. Jane had $\$3.75$.
She earned $\$2.95$.
How much money does
she have now?

Jane has _____.

ROUNDUP REVIEW

Fill in the oval next to the correct answer.

1 $7 + 8$
- ◯ 1
- ◯ 15
- ◯ 14
- ◯ NG

2 $\begin{array}{r} 16 \\ -\ 7 \end{array}$
- ◯ 9
- ◯ 23
- ◯ 19
- ◯ NG

3
- ◯ 326
- ◯ 263
- ◯ 236
- ◯ NG

4
- ◯ $1.88
- ◯ $1.28
- ◯ $1.83
- ◯ NG

5
- ◯ 4:45
- ◯ 3:45
- ◯ 9:18
- ◯ NG

6 $\begin{array}{r} 85 \\ +\ 67 \end{array}$
- ◯ 12
- ◯ 142
- ◯ 152
- ◯ NG

7 $\begin{array}{r} 238 \\ +\ 475 \end{array}$
- ◯ 703
- ◯ 603
- ◯ 713
- ◯ NG

8 $\begin{array}{r} 91 \\ -\ 48 \end{array}$
- ◯ 53
- ◯ 43
- ◯ 57
- ◯ NG

9 $\begin{array}{r} 315 \\ -\ 197 \end{array}$
- ◯ 118
- ◯ 512
- ◯ 328
- ◯ NG

10 $\begin{array}{r} 563 \\ -\ 274 \end{array}$
- ◯ 281
- ◯ 311
- ◯ 399
- ◯ NG

11 $\begin{array}{r} \$3.25 \\ +\ 2.75 \end{array}$
- ◯ $6.00
- ◯ $5.90
- ◯ $5.00
- ◯ NG

12 $\begin{array}{r} \$5.25 \\ -\ 2.98 \end{array}$
- ◯ $8.23
- ◯ $2.27
- ◯ $3.37
- ◯ NG

[ ] score

Name _____

13 GEOMETRY AND FRACTIONS

Plane Figures

circle   triangle   square   rectangle

Put **C** inside each circle.   Put **S** inside each square.
Put **T** inside each triangle.   Put **R** inside each rectangle.

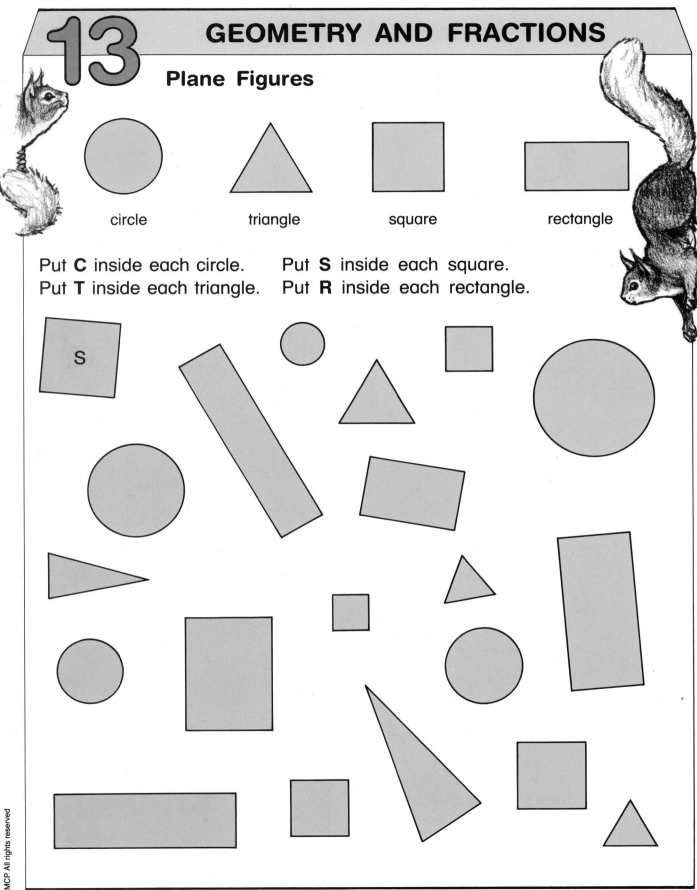

Circles, triangles, squares and rectangles   (two hundred thirty-seven) **237**

Practice

Color circles green.
Color squares red.

Color triangles purple.
Color rectangles orange.

Circles, triangles, squares and rectangles

Name _____

Sides and Corners

Put an X on each side. Circle each corner.
Then write the numbers.

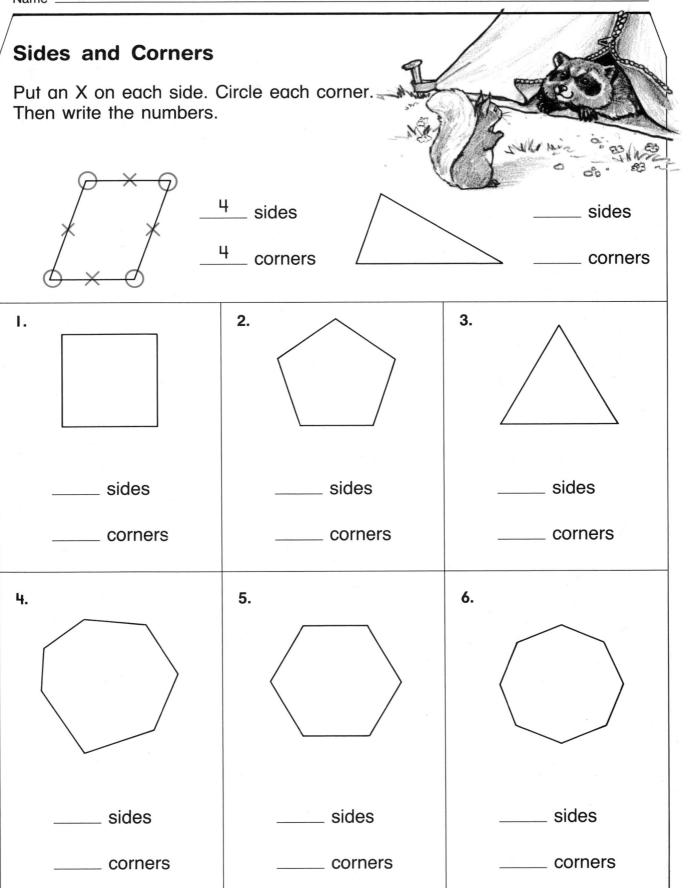

___4___ sides

___4___ corners

_____ sides

_____ corners

1.

_____ sides

_____ corners

2.

_____ sides

_____ corners

3.

_____ sides

_____ corners

4.

_____ sides

_____ corners

5.

_____ sides

_____ corners

6.

_____ sides

_____ corners

Sides and corners of figures

(two hundred thirty-nine) **239**

Practice

Some figures have square corners.
The corner of a piece of paper can be used for a check.

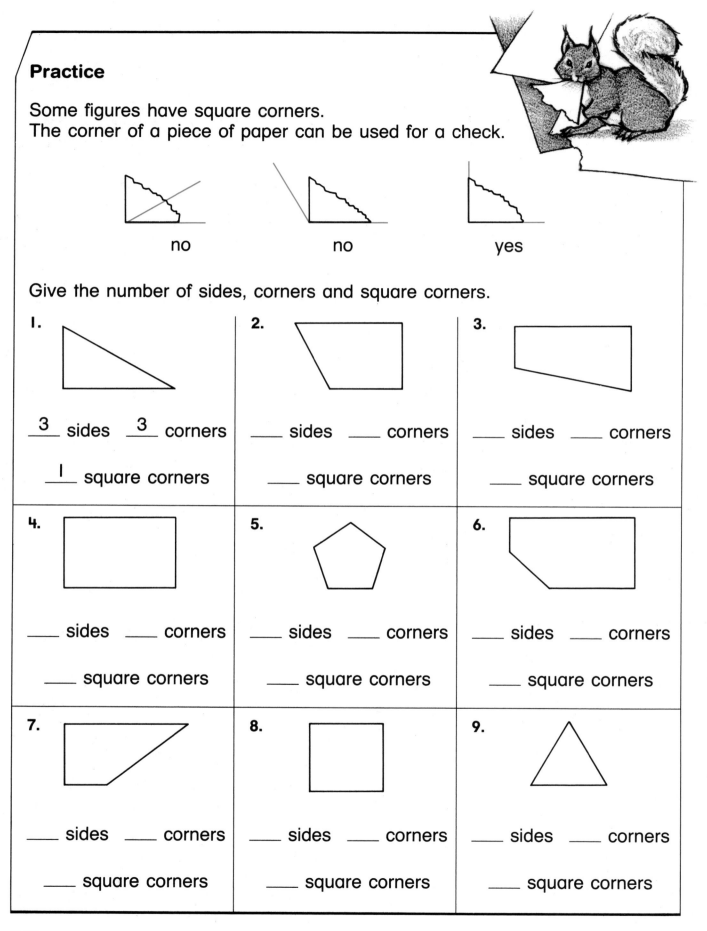

no   no   yes

Give the number of sides, corners and square corners.

1.

__3__ sides __3__ corners

__1__ square corners

2.

___ sides ___ corners

___ square corners

3.

___ sides ___ corners

___ square corners

4.

___ sides ___ corners

___ square corners

5.

___ sides ___ corners

___ square corners

6.

___ sides ___ corners

___ square corners

7.

___ sides ___ corners

___ square corners

8.

___ sides ___ corners

___ square corners

9.

___ sides ___ corners

___ square corners

Name _____

Symmetry

If you fold along a line of symmetry,
the two parts will match exactly.

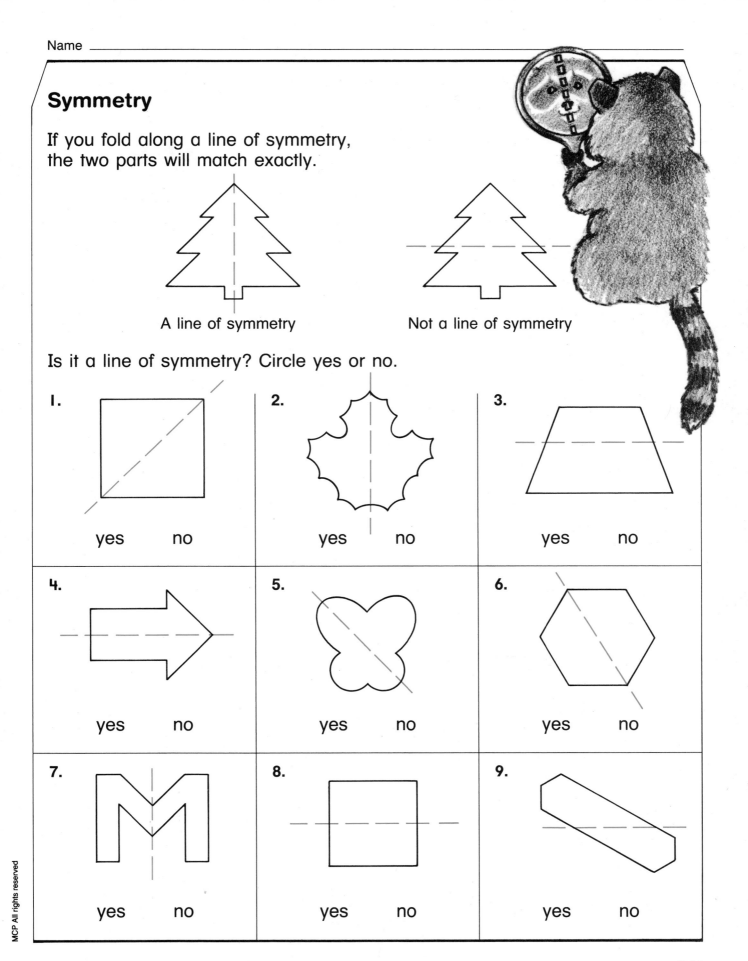

A line of symmetry   Not a line of symmetry

Is it a line of symmetry? Circle yes or no.

1. yes   no

2. yes   no

3. yes   no

4. yes   no

5. yes   no

6. yes   no

7. yes   no

8. yes   no

9. yes   no

Symmetric figures, congruent parts   (two hundred forty-one)   **241**

Practice

The line of symmetry in each figure below shows one part of a symmetric figure. Draw the missing part of each figure.

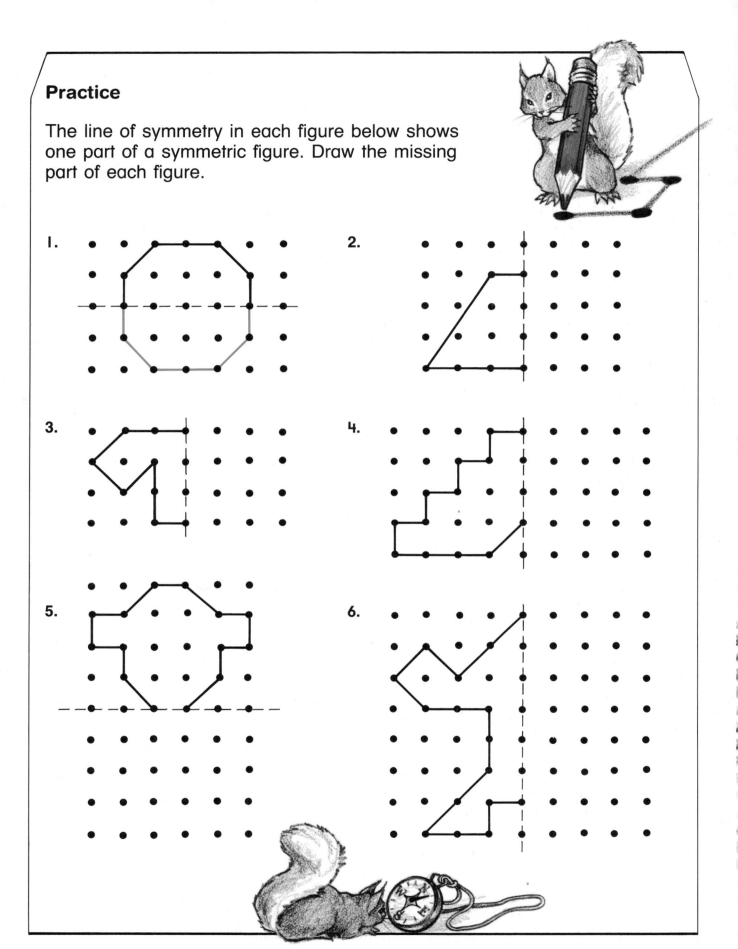

1.

2.

3.

4.

5.

6.

Drawing symmetric figures

Solid Figures

Match each shape with its name.

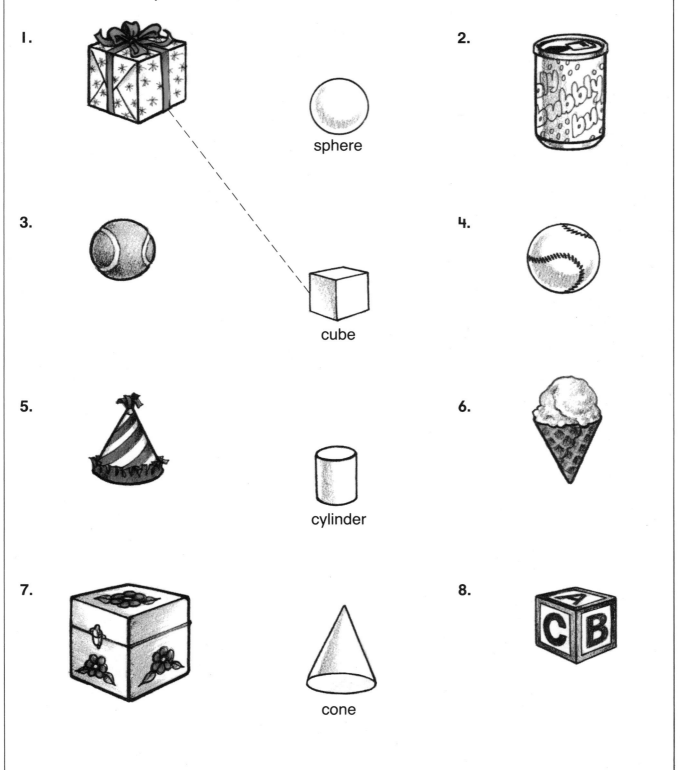

1.

sphere

2.

3.

cube

4.

5.

cylinder

6.

7.

cone

8.

Practice

Circle the shapes that match the first shape in each row.

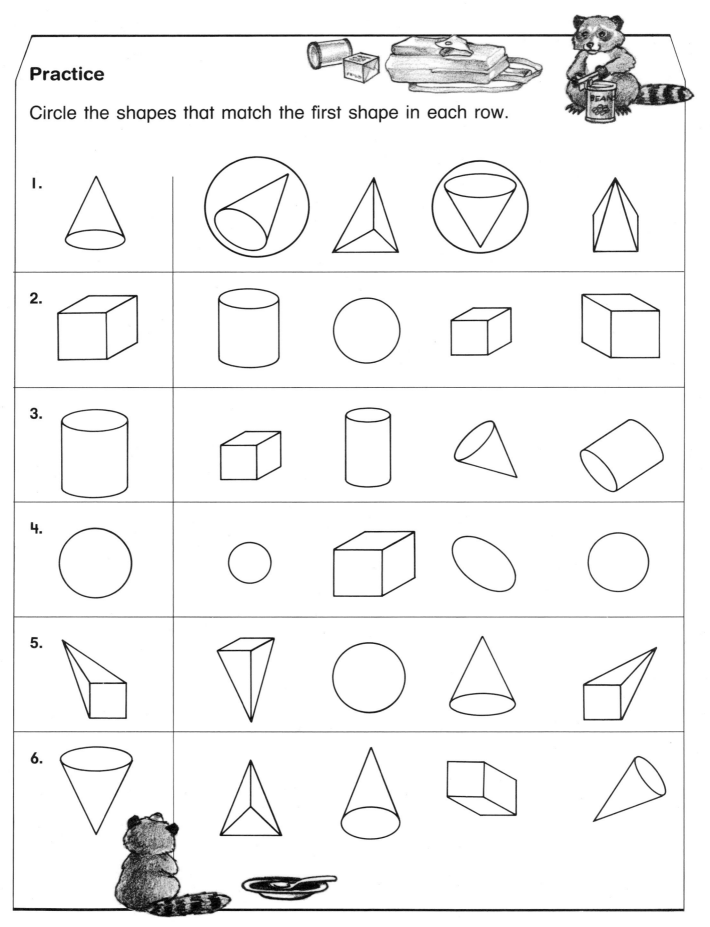

1.

2.

3.

4.

5.

6.

Solid figures

Fractions

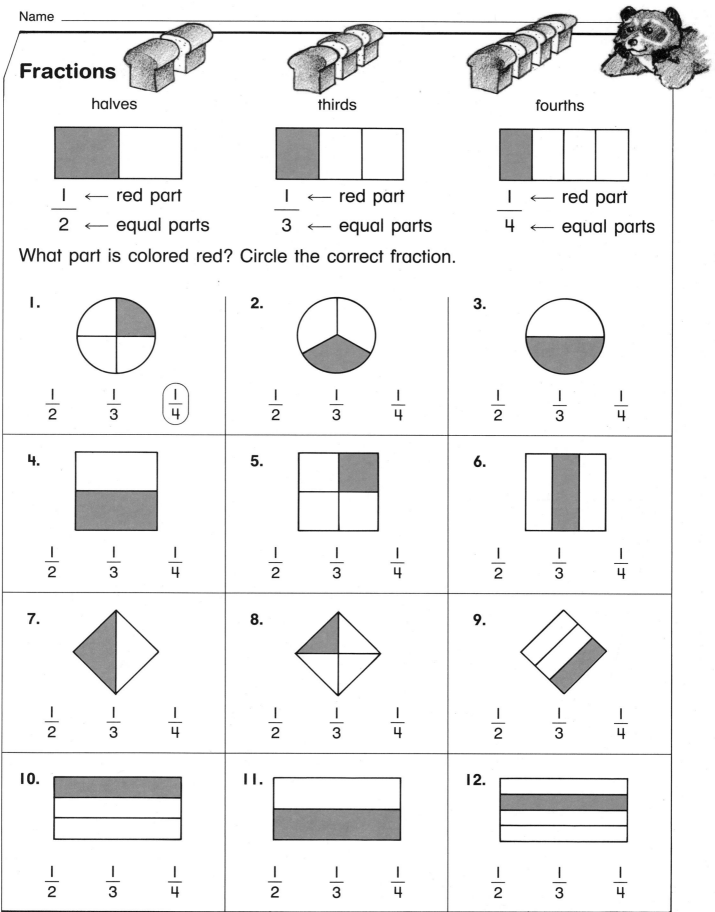

halves

$$\frac{1}{2}$$ ← red part
← equal parts

thirds

$$\frac{1}{3}$$ ← red part
← equal parts

fourths

$$\frac{1}{4}$$ ← red part
← equal parts

What part is colored red? Circle the correct fraction.

1. $\frac{1}{2}$ $\frac{1}{3}$ $\boxed{\frac{1}{4}}$

2. $\frac{1}{2}$ $\frac{1}{3}$ $\frac{1}{4}$

3. $\frac{1}{2}$ $\frac{1}{3}$ $\frac{1}{4}$

4. $\frac{1}{2}$ $\frac{1}{3}$ $\frac{1}{4}$

5. $\frac{1}{2}$ $\frac{1}{3}$ $\frac{1}{4}$

6. $\frac{1}{2}$ $\frac{1}{3}$ $\frac{1}{4}$

7. $\frac{1}{2}$ $\frac{1}{3}$ $\frac{1}{4}$

8. $\frac{1}{2}$ $\frac{1}{3}$ $\frac{1}{4}$

9. $\frac{1}{2}$ $\frac{1}{3}$ $\frac{1}{4}$

10. $\frac{1}{2}$ $\frac{1}{3}$ $\frac{1}{4}$

11. $\frac{1}{2}$ $\frac{1}{3}$ $\frac{1}{4}$

12. $\frac{1}{2}$ $\frac{1}{3}$ $\frac{1}{4}$

Halves, thirds and fourths

Practice

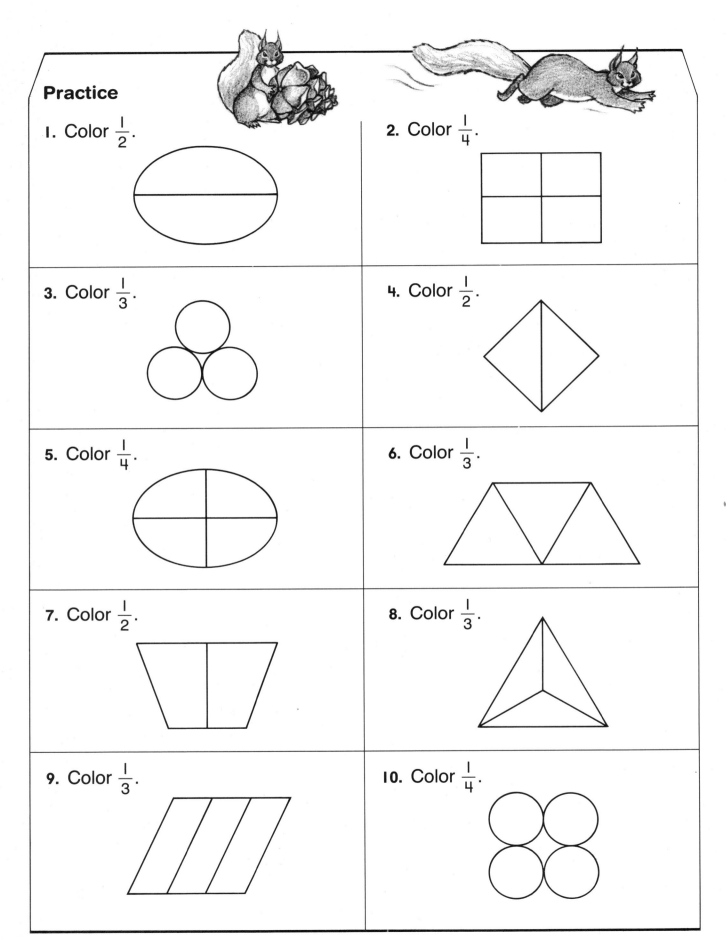

1. Color $\frac{1}{2}$.

2. Color $\frac{1}{4}$.

3. Color $\frac{1}{3}$.

4. Color $\frac{1}{2}$.

5. Color $\frac{1}{4}$.

6. Color $\frac{1}{3}$.

7. Color $\frac{1}{2}$.

8. Color $\frac{1}{3}$.

9. Color $\frac{1}{3}$.

10. Color $\frac{1}{4}$.

Halves, thirds and fourths

Name _____

Fractional Parts

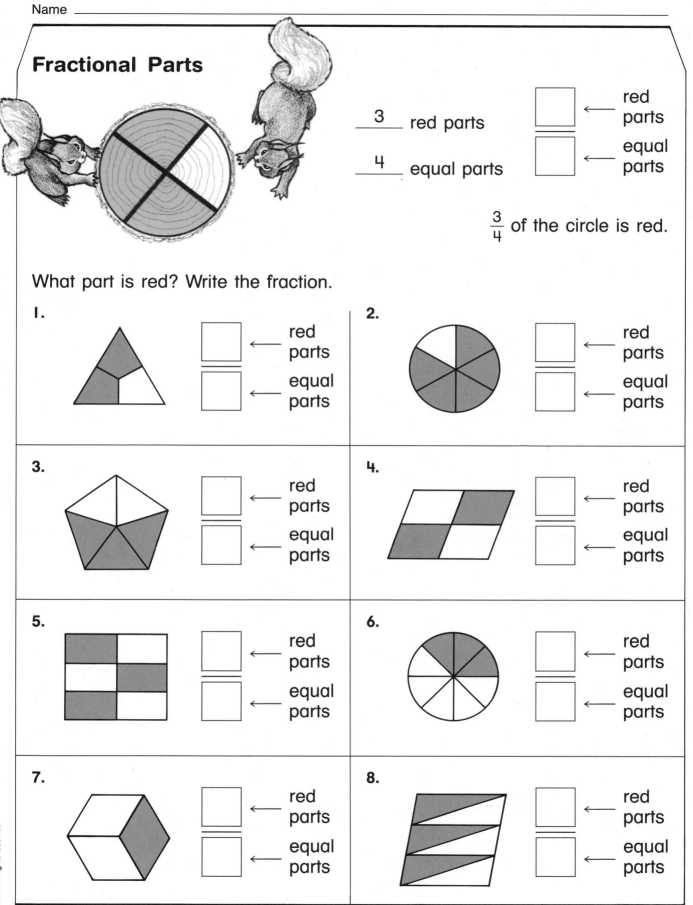

___3___ red parts

___4___ equal parts

□ ← red parts
□ ← equal parts

$\frac{3}{4}$ of the circle is red.

What part is red? Write the fraction.

1.
□ ← red parts
□ ← equal parts

2.
□ ← red parts
□ ← equal parts

3.
□ ← red parts
□ ← equal parts

4.
□ ← red parts
□ ← equal parts

5.
□ ← red parts
□ ← equal parts

6.
□ ← red parts
□ ← equal parts

7.
□ ← red parts
□ ← equal parts

8.
□ ← red parts
□ ← equal parts

Fractional parts of figures

(two hundred forty-seven) **247**

Practice

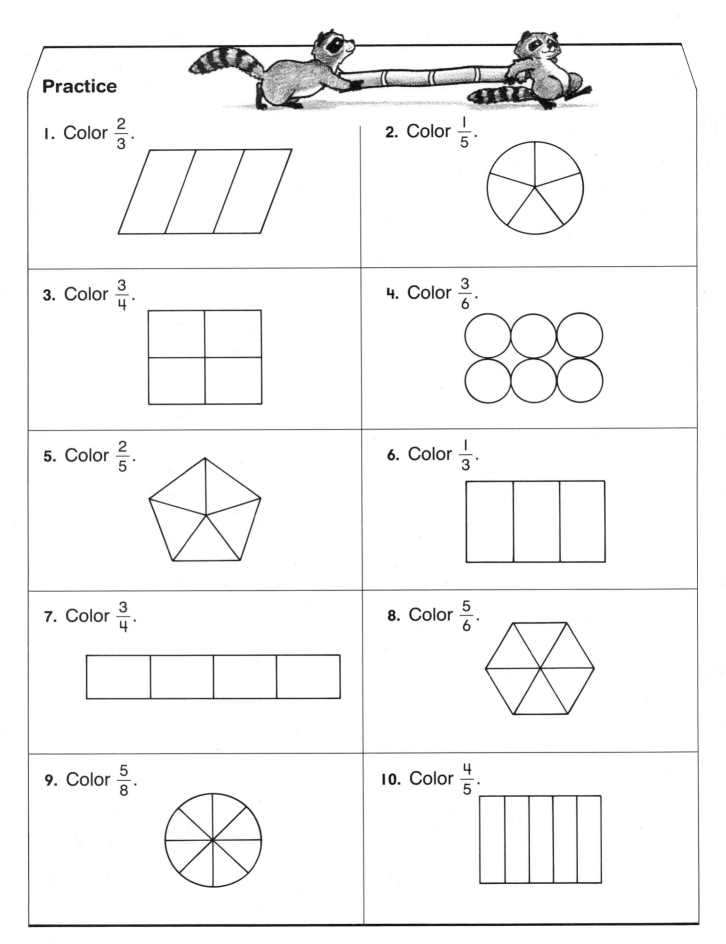

1. Color $\frac{2}{3}$.

2. Color $\frac{1}{5}$.

3. Color $\frac{3}{4}$.

4. Color $\frac{3}{6}$.

5. Color $\frac{2}{5}$.

6. Color $\frac{1}{3}$.

7. Color $\frac{3}{4}$.

8. Color $\frac{5}{6}$.

9. Color $\frac{5}{8}$.

10. Color $\frac{4}{5}$.

Fractional parts of figures

Parts of a Whole

Color the parts.

$\frac{1}{4}$ is white.

$\frac{3}{4}$ is red.

1. Color $\frac{1}{6}$ red.

   Color $\frac{5}{6}$ blue.

2. Color $\frac{2}{3}$ purple.

   Color $\frac{1}{3}$ yellow.

3. Color $\frac{3}{8}$ blue.

   Color $\frac{5}{8}$ green.

4. Color $\frac{7}{10}$ brown.

   Color $\frac{3}{10}$ yellow.

5. Color $\frac{3}{5}$ purple.

   Color $\frac{2}{5}$ yellow.

6. Color $\frac{2}{4}$ red.

   Color $\frac{2}{4}$ blue.

7. Color $\frac{1}{3}$ red.

   Color $\frac{2}{3}$ blue.

8. Color $\frac{4}{10}$ purple.

   Color $\frac{6}{10}$ yellow.

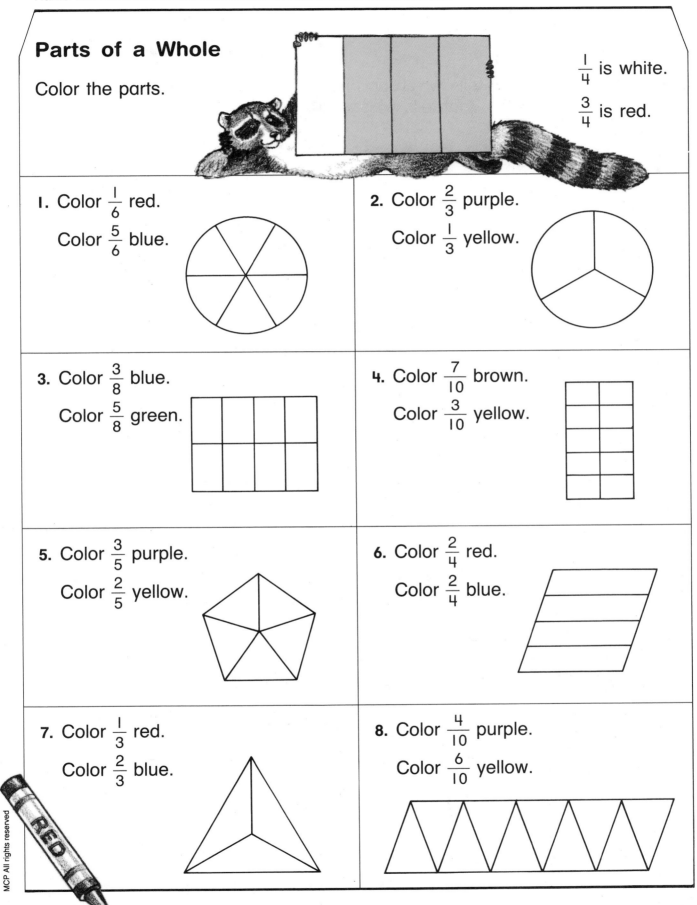

Fractional parts of figures

Practice

Write the fraction that tells which part is red.
Then write the fraction that tells which part is white.

1.

$\dfrac{2}{5}$ is red.

$\dfrac{3}{5}$ is white.

2.

$\dfrac{}{}$ is red.

$\dfrac{}{}$ is white.

3.

$\dfrac{}{}$ is red.

$\dfrac{}{}$ is white.

4.

$\dfrac{}{}$ is red.

$\dfrac{}{}$ is white.

5.

$\dfrac{}{}$ is red.

$\dfrac{}{}$ is white.

6.

$\dfrac{}{}$ is red.

$\dfrac{}{}$ is white.

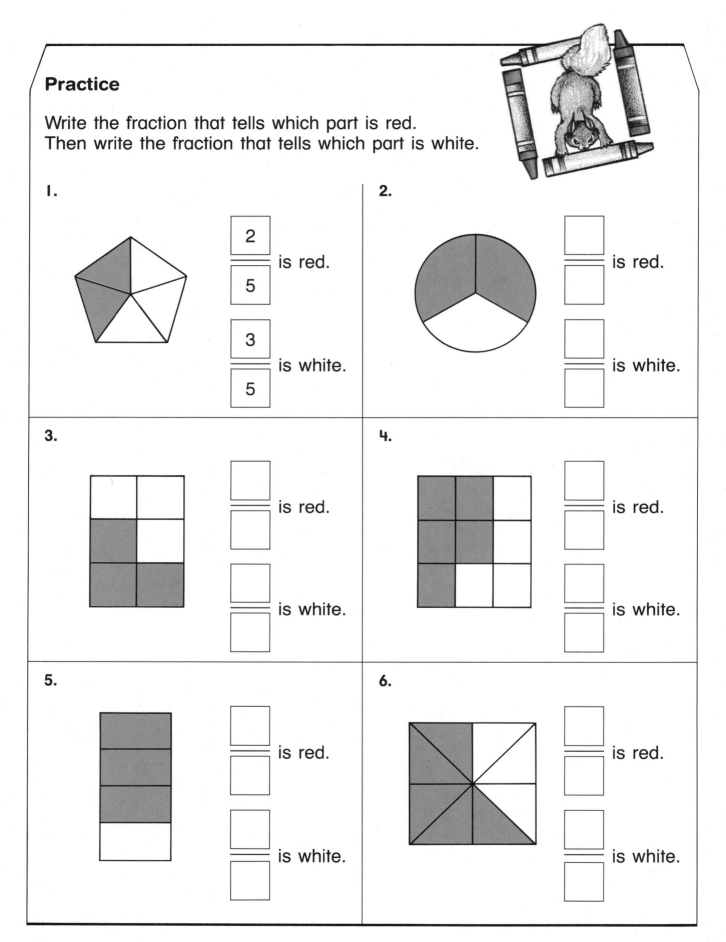

Fractional parts of figures

Name _____

Parts of Groups

Ann has 5 cars.
3 cars are red.
What part of the
cars are red?

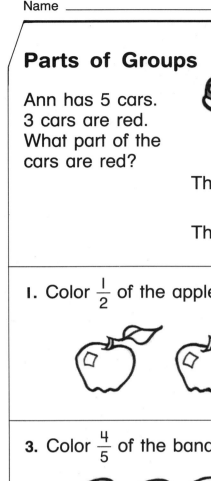

There are _____ red cars.

There are _____ cars in all.

$\dfrac{\square}{\square}$ of the cars are red.

1. Color $\frac{1}{2}$ of the apples.

2. Color $\frac{2}{3}$ of the oranges.

3. Color $\frac{4}{5}$ of the bananas.

4. Color $\frac{3}{10}$ of the cherries.

5. Color $\frac{3}{4}$ of the tomatoes.

6. Color $\frac{3}{6}$ of the peaches.

7. Color $\frac{4}{4}$ of the pears.

8. Color $\frac{5}{8}$ of the lemons.

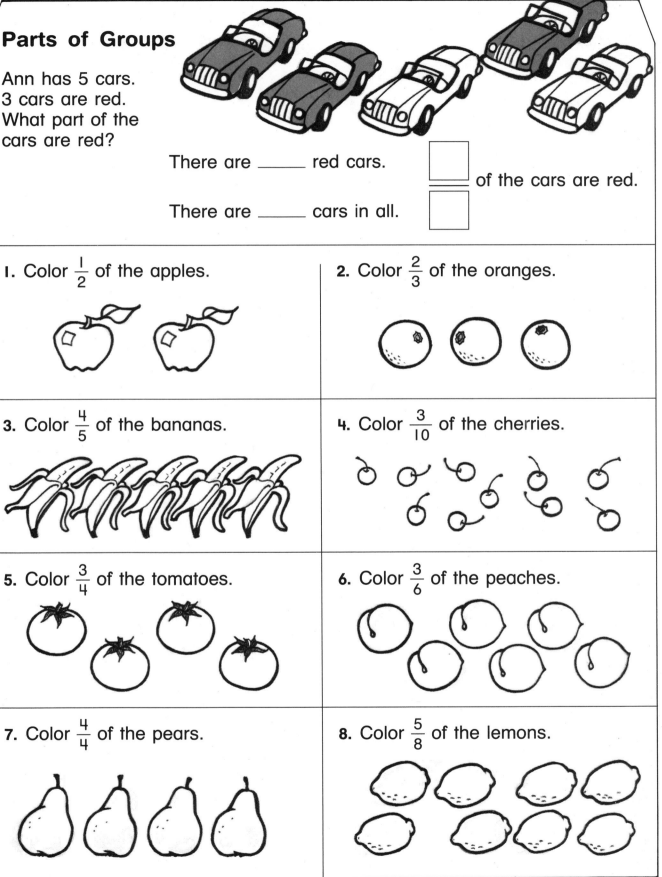

Fractional parts of groups

(two hundred fifty-one) **251**

Practice

What part is red? Write the fraction.

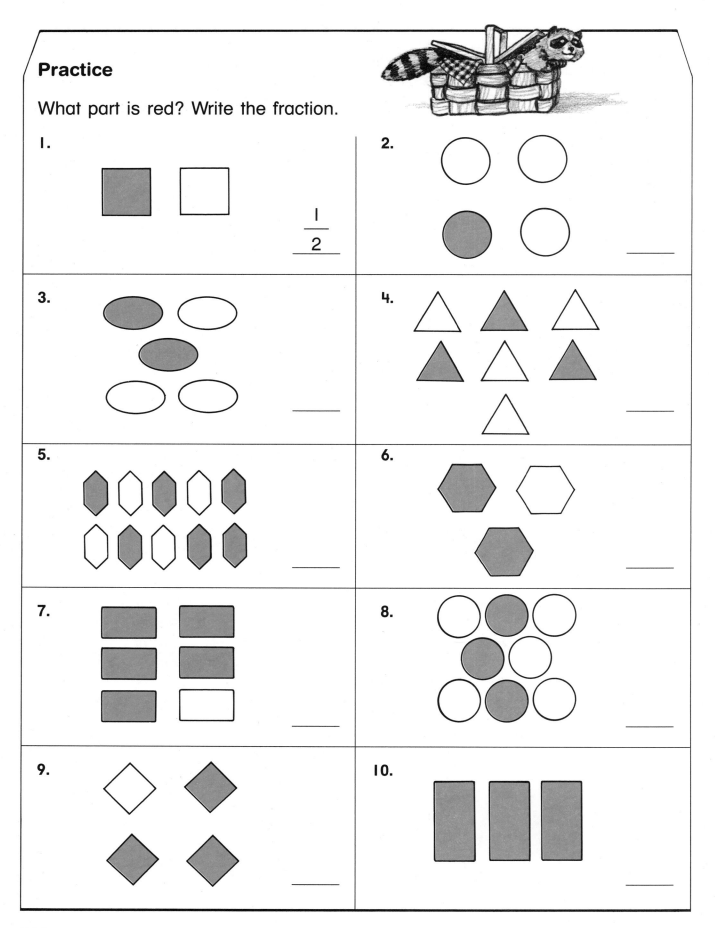

1.

$$\frac{1}{2}$$

2. _____

3. _____

4. _____

5. _____

6. _____

7. _____

8. _____

9. _____

10. _____

Fractional parts of groups

Parts of Groups

What part is stars?

3 stars

5 shapes in all

$\frac{3}{5}$

_____ of the shapes are stars.

What part is moons?

☐ moons

☐ shapes in all

_____ of the shapes are moons.

Write the correct fraction on the line.

1. _____ of the flowers are tulips.

2. _____ of the flowers are daisies.

3. _____ of the animals are cats.

4. _____ of the animals are dogs.

5. _____ of the vegetables are carrots.

6. _____ of the vegetables are corn.

7. _____ of the vegetables are cabbage.

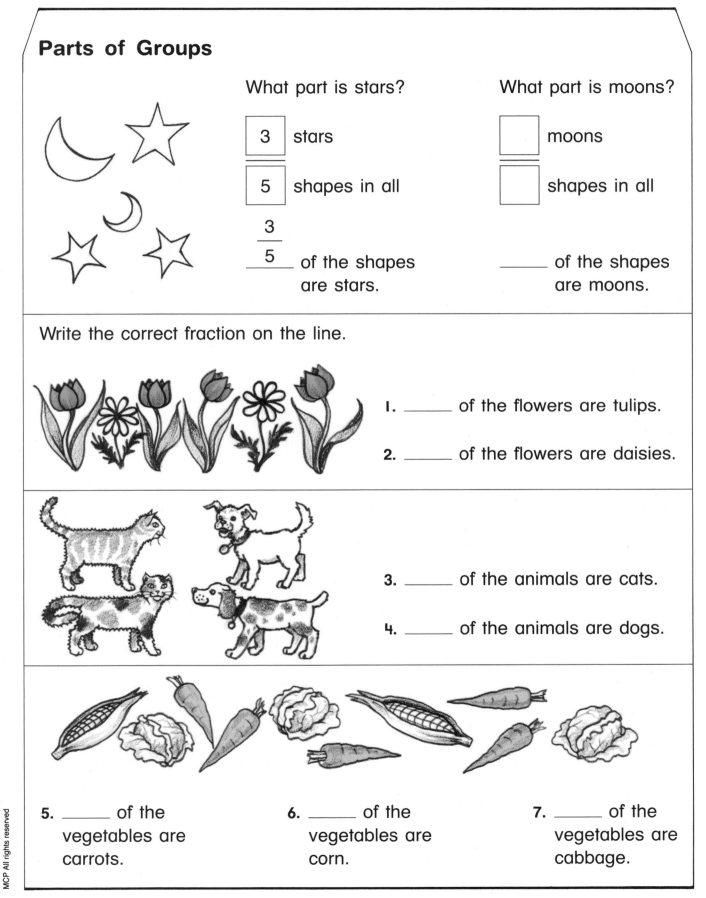

(two hundred fifty-three) **253**

Practice

Write the correct fraction on the line.

1. _____ of the shapes are circles.

2. _____ of the shapes are squares.

3. _____ of the shapes are rectangles.

4. _____ of the shapes are triangles.

5. _____ of the shapes are red.

6. _____ of the shapes are white.

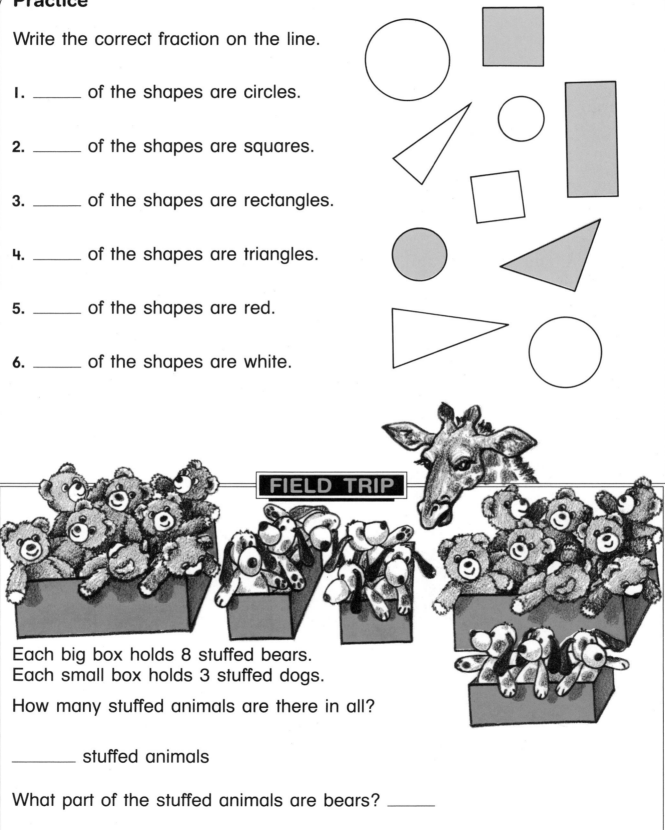

FIELD TRIP

Each big box holds 8 stuffed bears.
Each small box holds 3 stuffed dogs.

How many stuffed animals are there in all?

_____ stuffed animals

What part of the stuffed animals are bears? _____

CHAPTER CHECKUP

How many of each shape are there? Write the number.

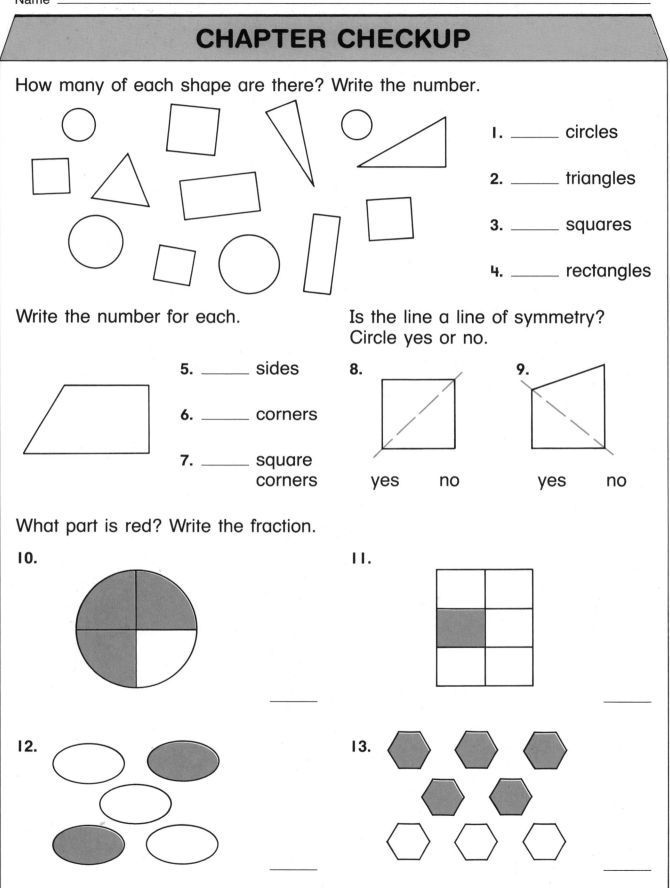

1. _____ circles

2. _____ triangles

3. _____ squares

4. _____ rectangles

Write the number for each.

5. _____ sides

6. _____ corners

7. _____ square corners

Is the line a line of symmetry? Circle yes or no.

8.

yes   no

9.

yes   no

What part is red? Write the fraction.

10.

11. _____

12. _____

13. _____

ROUNDUP REVIEW

Fill in the oval next to the correct answer.

1 $5 + 7$
- ⬭ 2
- ⬭ 12
- ⬭ 13
- ⬭ NG

2 $15 - 8$
- ⬭ 23
- ⬭ 3
- ⬭ 7
- ⬭ NG

3
- ⬭ 352
- ⬭ 235
- ⬭ 523
- ⬭ NG

4 $35 + 27$
- ⬭ 52
- ⬭ 8
- ⬭ 62
- ⬭ NG

5 $473 + 75$
- ⬭ 448
- ⬭ 548
- ⬭ 398
- ⬭ NG

6 $265 + 376$
- ⬭ 641
- ⬭ 631
- ⬭ 541
- ⬭ NG

7 $85 - 26$
- ⬭ 61
- ⬭ 59
- ⬭ 69
- ⬭ NG

8 $526 - 85$
- ⬭ 561
- ⬭ 541
- ⬭ 441
- ⬭ NG

9 $725 - 298$
- ⬭ 573
- ⬭ 427
- ⬭ 537
- ⬭ NG

10 What part is red?
- ⬭ $\frac{3}{4}$
- ⬭ $\frac{4}{3}$
- ⬭ $\frac{1}{4}$
- ⬭ NG

11 $455 + 345$
- ⬭ 800
- ⬭ 750
- ⬭ 700
- ⬭ NG

12 $\$4.59 + 2.82$
- ⬭ $7.31
- ⬭ $6.41
- ⬭ $7.41
- ⬭ NG

13 $\$7.15 - .48$
- ⬭ $6.67
- ⬭ $6.77
- ⬭ $7.33
- ⬭ NG

◻ score

14 MEASUREMENT

Inches and Half-Inches

Cindy needs 2 pieces of ribbon for a school project. One piece should be 4 inches long and the other should be $3\frac{1}{2}$ inches long. Mark each ribbon where Cindy needs to cut.

4 inches

$3\frac{1}{2}$ inches

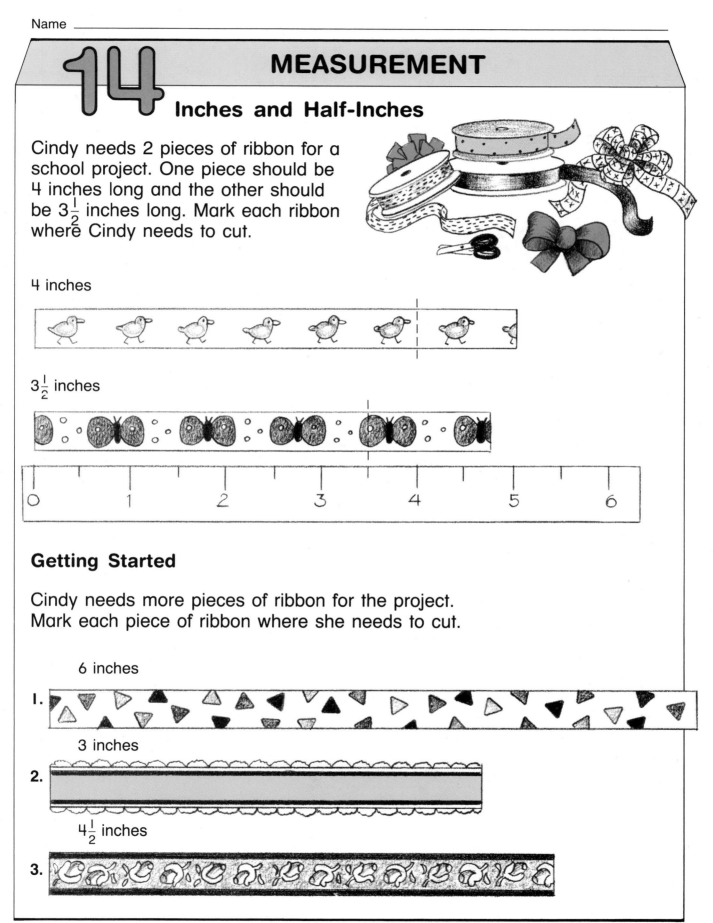

Getting Started

Cindy needs more pieces of ribbon for the project. Mark each piece of ribbon where she needs to cut.

6 inches

1.

3 inches

2.

$4\frac{1}{2}$ inches

3.

Practice

Cindy needs more pieces of ribbon for the project.
Mark each piece of ribbon where she needs to cut.

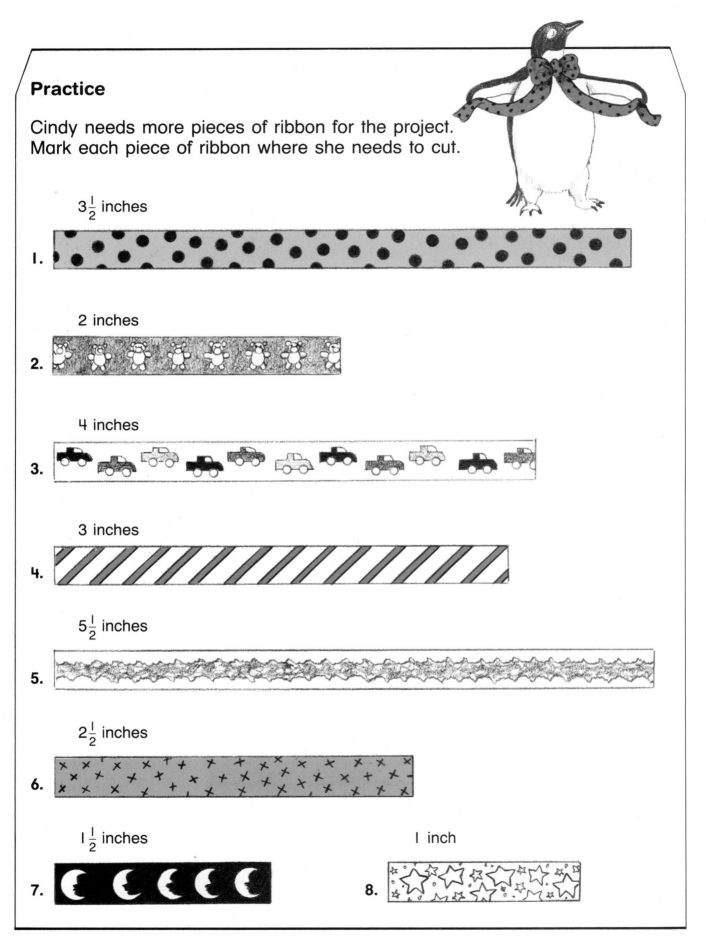

$3\frac{1}{2}$ inches

1.

2 inches

2.

4 inches

3.

3 inches

4.

$5\frac{1}{2}$ inches

5.

$2\frac{1}{2}$ inches

6.

$1\frac{1}{2}$ inches

7.

1 inch

8.

Measuring inches and half-inches

Name _____

Measuring to the Nearest Inch

Raul wants to find the length of his pencil to the nearest inch.

It is closer to 5.

It is between 4 and 5.

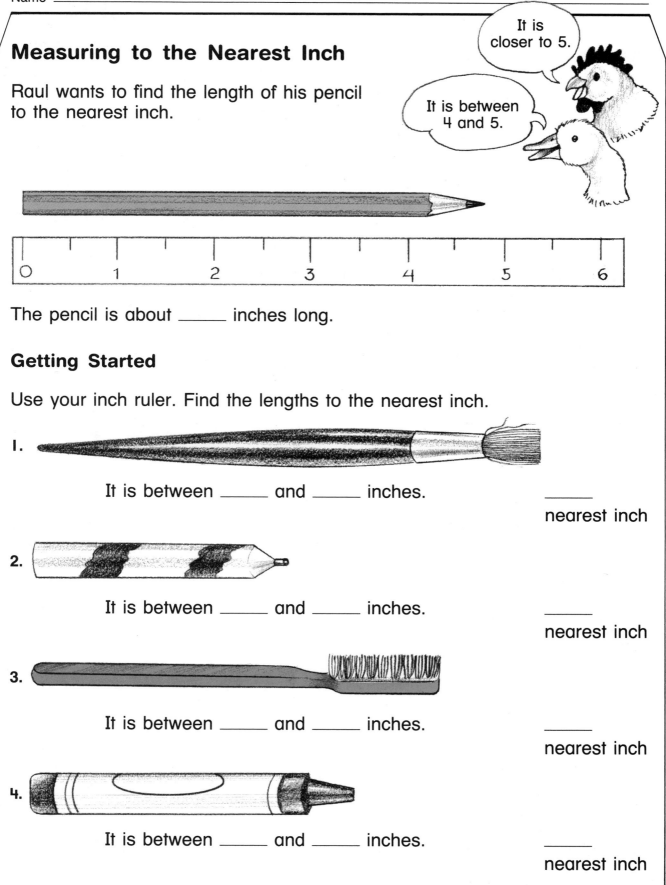

The pencil is about _____ inches long.

Getting Started

Use your inch ruler. Find the lengths to the nearest inch.

1. It is between _____ and _____ inches.

_____
nearest inch

2. It is between _____ and _____ inches.

_____
nearest inch

3. It is between _____ and _____ inches.

_____
nearest inch

4. It is between _____ and _____ inches.

_____
nearest inch

Practice

Use your inch ruler. Find the lengths to the nearest inch.

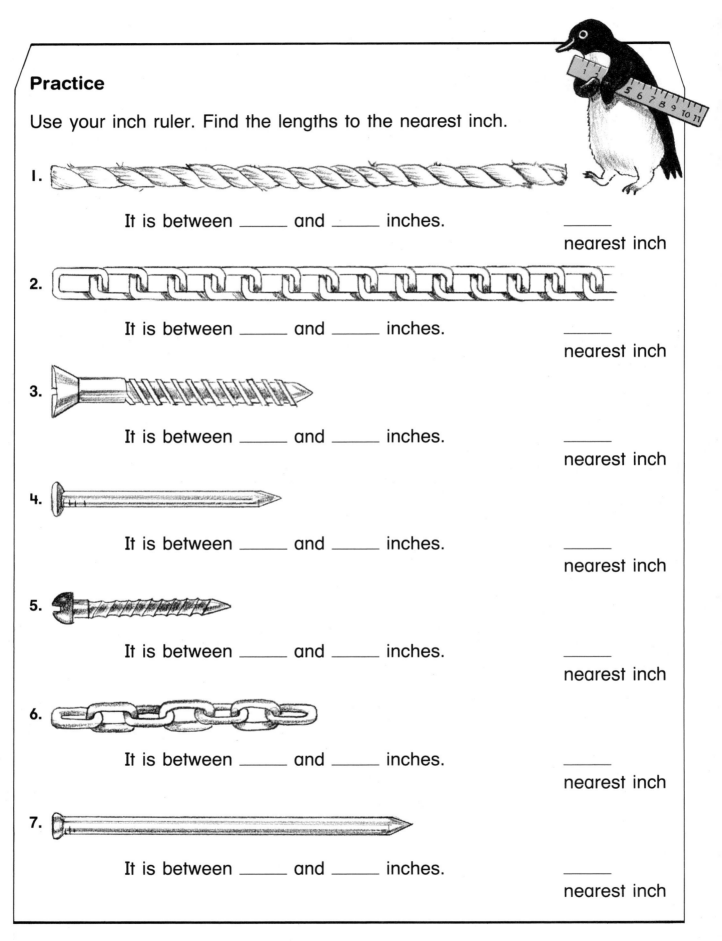

1. It is between _____ and _____ inches.

_____
nearest inch

2. It is between _____ and _____ inches.

_____
nearest inch

3. It is between _____ and _____ inches.

_____
nearest inch

4. It is between _____ and _____ inches.

_____
nearest inch

5. It is between _____ and _____ inches.

_____
nearest inch

6. It is between _____ and _____ inches.

_____
nearest inch

7. It is between _____ and _____ inches.

_____
nearest inch

Measuring to the nearest inch

Centimeters

Penny wants to use a centimeter ruler to measure a stick and mark it for a cut.

The stick is _____ centimeters long. Penny

marked the stick for a cut at _____ centimeters.

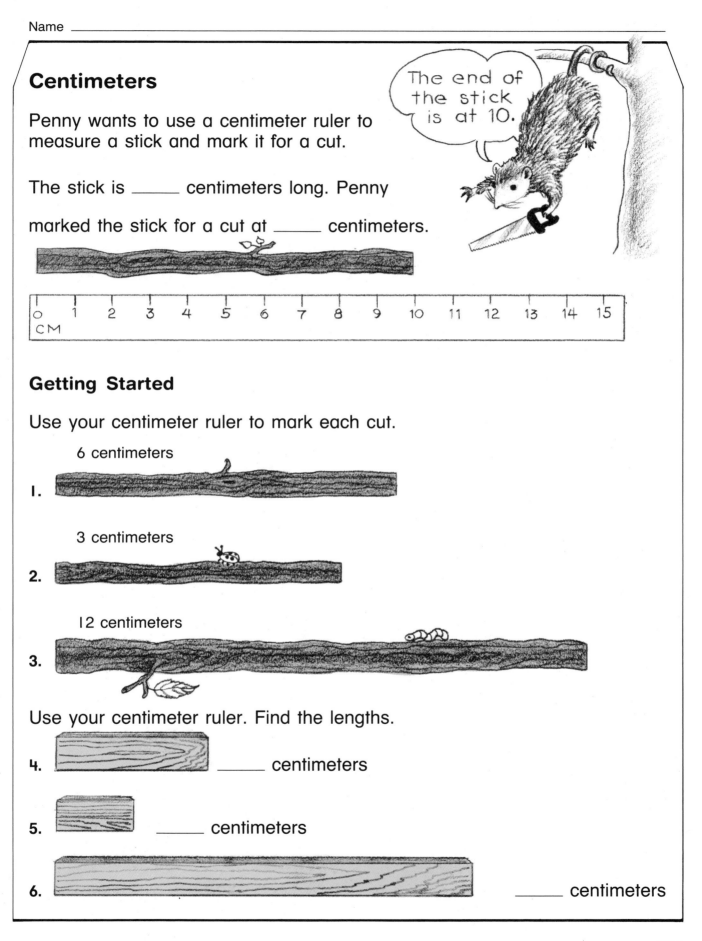

The end of the stick is at 10.

Getting Started

Use your centimeter ruler to mark each cut.

1. 6 centimeters

2. 3 centimeters

3. 12 centimeters

Use your centimeter ruler. Find the lengths.

4. _____ centimeters

5. _____ centimeters

6. _____ centimeters

Practice

Use your centimeter ruler to mark each cut.

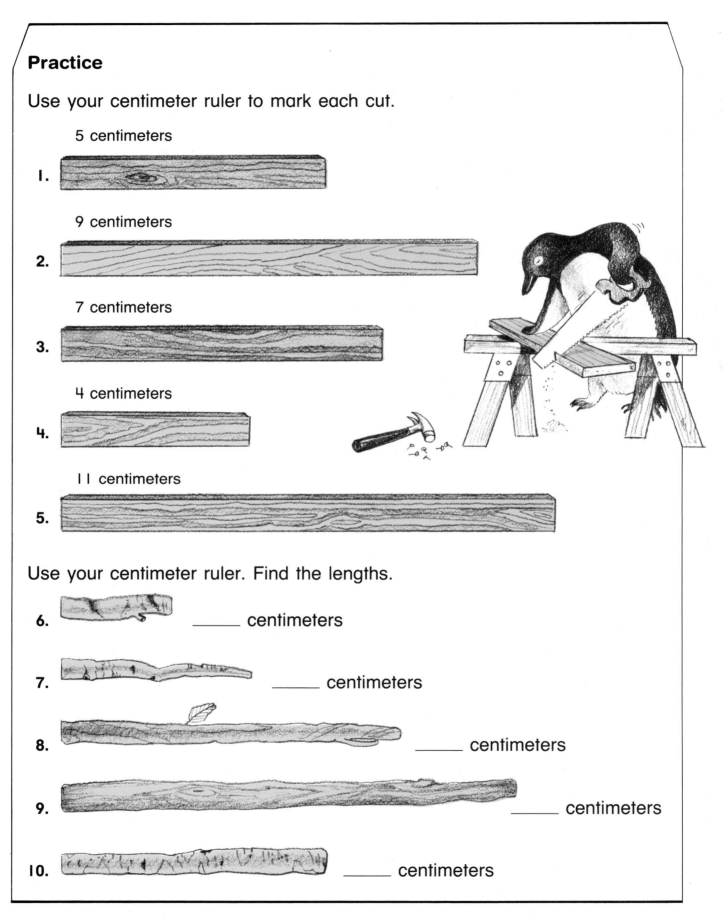

5 centimeters

1.

9 centimeters

2.

7 centimeters

3.

4 centimeters

4.

11 centimeters

5.

Use your centimeter ruler. Find the lengths.

6. _____ centimeters

7. _____ centimeters

8. _____ centimeters

9. _____ centimeters

10. _____ centimeters

Measuring centimeters

Measuring to the Nearest Centimeter

The nail is closer to 6 centimeters long.

Seth wants to know about how long the nail is. He uses his centimeter ruler to measure to the nearest centimeter.

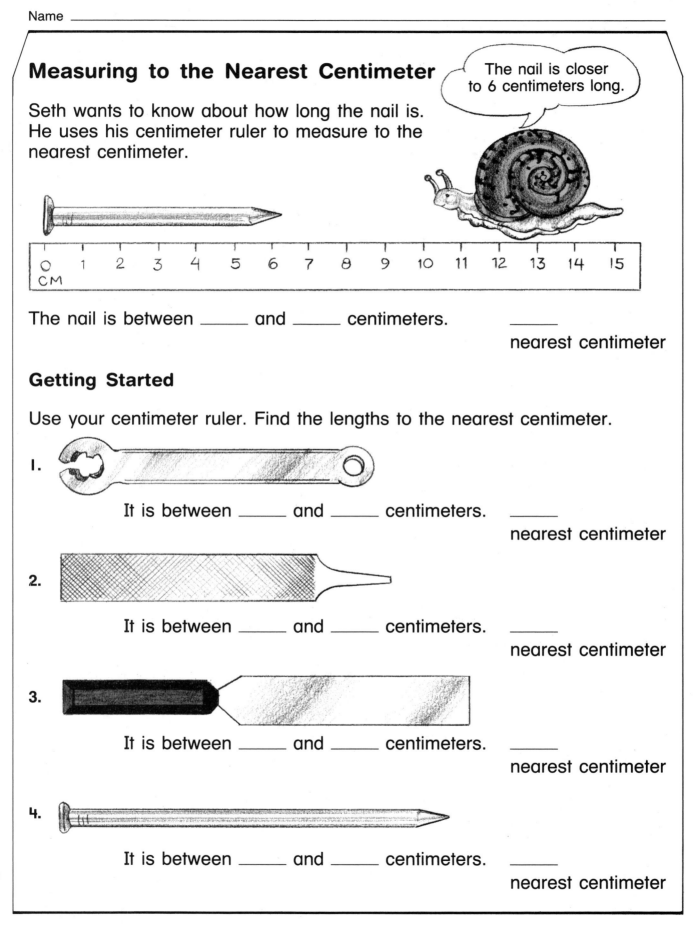

The nail is between _____ and _____ centimeters.

_____ nearest centimeter

Getting Started

Use your centimeter ruler. Find the lengths to the nearest centimeter.

1. It is between _____ and _____ centimeters.

_____ nearest centimeter

2. It is between _____ and _____ centimeters.

_____ nearest centimeter

3. It is between _____ and _____ centimeters.

_____ nearest centimeter

4. It is between _____ and _____ centimeters.

_____ nearest centimeter

Practice

Use your centimeter ruler. Find the lengths to the nearest centimeter.

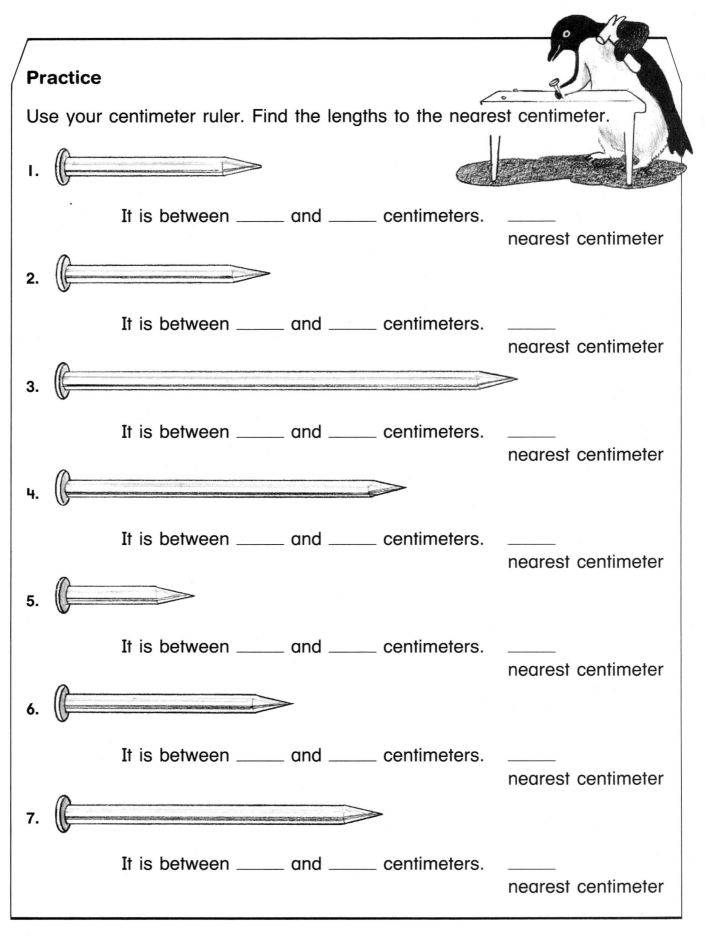

1.

It is between _____ and _____ centimeters. _____

nearest centimeter

2.

It is between _____ and _____ centimeters. _____

nearest centimeter

3.

It is between _____ and _____ centimeters. _____

nearest centimeter

4.

It is between _____ and _____ centimeters. _____

nearest centimeter

5.

It is between _____ and _____ centimeters. _____

nearest centimeter

6.

It is between _____ and _____ centimeters. _____

nearest centimeter

7.

It is between _____ and _____ centimeters. _____

nearest centimeter

Measuring to the nearest centimeter

Perimeter

The perimeter is the distance around a figure.

$$\underset{\text{A to B}}{3} + \underset{\text{B to C}}{3} + \underset{\text{C to D}}{3} + \underset{\text{D to A}}{3} = \underline{\qquad}$$

The distance around the figure is _____ centimeters.

Getting Started

Use your centimeter ruler. Measure around each figure.

1.

$$\underset{\text{X to Y}}{\underline{\qquad}} + \underset{\text{Y to Z}}{\underline{\qquad}} + \underset{\text{Z to X}}{\underline{\qquad}} = \underline{\qquad}$$

The perimeter is _____ centimeters.

2.

$$\underset{\text{A to B}}{\underline{\qquad}} + \underset{\text{B to C}}{\underline{\qquad}} + \underset{\text{C to D}}{\underline{\qquad}} + \underset{\text{D to A}}{\underline{\qquad}} = \underline{\qquad}$$

The perimeter is _____ centimeters.

3.

perimeter = _____ centimeters

4.

perimeter = _____ centimeters

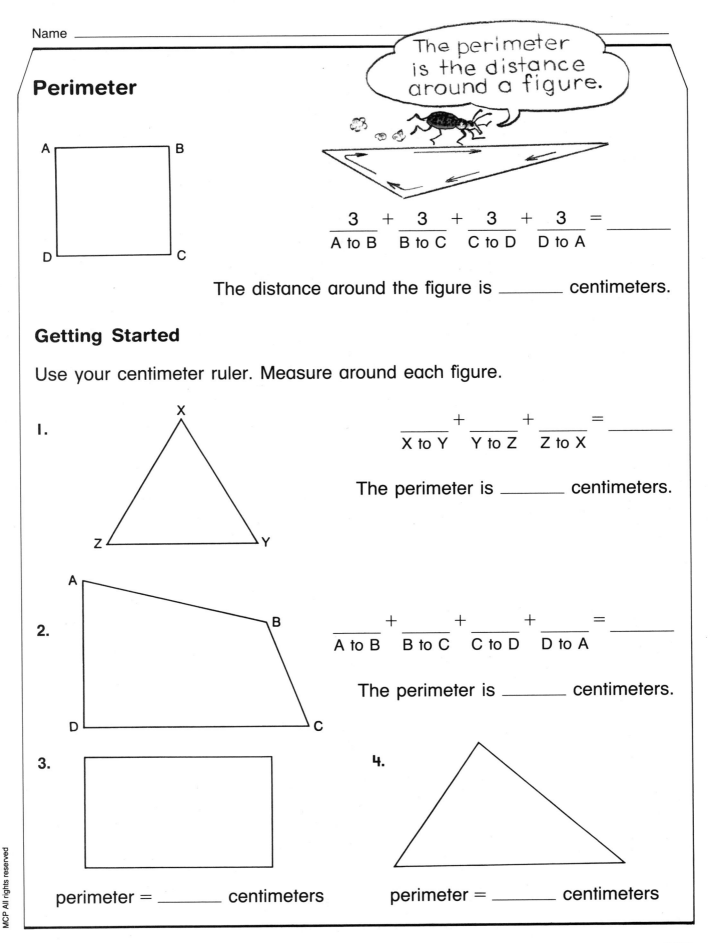

Practice

Use your centimeter ruler. Measure around each figure.

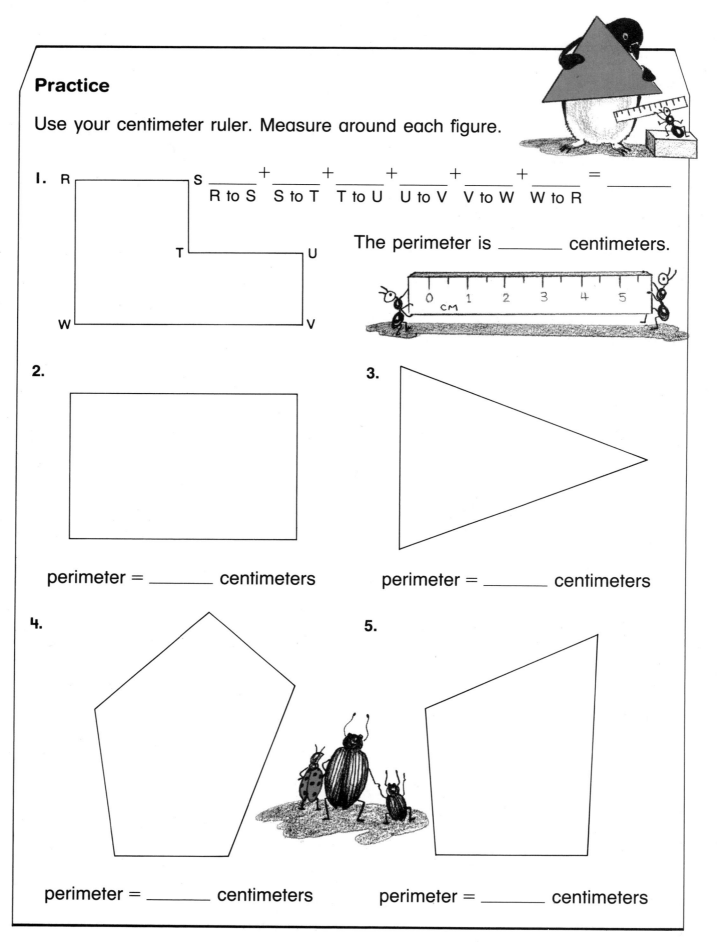

1. $\underset{\text{R to S}}{\rule{2cm}{0.4pt}} + \underset{\text{S to T}}{\rule{1.5cm}{0.4pt}} + \underset{\text{T to U}}{\rule{1.5cm}{0.4pt}} + \underset{\text{U to V}}{\rule{1.5cm}{0.4pt}} + \underset{\text{V to W}}{\rule{1.5cm}{0.4pt}} + \underset{\text{W to R}}{\rule{1.5cm}{0.4pt}} = \rule{2cm}{0.4pt}$

The perimeter is _____ centimeters.

2. perimeter = _____ centimeters

3. perimeter = _____ centimeters

4. perimeter = _____ centimeters

5. perimeter = _____ centimeters

Measuring to find perimeter

Area

This is a square centimeter.

I can count squares to find area.

The area of this figure is

_____ square centimeters.

Getting Started

Find the area of each figure.

1. _____ square centimeters

2. _____ square centimeters

3. _____ square centimeters

4. _____ square centimeters

5. _____ square centimeters

6. _____ square centimeters

(two hundred sixty-seven) **267**

Practice

Find the area of each figure.

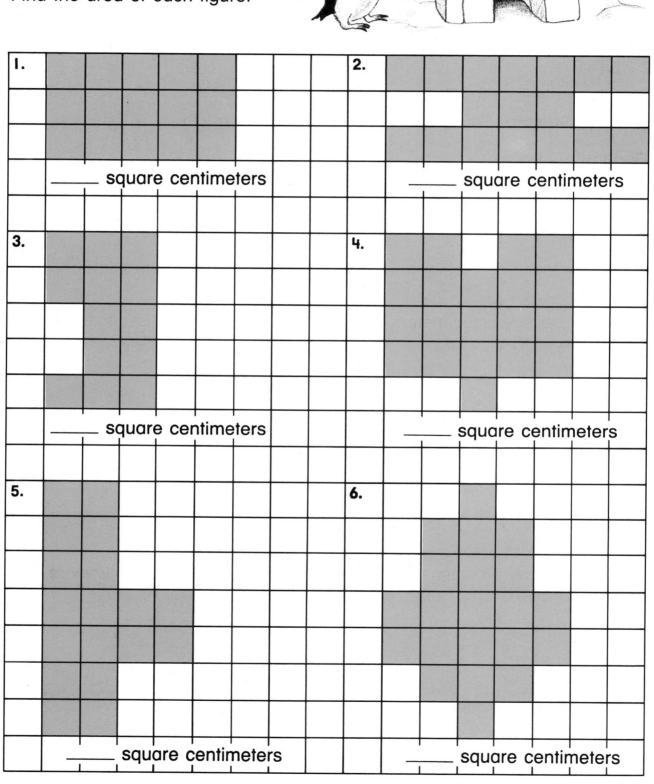

1. _____ square centimeters

2. _____ square centimeters

3. _____ square centimeters

4. _____ square centimeters

5. _____ square centimeters

6. _____ square centimeters

Finding area

Pounds and Ounces

A pound is a unit for measuring weight.

This weighs 1 pound.

This tennis ball weighs less than 1 pound.

My dog weighs more than 1 pound.

9 pennies weigh about 1 ounce.

An ounce is also a unit for measuring weight.

16 ounces = 1 pound

Getting Started

Circle the better guess for the weight.

1.

(More than 1 pound)

Less than 1 pound

2.

More than 1 pound

Less than 1 pound

3.

2 pounds   2 ounces

4.

4 pounds   4 ounces

Estimating weight   (two hundred sixty-nine) **269**

Practice

Circle the better guess for the weight.

1.

More than 1 pound

Less than 1 pound

2.

More than 1 pound

Less than 1 pound

3.

More than 1 pound

Less than 1 pound

4.

More than 1 pound

Less than 1 pound

5.

3 pounds   3 ounces

6.

20 pounds   20 ounces

7.

21 pounds   21 ounces

8.

1 pound   1 ounce

9.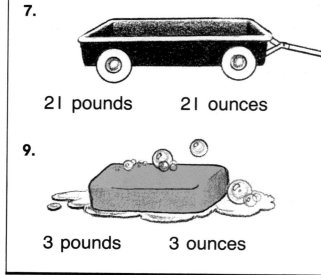

3 pounds   3 ounces

10.

15 pounds   15 ounces

Name _____

Cups, Pints and Quarts

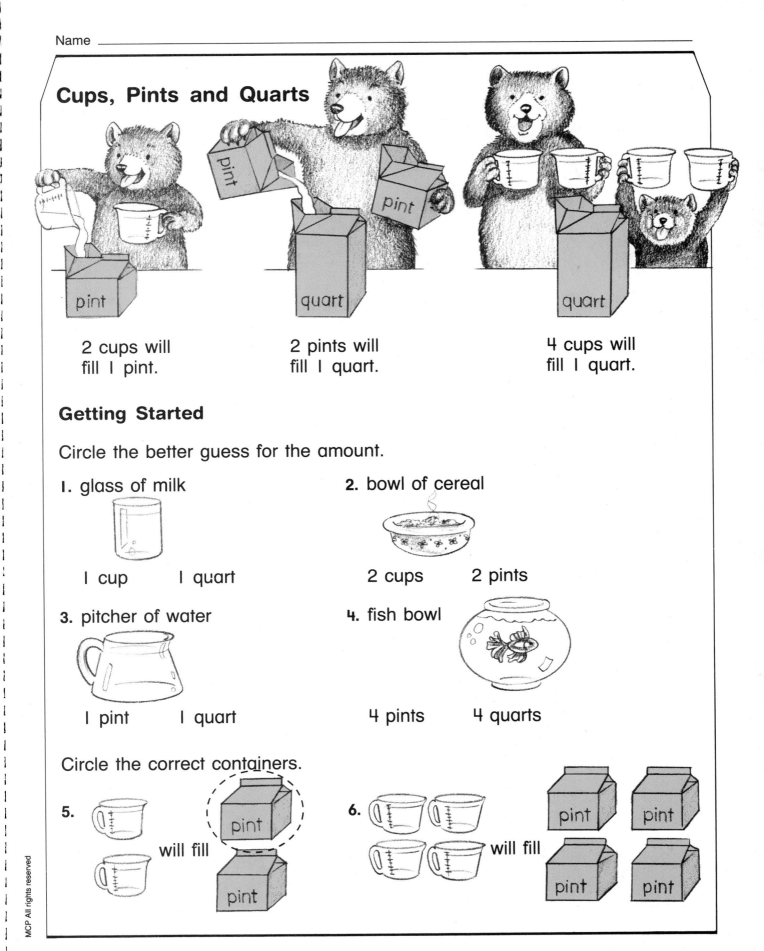

2 cups will fill 1 pint.

2 pints will fill 1 quart.

4 cups will fill 1 quart.

Getting Started

Circle the better guess for the amount.

1. glass of milk

1 cup   1 quart

2. bowl of cereal

2 cups   2 pints

3. pitcher of water

1 pint   1 quart

4. fish bowl

4 pints   4 quarts

Circle the correct containers.

5. will fill

6. will fill

(two hundred seventy-one) **271**

Practice

Circle the better guess for the amount.

1. coffee pot

8 cups   8 quarts

2. baking pan

2 cups   2 quarts

3. can of juice

2 cups   2 pints

4. water bucket

4 quarts   4 cups

Circle the correct containers.

5. will fill

6. will fill

7. will fill

8. will fill

9. will fill

10. will fill

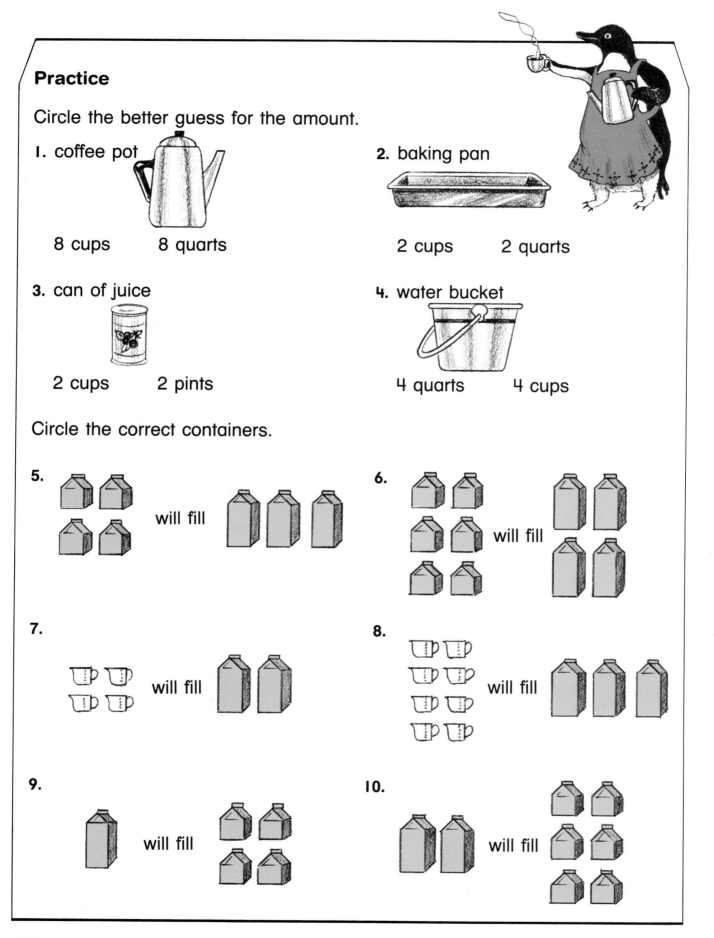

Temperature

Thermometers are used to measure temperature. This is a Fahrenheit thermometer.

This is a Celsius thermometer. It measures temperature using a different scale.

70°F

20°C

We read this _____ degrees Fahrenheit.

We read this _____ degrees Celsius.

Getting Started

Write the temperature.

1.

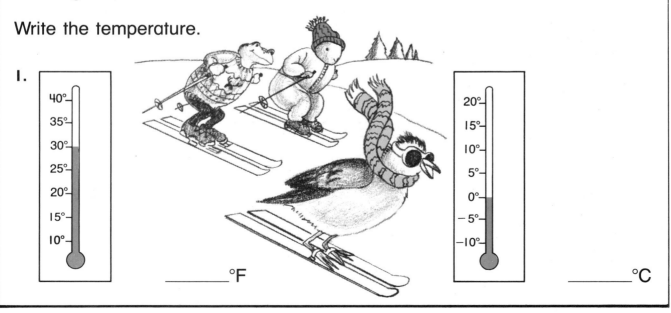

_____ °F

_____ °C

Practice

Write the temperature.

1. _____ °F   _____ °C

2. _____ °F   _____ °C

3. _____ °F   _____ °C

Fahrenheit and Celsius temperatures

CHAPTER CHECKUP

Find the length to the nearest inch.

I.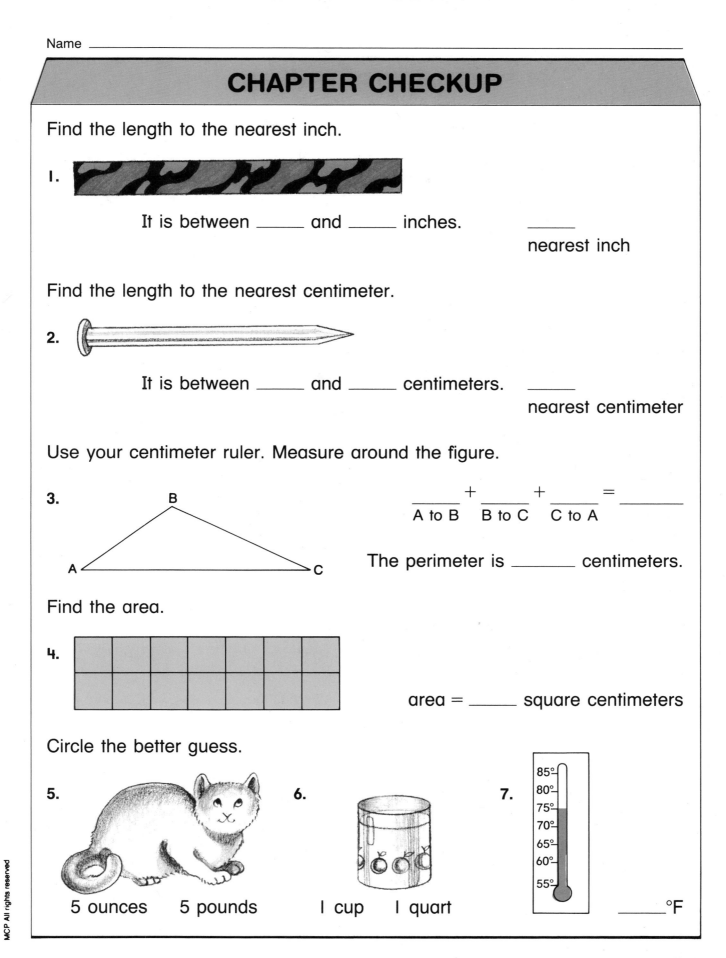

It is between _____ and _____ inches.   _____
                                              nearest inch

Find the length to the nearest centimeter.

2.

It is between _____ and _____ centimeters.   _____
                                              nearest centimeter

Use your centimeter ruler. Measure around the figure.

3.

$$\frac{\qquad}{\text{A to B}} + \frac{\qquad}{\text{B to C}} + \frac{\qquad}{\text{C to A}} = \underline{\qquad}$$

The perimeter is _____ centimeters.

Find the area.

4.

area = _____ square centimeters

Circle the better guess.

5.   5 ounces   5 pounds

6.   I cup   I quart

7.   _____ °F

ROUNDUP REVIEW

Fill in the oval next to the correct answer.

1
7
+ 5
- 2
- 12
- 13
- NG

2 17 − 8
- 8
- 25
- 11
- NG

3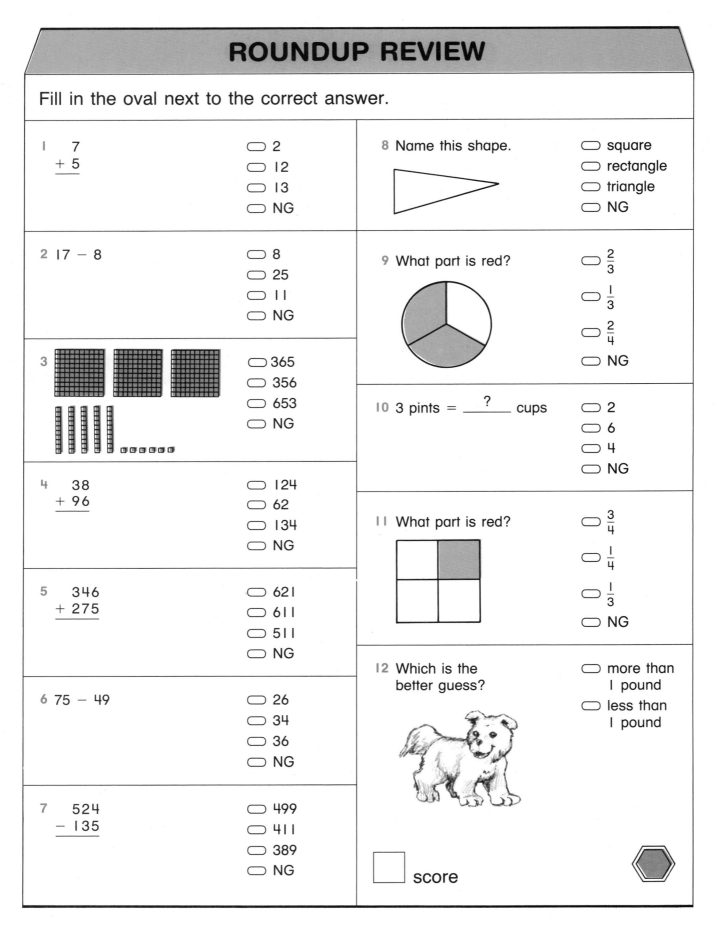
- 365
- 356
- 653
- NG

4
38
+ 96
- 124
- 62
- 134
- NG

5
346
+ 275
- 621
- 611
- 511
- NG

6 75 − 49
- 26
- 34
- 36
- NG

7
524
− 135
- 499
- 411
- 389
- NG

8 Name this shape.
- square
- rectangle
- triangle
- NG

9 What part is red?
- $\frac{2}{3}$
- $\frac{1}{3}$
- $\frac{2}{4}$
- NG

10 3 pints = _____?_____ cups
- 2
- 6
- 4
- NG

11 What part is red?
- $\frac{3}{4}$
- $\frac{1}{4}$
- $\frac{1}{3}$
- NG

12 Which is the better guess?
- more than 1 pound
- less than 1 pound

[ ] score

276 (two hundred seventy-six)

Cumulative review

15 MULTIPLICATION, THROUGH 5 × 5

2 as a Factor

Rona put 2 buttons in each box. She has 4 boxes. How many buttons does she have?

4 twos = ?

We are looking for the number of buttons.

Rona put _____ buttons in each box.

She has _____ boxes.
To find the number of buttons,

we can add _____ and _____ and _____ and _____,

or we can multiply _____ by _____.

Add.

$$\begin{array}{r} 2 \\ 2 \\ 2 \\ + 2 \\ \hline 8 \end{array}$$

or

Multiply.

$$\begin{array}{r} 2 \\ \times 4 \\ \hline 8 \end{array}$$

Rona has _____ buttons.

Getting Started

How many are there? Write the answers.

1.

$2 + 2 + 2 =$ _____

$3 \text{ twos} =$ _____

$3 \times 2 =$ _____

Multiply.

2. $\begin{array}{r} 2 \\ \times 4 \\ \hline \end{array}$ 3. $\begin{array}{r} 2 \\ \times 2 \\ \hline \end{array}$ 4. $\begin{array}{r} 2 \\ \times 1 \\ \hline \end{array}$

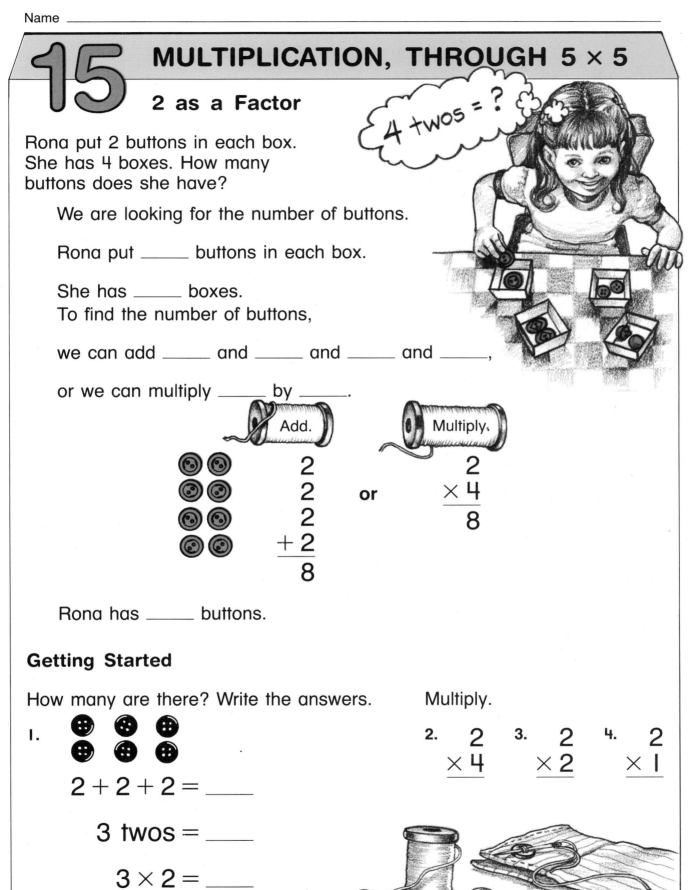

Practice

How many are there? Write the answers.

1.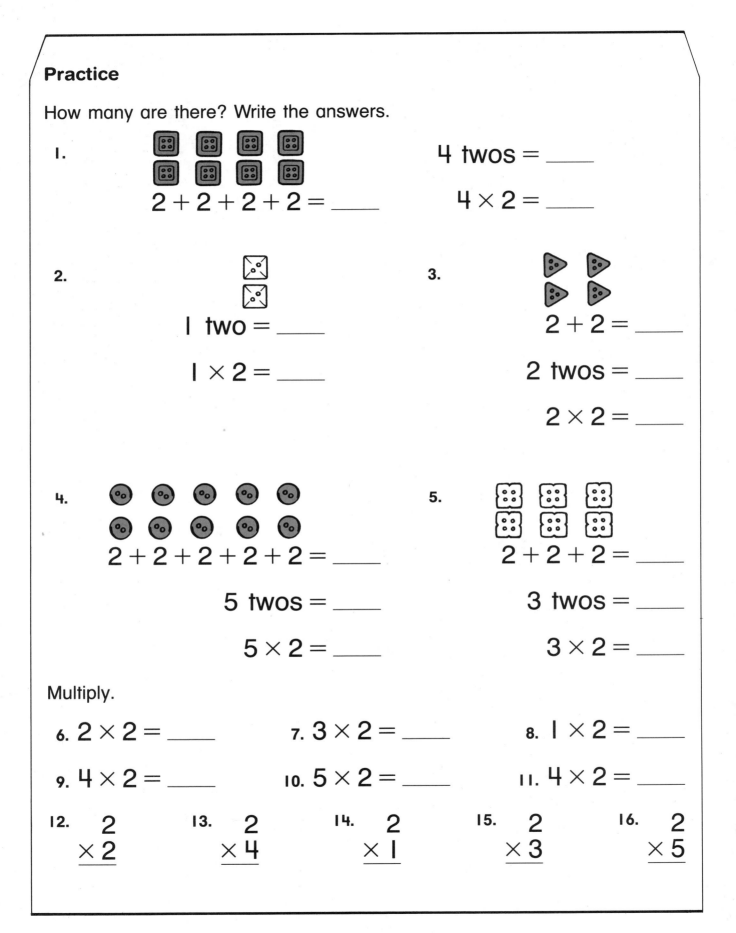

   $2 + 2 + 2 + 2 =$ _____

   4 twos $=$ _____

   $4 \times 2 =$ _____

2. 1 two $=$ _____

   $1 \times 2 =$ _____

3. $2 + 2 =$ _____

   2 twos $=$ _____

   $2 \times 2 =$ _____

4. $2 + 2 + 2 + 2 + 2 =$ _____

   5 twos $=$ _____

   $5 \times 2 =$ _____

5. $2 + 2 + 2 =$ _____

   3 twos $=$ _____

   $3 \times 2 =$ _____

Multiply.

6. $2 \times 2 =$ _____   7. $3 \times 2 =$ _____   8. $1 \times 2 =$ _____

9. $4 \times 2 =$ _____   10. $5 \times 2 =$ _____   11. $4 \times 2 =$ _____

12. $\begin{array}{r} 2 \\ \times 2 \\ \hline \end{array}$ 13. $\begin{array}{r} 2 \\ \times 4 \\ \hline \end{array}$ 14. $\begin{array}{r} 2 \\ \times 1 \\ \hline \end{array}$ 15. $\begin{array}{r} 2 \\ \times 3 \\ \hline \end{array}$ 16. $\begin{array}{r} 2 \\ \times 5 \\ \hline \end{array}$

Multiplication, 2 as a factor

3 as a Factor

Luke put 3 pictures on each card.
He has 3 cards. How many
pictures did he use?

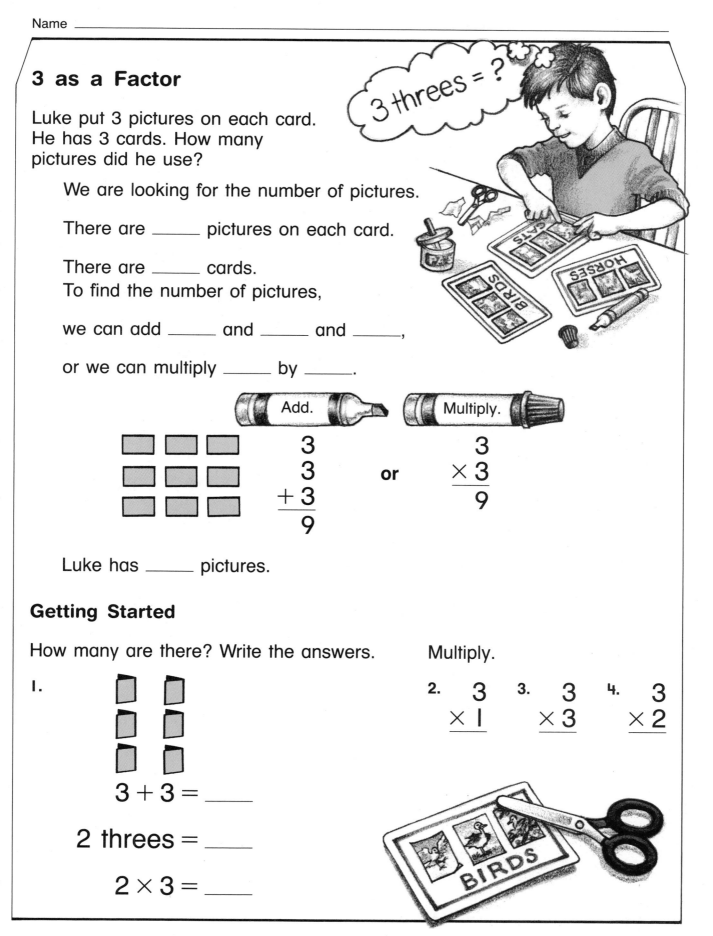

3 threes = ?

We are looking for the number of pictures.

There are _____ pictures on each card.

There are _____ cards.
To find the number of pictures,

we can add _____ and _____ and _____,

or we can multiply _____ by _____.

Add.

$$\begin{array}{r} 3 \\ 3 \\ +3 \\ \hline 9 \end{array}$$

or

Multiply.

$$\begin{array}{r} 3 \\ \times 3 \\ \hline 9 \end{array}$$

Luke has _____ pictures.

Getting Started

How many are there? Write the answers.

Multiply.

1.

$$3 + 3 = \_\_\_$$

2 threes = _____

$$2 \times 3 = \_\_\_$$

2. $\begin{array}{r} 3 \\ \times 1 \\ \hline \end{array}$

3. $\begin{array}{r} 3 \\ \times 3 \\ \hline \end{array}$

4. $\begin{array}{r} 3 \\ \times 2 \\ \hline \end{array}$

Practice

How many are there? Write the answers.

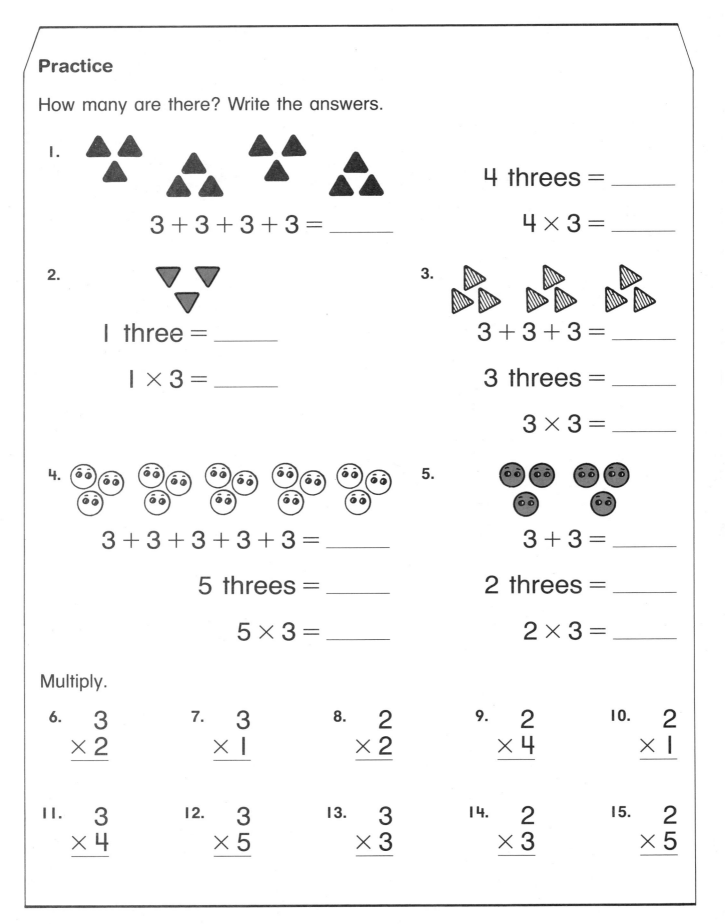

1. $3 + 3 + 3 + 3 =$ _____

   4 threes = _____

   $4 \times 3 =$ _____

2. 1 three = _____

   $1 \times 3 =$ _____

3. $3 + 3 + 3 =$ _____

   3 threes = _____

   $3 \times 3 =$ _____

4. $3 + 3 + 3 + 3 + 3 =$ _____

   5 threes = _____

   $5 \times 3 =$ _____

5. $3 + 3 =$ _____

   2 threes = _____

   $2 \times 3 =$ _____

Multiply.

6. $\begin{array}{r} 3 \\ \times 2 \\ \hline \end{array}$

7. $\begin{array}{r} 3 \\ \times 1 \\ \hline \end{array}$

8. $\begin{array}{r} 2 \\ \times 2 \\ \hline \end{array}$

9. $\begin{array}{r} 2 \\ \times 4 \\ \hline \end{array}$

10. $\begin{array}{r} 2 \\ \times 1 \\ \hline \end{array}$

11. $\begin{array}{r} 3 \\ \times 4 \\ \hline \end{array}$

12. $\begin{array}{r} 3 \\ \times 5 \\ \hline \end{array}$

13. $\begin{array}{r} 3 \\ \times 3 \\ \hline \end{array}$

14. $\begin{array}{r} 2 \\ \times 3 \\ \hline \end{array}$

15. $\begin{array}{r} 2 \\ \times 5 \\ \hline \end{array}$

Multiplication, 3 as a factor

4 as a Factor

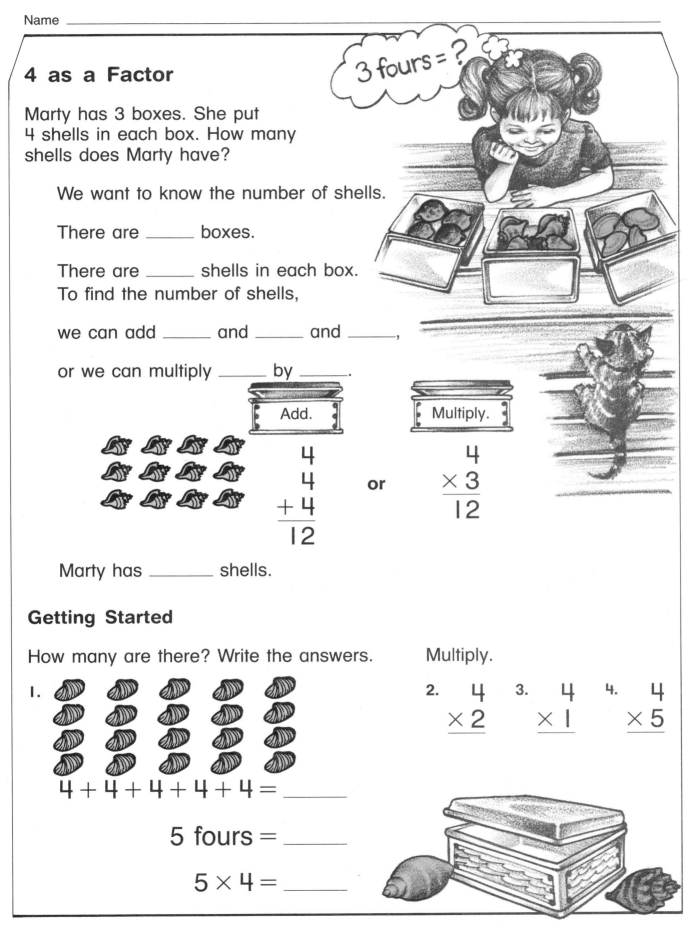

3 fours = ?

Marty has 3 boxes. She put 4 shells in each box. How many shells does Marty have?

We want to know the number of shells.

There are _____ boxes.

There are _____ shells in each box. To find the number of shells,

we can add _____ and _____ and _____,

or we can multiply _____ by _____.

Add.

$$\begin{array}{r} 4 \\ 4 \\ +4 \\ \hline 12 \end{array}$$

or

Multiply.

$$\begin{array}{r} 4 \\ \times 3 \\ \hline 12 \end{array}$$

Marty has _____ shells.

Getting Started

How many are there? Write the answers.

Multiply.

1.

$$4 + 4 + 4 + 4 + 4 = \underline{\hspace{2cm}}$$

$$5 \text{ fours} = \underline{\hspace{2cm}}$$

$$5 \times 4 = \underline{\hspace{2cm}}$$

2. $$\begin{array}{r} 4 \\ \times 2 \\ \hline \end{array}$$

3. $$\begin{array}{r} 4 \\ \times 1 \\ \hline \end{array}$$

4. $$\begin{array}{r} 4 \\ \times 5 \\ \hline \end{array}$$

Practice

How many are there? Write the answers.

1.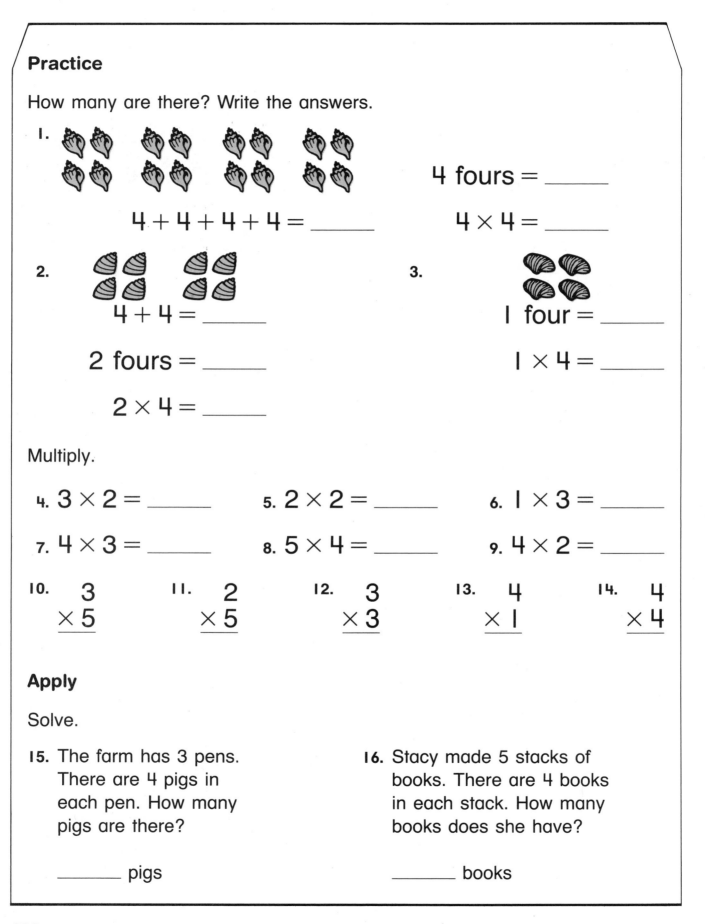

$4 + 4 + 4 + 4 =$ _____

4 fours = _____

$4 \times 4 =$ _____

2.
$4 + 4 =$ _____

2 fours = _____

$2 \times 4 =$ _____

3.
1 four = _____

$1 \times 4 =$ _____

Multiply.

4. $3 \times 2 =$ _____

5. $2 \times 2 =$ _____

6. $1 \times 3 =$ _____

7. $4 \times 3 =$ _____

8. $5 \times 4 =$ _____

9. $4 \times 2 =$ _____

10. $\begin{array}{r} 3 \\ \times 5 \\ \hline \end{array}$

11. $\begin{array}{r} 2 \\ \times 5 \\ \hline \end{array}$

12. $\begin{array}{r} 3 \\ \times 3 \\ \hline \end{array}$

13. $\begin{array}{r} 4 \\ \times 1 \\ \hline \end{array}$

14. $\begin{array}{r} 4 \\ \times 4 \\ \hline \end{array}$

Apply

Solve.

15. The farm has 3 pens. There are 4 pigs in each pen. How many pigs are there?

_____ pigs

16. Stacy made 5 stacks of books. There are 4 books in each stack. How many books does she have?

_____ books

5 as a Factor

Pablo has 4 bags. He put
5 rocks in each bag. How many
rocks does Pablo have?

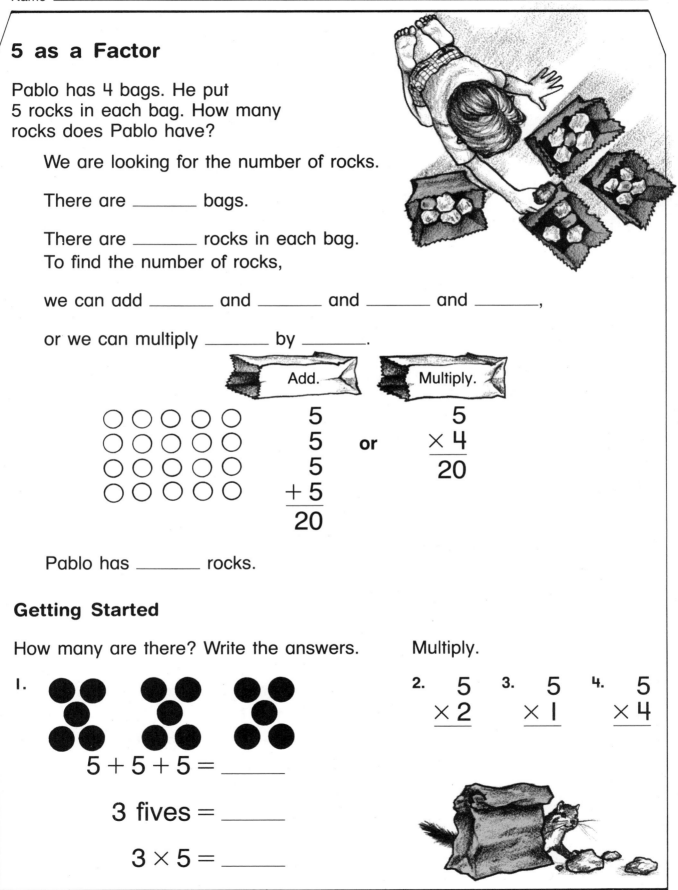

We are looking for the number of rocks.

There are _____ bags.

There are _____ rocks in each bag.
To find the number of rocks,

we can add _____ and _____ and _____ and _____,

or we can multiply _____ by _____.

Add.

$$\begin{array}{r} 5 \\ 5 \\ 5 \\ +5 \\ \hline 20 \end{array}$$

or

Multiply.

$$\begin{array}{r} 5 \\ \times 4 \\ \hline 20 \end{array}$$

Pablo has _____ rocks.

Getting Started

How many are there? Write the answers.

Multiply.

1.

$$5 + 5 + 5 = \underline{\quad}$$

$$3 \text{ fives} = \underline{\quad}$$

$$3 \times 5 = \underline{\quad}$$

2. $\begin{array}{r} 5 \\ \times 2 \\ \hline \end{array}$ 3. $\begin{array}{r} 5 \\ \times 1 \\ \hline \end{array}$ 4. $\begin{array}{r} 5 \\ \times 4 \\ \hline \end{array}$

Practice

How many are there? Write the answers.

1.

$5 + 5 + 5 + 5 + 5 =$ _____

5 fives = _____

$5 \times 5 =$ _____

2.

1 five = _____

$1 \times 5 =$ _____

3.

$5 + 5 =$ _____

2 fives = _____

$2 \times 5 =$ _____

Multiply.

4. $2 \times 5 =$ _____ 5. $2 \times 2 =$ _____ 6. $4 \times 5 =$ _____

7. $3 \times 4 =$ _____ 8. $3 \times 5 =$ _____ 9. $3 \times 3 =$ _____

10. $1 \times 2 =$ _____ 11. $2 \times 4 =$ _____ 12. $5 \times 4 =$ _____

13. $4 \times 3 =$ _____ 14. $5 \times 5 =$ _____ 15. $3 \times 2 =$ _____

16. $\begin{array}{r} 2 \\ \times 2 \\ \hline \end{array}$ 17. $\begin{array}{r} 5 \\ \times 4 \\ \hline \end{array}$ 18. $\begin{array}{r} 4 \\ \times 2 \\ \hline \end{array}$ 19. $\begin{array}{r} 3 \\ \times 3 \\ \hline \end{array}$ 20. $\begin{array}{r} 2 \\ \times 5 \\ \hline \end{array}$ 21. $\begin{array}{r} 5 \\ \times 5 \\ \hline \end{array}$

22. $\begin{array}{r} 4 \\ \times 3 \\ \hline \end{array}$ 23. $\begin{array}{r} 5 \\ \times 2 \\ \hline \end{array}$ 24. $\begin{array}{r} 5 \\ \times 3 \\ \hline \end{array}$ 25. $\begin{array}{r} 2 \\ \times 4 \\ \hline \end{array}$ 26. $\begin{array}{r} 5 \\ \times 1 \\ \hline \end{array}$ 27. $\begin{array}{r} 4 \\ \times 4 \\ \hline \end{array}$

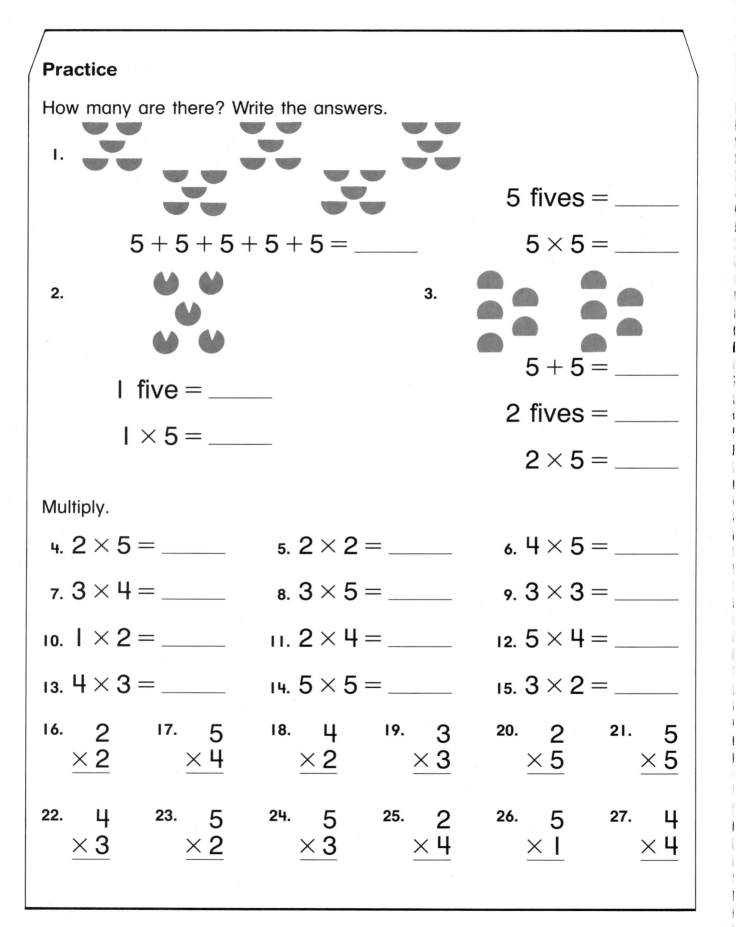

Multiplication, 5 as a factor

Order in Multiplication

Here is an important idea that makes multiplication easy.

We can multiply in any order.
The answers will always be the same.

$$2 \times 3 = 6 \qquad 3 \times 2 = 6$$

Getting Started

Multiply.

1. $3 \times 4 =$ _____

   $4 \times 3 =$ _____

2. $2 \times 5 =$ _____

   $5 \times 2 =$ _____

3. $2 \times 4 =$ _____

   $4 \times 2 =$ _____

4. $1 \times 3 =$ _____

   $3 \times 1 =$ _____

5. $\begin{array}{r} 2 \\ \times 3 \\ \hline \end{array}$ $\begin{array}{r} 3 \\ \times 2 \\ \hline \end{array}$

6. $\begin{array}{r} 5 \\ \times 4 \\ \hline \end{array}$ $\begin{array}{r} 4 \\ \times 5 \\ \hline \end{array}$

7. $\begin{array}{r} 3 \\ \times 5 \\ \hline \end{array}$ $\begin{array}{r} 5 \\ \times 3 \\ \hline \end{array}$

Find the total cost.

8. $\begin{array}{r} 3¢ \\ \times 2 \\ \hline \end{array}$

   2

   Total cost _____

9.

   3

   Total cost _____

Practice

Multiply.

1. $5 \times 4 = \underline{\hspace{1cm}}$

   $4 \times 5 = \underline{\hspace{1cm}}$

2. $1 \times 5 = \underline{\hspace{1cm}}$

   $5 \times 1 = \underline{\hspace{1cm}}$

3. $4 \times 1 = \underline{\hspace{1cm}}$

   $1 \times 4 = \underline{\hspace{1cm}}$

4. $3 \times 5 = \underline{\hspace{1cm}}$

   $5 \times 3 = \underline{\hspace{1cm}}$

5.
$$\begin{array}{r} 5 \\ \times 2 \\ \hline \end{array} \qquad \begin{array}{r} 2 \\ \times 5 \\ \hline \end{array}$$

6.
$$\begin{array}{r} 4 \\ \times 2 \\ \hline \end{array} \qquad \begin{array}{r} 2 \\ \times 4 \\ \hline \end{array}$$

7.
$$\begin{array}{r} 3 \\ \times 4 \\ \hline \end{array} \qquad \begin{array}{r} 4 \\ \times 3 \\ \hline \end{array}$$

Find the total cost.

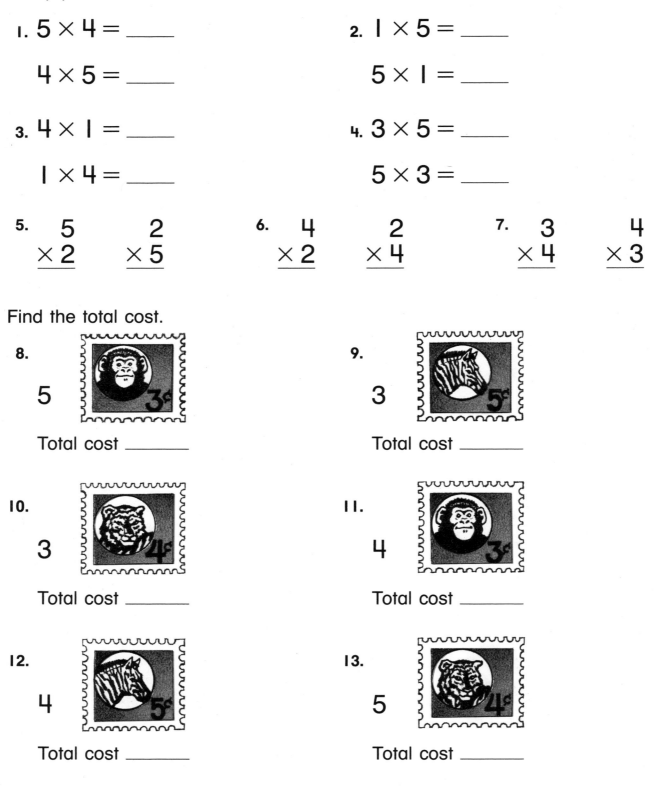

8. 5 [3¢ stamp]

   Total cost $\underline{\hspace{1.5cm}}$

9. 3 [5¢ stamp]

   Total cost $\underline{\hspace{1.5cm}}$

10. 3 [4¢ stamp]

   Total cost $\underline{\hspace{1.5cm}}$

11. 4 [3¢ stamp]

   Total cost $\underline{\hspace{1.5cm}}$

12. 4 [5¢ stamp]

   Total cost $\underline{\hspace{1.5cm}}$

13. 5 [4¢ stamp]

   Total cost $\underline{\hspace{1.5cm}}$

Order in multiplication

Problem Solving

Solve.

Each chair has 4 legs.

1. 2 chairs have _____ legs.

2. 5 chairs have _____ legs.

3. 3 chairs have _____ legs.

4. 4 chairs have _____ legs.

Each bird has 2 legs.

5. 3 birds have _____ legs.

6. 1 bird has _____ legs.

7. 2 birds have _____ legs.

8. 5 birds have _____ legs.

9. 4 birds have _____ legs.

10. 2 hands have _____ fingers.

11. 4 hands have _____ fingers.

12. 3 hands have _____ fingers.

13. 1 hand has _____ fingers.

14. 5 hands have _____ fingers.

Each hand has 5 fingers.

More Problem Solving

Write the number sentence. Solve.

1.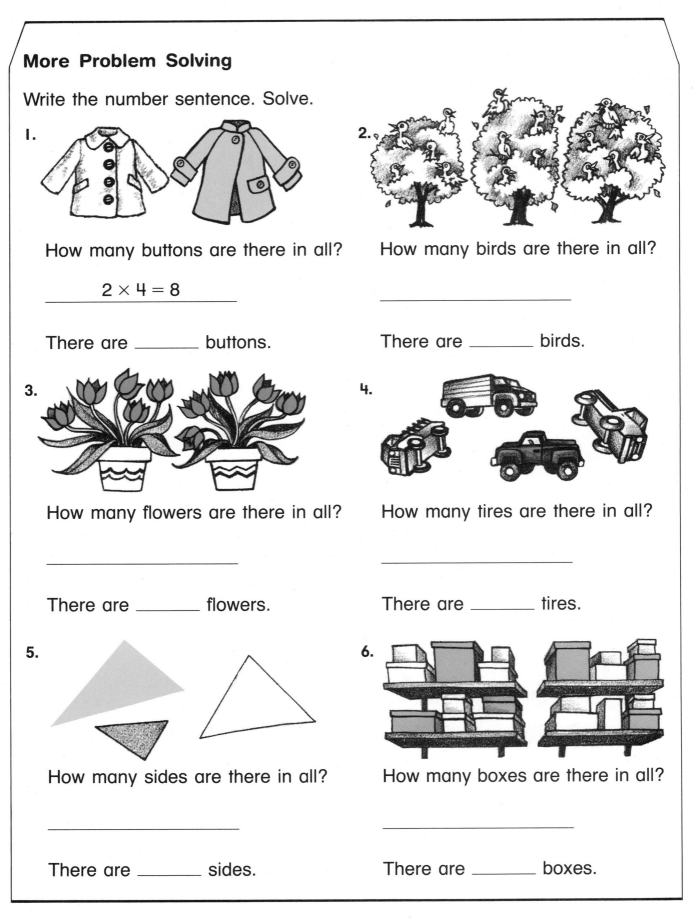

How many buttons are there in all?

$$2 \times 4 = 8$$

There are _____ buttons.

2. How many birds are there in all?

_____

There are _____ birds.

3. How many flowers are there in all?

_____

There are _____ flowers.

4. How many tires are there in all?

_____

There are _____ tires.

5. How many sides are there in all?

_____

There are _____ sides.

6. How many boxes are there in all?

_____

There are _____ boxes.

Picture Graphs

Mary made a graph to show
the books she read in January.

First Week	📖 📖
Second Week	📖 📖 📖 📖
Third Week	📖 📖 📖
Fourth Week	📖 📖 📖 📖 📖

Each 📖 means 2 books.

Write the answers on the lines.

1. How many books did Mary read

   the first week? _____   the third week? _____

   the second week? _____   the fourth week? _____

2. Mary read the most books during the _____ week.

3. She read the fewest books during the _____ week.

4. How many more books did Mary read the fourth week than
   the first week?

   _____ − _____ = _____

5. How many books did Mary read the first two weeks?

   _____ + _____ = _____

5 children made a tally of the shells they found at the beach.

Del TTTT TTTT
Jennifer TTTT TTTT TTTT
Rosa TTTT TTTT TTTT TTTT TTTT
Joseph TTTT TTTT TTTT TTTT
Rodney TTTT

Color the number of shells to show how many shells each child found.

1.	Del	🐚	🐚	🐚	🐚	🐚
2.	Jennifer	🐚	🐚	🐚	🐚	🐚
3.	Rosa	🐚	🐚	🐚	🐚	🐚
4.	Joseph	🐚	🐚	🐚	🐚	🐚
5.	Rodney	🐚	🐚	🐚	🐚	🐚

Each 🐚 means 5 shells were found.

Answer these questions.

6. Who found the most shells? _____

7. Who found the fewest shells? _____

8. How many shells were found by Del and Jennifer? _____

9. How many shells were found by Joseph and Rodney? _____

10. How many more shells were found by Rosa than Rodney? _____

CHAPTER CHECKUP

Multiply.

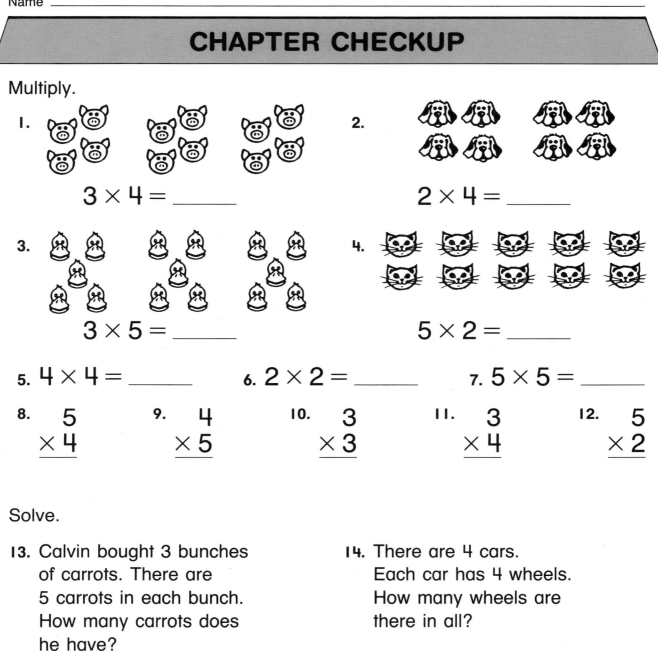

1. $3 \times 4 =$ _____

2. $2 \times 4 =$ _____

3. $3 \times 5 =$ _____

4. $5 \times 2 =$ _____

5. $4 \times 4 =$ _____   6. $2 \times 2 =$ _____   7. $5 \times 5 =$ _____

8. $\begin{array}{r} 5 \\ \times 4 \\ \hline \end{array}$ 9. $\begin{array}{r} 4 \\ \times 5 \\ \hline \end{array}$ 10. $\begin{array}{r} 3 \\ \times 3 \\ \hline \end{array}$ 11. $\begin{array}{r} 3 \\ \times 4 \\ \hline \end{array}$ 12. $\begin{array}{r} 5 \\ \times 2 \\ \hline \end{array}$

Solve.

13. Calvin bought 3 bunches of carrots. There are 5 carrots in each bunch. How many carrots does he have?

_____ carrots

14. There are 4 cars. Each car has 4 wheels. How many wheels are there in all?

There are _____ wheels.

Find the total cost.

15. 5

Total cost _____

16. 3

Total cost _____

ROUNDUP REVIEW

Fill in the oval next to the correct answer.

1 7
$+ 8$
- ⬭ 16
- ⬭ 1
- ⬭ 15
- ⬭ NG

7 81
$- 55$
- ⬭ 36
- ⬭ 26
- ⬭ 34
- ⬭ NG

2 $13 - 6$
- ⬭ 7
- ⬭ 13
- ⬭ 19
- ⬭ NG

8 623
$- 298$
- ⬭ 325
- ⬭ 335
- ⬭ 435
- ⬭ NG

3
- ⬭ 3:45
- ⬭ 8:15
- ⬭ 8:03
- ⬭ NG

9 What part of the figure is red?
- ⬭ $\frac{2}{4}$
- ⬭ $\frac{1}{4}$
- ⬭ $\frac{3}{4}$
- ⬭ NG

4
- ⬭ 85¢
- ⬭ 80¢
- ⬭ 75¢
- ⬭ NG

10 5
$\times 3$
- ⬭ 8
- ⬭ 15
- ⬭ 2
- ⬭ NG

5 37
$+ 54$
- ⬭ 23
- ⬭ 81
- ⬭ 83
- ⬭ NG

11 $\$8.35$
$- 4.26$
- ⬭ $4.11
- ⬭ $4.19
- ⬭ $4.09
- ⬭ NG

6 356
$+ 575$
- ⬭ 931
- ⬭ 921
- ⬭ 821
- ⬭ NG

12 4×4
- ⬭ 8
- ⬭ 20
- ⬭ 12
- ⬭ NG

☐ score

292 (two hundred ninety-two)

Cumulative Review

Name _____

Add.

1. $0+5$ $3+2$ $0+4$ $2+1$ $0+7$ $3+4$ $3+1$ $3+8$ $1+1$ $1+6$

2. $1+5$ $0+1$ $8+2$ $7+3$ $6+5$ $7+1$ $1+4$ $6+0$ $5+1$ $0+8$

3. $9+8$ $0+3$ $4+0$ $6+7$ $5+3$ $0+2$ $5+7$ $4+1$ $2+2$ $0+6$

4. $8+0$ $9+0$ $1+8$ $6+3$ $5+6$ $2+4$ $1+7$ $6+1$ $4+7$ $3+0$

5. $4+8$ $7+9$ $7+0$ $1+2$ $2+6$ $5+5$ $7+4$ $1+9$ $1+3$ $4+3$

6. $2+9$ $3+7$ $0+0$ $3+5$ $7+2$ $8+9$ $9+5$ $1+0$ $4+5$ $7+5$

7. $6+9$ $7+6$ $4+6$ $3+3$ $9+9$ $9+4$ $8+1$ $9+3$ $2+0$ $6+4$

8. $8+6$ $4+2$ $5+2$ $2+3$ $2+8$ $3+6$ $8+3$ $9+7$ $2+7$ $3+9$

9. $6+6$ $9+2$ $2+5$ $6+8$ $5+0$ $0+9$ $8+5$ $4+4$ $7+7$ $6+2$

10. $5+4$ $8+7$ $9+6$ $4+9$ $7+8$ $5+9$ $8+8$ $8+4$ $5+8$ $9+1$

100 addition facts   (two hundred ninety-three) **293**

Subtract.

1.
2	3	5	6	9	5	2	5	11	2
−1	−2	−1	−6	−8	−0	−0	−4	− 3	−2

2.
4	8	8	7	8	11	8	9	3	10
−3	−6	−1	−0	−2	− 4	−0	−3	−1	− 3

3.
10	6	10	13	7	9	7	6	11	15
− 7	−3	− 1	− 4	−1	−9	−2	−4	− 5	− 8

4.
0	6	4	4	14	15	9	4	8	8
−0	−1	−4	−2	− 9	− 6	−7	−1	−7	−3

5.
8	3	12	14	14	4	6	9	9	6
−5	−3	− 5	− 5	− 6	−0	−0	−5	−2	−2

6.
12	5	7	16	17	7	1	10	5	8
− 7	−2	−3	− 8	− 9	−4	−1	− 8	−5	−4

7.
16	6	7	12	13	8	7	13	10	11
− 9	−5	−5	− 9	− 9	−8	−7	− 5	− 6	− 8

8.
9	10	11	10	15	15	11	13	5	9
−0	− 9	− 6	− 5	− 9	− 7	− 2	− 6	−3	−6

9.
12	12	16	12	11	10	10	1	13	12
− 6	− 3	− 7	− 4	− 9	− 4	− 2	−0	− 8	− 8

10.
17	14	9	11	18	14	9	3	7	13
− 8	− 7	−1	− 7	− 9	− 8	−4	−0	−6	− 7

294 (two hundred ninety-four)

100 subtraction facts

Name _____

ALTERNATE CHAPTER 7 CHECKUP

Add. Trade if needed.

1.	2.	3.	4.	5.	6.
43 + 6	65 + 9	76 + 7	70 + 40	20 + 90	50 + 60

7.	8.	9.	10.	11.	12.
53 + 45	83 + 9	27 + 77	59 + 50	45 + 6	98 + 61

13.	14.	15.	16.	17.	18.
28 + 27	69 + 74	88 + 5	36 + 36	17 + 44	64 + 8

19.	20.	21.	22.	23.	24.
40 + 87	55 + 98	91 + 71	73 + 68	54 + 53	87 + 8

Add. Then write your answers in dollar notation.

25.	26.	27.	28.	29.
57¢ + 8¢	80¢ + 50¢	74¢ + 13¢	85¢ + 22¢	97¢ + 7¢

Solve.

30. There were 72 girls and 69 boys in the swimming pool. How many children were swimming?

_____ children

31. Tony has 99¢. Young Mi has 85¢. How much money do they have in all?

_____

Name _____

ALTERNATE CHAPTER 8 CHECKUP

Subtract. Trade if needed.

1. $47 - 3$

2. $85 - 9$

3. $76 - 7$

4. $61 - 5$

5. $70 - 20$

6. $90 - 50$

7. $40 - 10$

8. $55 - 31$

9. $74 - 15$

10. $92 - 45$

11. $67 - 38$

12. $75 - 45$

13. $91 - 15$

14. $87 - 69$

15. $48 - 19$

16. $56 - 38$

17. $64¢ - 25¢$

18. $71¢ - 54¢$

19. $38¢ - 29¢$

20. $95¢ - 56¢$

Solve.

21. Jason saved 57 marbles. He gave Sonja 18 of them. How many marbles did he have left?

_____ marbles

22. The pet store had 84 hamsters. They sold 39 of them. How many did they have left?

_____ hamsters

Name _____

ALTERNATE CHAPTER 9 CHECKUP

Add or subtract.

1. $63 + 9$
2. $58 + 31$
3. $23 + 76$
4. $41 + 48$
5. $57 + 34$
6. $62 + 19$

7. $26 + 45$
8. $83 + 38$
9. $63 + 77$
10. $14 + 88$
11. $45 + 46$
12. $98 + 61$

13. $76 - 22$
14. $52 - 31$
15. $91 - 47$
16. $65 - 58$
17. $74 - 19$
18. $86 - 68$

19. $44 + 15 + 26$
20. $58 + 21 + 43$
21. $72 + 16 + 33$
22. $27 + 35 + 68$
23. $54 + 62 + 19$
24. $67 + 26 + 55$

25. $16 + 69 + 8$
26. $32 + 21 + 49$
27. $47 + 43 + 14$
28. $86 + 33 + 28$
29. $63 + 68 + 53$
30. $27 + 19 + 42$

Add or subtract. Then write the answers in dollar notation.

31. $57¢ + 18¢$
32. $82¢ + 59¢$
33. $74¢ - 27¢$
34. $85¢ + 36¢$
35. $97¢ - 18¢$

_____ _____ _____ _____ _____

Name _____

ALTERNATE CHAPTER 10 CHECKUP

Add. Trade if needed.

1. $543 + 6$
2. $666 + 7$
3. $432 + 9$
4. $715 + 5$
5. $136 + 5$

6. $329 + 60$
7. $455 + 16$
8. $376 + 29$
9. $528 + 73$
10. $409 + 54$

11. $48 + 333$
12. $26 + 178$
13. $77 + 460$
14. $143 + 109$
15. $321 + 538$

16. $177 + 304$
17. $326 + 176$
18. $265 + 416$
19. $531 + 199$
20. $428 + 275$

21. $\$2.37 + 0.42$
22. $\$3.42 + 1.39$
23. $\$4.11 + 3.79$
24. $\$5.28 + 3.72$

Solve.

25. Kathy spent $3.74. Matt spent $4.33. How much did they spend altogether?

_____

26. The Jacksons drove 313 miles on Tuesday. They drove 178 miles on Wednesday. How many miles did they drive altogether?

_____ miles

Name _____

ALTERNATE CHAPTER 11 CHECKUP

Subtract. Trade if needed.

1. 432
    − 6

2. 833
    − 7

3. 715
    − 10

4. 168
    − 50

5. 917
    − 60

6. 329
    − 81

7. 456
    − 92

8. 376
    − 35

9. 528
    − 38

10. 401
    − 78

11. 177
    − 89

12. 326
    − 27

13. 265
    − 174

14. 534
    − 243

15. 428
    − 278

16. 483
    − 365

17. 258
    − 179

18. 734
    − 585

19. 672
    − 433

20. 916
    − 558

21. $2.75
    − 0.24

22. $5.64
    − 2.42

23. $7.17
    − 1.58

24. $4.12
    − 3.23

25. $3.45
    − 2.98

Solve.

26. The music store had 765 CDs. Lucy sold 177 of them. How many CDs are left?

    _____ CDs

27. Sam had $8.42. He bought a book for $3.85. How much money does he have left?

    _____

Name _____

ALTERNATE CHAPTER 12 CHECKUP

Add or subtract.

1. $\begin{array}{r} 465 \\ +\ 34 \\ \hline \end{array}$
2. $\begin{array}{r} 638 \\ +\ 38 \\ \hline \end{array}$
3. $\begin{array}{r} 313 \\ -\ 49 \\ \hline \end{array}$
4. $\begin{array}{r} 752 \\ +139 \\ \hline \end{array}$
5. $\begin{array}{r} 278 \\ +610 \\ \hline \end{array}$

6. $\begin{array}{r} 329 \\ 143 \\ +333 \\ \hline \end{array}$
7. $\begin{array}{r} 251 \\ 227 \\ +295 \\ \hline \end{array}$
8. $\begin{array}{r} 406 \\ 118 \\ +276 \\ \hline \end{array}$

9. $\begin{array}{r} 593 \\ +248 \\ \hline \end{array}$
10. $\begin{array}{r} 888 \\ -359 \\ \hline \end{array}$
11. $\begin{array}{r} 656 \\ -447 \\ \hline \end{array}$
12. $\begin{array}{r} 451 \\ -167 \\ \hline \end{array}$
13. $\begin{array}{r} 923 \\ -278 \\ \hline \end{array}$

14. $\begin{array}{r} \$6.95 \\ +\$2.24 \\ \hline \end{array}$
15. $\begin{array}{r} \$4.37 \\ +\$3.33 \\ \hline \end{array}$
16. $\begin{array}{r} \$6.14 \\ -\$2.69 \\ \hline \end{array}$
17. $\begin{array}{r} \$8.21 \\ -\$3.54 \\ \hline \end{array}$

Subtract. Then check your answers.

18. $\begin{array}{r} \$3.49 \\ -\ 1.67 \\ \hline \end{array}$
19. $\begin{array}{r} 852 \\ -564 \\ \hline \end{array}$
20. $\begin{array}{r} \$6.21 \\ -\ 2.45 \\ \hline \end{array}$

Solve.

21. Soo had $5.35.
    She spent $4.58.
    How much money does
    she have now?

    Soo has _____.

22. Mike had $3.42.
    He spend $1.58.
    How much money does
    he have left?

    Mike has _____ left.

Name _____

ALTERNATE CHAPTER 13 CHECKUP

How many of each shape are there? Write the number.

1. _____ triangles

2. _____ rectangles

3. _____ circles

4. _____ squares

Write the number for each.

5. _____ sides

6. _____ corners

7. _____ square corners

Is the line a line of symmetry? Circle yes or no.

8.

yes   no

9.

yes   no

What part is red? Write the fraction.

10.

_____

11.

_____

12.

_____

13.

_____

ALTERNATE CHAPTER 14 CHECKUP

Find the length to the nearest inch.

1.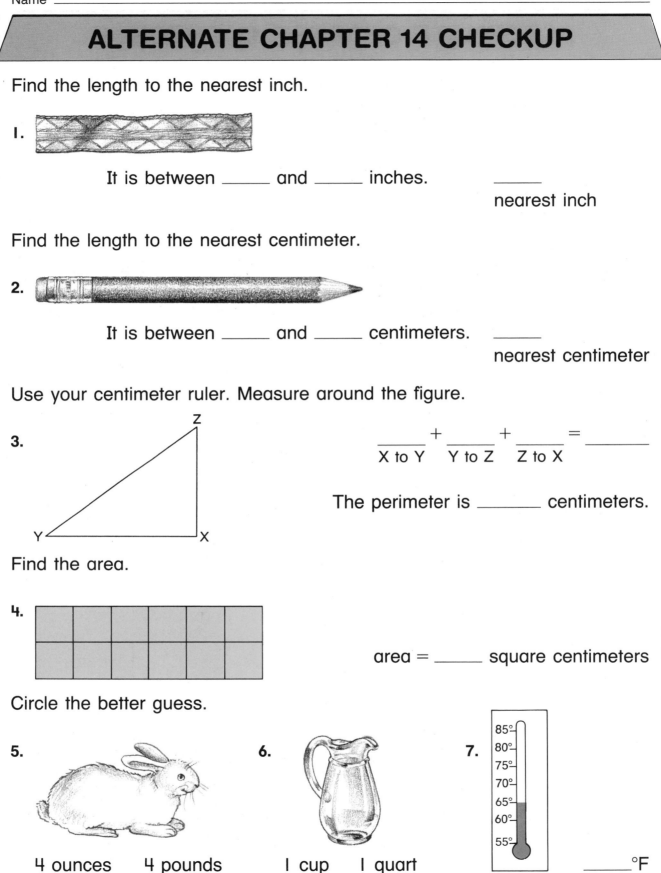

It is between _____ and _____ inches.

_____
nearest inch

Find the length to the nearest centimeter.

2.

It is between _____ and _____ centimeters.

_____
nearest centimeter

Use your centimeter ruler. Measure around the figure.

3.

$$\underline{\qquad}_{\text{X to Y}} + \underline{\qquad}_{\text{Y to Z}} + \underline{\qquad}_{\text{Z to X}} = \underline{\qquad}$$

The perimeter is _____ centimeters.

Find the area.

4.

area = _____ square centimeters

Circle the better guess.

5. 4 ounces   4 pounds

6. 1 cup   1 quart

7. 85° 80° 75° 70° 65° 60° 55°

_____ °F

ALTERNATE CHAPTER 15 CHECKUP

Multiply.

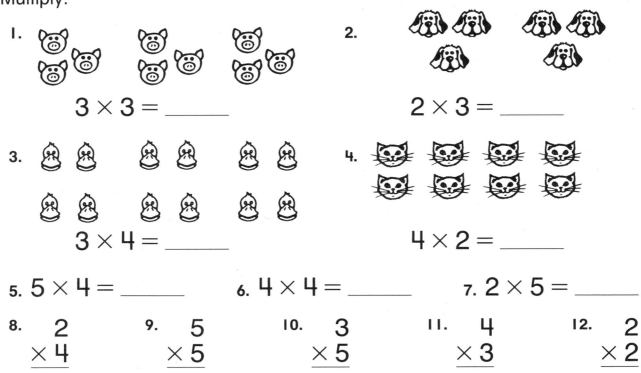

1. $3 \times 3 =$ _____

2. $2 \times 3 =$ _____

3. $3 \times 4 =$ _____

4. $4 \times 2 =$ _____

5. $5 \times 4 =$ _____   6. $4 \times 4 =$ _____   7. $2 \times 5 =$ _____

8. $\begin{array}{r} 2 \\ \times 4 \\ \hline \end{array}$
9. $\begin{array}{r} 5 \\ \times 5 \\ \hline \end{array}$
10. $\begin{array}{r} 3 \\ \times 5 \\ \hline \end{array}$
11. $\begin{array}{r} 4 \\ \times 3 \\ \hline \end{array}$
12. $\begin{array}{r} 2 \\ \times 2 \\ \hline \end{array}$

Solve.

13. Peter bought 4 bunches of grapes. There are 5 grapes in each bunch. How many grapes does he have?

    _____ grapes

14. There are 3 cars. Each car has 4 wheels. How many wheels are there in all?

    There are _____ wheels.

Find the total cost.

15. 4

    Total cost _____

16. 5

    Total cost _____